BLOCKCHAIN
THE UNTOLD STORY

by

Srinivas Mahankali

Distributors:

BPB PUBLICATIONS

20, Ansari Road, Darya Ganj
New Delhi-110002
Ph: 23254990/23254991

MICRO MEDIA

Shop No. 5, Mahendra Chambers
150 DN Rd. Next to Capital Cinema,
V.T. (C.S.T.) Station,
MUMBAI-400 001
Ph: 22078296/22078297

BPB BOOK CENTRE

376 Old Lajpat Rai Market,
Delhi-110006
Ph: 23861747

DECCAN AGENCIES

4-3-329, Bank Street,
Hyderabad-500195
Ph: 24756967/24756400

Published by Manish Jain for BPB Publications, 20, Ansari Road, Darya Ganj, New Delhi-110002 and Printed by Repro India Ltd., Mumbai

Dedication

Dedicated to all those curious and passionate about Blockchain & have strived hard to take the benefit of Blockchain paradigm to all the stake holders, this work is the first book to:

1. Trace the origin of internet to Blockchains of the future & written like a story to make the Blockchain concept well understood in the right perspective and context of digital world's challenges!

2. To talk about Blockchain 1.0 to Blockchain 4.0

3. To comprehensively link Blockchain development process to 'Process excellence' methodologies

4. To trace and link the DNA of Blockchain paradigm to real world entities

5. To discuss comprehensively the relation of Blockchain to the cutting edge technologies today

6. To discuss the role of the leading global technology organisations in promoting the Blockchain ecosystems

7. To focus on taking the knowledge of Blockchain to the real investors of the Blockchain and offer the rationale of doing so, the corporate user group & the Governments.

8. To offer a balanced perspective on cryptoasset based and enterprise Blockchains

9. Focus on the impact of Blockchain technology on the human resources function through a comprehensive case study.

10. Written by a technology evangelist experienced in both technology and business development roles as both a customer and marketer.

Preface

Blockchain - The Untold story!

I have read many books on Bitcoin and Blockchain. The amount of information out there in the open is indeed mind-boggling. It is humongous, but never comprehensive! It seems clarifying, but leaves you confused. It seems conceptually simple, but technologically looks very complicated!

After all, how can a 'Distributed Ledger' be imparted with so many properties and powers to be able to 'Disrupt' the fundamental way in which we can operate?

In most of the books you will find that it teaches the same points again and again. After all RFID can be used in hundreds of situations giving us numerous benefits in every situation. In the same way, an augmented distributed ledger like Blockchain can also serve a variety of purposes in different situations.

Either we have a book which gives the numerous benefits describing the revolution that this new paradigm can unleash, or we have books explaining the various platforms and their working.

In this book, I am trying a new approach to balance write-ups, code and explanations. By using a judicious mix of text, illustrations, images and references, I will try to cut across the timelines and the technologies to give a perspective of the past, present and the future.

While a lot of what written is 'original', I would not like to pretend that a number of times you come across concepts and visuals that sound & look familiar. The influence of many a great work is visible, and I believe, it has to be, to provide the best information available. At the same time, I will be too pleased if any other authors use the words in this book to put across their points in any forum even without referencing me. After all, 'Blockchain' is a religion, proliferated by missionary people through freely available open source technologies to decentralize and democratize the world we live in! I would like this book to be known as something that 'Speaks less, Shows more & Provokes thought'.

At the end, it is still possible that you are left with a number of questions unanswered, some concepts either explained in a wrong way or already challenged by another upcoming platform (for example the high level of immutability of Bitcoin platform could be challenged through Quantum computing) and many more issues. That is the way this technology is. Evolving rapidly, offering different interpretations at times, contradicting at times, it indeed offers a lot of food for thought, feeds your curiosity and challenges your brain!

To read most of the books today, either you have to be profuse reader, or you have to be a great programmer.

They write the same thing in a different style. No book teaches you:

- How to architect a solution.
- How to think
- How to act and above all,
- The real action ahead.

Though there has been a huge crash in the prices of cryptocurrencies in the past one year, many indicators are revealing a dramatic improvement in the Blockchain adoption across the world for enterprise applications, with over 30% of the 4000 odd projects entering Pilot or Production stage from the Proof of Concept stage across the world.

In this second edition, I have tried to leverage my experience and observation in the recent past to offer the readers, a real life account of practical use cases that are currently under implementation across the world. Blockchain approach is being leveraged across different areas of enterprise, public, private and government domains including police and judicial systems. Countries are slowly beginning to understand the importance of bringing Blockchain into mainstream through proper regulation. If police departments & judiciary across the world are exploring the use of Blockchain, it implies that there is nothing to stop this disruptive paradigm any longer. Estonia, Dubai and some Indian states are implementing Blockchain versions of distributed technologies as illustrated below.

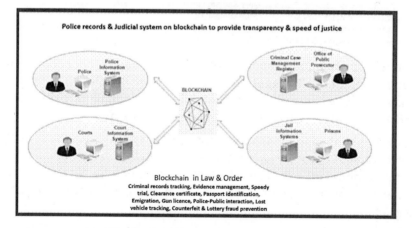

In the past one year, though the bitcoin and most of the cryptocurrencies and cryptoassets have come down a lot in their value, government and enterprises have discovered that the underlying Blockchain technology can be used for a variety of purposes. Another interesting use case is that of managing the autonomous vehicles like drones for the welfare of citizens and also protection of these vehicles for unauthorized hacking to use them for illegal & criminal activities. One such illustration is given below.

Secured Drone network for disaster relief through blockchain

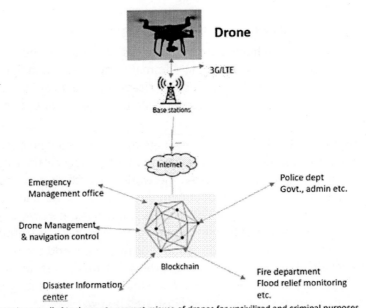

- Access is controlled to drones to prevent misuse of drones for uncivilized and criminal purposes
- Rapid response through shared imagery & related information for disaster management response across government machinery & infrastructure companies
- Shared updated information regarding fire, floods, damaged roads, power outages and bridges etc., helps in quick & timely relief to affected citizens

With its cooperative style approach of i) Disintermediation, ii) Transparency,iii) Democratic approach iv) Equitable distribution of investments, expenses and returns and vi) Openness of participation & involvement, Blockchain is also being viewed as a digital version of the co-operative movement.

Indian leaders of co-operative enterprise ecosystem like ULCCS (Uralungal Labour Contract Co-operative Society Ltd.) GCMMF (Gujarat Cooperative Milk Marketing Federation) are actively looking at implementing Blockchain solutions in cooperatives operating farm, food, diary, fish, perishable product, construction projects etc.

Organisations like IBM have launched major initiatives for implementing Blockchain solutions for tracking minerals, precious products, food products and many more.

With a lot of PoCs now going into production, leading companies in the ecosystem like IBM are coming out with research and guidance for appropriate returns on investments for Blockchain business. 'Emerging Technology Projection-The total economic impact of IBM Blockchain'. a total economic impact tool by Forrester, is an interesting effort and a resource to be referred.

Successful re-platforming of global leader in clearing and settlement DTCC's TIW (Trade Information Warehouse) that plays a central role in credit derivatives market in May 2019 will be one of the first major capital market related projects to enter into production. TIW's project to move from a traditional relational database to a distributed ledger permissioned blockchain based ledger is truly a ground-breaking effort pushing the boundaries of distributed ledger technology. This forebodes the coming of age of Blockchain technology and its break thorough into the mainstream of fin ancial services.

In a landmark move, on February 14th, 2019, JP Morgan one of the world's largest banks that moves more than $5 trillion in wholesale payments each day, announced that it will launch a digital coin, namely JPM Coin to move corporate payments across the world.

Though the JPM Coin operates in a closed network of over 150 global multinational clients, eliminating the controversial issues relating to KYC & AML that could clash with the regulators, this lends a lot of legitimacy to the cryptocurrency world that has often been rocked by volatility and branded illegitimate and also ratifies the fact that the world's experiments on cryptocurrency are firmly out of the lab, while underscoring the need for enhanced speed, trust and secured automation.

JPM Coin paves way for the usage of digital versions of many national currencies by respective countries in a permissioned & compliant manner offering disintermediation and decentralisation to a large extent. These digital currencies can then be integrated into the global cryptocurrency eco-system in a seamless manner. This enables the ability to monetise lots of data, generated by the proliferation of IoT devices across entities, globally through data broking arrangements. For countries like India with a huge data generation & consumption across media that could be monetised, this bodes a new era of prosperity!

In this edition we examine many such use cases and illustrations as to how, Blockchain can facilitate safe, secure and automated future full of exciting possibilities. Let us delve into the past, present and future of the Blockchain with Blockchain the Untold Story.

Happy Blockchaining!

Disclaimers

Blockchain is a fast-evolving young field with a lot of action happening every day. There is no definitive approach or answer on any topic or problem. A lot of information in this book is provided after a tremendous research on available resources online to cut down the learning curve of the BCT adopters. Hence, while investing any resources on any projects inspired by the information in this book, the readers are kindly advised to do their own diligent research and the author is not responsible for any liabilities.

A large amount of available information made available online & in person by generous organisations and individuals is used in the book to make the learning experience comprehensive and enjoyable. Those owning respective copyrights can file their objection for removal of the same or for insertion of credits in appropriate places, to the author. It will be actioned immediately.

Happy learning. Welcome to the Blockchain Religion!

Acknowledgement

I am especially thankful on behalf of myself as an author and all the readers, to world's leading companies & organisations like IBM, Microsoft, Google, KPMG, Persistent systems, Deloitte, Ernst & Young, Price Waterhouse Coopers, TCS, Infosys, William Mougayar, Stellar, L&T Infotech, Mindtree, Oracle and many more for their contributions to the Blockchain learners' community and the same have been referred in many places in this book.

I would like to thank, Hari TN, HR Head, Bigbasket, for inspiring me as he does to millions of aspiring professionals and entrepreneurs.

Raghavendra Prasad, Ganesh Ramakrishnan, APS Bhalla, JV Raman, Robert Pancras, Jayavel Soundara Rajan, Jariff Ali Abdul Hameed, Siddharth Maheshwari.

Thanks so much for believing in me.

Satish Salivati, Seetharaman GR, Vasanth Kumar (Graphic designer), Sanath Bhat, Ratna Sathappan and so many angels and experts who have helped me in my effort to put this book together. Thank you so much in helping me with the edits and support during the making of the book.

I am extremely thankful to Ms Shradha Sharma, founder and CEO at YourStory Media & Ms Mansi Kelkar, News Editor at YourStory Media for their help un augmenting the second edition, a lot.

My family members, my daughter Deepika, my son Sai Prateek & my wife Anuradha for putting with my indifference during the making of the book and yet being with me constantly & egging me on.

Inspiration for the Second edition

Blockchain the Untold Story, has been received very well by many who could now understand the all pervasive & disruptive implications of this technology.

The all pervasive implications of the Blockchain paradigm are now being felt across many businesses who are able to understand the exponential benefits of a collaborative ecosystem which was hitherto not possible, before the arrival of this technology, made possible by the coming together & synthesis of a number of platforms & paradigms at the same time.

Various use cases & applications of Blockchain technology that we are now able to envisage more concretely, are explored in this second edition. Some of them are listed below:

1. Birth to Death - Issue and storage of all certificates including identity, academic & non academic, medical records, licenses, municipal certificates etc.

2. Supply chain applications from 'Farm to fork', 'Raw material to Customer' and many more.

3. Application of Blockchain in insurance, pharma, medical records & related domains

4. Financial applications including complete life cycle management of transactions including 'Letter of Credit', 'Cross border remittance', 'Interbank transfers' and many more.

5. Disruptions that large business areas like Ecommerce & Social media are going to face in the future

6. Cybersecurity implications for IoT & many more areas currently operating with 'SPOF' or Single point of failure related vulnerabilities

This book will surely be a treasure for all those who are eager to know the disruptive impact & possibilities of this amazing paradigm!

Table of Contents

CHAPTER 1

Introduction - How it started
Rise of Blockchain Religion

1969 was a land mark year for the world. It was the year in which Internet was born.

In response to the launch of Sputnik by Russia, in 1957, US President Dwight Eisenhower created the ARPA agency, now known as DARPA (Defense Advanced Research Projects Agency) under the leadership of JCR Liklider, to regain the technological lead in the arms race& also protect America against a space based nuclear attack from Russia. Liklider evangelized within the IPTO about the potential benefits of a country-wide communications network and the ARPANET went live in October, 1969. By collaborating with academic, industry, and government partners, DARPA formulates and executes research and development projects to expand the frontiers of technology and science, often beyond immediate U.S. military requirements

On 29th October 1969, the first communications was made over a 50 Kbps AT&T line October, 1969, the first communications were between Leonard Kleinrock's research center at the University of California at Los Angeles, and Douglas Engelbart's center at the Stanford Research Institute and a two node ARPANET was born.

Thus, internet as we know today, came into existence as an outcome of the constructive competition between the two super powers of the post-World war-2 era, USA & Russia

The first networking protocol used on the ARPANET was the Network Control Program. In 1983, it was replaced with the TCP/IP protocol invented by Robert Kahn, Vinton Cerf and others which quickly became the most widely used network protocol in the world.

The birth of the Internet was facilitated by the confluence of many technologies and owes its existence to a collective vision of many visionary technologists. Some of them are outlined below:

- Vannevar Bush was the first to envision the benefits of Information Technology by describing, "memex" automated library system.

- Norbert Wiener the inventor of Cybernetics (the science of control and communications in the animal and machine) inspired the research to extend human capabilities through technology.

- The 1956 Dart mouth Artificial Intelligence conference inspired the world to seriously consider leveraging the Technology for the benefits of humanity.
- Marshall McLuhan envisioned a global village interconnected by an electronic nervous system.

The two node ARPANET born in October 1969 metamorphosed to connect, first the Universities around North America, and then to the research facilities in Europe through EUnet as the 'Internet' as we know today.

The use of the Internet exploded after 1990, causing the US Government to transfer management by first opening up to the world on April 30th 1993 as 'World Wide Web' and later to independent organisations to manage the entire eco-system.

The adoption of the World wide web grew exponentially through the late 1990s and the early 21st century with the development and adoption of cutting edge technologies like Digital marketing, Customer Relationship Management, Enterprise Resource Planning, Internet of Things, Artificial Intelligence , Machine learning, Robotics and the like. They helped the citizens of the world to dramatically improve their productivity and quality of life, but also gave rise to a number of side effects that intruded into the privacy of their lives and threatened security of the digitally influenced lifestyles.

This has resulted in the world searching for ways to protect themselves from the negative impacts of the technological advancements that exposed their vulnerabilities due to the oligopolistic tendencies of the digital giants exposed to the 'Internet villains' that focused on cyberattacks and unauthorized information leaks.

Blockchain that came into existence on 3rd January 2009 through the launch of the cryptocurrency by name bitcoin, promises to offer answer to many of these problems.

Many people in the world still think, Blockchain is nothing but Bitcoin! Such is the impact that bitcoin has created on people and systems across the world. It is 'Disruption' at the very best indeed! Shaking the very roots of convention and centralization, being mystical, yet building trust, being process driven, yet boosting entrepreneurial culture, being mostly limited to 'Transactions and States' yet impacting every possible business one can think of , not being run by any 'owner' but still creating enormous value and economic activity, the story of Blockchain without us ever knowing who it is, who started it all, is nothing but a Whodunnit Mystery that continues to impact us in many ways. While it is unknown, that who is the inventor of the Blockchain, it is indeed heartening to note the collective power of the giant 'centralized' organisations like Microsoft, IBM, Cisco, Intel, Oracle, Huawei, Amazon, SAP throwing their weight behind this movement even though this could disrupt their business models in many ways!

The birth of the Blockchain, through the birth of bitcoin coincided with the inception of the Big Data and the growing power of & vexation against the powers of centralization.

By putting the power back in the hands of the individual users and also the connected devices, while protecting their identities to a large extent, Blockchain has spurred an era of empowered customers and entrepreneurs while promising to mitigate the risk to the organizations.

Blockchain being a new domain, is rapidly growing in adoption across the world in the form of crowd funding & launch of cryptocurrencies, aided by the increasing trend towards 'Decentralization, Open source technologies and Cloud computing enabled Pay as you use approach' sweeping the world.

While currently there is no structured program across the global educational system, offering Blockchain related courses, this rapidly growing field has to be learnt through experience, where new approaches are discovered every day while old myths, approaches and realities are challenged.

It is important to learn about the Blockchain paradigm in the context of the various technologies that are operating in tandem and to understand the impact of Blockchain beyond the use of cryptocurrencies, currently dominated by bitcoin.

It is important to explain this concept in a way which facilitates proper understanding by all concerned including the users and enterprises who are supposed to fund its adoption, not just those technologists who are executing these projects.

Most importantly, we need to examine the potential impact of Blockchain, beyond the bitcoin!

Those who can embrace the change, are able to harness the enormous powers that a well-conceived and executed Blockchain platform can offer, while the rest could well transition their way into the oblivion.

Embrace the new paradigm and welcome to the new religion!

In this book, we traverse the technological journey of the world from the birth of the Internet to the future of Blockchain. Hope you enjoy the journey.

CHAPTER 2

Whodunnit- Unravelling the Mystery of Bitcoin's Origin

"The Times 3/Jan/2009 Chancellor on the verge of second bailout for banks"

-Satoshi Nakamoto - Genesis Block

Who do you think is the real Satoshi Nakamoto? A question plaguing millions of people across the world. It is indeed a Brilliant work of A Genius digital currency specialist, Cryptographer, Mathematician, Computer Programmer, A Super Grand Master of Chess, Marketer, A Passionate Activist against Centralization & Excessive Regulation and above all, someone who has no need for a Million Bitcoins available in his account, no need for the associated fame in return for the Anonymity that is needed to stand by the values of the Cryptocurrency he invented or someone who has the capacity to command respect from , employ/ work with all such persons combined for a cause?!

Let us examine the key suspects:

Satoshi Nakamoto, the name used by the unknown person or people who designed bitcoin and created its original reference implementation. As a part of the implementation, they also devised the first Blockchain database. In the process they were the first to solve the double-spending problem for digital currency. Incidentally, Hal Finney is the neighbour of a person by name 'SATOSHI NAKAMOTO' who did not have any clue about the technology aspects of Bitcoin, when interrogated.

Harold Finney was a cypher punk advocating the use of cryptography for the world's benefit, and said: "It seemed so obvious to me: 'Here we are faced with the problems of loss of privacy, creeping computerization, massive databases, more centralization - and David Chum offers a completely different direction to go in, one which puts power into the hands of individuals rather than governments and corporations. The computer can be used as a tool to liberate and protect people, rather than to control them'. "He was an early <u>bitcoin</u> user and received the first bitcoin transaction from Bitcoin's creator <u>Satoshi Nakamoto</u>. **Finney lived in the same town for 10 years that Dorian Satoshi Nakamoto lived (Temple City, California)**, adding to speculation that he may have been Bitcoin's creator. Finney denied that he was <u>Satoshi Nakamoto</u>.

Let us examine the properties of Cryptocurrencies like Bitcoin with respect to other forms of value exchange like Fiat currencies and Gold.

Ae we know, the traditional concept of currency, which is traditionally used by all world citizens should have the following desirable characteristics

Wei Dai is a computer engineer and cypherpunk best known as creator of money and the developer of the Crypto++ library. Dai is listed as inventor on U.S. patents 5724279 and 6081598 which were assigned to Microsoft.

Mr. Dai worked in the Cryptography Research Group at Microsoft Corporation in Redmond, Washington. While at Microsoft, he was involved in the study, design and implementation of cryptosystems for specialized applications. Prior to joining Microsoft, Mr. Dai was a programmer with Terra Sciences of Acton, Massachusetts. Mr. Dai holds a Bachelor of Science degree from the University of Washington in computer science, with a minor in mathematics. "Dai has made numerous contributions to the field of cryptography and has identified critical Cipher Block Chaining (CBC) vulnerabilities affecting SSH2 and the browser exploit against SSL/TLS known as BEAST (Browser Exploit against SSL/TLS).

Nick Szabo is a computer scientist, legal scholar and cryptographer known for his research in digital contracts and digital currency. He was graduated from the University of Washington in 1989 with a degree in computer science. In 1998, Szabo designed a mechanism for a decentralized digital currency he called "bit gold". Bitgold was never implemented but has been called "a direct precursor to the Bitcoin architecture. Research by financial author Dominic Frisby provided circumstantial evidence but, as he admits, no proof that Satoshi is Szabo. Speaking on RT's Keiser Report, he said "I have concluded there is only one person in the whole world that has the sheer breadth but also the specificity of knowledge and it is this chap...". In an email to Frisby, in July 2014, Szabo said "Thanks for letting me know. I'm afraid you got it wrong doxing me as Satoshi, but I am used to it".

At this juncture it is important to review the various options used as currency for value exchange among global citizens available today. The currency that we use, must have the following desirable characteristics:

(i)   **Scarcity:** Limited supply of units represented by a common symbol (Example-$)

(ii)   **Fungibility:** Interchange ability of unit is represented by the same symbol.

(iii)   **Divisibility:** Ability to be divided into fractional units for varying transaction sizes.

(iv)   **Durability:** The representative single unit should be available across time periods.

(v)   **Transferability:** The units can be transferred from person to person into respective accounts.

In the real world today, Gold and US Dollar are seen as the standards for value transfer representing Precious metal and Fiat currency respectively.

Bill Gates, the co-founder of Microsoft has once famously said, 'Bitcoin is better than money'.

The differences between the various forms of value transfer are given in the table below:

Comparison of charactersitics of Cryptocurrencies(bitcoin) versus Fiat (Regular cash) versus Precious metal (Gold)					
Desirable properties of a Currency	Description of property	Cryptocurrency- Example bitcoin)	Precious metal- Example Gold	Fiat currency (Example- US Dollar)	Cryptocurrency Versus Fiat
Divisible	Availability in Varying increments	Yes	No	Yes	Equal
Durable	Long lasting	Yes	Yes	Yes	Equal
Fungible	Mutually Interchangeable	Yes	Yes	Yes	Equal
Portability	Ability to carry from place to place	Yes	No	Yes	Equal
Scarce	Limit on overall supply	Yes	Yes	No	Better
Transferability	Ease of Person to Person transfer	Yes	Yes(Restricted by regulation)	Yes(Restricted by regulation)	Better
Non Counterfeitability	Replicaility by fakes	Yes	No	No	Better
Decentralised	No central authority regulation	Yes	Yes	No	Better
Global	Univerally acceptable at same value	Yes	No	No	Better
Pseudonymous	Representative name for owner	Yes	No	No	Better
Irreversible	Modification of transaction	Yes	No	No	Better
Cybersecurity	Cryptography enabled protection of transactions and identities	Yes	Yes	No	Better
Inflation resistant	Controlled value fluctuation	Yes	Yes	No	Better
Transparent		Yes	No	No	Better
Traceable	Tracing of the currency unit from origin to final user	Yes	No	No	Better
Machine to Machine transfer	Enabling IOT asset exchange	Yes	No	No	Better
Intrinsic value		No	Yes	Partly	Worse
Protection against loss	Support from regulatory authorities against loss	No	Yes	Yes	Worse
Backed by an Asset aggregate		No	Yes	Partly	Worse

It can be easily observed that, Bitcoin though having some limitations over a fiat currency like US Dollar, scores better across a range of desirable characteristics of a currency. No wonder, Bill Gates, went on to remark that 'Bitcoin is exciting because, it shows how cheap it can be. Bitcoin is better than currency in that you don't have to be physically in the same place and of course, for large transactions, currency can get pretty inconvenient.'

Let us look at some of famous quotes that are relevant to our discussion:

The crypto boom is like the dotcom bubble but that's not a bad thing: 'Selling crypto now is like selling Apple in 2001'- **Yoni Assia, the CEO of eToro**, a social trading platform that supports a range of cryptocurrencies. Business Insider , Oscar WilliansGrut- 18th June 2018

Some notable quotes by **VitalikButerin, Co-founder, Ethereum** are worth taking note of.

"The industrial revolution allowed us, for the first time, to start replacing human labour with machines.

Whereas most technologies tend to automate workers on the periphery doing menial tasks, Blockchains automate away the center. Instead of putting the taxi driver out of a job, Blockchain lets the taxi drivers work with the customer directly.

There are definitely a lot of banks that are interested in private Blockchains. In some cases, they are happy with public Blockchains as well. The opposition to just doing things on a public Blockchain is definitely smaller than some of the strongest detractors think.

Blockchains will drop search costs, causing a kind of decomposition that allows you to have markets of entities that are horizontally segregated and vertically segregated. **VitalikButerin, Co-founder, Ethereum.**

It is only in the recent past that **Steve Wozniak, co-founder** of the world's leading Technology giant, Apple Inc. commented that, "Ethereum interests me because it can do things and because it's a platform. In the long term, Ethereum can become as influential as **Apple**. Blockchain is the next major revolution about to happen." He also is taking an active interest in Blockchain training across the world.

It seems so obvious that **Satoshi Nakamoto** is the name given to the **Project Bitcoin** by one of the greatest legends of all times to come, we have in our midst (no guess needed!) who was instrumental in bringing together genius professionals who combined all the above skills narrated at the beginning, possible only by the collusion of all or some of the persons including those whose quotes are mentioned so far (one of them being an unsuspecting lender of the name to the project)!

No one else has the 'Greatness' to be behind such a monumental Technology like the Blockchain, leave alone the phenomenal innovation behind bitcoin and still have the magnanimity and the poise, not to stake claim for such a stupendous invention.

Now let us examine the organisations led by iconic leaders who can be behind the project that led to the launch of bitcoin.

1. If Blockchain is now considered as a religion by many passionate followers of this paradigm, most of us know of another iconic brand that always has been considered as a cult, 'The Apple'.

2. It's a common fact that anybody who experienced apple's products I-MAC, iPod, iPhone, iPad, etc., finds it very difficult to switch to any other brands products for the same activity. Similarly, anybody who has understood Blockchain technology are finding it very difficult to focus & specialize in any other area.

3. It's a well-known fact that Apple Brand was purely built on word of mouth, nil advertisements & sheer utility & experience of their products offered to consumers. Similarly Blockchain technology has gathered so much of steam by its sheer utility & value that it offers to its users despite the opposition or ignorance or lack of understanding from most of the giant adopters of traditional technologies.

4. Like Apple, Bitcoin, the first application of Blockchain technology was born to challenge the status quo & do things differently.

5. Blockchain Aims to promote a decentralized world of autonomous organisations accessible to any person and organisations to conduct secure transactions unlike the current centralized approach of most of the enterprises today.

6. Apple products were built to support & create an ecosystem of millions of applications, application developers offering enormous user experience to iPhone users.

7. In a similar way, Blockchain technology has gained immense popularity due to the amazing open source ecosystem leading to the launch of numerous DAPPS (Decentralized Applications) leading to the huge growth of a huge ecosystem of related products & service providers. This in turn is encouraging users & adopters to embrace Blockchain technology leading to its proliferation.

8. We know that when any new product is launched by Apple, the teams that work on the project work in extremely independent, confidential & isolated but interrelated cells that are stitched together only at almost absolute end of the project to deliver the product holistically. This is very similar to the approach we have seen where we observed that Bitcoin project comprising of numerous technologies harnessed together for an unimaginable and comprehensive fool proof platform.

9. Most important of all, the incorporation date of Apple that is 3rd January (1977) which seems to coincide with that of the launch of Bitcoin (3rd January 2009). Looks too much serendipitous.

The Analysis of the above seems to suggest the Bitcoin platform and Apple products have the same genes and therefore perhaps the same father, could be the Iconic Steve Jobs? But is it so obvious?

Or is it from the stable of another iconic personality wanting to give rise to a platform with the same genes as that of Apple's products, having been otherwise boxed into a different positioning due to the legacy track record.

Let's look at another iconic organisations, Microsoft. If Microsoft always stood for conventional technologies with absolute domination in most of the areas of its operation, it is led by iconic founders like Bill Gates who is capable of everything possible leading to the launch of a project like Bitcoin. It is well possible that Bill Gates& his team also nursed the ambition of doing something that stood exactly the opposite with a cult like status as that of Apple. The date of launch of the project could well have been deliberately coincided to divert the attention of people from itself to some other potential suspect. After all, one of the fundamental ideas behind the blockchain project is to encourage peer to peer transactions without any "known "centralized organisations. It is very much in the scheme of things for somebody like Bill Gates & his organisations to launch this project & give it all attributes that divert attention from itself.

While it is potentially possible to conclude by analyzing even more inferences as to who could be behind the Bitcoin project, it makes sense for all of us to let the ambiguity prevail as it is against the ethos of Blockchain technology to focus on a "known" originator that could bias the world once again.

Sources: www.cnbc.com, Slide share presentation by GalinDinkov, Wikipedia, Bitcoin Aliens & steemit.com

CHAPTER 3

Blockchain- Some Faqs.
What is Blockchain? Some Fundamentals

What is Blockchain?

Bitcoin Blockchain

Cryptocurrency based Blockchains like Bitcoin define Blockchain as a linked list of blocks containing a full copy of the Bitcoin ledger giving the UTXOs (Unspent Transaction Output) in the form of a crypto currency unit named Bitcoin or its fraction (1 Bitcoin = 1 million Satoshis) of each of the address mapped in groups to respective wallets. Each of the addresses has a public key and a password named Private Key. Public key is used to check the details if the transactions and private keys allows the holder to spend the UTXO units and then Private key allows the holder to spend the UTXOs associated with the respective public key.

The Blockchain is thus a store of and a means to transfer immense value, underlining the importance of keeping the password (pass phrase of wallet and the private key for every address) a closely guarded secret.

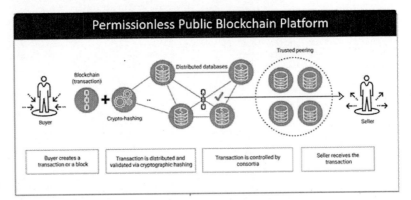

BITCOIN & ETHEREUM are examples of Public Blockchains

Blockchain with Turing complete state machine (Smart contract + Cryptocurrency).

In a permission less public Blockchain platforms any one can conduct transactions & view the transactions and anyone can download the mining program to be a part of the decision making process.

Ethereum Virtual Machine unlike Bitcoin core is known as **World Computer** and is capable of processing a wide range of applications. It not only stores the transactions but also updated values of each address in the revised state.

Ethereum has made it possible for any type of business to be transacted in peer to peer manner and that to be in a sustainable manner through the concept of Smart contracts and decentralized autonomous where decisions are taken with little human intervention.

Enterprise Blockchains (Private and Consortium Permissioned)

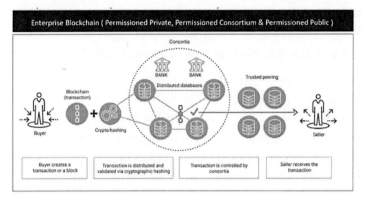

Hyperledger, Enterprise Ethereum, Quorum, Corda are examples of Enterprise Blockchain Platforms

In the case of enterprise applications like Hyperledger, Multiledger, Quorum, Corda etc., Blockchain is defined by IBM as 'A Peer to Peer Distributed Ledger Technology for a new generation of transactional applications that vastly improve the security, transparency and accountability while streamlining organizational processes.

In case of permissioned Blockchain for public use, anyone can have an access to view the ownership of assets after creating an account on the platform.

Who are the participants of the Blockchain?

In both Bitcoin and Ethereum, the transactions take place between peers identifies through their public keys/ addresses or pseudonyms which are difficult to be traced back to the real world entities unless an enormous effort is out on IP address tracking.

Who are the original founders of Bitcoin, is still a mystery, but the addresses supposedly corresponding to the initial inventors carry close to a million bitcoin worth close to 8 billion US dollars as on 1st May 2018.

In Ethereum, the founders are a part of a foundation that plays very little part in the functioning of the network, transacted through pseudonymous parties.

In the case of Enterprise Blockchain, the transactions are conducted between untrusting peers with established identity and credentials validated through a proper member identification methodology. How the participants are incentivized in the Blockchain based businesses?

Bitcoin and Ethereum public Blockchain based businesses rely on a cryptoasset based mechanism to incentive economic and value creation activity, in the case of Enterprise Blockchain, promoted and run by established member or member consortiums, the incentive arises out of the various benefits

Derived from a Blockchain based approach that vastly increase the accountability, transparency & efficiency of operations while streamlining business processes.

What is the data stored in the Blockchain?

The Blockchain contains details of every public key along with its address ever created and also all the transactions ever done on the platform while the wallets contain all the addresses and their associated public and respective private keys.

The wallet used to transact with the Blockchain through the nodes (a wallet can be embedded in a node and store all the transactions or be a separate .dat file containing only the transactions of all its addresses required to calculate the address balances).

Bitcoin Blockchain uses Level DB database to store all the key value pairs and transactions that can be queried through a block explorer website.

Where is all the data stored?

https://en.bitcoin.it/wiki/Data_directory

Blocks subdirectory

[v0.8 and above] Contains Blockchain data.

- blk*.dat
  - o   Stores Bitcoin blocks, in network format, dumped to raw disk. They are only needed for re-scanning the missing transactions in a wallet, reorganizing to a different part of the chain, and serving the block data to other nodes that are synchronizing.
- blocks/index subdirectory
  - o   [v0.8 and above] A LevelDB database that contains metadata about all known blocks, and where to find them on disk. Without this, finding a block would be very slow.

Chain state subdirectory

[v0.8 and above] A LevelDB database with a compact representation of all currently unspent transaction outputs and some metadata about the transactions they are from. The data here is necessary for validating new incoming blocks and transactions. It can theoretically be rebuilt from the block data (–re-index command line option), but this takes a rather long time. Without it, you could still theoretically do validation indeed, but it would mean a full scan through the blocks (150 GB as of Nov 2017) for every output being spent.

Ethereum

Ethereum uses hashes exclusively for identifying anything. However, hashes are uniformly randomly distributed identifiers. LevelDB keeps keys organized. Hence, the client Geth uses LevelDB. Some of the reasons behind choosing it was:

- In process database (i.e. It don't need to run an additional software)
- Native implementation in Go (i.e. cross platform to everything Go supports)
- Key/value store (i.e. values are arbitrary binary blobs, no schema constraints)
- Modern data storage (i.e. multiple layers on disk, organized in the background)
- Proven track record (i.e. many companies and other databases build on top)

Hyperledger

There are two place which "store" data in Hyperledger Fabric, the ledger and the state database the ledger is the actual "Blockchain". It is a file-based ledger which stores serialized blocks. Each block has one or more transactions. Each transaction contains a read-write set which modifies one or more key/value pairs. The ledger is the definitive source of data and is immutable.

The state database holds the last known committed value for any given key. It is populated when each peer validates and commits a transaction. The state database can always be rebuilt from re-processing the ledger. There are currently two options for the state database: an embedded LevelDB or an external CouchDB.

Further, Hyperledger Fabric uses channels for each private connection between transacting parties.

There is a separate ledger for each channel as well.

Bitcoin stores the details of all the transactions giving the address wise inputs and outputs ever done on the Blockchain along with all the public keys & respective addresses ever created.

Also, Bitcoin allows to store message in the Blockchain using the OP_RETURN function. This will allow senders to store up to 40 bytes of data into a block as output, which is a non-spendable transaction output.

In the genesis block, the inventor of Bitcoin, 'Satoshi Nakamoto' embedded into the Genesis block, The Times 03/Jan/2009 Chancellor on brink of second bailout for banks'.

Who owns Bitcoin Blockchain? What is the ownership structure in other Blockchains and applications?

Bitcoin Blockchain is a publicly owned Blockchain and is open for anyone to transact, download, store and mine. It works like a decentralized autonomous Organization without any owner group. Any decisions regarding the upgradation of the software etc., are uploaded in the form of suggestions in public portals like GitHub and voted upon by the community. Major proposals need to be adopted by over 95% votes for inclusion.

While the upgradations, core network are supposed to cause, 'Soft Fork', new Blockchain arising out of the core Blockchain due to disagreements in the proposed implementation leading to breaking away of a set of miners to start a new Blockchain with different features are a result of 'Hard fork'.

Bitcoin cash & Bitcoin Gold are new cryptocurrencies formed out of such hard forks.

In case of Ethereum, while the public Blockchain operates like a DAPP but which is overseen from a distance by the Ethereum foundation, the private Blockchain version, as in the case of Hyperledger Fabric, Corda, Quorum, Multichain etc., the governance is done by an identified promoter in case of a single party promoted Blockchain and by a quorum represented by a promoter group in case of Consortium Blockchains.

In DAOs created with public Blockchains as the backend, the decision making is driven programmatically while the promoters oversee the governance through a pre-declared code of conduct as per the consensus mechanism adopted.

Some of the different types of decentralized applications for which DAPP concept has been used are given in the above figure. Courtesy https://dappbuilder. io/ . dApp Builder is a platform to create Ethereum DAPPs from prebuilt smart contracts (no coding) and instantly deploy them to Blockchain.

How are the public Blockchains like Bitcoin, Ethereum planning to scale up in view of the rapid increase in usage?

Bitcoin and Ethereum platforms are supported by the improvement projects namely BIP & EIP. All other public platforms are actively supported by a number of improvement projects that are generally incentivized by using a mechanism involving native currencies and tokens. While in Bitcoin, the proposals are listed in GitHub brought to the notice of the informal leadership bodies overseeing bitcoin. org and then put to the notice of mining members for voting and adoption, in case of other Blockchains, the foundation or the governing body consisting of the founders and associates oversees the implementation of the improvement proposals.

Some of the strategies being discussed and implemented by the leading platforms to manage scale are as follows:

(A)   Changing the Consensus algorithm:

Proof of Work followed by Bitcoin Blockchain, some versions of Ethereum Blockchain consume huge resources for arriving at a deterministic consensus. Ethereum platform would soon be shifting to a 'Proof of Stake' based consensus that involves negligible energy consumption.

Some new generation public platforms use variations of 'POW' & 'POS' based consensus algorithms like PoET, DPOS, respectively to minimize resource utilization and wastage.

Enterprise Blockchains use energy efficient algorithms like 'Proof of Authority (POA)', 'PBFT (Practical Byzantine Fault tolerant)' , 'N2N (Node to Node)'and their variations to arrive at deterministic consensus.

To prevent Blockchain bloating, external databases linked through IPFS or Swarm, Giant scale databases like BigChainDB, FlureeDB, cloud databases like IPDB as well as decentralized storage systems like Storj, SIA etc., are used.

Sharding, Segwit, Sidechains etc., are some of the concepts being used to improve the processing power of the public Blockchains.

Sharding

A database shard is a horizontal partition of data in a database or search engine. Each individual partition is referred to as a shard or database shard. Each shard is held on a separate database server instance, to spread load.

Segwit (Segregated Witness consensus layer)

Bitcoin Improvement Proposal number BIP141.The purpose was to solve the transaction malleability that allowed a possibility to double spend by changing transaction code before confirmation while being mined. It was also intended to mitigate size limitation problem that reduces Bitcoin transaction speed. It does this by splitting the transaction into two segments, removing the unlocking signature ("witness" data) from the original portion and appending it as a separate structure at the end.

Sidechains

Sidechains allow organizations to leverage the power of main Blockchain platform like Bitcoin by creating a pegged chain with much more versatile features and having interoperability of their assets with the assets on the main chain (bitcoins). However, sidechains are still considered vulnerable to double spend and are awaiting confirmation of results from approaches like NiPoPoW (Non-Interactive Proofs of Proofs of Work) that could address this issue.

What are the prominent use cases Blockchain being implemented across the world?

SI No	APPLICATION	Organization	USE CASE
1	ADVERTISING	NYLAX	Ads marketplace using Blockchain by New York Interactive Advertising Exchange
2	BORDER CONTROL	Essentia One	Cross border passenger lists tracked through Blockchain in Netherlands
3	BORDER CONTROL	Essentia One	Customs Agents record & safely store passenger data from various input sources
4	CARBON OFFSETS	IBM & Hyperledger	Carbon offset trading through Blockchain
5	COMPUTATION	Digital Currency Group	Improving Data Base security through Blockchain at Amazon Web services
6	DIAMONDS	DEBEERS Group	Tracking Importation and sale of Diamonds using Blockchain
7	ENDANGERED SPECIES PROTECTION	WWF	Blockchain based recording and tracking of rare animals
8	ENERGY	Essentia One	Real time and confidential tracking of resources supplied by Energy suppliers.
9	ENERGY	China National Energy Network	Certifying and storing data of new energy produced & used
10	ENTERPRISE	Microsoft Azure	Blockchain as a Service platform using Ethereum
11	ENTERPRISE	ALPHABET Inc.	Google integrating Blockchain with cloud based servers for

			customers to store data
12	FINE ART	Ascribe	Certificate of Authenticity stored on Blockchain to eliminate forgeries
13	FISHING	Fisheries Trading	Track the movement of fish from capture to consumption
14	GOVERNMENT	Essentia One	Blockchain Solution for managing Logistics Hub by Finnish Government
15	HEALTHCARE	Health Rec	Medical records Storing and Management
16	IDENTIFICATION	Uport	Voter registration in Switzerland through Blockchain
17	INSURANCE	AIG	Blockchain based insurance settlement to cut costs and increase transparency
18	INSURANCE	Estonia	Medical records of all citizens stored and managed through Blockchain
19	JOURNALISM	CIVIL	Decentralized journalism to prevent censorship and increase transparency
20	LAND REGISTRY	National Agency of Public Registry	Land Registry files stored in Blockchain in Georgia
21	MEDICAL RECORDS	Singapore Government	Insurance of Pregnant women managed through Blockchain
22	MOBILE PAYMENT	Ripple	Quick Mobile payments through Blockchain ledger by Japanese Banks
23	MUSIC	Arbit	Blockchain tech. to enable musicians to store and monetize faster in secure manner
24	NATIONAL SECURITY	US Dept. of National Security	Record keeping of CCTV & surveillance camera data on Blockchain
25	NGO	World Food Program	Aid to Syrian refugees transferred through Blockchain for speedy process without middlemen.

26	PHARMACEUTI-CALS	USA	Pharma companies to demonstrate traceability of drugs through Blockchain by 2020.
27	RAILWAYS	Novotrans	Storing repair requests and rolling stocks by Russian Railways
28	REAL ESTATE	PROPY	Complete real estate data& records management
29	SHIPPING	IBM-MAERSK	Cross Border trading for Marine Logistics Industry
30	SUPPLY CHAINS	IBM & Walmart	Farm to Fork Tracking application for food safety
31	SUPPLY CHAINS	LDC(Louis DereyfusCo)	Soybean Importation Operation using Blockchain
32	TAXATION	Miascal Network	Storing electronic invoices and Tax records
33	TOURISM	HAWAI State	Accepting cryptocurrencies across state to boos tourism
34	WASTE MANAGEMENT	Waste on chain on Blockchain in China	Storing Waste Management Data

Compare Transaction speeds of prominent Blockchain platforms with Non Blockchain financial transaction platforms:

Approximate Transaction speed comparison of applications and platforms as on 31-5-2018	
Platform/Application	**Transactions per second**
Bitcoin	10
Bitcoin Cash	70
Litecoin	80
Ethereum	30
Dash Coin	60
Ripple	1500
KOMODO	45000
Auxledger	100000
Paypal-Non Blockchain Platform	200
VISA- Non Blockchain Platform	24000

How does Blockchain secure Internet of Thing (IoT) devices?

The Internet of Things (IoT) refers to the interconnection of smart devices, for communication with the rest of the world through internet and other various wireless technologies, to collect data for making intelligent decisions. However, a lack of intrinsic security measures, inherent security resilience capabilities & sophisticated approach of cyber criminals makes IoT devices vulnerable to privacy and security threats. Blockchain's "security by design" & other capabilities like immutability, transparency, auditability, data encryption, identity management, secured access and operational resilience can help solve most architectural shortcomings of IoT & major security requirements in IoT.

What makes the Blockchain technology unique and disruptive?

Currently most of the existing technologies like ecommerce, market places, Supply chain management, ERP, CRM etc., are focused on developing the productivity and organisational performances within the organisation or between organisation & its buyers and suppliers. Blockchain technology makes hitherto unknown parties, organisations, governments and a host of transacting parties to work with each other with trust guaranteed through advanced automation technologies abstracted through different open source & permissioned platforms.

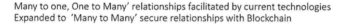

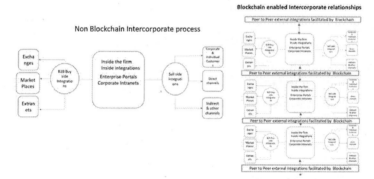

This along with Cloud, in turn enables the organisations to take advantage of IoT, Analytics and other advanced disruptive technologies to expand the organisational reach for complex transactions across the world through a consortium-based approach.

What is Quantum computing and what are its implications for Blockchains?

Quantum computers are computers which exploit quantum mechanics to do certain computations far more quickly than traditional computers. A sufficiently powerful quantum computer would cause some trouble for Bitcoin, though it would certainly not be insurmountable.

It is expected that the current public key cryptography based digital signature algorithms can be broken by quantum computers. The capacity of quantum computers is measured in terms of Qbits and it is expected that a quantum computer with a capacity of 1500 Qbit is required to break Bitcoin's key generation system. While in the case of private & permissioned network, the need for revealing the identity of all the participants & decision makers along with the corresponding consensus mechanisms make them immune to quantum attacks, the private key, public key pairs generated through the current public key cryptography-based systems could be vulnerable. Hence a new system is expected to be evolved to make the same quantum resistant. In such a scenario, the current set of private key, public key pairs need to be replaced by new pairs generated by a corresponding quantum resistant cryptographic system evolved to counter such threats.

What is the Consortium Approach Facilitated by Blockchain

The idea of Supply chain consortiums in the past is not new. The efforts have not been fruitful in the past due to lack of proper frameworks and facilitating infrastructure & view of demonstrable disruption potential

The centre for advanced purchasing studies, highlights the following critical factors for this approach:

1.   Channel master should formulate & articulate the returns and rewards of participation in the consortium well to the potential participants.

2.   Relationship between the trading partners should be based on trust and cooperation. This has always been difficult to achieve till the launch of Blockchain paradigm

3.   It should be cost beneficial to all the trading participants to participate in the program

4.   Channel Master mandating the participants by implicit & explicit means is not desirable in the long run, implying that the benefits should be demonstrable over a defined period for sustainability of the consortium.

5.   The channel master and he trading partners should ensure adherence to all the region specific prevailing laws

Information related to transactions should be secured and not be made available to competing parties.

By facilitating this, blockchain technology offers an immense disruption potential to give a new trajectory for reducing costs & increase productivity & profitability through effective cross border & cross enterprise collaboration.

How is Blockchain technology used in Estonia, the pioneer in Blockchained world? Some FAQs..

Source (https://e-estonia.com/wp-content/uploads/faq-a4-v02-blockchain.pdf, http://www.egov.ee/media/1374/martinovic-blockchains-design-principles-applications-and-case-studies.pdf)

What is Blockchain technology and how is it related to e-Estonia?

Blockchain is a mathematically ensured cyber security technology for rapid and immutable identification of modifications in digital data and intelligent devices. Blockchain technology makes it possible to discover any and all changes made to digital data, no matter how small, no matter by whom, immediately and with zero error.

How is Blockchain used in e-Estonia?

Although Blockchain has only become hot technology in recent years, Estonia has been testing the Blockchain technology since 2008 in the form of "hash-linked time-stamping". Since 2012, Blockchain has been in production use in Estonia's data registries, such as the national health, judicial, legislative, security and commercial code systems, with plans to extend its use to other spheres such as personal medicine, cybersecurity and data embassies.

How does Blockchain work?

One way to look at the Blockchain technology is to view it as a "digital defence dust" that covers all the data and smart devices that need to be protected from corruption and misuse. • Every change in data can be instantly detected based on traces left in the pattern of the "digital defence dust" that covers the data • Blocks of "digital defence dust" are connected to each other and make up a chain that is distributed in millions of computers all over the word, which makes it impossible to change data so that nobody knows – the chain instantly reflects all changes that mismatch the mathematical code in the chain. This way millions of lives and resources are saved, while the potential manipulation of sensitive data (such as health data, intelligence information, legislation related records, etc.) or smart devices (such as military machinery, hospital equipment, intelligent cars etc.) is prevented or instantly detected.

What is KSI (Keyless Signature Infrastructure) & how is it used in Estonia?

The KSI Blockchain

In Estonia, the KSI Blockchain is used to provide a *signature service:* a customer transmits the asset's hash and in return receives a token, which proves participation in the Blockchain.

This creates a so-called proof of existence. Data never leave customer premises, because only the hash is sent to the KSI service. The main security claims provided by the KSI signatures are: *proof of integrity, time, and signing entity.* The signatures can be independently verified, and the system supports a high level of parallelisation and scalability.

X-Road

The X-Road is Estonia's interoperability platform; it integrates different interfaces, security services, and the surrounding regulatory framework. Its main purpose is to connect different governmental institutions and to facilitate state governance via the use of digital technologies. It is used as the main communication system of government services and supports writing to multiple databases, transmitting large data sets, and performing searches across several databases. The main security guarantees offered by the X-Road are authenticity, integrity, and non-repudiation of exchanged data; high availability of services; and confidentiality of exchanged data. These features enable a communication channel over which data are ***digitally signed and encrypted*** and by which all incoming data are ***authenticated and logged***. The X-Road system is the technical backbone of e-Estonia: it underpins various e-services in both the public and private sectors. As a citizen portal to government e-services, the X-Road supports the following kinds of vital activity (*inter alia*):

Registration services: The X-Road enables digital transactions in the following areas: residency; electronic declaration of taxes; validation of driving licenses and registered vehicles; application for child benefits and municipal day care; and exchange of documents among government agencies.

E-health system: The X-Road interconnects hospitals, clinics, and other organisations. It implements a unified Electronic Health Record that supplies medical practitioners with information about patients' health while protecting their privacy. For example, the "e-prescription" system allows doctors to create prescriptions and make them immediately available to pharmacies, patients can then collect their medicines directly from the pharmacy without having to visit the doctor for a hard copy of the prescription.

Judicial and police functions: The "E-File" system uses the X-Road to connect the business processes of courts, police, public prosecutors, prisons, lawyers, and ordinary citizens. Similarly, the Ministry of Interior uses the "e-police" system to provide police officers with access to state registers such as the vehicle register. The police can use this system to check whether a vehicle has been reported as stolen, for example. (Remarkably, Estonian citizens do not need to carry a driver's license or vehicle documents, because authorities can verify such information online directly from the source.)

Why should Blockchain technology be trusted?

No data is ever stored on a Blockchain - instead Blockchain works like a speed camera that detects who has violated the law, when and how. Due to the fact that data, protected by Blockchain technology, is covered with the "digital defence dust", every change in the data can be detected because it leaves a trace in the pattern.

The particular Blockchain technology used by Estonia – KSI Blockchain by Guardtime – has been proven to work and is today even used by NATO and US Department of Defence.

What makes Blockchain technology so special?

The Blockchain technology used in Estonia is different from mainstream Blockchains due to its scalability. This means that even large amounts of data can be covered with "digital defence dust", since the parts of the dust (blocks) are connected to each other using a mathematically verifiable code that connects the blocks into a chain, which cannot be changed without leaving a trace behind.

What is the difference between Blockchain and Bitcoin?

"Blockchain" and "Bitcoin" are two separate terms and should not be confused. While Blockchain is a technological concept, Bitcoin is one of the use cases for a particular type of a Blockchain technology. It is important to keep in mind that even though both, Estonian public e-services and international unregulated digital currencies such as Bitcoin are covered with "digital defence dust", the value of the digital currency may vary (increase or decrease), whereas the value of the data covered with "digital defence dust" does not change and this very fact makes the data even more valuable.

Who controls Blockchain?

The chain of blocks of "digital defence dust" (aka Blockchain) reaches a great number of computers all over the world and can therefore be controlled and verified by great number of parties. The Blockchain is, after all, just an internet-hosted network which stores information as a shared database. That means the information isn't stored in a single location and no centralised version exists for a hacker to corrupt, making it safe to use. It is important to point out that although Blockchain may not prevent the crime itself, it is 100% effective in detecting it.

Blockchain-based cryptomoney frauds are common. So how can a state trust and use Blockchain to protect the private data of its citizens?

When dealing with any sensitive data, it is obvious that this data should not be kept on the Blockchain - after all, Blockchain relies on a large number of eyes to keep it secure! Instead, in order to secure sensitive data, what is kept on the Blockchain are the "hash values" - essentially digital fingerprints of the original data. Just like your own fingerprints uniquely represent you, but don't tell anything about your race, eye colour or thoughts, the same applies to digital fingerprints - while uniquely representing the original data, it is impossible to know anything about the data itself based on the "hash values". Therefore - it does not matter if anyone gets their hands on the Blockchain - there is absolutely no original data there to be compromised!

Can you provide any examples of Blockchain technology actually being useful in protecting the data of some important state or company?

- Millions of lives and resources are saved as the potential manipulation of defence data or smart war machines is prevented using Blockchain technology.

- In order to keep health information completely secure and at the same time accessible to authorised individuals, the electronic ID-card system used by the Estonian e-Health Record uses Blockchain technology to ensure data integrity and mitigate internal threats to the data. In this way every occurrence of data use and misuse is detectable and major damages to a person's health can be prevented (such as the wrong medicine or the wrong dose).

- The Estonian KSI Blockchain technology protects Estonian e-services such as the e-Health Record, e-Prescription database, e-Law and e-Court systems, e-Police data, e-Banking , e-Business Register and e-Land Registry.

- The same KSI Blockchain technology is used by the NATO Cooperative Cyber Defence Centre of Excellence, European Union IT Agency, US Defence Department and also by Lockheed Martin, Ericsson and others.

What happens if a Blockchain company goes bankrupt, how is data protection assured then?

The company itself can NEVER see the actual data that is protected, it only provides the "digital defence dust" solution that can ensure its integrity and mitigate internal threats. So nothing happens when a Blockchain company disappears, all the data protected will remain verifiable for its integrity for forever based on the shared Blockchain, and if applicable for a particular Blockchain technology, also based on the physical publication of the Blockchain in the world's newspapers.

How does Blockchain technology contribute to the well-being of a layman?

Blockchain technology helps to ensure that data concerning the person is not misused.

For example:

- Blockchain technology helps detect who looks at a person's digital health data and changes it and when;

- Blockchain technology helps to see when information about a company in the e-Business Register was changed and why;
- Blockchain technology helps to detect who changed data about real estate in the e-Land register or statements documented in the e-Court system as well as when and how;
- Blockchain technology helps to ensure that no one has manipulated smart devices such as intelligent transportation or smart war machines that could become life-threatening.

How quickly can the misuse of data be detected using Blockchain technology?

According to the research by FireEye, one of the leading cyber security vendors in the world today, it currently takes organizations on average of about 7 months to detect breaches and manipulations of electronic data.

With Blockchain solution like the one Estonia is using, these breaches and manipulations can be detected immediately.

CHAPTER 4

It's 'Data' Stupid! - The Rising Power of Data Exponents

"In God we trust; all others bring data."

— *W. Edwards Deming*

A quote known by many in the corporate world has never been more relevant even after decades of technological developments.

Data Scientist, Data Analyst, Cryptographer, Internet Security Expert are deemed to be the best jobs of the current generation. Why not? Data collection, Analysis, Management, Manipulation and corruption are supposedly behind the biggest success stories of the current generation.

Whether it is the victories in US Presidential elections, term after term, rise of gigantic companies like Google, Amazon, Facebook, Netflix, Microsoft, Walmart, Apple, Tesla and the like to their gigantic and invincible status and the rise of countries like China from nowhere to the most coveted exponent of the cutting edge technologies of Artificial Intelligence and Machine Learning is linked to their exploits of leveraging Data Management technologies. After-all there is no Machine learning without Data sets collection.

There was a time when they said, 'Data is Garbage and Information is Power'. Countries, Kings, Cops and Companies used to go to any extent to plant their people in right places to get right information at right time that enabled them to manage opinion, win wars and get ahead of the competition.

The advent of the internet in the last part of the 20th century, enabled various entities publish relevant information that enabled them to communicate the details that they wanted their subjects to know through Web 1.0, a medium that allowed for one-way communication.

Web 2.0 allowed the users to interact with the publishers and provide them feedback about their experiences, needs and thoughts. The advent and proliferation of e-commerce allowed the consumers to undertake transactions and provide more information about themselves, their purchasing behavior and much more. The convenience the web offered to consumers enabled the users to offer crucial information about themselves that in turn paved way for marketing companies to pin point their targets.

The advent of advanced Search engines like Google and Yahoo while offering massive convenience to consumers, effectively made every citizen totally dependent on them for everything and anything.

Digital Marketing coupled with Ecommerce became the hot subject in early 2000s which led to the rise of Google, Facebook as the run-away super stars of wealth creation for their promoters and investors while becoming the most sought after companies by the customers for the facilities, convenience and modes of self-expression they offered.

Web 3.0 that followed enabled P2P (Peer to Peer) communication possible while Intelligence started getting embedded into the services provided by the giants like Google, Apple and Facebook.

The 'Semantic Web' allowed the consumers to talk their needs to chatbots that offered them instant answers. The IoT revolution that emerged in the recent past has enabled the companies to monitor the activities of their consumers in a 360 degree manner through web connected devices and tracking, which in turn while collecting the data, also offered an unforeseen convenience to their users. Home automation, intelligent spaces, automated companions and friendly chatbots started getting embedded into the lives of the citizens across the world.

All these developments were not without side-effects. The loss of privacy, the threat of data leaks and the all-round embedded risks due to the failure of 'Single Point of Ownership and Control' led the world to unforeseen consequences.

The obsession of the marketers with data and the subsequent developments leading to evolution of data management tools to manage unbelievable large sets of data that, when clubbed with the Analytics, Artificial Intelligence and Machine Learning Algorithms have tilted the odds away from the customers to the giant centralized corporations. The power offered by the knowledge of data that enabled the companies to build fortunes and the unscrupulous to hold their subjects to ransom ware attacks to say the least, opened up the eyes of the regulators and the citizens to the need to safeguard their identities. After all it is better late than being too late.

The risks associated with such an environment have now been well exposed leading to regulatory actions like GDPR (General Data Protection Regulations) and Non-regulated platforms like Blockchain that help manage the risks, while posing challenges at the same time.

This has led to the rise of Blockchain technologies on one hand and also to the regulations like GDPR by European Union, which could soon spread across the world.

Estonia, a land of 1.3 million people, one of the smallest in the world, is well known as the birth place to Skype. One of the most digitally advanced countries in the world, Estonia is a part of the D5 Nations, including UK, South Korea, Israel, New Zealand and is truly one of the wonders of the modern era. Its 'Digital Citizen

Identity card' is known to be the most advanced in the world. It is ranked as the world's top most in Digital awareness and Health records as the entire population is secured by the Blockchain Technology by Guard time. Estonia is also ranked best on the Internet freedom index and is one of the biggest exponents of 'Internet of Things' (IoT) technology. While most people are still to hear of the coming explosion of IOT devices and Edge computing, Estonia is researching about 'Mist' Computing, which is two steps ahead of Edge computing and the next step to Fog computing that is supposed to empower IOT devices in the fight against the Malware attacks, in conjunction with the security offered by Blockchain technology.

The world is still reeling under the DDOS (Distributed Denial of Service) attack of October 2016, when a mere 6 lakh IoT endpoints compromised by a botnet brought down many of the world's top internet portals, through a flood of maliciously directed traffic. How do we avoid such attacks, when the world is already flooded with over 20 billion internet connected devices as per an IHS survey?

In many ways, Estonia, with highest penetration of IoT devices, has secured itself against any such attacks in the future by leveraging the IoT and also securing its devices by empowering technologies like Edge computing, Fog computing and Blockchain technologies. Is it the way forward for the rest of the world?

While we are living in most exciting times, we are also living in some of the most dangerous times. World Economic Forum's Global Risks Report 2018 cited Cyber-attacks and data fraud as the two of the top five threats to global stability in the coming years. We have already seen these in action in the recent past with such audacious assaults involving almost all global leading companies including Google, Yahoo, Facebook and many more Transnational Banks, which are supposed to maintain high standards of Internet security and safe guard their users' interests.

Thank fully, companies like Microsoft, IBM, Google, Cisco and Intel are working in tandem to empower us with all the technologies and learning needed to manage the burgeoning risks.

The centralized organizations which are in one way responsible for the loss of our privacy, are also now coming together to make this world, a safer and secure place.

We are witnessing three major trends that are coming together to spur the development and adoption of the latest technologies in tandem. They are:

(A) **Increasing tendency for decentralization:** While decentralization is considered to be having three dimensions, namely i) Political ii) Administrative and iii) Logical. Increasing skepticism about the centralized control and their potential of becoming single point of failure is a strong catalyst for the tendency on the part of the subjects for asserting self-expression. While ironically, the need to trust a central organisations has led to the proliferation of Ecommerce, the very lackof trust in these centralized organisations and their vulnerability to act as Single Points of Failure, is accelerating the trend towards Political and Administrative decentralization, though it may still be acceptable to be logically centralized as this is required to add a method to the process.

(B) **Increasing availability of Open Source Technologies:** The trend towards open source technologies like Linux, Android operating systems and programming languages like Java, PHP has now spread across all technological paradigms putting immense power in the hands of the developers to rapidly develop programs and applications at minimal cost.

(C) **Availability of Cloud computing enabled 'Pay as you use' services:** During the early days of Internet, for an organisations to develop any applications, it had to invest heavily in a lot of hardware. Now, the availability of the entire development environment as PAAS (Platform as a Service), IAAS (Infrastructure as a Service) and SAAS (Software as a Service) has enabled a large number of entrepreneurs with limited resources, to undertake application development and thus implement Proof of Concepts (POCs) and launch new products and services with a very low investment.

These trends are catalyzing the growth and adoption of new age technologies like Blockchain at a rapid rate.

Join me to recount the enthralling journey from 'Data' for Quality paradigm, to 'Data' for control and the shifting of the power back into the hands of the 'Intelligent' end points that we all are!

Points to note:

- Cloud computing fulfils the need for large amounts of data to be accessed quickly.

- Edge computing allows data produced by IoT devices to be processed closer to where it is created with the help of devices, gateways, software and computing equipment instead of sending it across long routes to data centers or clouds.

- Fog computing refers to the network connections between the edge devices and cloud. Fog computing extends the cloud computing paradigm to the edge of the network and aims at transferring only valuable data through cloud computing networks. Thus, it helps devices to identify potential intruders/threats.

- Mist computing is lightweight form of computing power, employing microcomputers and microcontrollers, that resides at the very edge of the network fabric. Mist computing feeds data into edge computing nodes and potentially to fog computing nodes after which data is sent to cloud computing platforms.

CHAPTER 5

The Rise of Digital Marketing: How it All Started...

In early days of the 21st century, all you needed to know about your consumer or website visitor were the following:

Name, Age, Location, Sex, email Id, the preferred time of surfing and the approximate socio-economic status.

This has led to the burgeoning digital marketing industry that trailed potential customers as they traversed through websites and portals in search of information, products and services.

The launch and subsequent explosion of Mobile & Smart phone technologies while putting the power in the hands of the consumers, also exposed them to unwarranted tracking, targeting and solicitation by the 'Smart' marketers who ran away with their business all the way to their banks. Companies that were not into Digital Marketing lost big or could find the going tough. While Facebook and LinkedIn were the darlings of the online marketers, a number of other social media platforms such as Twitter, Pinterest, Instagram and WhatsApp enveloped their audience and provided valuable information across various psychographic and social angles.

Learn More: http://rad-students.wikia.com/wiki/Web_3.0_%26_Beyond

Evolution of Internet			
	Web 1.0	Web 2.0	Web 3.0
Communication	Broadcast	Interactive	Engaged / Invested
Information	Static / Read-only	Dynamic	Portable & Personal
Focus	Organisation	Community	Individual
Personal	Home Pages	Blogs / Wikis	Lifestreams
Content	Ownership	Sharing	Curation
Interaction	Web Forms	Web Applications	Smart Applications
Search	Directories	Key Words / Tags	Contex / Relevance
Metrics	Page Views	Cost Per Click	User Engagement
Advertising	Banners	Interactive	Behavioral
Resarch	Britannica Online	Wikipedia	The Sementic Web
Technologies	HTML / FTP	Flash / Java / XML	RDF / RDFS /OWL

The World Wide Web was first dedicated open to the world on 30th April 1993, approximately 25 years ago by Sir Tim Berners Lee, who declared it as an open source project and open for everyone to use.

Earlier in March 1989, Tim laid out his vision for what would become the web in a document called "Information Management: A Proposal". He envisioned a world in which millions of computers across the world could work in conjunction with each other through a common platform.

By October of 1990, Tim had written the three fundamental technologies that remain the foundation of today's web (and which you may have seen appear on parts of your web browser):

- **HTML:** Hypertext Mark-up Language. The mark-up (formatting) language for the web.

- **URI:** Uniform Resource Identifier. A kind of "address" that is unique and used to identify to each resource on the web. It is also commonly called a URL.

- **HTTP:** Hypertext Transfer Protocol. Allows for the retrieval of linked resources from across the web.

Growing under the aegis of CERN, the web was made open to public on royalty free basis in April 1993. Tim moved to MIT, USA in 1994 and founded W3 C (World Wide Web consortium) of which he continues till today as its Chairperson.

Ironically, the early web community was founded by TIM with the very basic tenets that are underlining the foundations of Blockchain technology.

- **Decentralization:** Permission less, leaderless, no single point of failure, and no indiscriminate control or censorship.

- **Non-discrimination:** Equality of consumers subscribing to different levels of service,

- Bottom-up design Open sourced implementation with everyone's participation,

- **Universality:** Borderless communication cutting across all segments of world populations

- **Consensus:** Transparent, participatory process at W3C for creating open standards.

Starting as an open source tool to connect communities across the world, the world wide web grew by leaps and bounds and evolved into one of the biggest killer apps of all times.

Timelines

While the web evolved with the launch and proliferation of new technologies, the number of users grew by leaps and bounds.

Web 1.0 was all about communicating one's proposition and informing of their presence to the potential users and the communication was mostly one sided.

Evolution of Digital Marketing

1990	Prodigy, Compu serve
1991	America Online
1992	SMS Messaging
1994	First Onlne Display AD
1995	Yahoo Search Engine
1996	Email Marketing
1997	AIS Media Launched, Mobile Payments, SEO
1998	SEM & Google
2000	PPC, Adwords, Google Mobile Adverstising
2003	LinkedIn, Word Press, MySpace
2004	Mobile First, Yelp, Responsive Web Design, Facebook
2005	Google Analytics SEO YouTube
2006	Twitter, Marketing Automation
2007	iPhone, App Store, Geotargeting, Tumblr
2008	Facebook Ads
2009	Bling
2010	iPad, Instagram, Internet Surpasses, Newspaper
2011	Google+, Pinterest, Snapchat
2012	Infographics, Visual Content Marketing
2013	iBeacon, Micro-location
2014	Mobile Surpasses, Desktop Users, Omni Channel
2015	Wearables
2016+	Internet of Things, Mobile Overtakes Email & Social, Online Ad Spend Equivalent to TV Spend

Web 2.0 involved users communicating with the website owners and the companies on a live basis. This led to a lot of user generated data and a multiplying stream of people joining the bandwagon of internet users to experience the unimaginable convenience. Trade over the internet and social media explosion was the offshoot of this revolution.

Web 3.0 involved the communication among the people further boosted by the ubiquitous connectivity catalyzed by the growing trend of smartphone usage and high bandwidths.

And the numbers...

All these led to the explosion of data streams being generated, which were used by the powerful marketers to analyses with latest tools and technologies to gain unimaginable insights into buyer behavior. The era that started with a vision of decentralized world, ended by going into the hands of a select few, while also increasing the risk of SPOF (Single Point of Failure) a threat that was supposed to be addressed by the early web community. The dominance of the powerful marketing organizations, that were the best exponents of data generated, can be depicted in a humorous way in the following example where the marketer is able to not only predict the way, the consumer behaves, but also prescribe the suggested course of action!

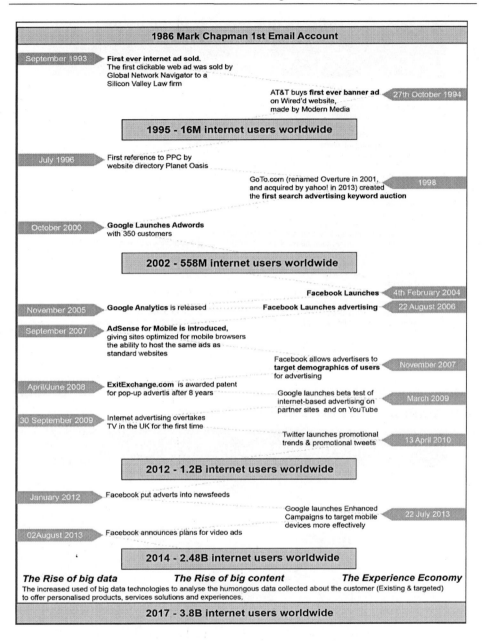

1986 Mark Chapman 1st Email Account

September 1993 — **First ever internet ad sold.**
The first clickable web ad was sold by
Global Network Navigator to a
Silicon Valley Law firm

AT&T buys **first ever banner ad**
on Wired'd website,
made by Modern Media — 27th October 1994

1995 - 16M internet users worldwide

July 1996 — First reference to PPC by
website directory Planet Oasis

GoTo.com (renamed Overture in 2001,
and acquired by yahoo! in 2013) created
the **first search advertising keyword auction** — 1998

October 2000 — **Google Launches Adwords**
with 350 customers

2002 - 558M internet users worldwide

Facebook Launches — 4th February 2004

November 2005 — **Google Analytics** is released   **Facebook Launches advertising** — 22 August 2006

September 2007 — **AdSense for Mobile is introduced,**
giving sites optimized for mobile browsers
the ability to host the same ads as
standard websites

Facebook allows advertisers to
target demographics of users
for advertising — November 2007

April/June 2008 — **ExitExchange.com** is awarded patent
for pop-up advertis after 8 years

Google launches beta test of
internet-based advertising on
partner sites and on YouTube — March 2009

30 September 2009 — Internet advertising overtakes
TV in the UK for the first time

Twitter launches promotional
trends & promotional tweets — 13 April 2010

2012 - 1.2B internet users worldwide

January 2012 — Facebook put adverts into newsfeeds

Google launches Enhanced
Campaigns to target mobile
devices more effectively — 22 July 2013

02 August 2013 — Facebook announces plans for video ads

2014 - 2.48B internet users worldwide

The Rise of big data   **The Rise of big content**   **The Experience Economy**

The increased used of big data technologies to analyse the humongous data collected about the customer (Existing & targeted)
to offer personalised products, services solutions and experiences.

2017 - 3.8B internet users worldwide

A Google joke that reflects this mood is given below:

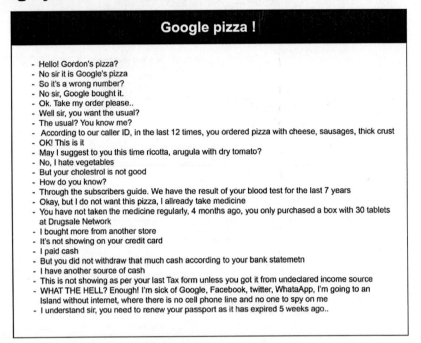

Today, the Digital marketing ecosystem could be broadly represented as per the following diagram:

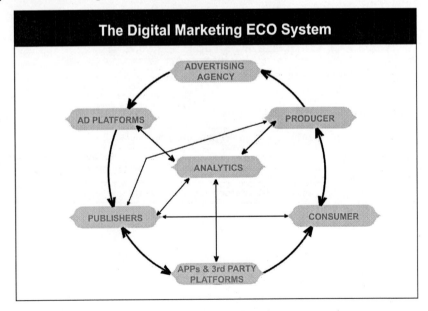

Consumers

Consumers surf the web for information, purchase from producers and platforms online or offline leaving a huge digital footprint.

Producers/ Advertisers

Manufacturers & Distributors provide goods and services to the consumers and enlist the services of the advertising agencies or online platforms directly to target consumers in order to maximize sales.

Publishers

Publishers collect the data of their visitors and create visitor profiles that will allow them to access the complete information on their traffic sources, demographics, psychographic and social profiles. They can analyses the information directly or with the help of Analytics consultants.

Some of the top publishers and their characteristics are given below:

	FACEBOOK	TWITTER	LINKEDDIN	GOOGLE+	YOU TUBE	PINTEREST
INDUSTRY	B2C	B2B/B2C	B2B	B2C	B2C	B2C
FOCUS AREA	Share - News, contents, stories etc...	Share - News, contents, stories etc...	Share - Corporat and Industry News/Info etc...	Share - News, contents, stories etc...	Share - Videos	Share - products, info, websites etc.
BRAND VISIBILITY	Facebook Business pages	Profile pages	Company pages & recommendations both from Industry & networking groups	Google+ page	Dedicated Brand Channel	Boards
BRAND INFLUENCERS	Likes/ Comments	Tweets/ retweets	Likes/ Comments/ Discussions	Shares, Comments & Add to Circle	Subscribe & Share	Likes Comments
WEBSITE CONNECTS	Direct Links/ & eCommerce apps	Direct Links	Direct Links	Direct Links/ Google+ Activity Influences	Direct Links	Direct Links
ADVERTISEMENTS	Facebook Ads Premium Ads Sponsored Stories	Promoted Tweets/Trends/ Enhanced Accounts Profile	Ads	N/A	Ads- Video/Display	N/A

Advertising Agencies

Adverting agencies work with their clients & producers of various products and services to plan and invest their marketing budgets across media platforms for an integrated and cumulative impact that yield desired results. Online advertising has become a major component of the media plans due to the traceability of the ROIs in such investments by organizations on a live basis enabling fine tuning of campaigns.

Advertising Platforms

Advertising Platforms leverage sophisticated algorithms to provide a bridge between the Publishers on one hand and the producers / advertising agencies on the other, serving huge impressions in front of the online traffic thus playing the role of an intelligent middle person effectively.

A comprehensive digital marketing strategy for any organization is reflected in the following table:

DIGITAL MARKETING					
MARKETING	People	Positioning	Messaging		
SEO	Links	Page Optimization	Site Architecture	Technical Challenges	
MOBILE MARKETING	Knowledge of Audience & opportunities	Effecting & Measuring Campaigns			
ADVERTISING	Display	Search			
SOCIAL MEDIA MARKETING	Strategy	Content			
EMAIL MARKETING	Demographics & Segmentation	Cutomize Content	Scheduling		
WEBSITE OPTIMIZATION	Multivariate testing	Usability testing	Entry/Exit surveys/tests	Web Analytics	Click Analysis & Mapping
CONTENT STRATEGY	Benefits driven content	Corporate blog	Creation of Linkable Assets	Promotional Strategy	

Analytics services

Analytics service providers excel in the art of thorough analysis and profiling of the traffic constituents and provide insights to the publishers and their contractors. These insights enable the publishers to target their customers with pin point accuracy.

Here is where companies like Cambridge Analytica which is caught up in the scandal encompassing US Presidential elections and Facebook users excel.

Cambridge Analytica collected the information of Facebook users and their friends. This information was acquired through an app it published.

The data of about the 50 million Facebook users was acquired from 270,000 Facebook users who shared the data with the app "this is your digital life". By giving this third-party app permission to acquire their data, back in 2015, this also gave the app information about the friend network of those people, which resulted in information of about 50 million users which later was expanded to 87 million users. The app developer breached Facebook's terms of service by giving the data to Cambridge Analytica (CA). CA collects data on voters using sources such as demographics, consumer behavior, internet activity, and other public and private sources. According to The Guardian, CA is using psychological data derived from millions of Facebook users, largely without users' permission or knowledge. Another source of information was the "Cruz Crew" mobile app that tracked physical movements and contacts and according to the Associates Press, invaded personal data more than any other app of presidential candidates.

> "Today in the United States we have somewhere close to four or five thousand data points on every individual. So we model the personality of every adult across the United States, some 230 million people."

> — *Alexander Nix, chief executive of Cambridge Analytica, October 2016.*

The company claims to use "data enhancement and audience segmentation techniques" providing "psychographic analysis" for a "deeper knowledge of the target audience". The company uses the OCEAN scale of personality traits. Using what it calls "behavioral micro targeting" the company indicates that it can predict "needs" of subjects and how these needs may change over time. Services then can be individually targeted for the benefit of its clients from the political arena, governments, and companies providing "a better and more actionable view of their key audiences." According to Sasha Issenberg, CA indicates that it can tell things about an individual he might not even know about himself

The use of personal data collected without knowledge or permission to establish sophisticated models of user's personality raises ethical and privacy issues. CA operates out of the United States; its operations would be illegal in Europe with its stricter laws. While Cruz is outspoken about protecting personal information from the government, his database of CA has been described as "political-voter surveillance".

Regarding CA's use of Facebook users, a speaker for CA indicated that these users gave permission while signing up with the provider, while Facebook declared that "misleading people or misusing information" is in violation of Facebook's policies. In 2015, Facebook indicated that it was investigating the matter. In March 2018, Facebook announced that it had suspended the accounts of Strategic Communication Laboratories for failing to delete data on Facebook users that had been improperly collected. (Source Wikipedia)

APPs and 3rd Party Platforms

These are the numerous applications that run on the internet and on various platforms that enable the websites to increase engagement, provide entertainment and additional revenues. These app owners get access to the details of the platform traffic and are bound by confidentiality agreements n not to use such information for commercial purposes and also expose the details to unauthorized sources. Cambridge Analytica obtained such information from an app provider on Facebook platform and utilized the same for targeting the consumers and apparently helped shape the public opinion in favor of Donald Trump, thus adding to his popularity in the process.

While Alexander Nix suggests that data collection and micro targeting benefits the voters because they receive messages about issues they care about, digital rights protection groups are concerned that private information is collected, stored, and shared while individuals are "left in the dark about [it]" and have no control.

Significant backlash against Facebook came to light in March 2018, resulting in controversy as well as a $37 billion drop in the market capitalization of Facebook, as of 20 March. Due to the scandal of enabling monetization of Facebook personal data, one assessment was that only 41% of Facebook users trust the company. On 26 March, the US Federal Trade Commission announced it is "conducting an open investigation of Facebook Inc.'s privacy practices following the disclosure that 50 million users' data got into the hands of political consultancy Cambridge Analytica."(https://en.wikipedia.org/wiki/Cambridge_Analytica)

Whatever be the intentions of Facebook or Cambridge Analytica, the damage has been done and a huge overhauling of the global organizational approach to preserve and protect the Privacy of their users is now underway. The top Social Media Monitoring tools are summarized in the following diagram:

Companies like Hubspot & Google offered amazing education and structured programs to the learners and exponents that enable organizations to leverage the power of the Digital Marketing.

One can find excellent resources at https://academy.hubspot.com/certification& https://learndigital.withgoogle.com/digitalunlocked/certification

It is very important for the organizations to be on top of all the communication that is happening around their offerings, whether it is between customers, competitors, media, partners and employees across various social media platforms. Analyzing the same will help them in managing their impact in a positive manner. This is called online reputation management and once again involves churning enormous amounts of data using advanced analytical tools. Some of the top social media monitoring tools employed by organizations to monitor the effectiveness of the campaigns and take appropriate action are given below:

Social Mention

Social Mention is a social media search engine that searches for keywords on social media platforms (blogs, comments, bookmarks, events, news, videos) and provides graphic illustrations or charts showing mentions per day or week

Twitter

Twitter Advanced Search is the best way to ferret out tweets about a targeted sector. Look for keywords, serach by location, date or with other filters. Track is a litte known Twitter feature that lets you track keywords and have them sent directly to your mobile phone as soonas they are posted.

Addict-o-matic

Addict-o-matic lets you instantly create a custom page with the latest buzz on a given topic. The browser-based tool offers a one stop customized site for seeing results across multiple social media channels.

Sprout Social

Chicago-based Sprout Social lets you target and discover new customers or supporters, monitor yoar brand across social Web, organise your social netweoks and manage up to five identities with the basic plan. The service offers an easy-to-digest summary of what's happening online around your social presence.

Wildfire

Wildfire, which creates interactive promotions on social sites, has a tool, Social Media Monitor, that tracks and compares how nonprofits and brands are performing on Facebook and Twitter.

HootSuite

HootSuite issocial media dashboard. You can track results and use Twittet lists to check on what people in a specific sector are talking about. Free for one person, $5-$15/mo, for other team members.

Topsy

Enter a search term on TOPSY, such as the name of your cause or nonprofit, and you'll get results showing what users are saying on Twitter and Google+. Fine-tune your results to see only what users are saying within the hour, or up to 30 days.

Trackur

AN online reputation management tooland social media monitoring tool, Trackur is Google Alerts on steriods. It will deliver results to your inbox, RSS feed or web based dashboard. Quickly monitor your reputatiion, check on trends and analyze media mentions for your brand. 4 plans cost $18-$377/,onth.

Thrive

Thrive is an all in one social media tool that lets you listen, publish, report and engage with donors and supporters. Features like contact tagging and sorting, automated keyword searching and conversation archiving help you cultivate relationships over time, turningfans into donors.

WatchThatPage

Sometimes you'd like to know when up-dates takeplace to an important Web page - say, your Wikipedia page or key pages on your competitors sites. Instruct WatchThatPage to keep tabs on any Web page, and you will receive an alert any time a change is made to the page.

CHAPTER 6

Customer Relationship Management

Customer Relations Management CRM is an important tool in the hands of the marketers to maximize the life time value of the business opportunity provided to them. CRM aims at:

- Maximizing sales force coverage effectiveness.
- Maximizing conversion of potential customers.
- Maximizing uptime of customers & their satisfaction leading to customer advocacy.

This involves tracking the customer through the lead generation lifecycle till the end of his association to maximize the business provided. While progressive organizations adopt a number of proactive steps resulting in customer delight and customer advocacy, this again results in a collection of data sets across the life cycle of the association.

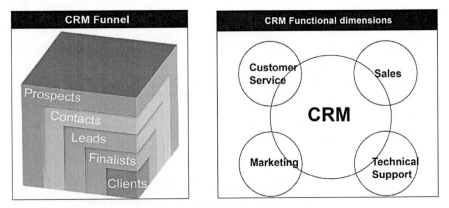

Customer relationship management aims to track the journey of the prospects across various stages of interactions depending on the level of interaction, closeness of the prospect to conversion and the interactions of the respective sales team members through this journey.

A well-managed CRM solution ensures that all the potential customers are addressed with due respect and attention by all the various departments.

While it is the sales and marketing department that is involved during the order generation and execution process, the duty of the customer service department is to ensure that any complaints are properly addressed on the post to minimize the agony of the grieving customer's ad and also keep them delighted. The duty of the Technical support department is to ensure minimal downtime and maximum productivity of the assets employed with the customer, thus maximizing their return on investments.

Technology plays very important role in the CRM of any organization. There are various stages of interaction corresponding to various activities; some of them are aided by technology and most of them through an appropriate well-oiled system involving the following activities:

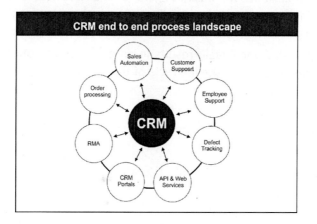

Most of the organizations employ websites to communicate and interact with their potential customers and also use landing pages for their online campaigns

Data is collected across the various stages of the customer's journey from visiting online portals or getting into contact with a company representative in some way to processing grievances and merchandise returns through appropriate authorizations and redressal.

These are mapped against industry benchmarks to ensure that customer handling machinery of the organization is constantly challenged, thus maximizing the life time revenue potential conversions.

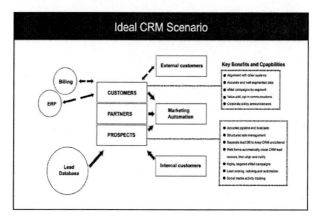

All these activities once again result in churning of huge data and the organizations

which have mastered this process stood to gain the biggest chunks of customers' pockets.

The ideal CRM system for any organization is expected to integrate with all the backend and front end systems across the entities to provide a single view of the customer, customer needs, potential and issues that can be proactively traced and handled to maximize the business generated and serviced. Most businesses dream of having a customer who is delighted and advocates for their product or service in turn generating referral customers while increasing consumption.

Needless to say, this once again results in an enormous amount of data to be tracked and managed across the life cycle of the engagement.

CHAPTER 7

Big Data Evolution, Landscape, Exponent & Implications

The huge interaction provided by the Web 2.0 and the increasing commercial interaction led to the generation of vast amount of data that not only provided huge opportunity for publishers to gain insights, but also was problematic to handle in the short run.

UNIT	ABBREVIATION	STORAGE
Bit	B	Binary Digit, Single 1 or 0
Nibble	-	4 bits
Byte/Octet	B	8 bits
Kilobyte	KB	1024 bytes
Megabyte	MB	1024 KB
Gigabyte	GB	1024 MB
Terabyte	TB	1024 GB
Petabyte	PB	1024 TB
Exabyte	EB	1024 PB
Zettabyte	ZB	1024 EB
Yottabyte	YB	1024 ZB

The world's technological per-capita capacity to store information has roughly doubled every 40 months since the 1980s; as of 2012, every day 2.5 exa-bytes (2.5×1018) of data are generated. Based on an IDC report prediction, the global data volume will grow exponentially from 4.4 zettabytes to 44 zettabytes between 2013 and 2020.By 2025, IDC predicts there will be 163 zettabytes of data.

One question for large enterprises is determining who should own Big Data initiatives that affect the entire organization.

Source: Wikipedia

The increasing number of Data sources in an organization and their complexity led to reduction in speed of processing time and operations.

Data is characterized by its:

- Variety
- Velocity

- Volume
- Veracity &
- Value (embedded in the data that needs to be mined)

While there have always been a number of Statistical tools and techniques to analyses data to come out with right inferences and corresponding actions, the increasing volumes of data prove to be unmanageable.

The different types of analytics that are performed on the data, summarized in the following figure, gave immense power to those using the same to target their customers with precision and walk away with high market shares. In other words, the exponent of Data Management Technologies will be able to mine the value that is embedded in it.

There are five categories of analytics which create business value opportunities for manufacturers across the enterprise. The complexity of the analytics capabilities required and magnitude of the business value opportunity increase across these five categories of analytics:

- **Descriptive:** Analysis of historical data that provides simplistic insight into past activities and performance to understand previous behavior and/or outcomes;
- **Diagnostic:** Utilization of historical data to identify a product failure pattern and determine the failure's root cause. Once the root cause is understood and diagnosed, the resolution can also be identified through mapping to knowledge management tools;
- **Predictive:** Use of modelling, data mining, and machine learning to analyses both real-time and historical data to predict and anticipate future events based on patterns found in the data;
- **Prescriptive:** Once a future event (outcome) is predicted, a suggested next step and/or decision is identified, evaluated, and can be automatically enabled.
- **Cognitive:** Provides the right sight and vision for the business to move forward by not only providing answer to questions, but also enabling the management to look beyond and ask the right questions, proactively predicting and preparing for the future.

Source: Frost and Sullivan report.

Progressive organizations are pro-actively leveraging the data available to them across various internal and external sources. Any Organization has to have a structured approach to various streams of data that it can capture and leverage the same to maximize the business impact arising out of analysis and applications to predict the future performance. A typical five phase approach to implementing data analytics as observed in the case of an insurance services company is depicted in the following figure:

Understanding Data Volume

Bytes(8 Bits)
0.1 bytes: A binary decision
1 byte: A single character
10 bytes: A single word
100 bytes: A telegram

Kilobyte (1000 Bytes)
1 Kilobyte: A very short story
2 Kilobytes: A Typewritten page
10 Kilobytes: An encyclopaedic page
50 Kilobytes: A compressed document image page
100 Kilobytes: A low-resolution photograph

Megabyte (1 000 000 Bytes)
1 Megabyte: A small novel
5 Megabytes: 30 seconds of TV-quality video
10 Megabytes: A digital chest X-ray

Gigabyte (1 000 000 000 Bytes)
1 Gigabyte: A pickup truck filled with paper OR A movie at TV quality
2 Gigabytes: 20 meters of shelved books
20 Gigabytes: A good collection of the works of Beethoven
50 Gigabytes: A floor of books
100 Gigabytes: A floor of academic journals OR A large ID-1 digital tape

Terabyte (1 000 000 000 000 Bytes)
1 Terabyte: 50000 trees made into paper and printed
2 Terabytes: An academic research library
50 Terabytes: The contents of a large Mass Storage System

Petabyte (1 000 000 000 000 000 Bytes)
2 Petabytes: All US academic research libraries
20 Petabytes: Production of hard-disk drives in 1995

Exabyte (1 000 000 000 000 000 000 Bytes)
5 Exabytes: All words ever spoken by human beings.

Zettabyte (1 000 000 000 000 000 000 000 Bytes)

Yottabyte (1 000 000 000 000 000 000 000 000 Bytes)
Xenottabyte (1 000 000 000 000 000 000 000 000 000 Bytes)
Shilentnobyte (1 000 000 000 000 000 000 000 000 000 000 Bytes)
Domegemegrottebyte (1 000 000 000 000 000 000 000 000 000 000 000 Bytes)

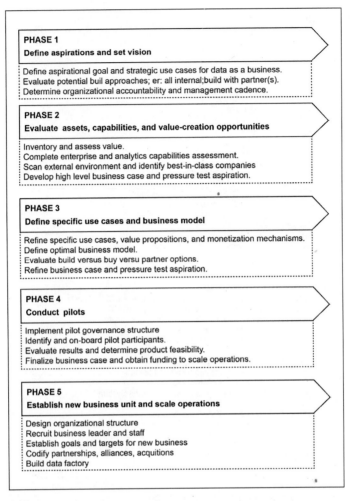

PHASE 1

Define aspirations and set vision

Define aspirational goal and strategic use cases for data as a business.
Evaluate potential buil approaches; er: all internal;build with partner(s).
Determine organizational accountability and management cadence.

PHASE 2

Evaluate assets, capabilities, and value-creation opportunities

Inventory and assess value.
Complete enterprise and analytics capabilities assessment.
Scan external environment and identify best-in-class companies
Develop high level business case and pressure test aspiration.

PHASE 3

Define specific use cases and business model

Refine specific use cases, value propositions, and monetization mechanisms.
Define optimal business model.
Evaluate build versus buy versu partner options.
Refine business case and pressure test aspiration.

PHASE 4

Conduct pilots

Implement pilot governance structure
Identify and on-board pilot participants.
Evaluate results and determine product feasibility.
Finalize business case and obtain funding to scale operations.

PHASE 5

Establish new business unit and scale operations

Design organizational structure
Recruit business leader and staff
Establish goals and targets for new business
Codify partnerships, alliances, acquitions
Build data factory

Sources of Data

As the activities and the organizations grew, the scale of data generation and consumption across the world grew rapidly.

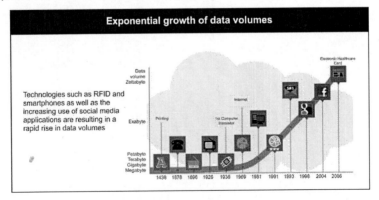

The Data corresponding to an organization is gleaned from various sources internal and external in various forms such as text, images, json files, videos, audios etc. and stored in a streamlined fashion for onward processing. This has led to the creation of Data Lakes.

The increasing adoption of technology across all aspects of organizational functioning led to the proliferation of all types of data and correspondingly the necessity for advanced technologies for extraction, storage, processing and analysis.

This led to the launch of Hadoop project by co-founders, Doug Cutting and Mike Cafarella.

Apache Hadoop is a collection of open-source software utilities that facilitate using a network of many computers to solve problems involving massive amounts of data and computation.

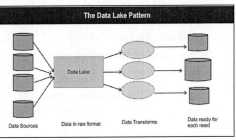

It provides a software framework for distributed storage and processing of big data using the MapReduce programming model. Originally designed for computer clusters built from —still the common use—it has also found use on clusters of higher-end hardware. All the modules in Hadoop are designed with a fundamental assumption that hardware failures are common occurrences and should be automatically handled by the framework.

The core of Apache Hadoop consists of a storage part, known as Hadoop Distributed File System (HDFS), and a processing part which is a MapReduce programming model. Hadoop splits files into large blocks and distributes them across nodes in a cluster. It then transfers packaged code into nodes to process the data in parallel. This approach takes advantage of data locality, where nodes manipulate the data, they have access to. This allows the dataset to be processed faster and more efficiently than it would be in a more conventional

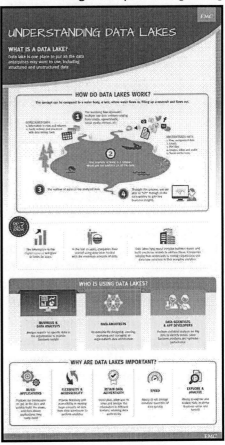

supercomputer architecture that relies on a parallel file system where computation and data are distributed via high-speed networking.

The base Apache Hadoop framework is composed of the following modules:

- **Hadoop Common** – contains libraries and utilities needed by other Hadoop modules; **Hadoop Distributed File System (HDFS)** – a distributed file-system that stores data on commodity machines, providing very high aggregate bandwidth across the cluster;

- **Hadoop YARN** – introduced in 2012 is a platform responsible for managing computing resources in clusters and using them for scheduling users' applications; and

- **Hadoop MapReduce** – an implementation of the MapReduce programming model for large-scale data processing.

The term *Hadoop* has come to refer not just to the aforementioned base modules and sub-modules, but also to the ecosystem, or collection of additional software packages that can be installed on top of or alongside Hadoop, such as Apache Pig, Apache Hive, Apache HBase, Apache Phoenix, Apache Spark, Apache Zookeeper, Cloudera Impala, Apache Flume, Apache Sqoop, Apache Oozie, and Apache Storm.

Apache Hadoop's MapReduce and HDFS components were inspired by Google papers on their MapReduce and Google File System.

The Hadoop framework itself is mostly written in the Java programming language, with some native code in C and command line utilities written as shell scripts. Though MapReduce Java code is common, any programming language can be used with "Hadoop Streaming" to implement the "map" and "reduce" parts of the user's program. Other projects in the Hadoop ecosystem expose richer user interfaces.

The genesis of Hadoop was the "Google File System" paper that was published in October 2003. This paper spawned another one from Google – "MapReduce: Simplified Data Processing on Large Clusters". Development started on the Apache Nutch project, but was moved to the new Hadoop subproject in January 2006. Doug Cutting, who was working at Yahoo at the time, named it after his son's toy elephant. The initial code that was factored out of Nutch consisted of about 5,000 lines of code for HDFS and about 6,000 lines of code for MapReduce.

Hadoop can be deployed in a traditional onsite data centre as well as in the cloud. The cloud allows organizations to deploy Hadoop without the need to acquire hardware or specific setup expertise. Vendors who currently have an offering for the cloud include Microsoft, Amazon, CenturyLink Cloud IBM, Google and Oracle.

The Hadoop file system

Hadoop distributed file system

The HDFS is a distributed, scalable, and portable file system written in Java for the Hadoop framework. Some consider it to instead be a data store due to its lack of POSIX (Portable Operating System Interface) compliance, but it does provide shell commands and Java application programming interface (API) methods that are similar to other file systems. A Hadoop cluster has nominally a single name node plus a cluster of data nodes, although redundancy options are available for the name node due to its criticality. Each data node serves up blocks of data over the network using a block protocol specific to HDFS. The file system uses TCP/IP sockets for communication. Clients use remote procedure calls (RPC) to communicate with each other.

HDFS stores large files (typically in the range of gigabytes to terabytes across multiple machines. It achieves reliability by replicating the data across multiple hosts, and hence theoretically does not require redundant array of independent disks (RAID) storage on hosts (but to increase input-output (I/O) performance some RAID configurations are still useful). With the default replication value, 3, data is stored on three nodes: two on the same rack, and one on a different rack.

Data nodes can talk to each other to rebalance data, to move copies around, and to keep the replication of data high. HDFS is not fully POSIX-compliant, because the requirements for a POSIX file-system differ from the target goals of a Hadoop application. The trade-off of not having a fully POSIX-compliant file-system is increased performance for data throughput and support for non-POSIX operations such as Append.

Source: Wikipedia

Storing and Data querying in HDFS Is depicted in the following picture:

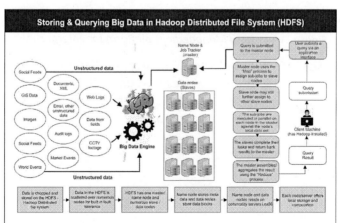

Hadoop facilitates the collection of different types of data across various activities and outposts of an organization to be stored, queried, analyzed and reported through appropriate dashboards for real time monitoring and performance optimization.

The important aspect of the Hadoop ecosystem is that it provided for inherent fault tolerance and a Disaster recovery model for valuable data stored, by offering back up nodes for the Master Node that contains Meta data and pointers to the actual data stored in Data Nodes with a general replication factor of three.

The evolution of Big Data technology enabled organizations to create Data repositories in the form of Data Lakes (suitable for unstructured data) and Enterprise Data Warehouses that contain structured and schema applied data to be further analyzed as per the organizational requirements.

The following picture offers a view of the Azure Data Management platform that reflects the use of Enterprise Data warehouse and Hadoop based Data lakes used for storing and processing different types of data.

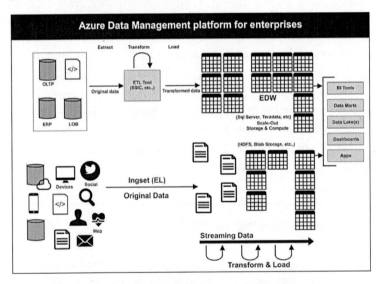

Figure: Azure Data Management platform for enterprises.

Hadoop Data lake platform complements the standard Enterprise Data Warehouse through a variety of tools and techniques that offers flexibility to handle a wide variety of data with agility and speed thus forming the base for embedding intelligence into the organizational operations through state-of-the-art analytics.

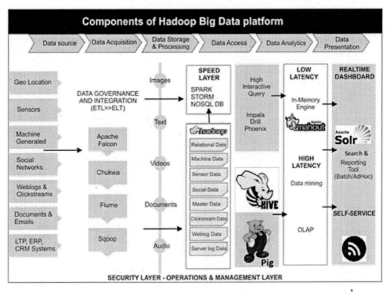

Figure: Components of Hadoop Big Data platform.

A high level architecture of Hadoop ecosystem that has become de facto technology backbone for organizations handling large data sets is represented in the following diagram:

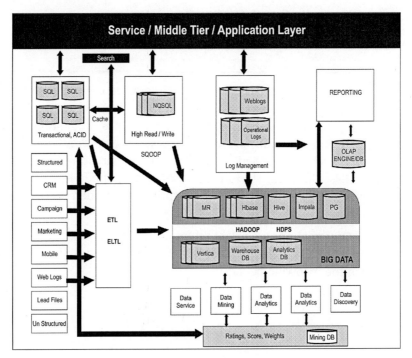

Key components of the Big Data Eco system with Hadoop at the center

of action:

Key components of the Big Data Eco system with Apache Hadoop as the centre of action	
OLTP	Online Transactional Processing
OLAP	Online Analytical Processing
HTAP	Hybrid transaction/analytical processing (HTAP),
ETL	Extract, Transform, Load
Name Node	Master node in HDFS storing Metadata of the Hadoop cluster
Data Node	Slave nodes in HDFS containing actual data with a replciation factor
Secondary Name Node	Dedicate node that checkpoints namenode's file system namespace of Name Node for quick start up of the cluster
Apache Hadoop	Open source framework to handle, process & store large volumes of data using a network of many computers
HDFS	Hadoop distributed file system that runs on commodity hardware
HUE	Opens source web interface for Hadoop
MAP REDUCE	Java based Programming framework for processing and generating big data sets with a parallel, distributed algorithm on a cluster.
HIVE	SQL like data warehouse software used to query data in HDFS
TEZ	Application Framework built on top of Yarn to process Big data much faster than Map Reduce
YARN	Resource management and job scheduling technology for Hadoop ecosystem
PIG	High-level platform for creating programs using Pig Latin Language on HDFS
SPARK	Unified analytics processing engine with built-in modules for streaming, SQL, machine learning and graph processing.
SCALA	General-purpose programming language with support for functional programming & a strong static type system.
AVRO	Row-oriented object container storage format for Hadoop with RPC and data serialization framework
CLOUD ERA/ HORTONWORKS	Leading IT companies offering Software, support, training and certification for Hadoop co system
RDBMS	Relational Data Base Management systems
NO SQL	Not Only SQL
IMPALA	Open source massively parallel processing SQL query engine for HDFS
CASSANDRA	Opensource NoSQL database for handling large volumes of data
MONGODEB	Open-source cross-platform document-oriented NoSQL database program
SQOOP	Command-line interface application to transfer data between RDMS and Hadoop
OOZIE	Server-based workflow scheduling system to manage Hadoop jobs.
ZOOKEEPER	Centralized service for maintaining configuration information, naming, providing distributed synchronization, and providing group services in HDFS
CLOUD SERVICE PROVIDERS	Company offering cloud service as DaaS, SaaS, PaaS, IaaS on pay as per use basis
DAAS	Database as a service
SAAS	Software as a service
PAAS	Platform as a service
IAAS	Infrastructure as a service

Thus the open sourced Apache Hadoop technologies enable organizations to create a large pool of data from various sources, also referred as 'Data Lake' that enables organization to run near real time analytics. Organizations can also create Data Warehouses that have more structured data drawn out of various sources and have schema applied on them for a more structured representation. Organizations like Cloudera, Horton Networks offer various levels of managed services to organizations to set up and run the Big Data operations with varying levels of intervention and corresponding charges.

While several Organizations are still at infancy stage in the continuum of adoption of Data Analytics and Big Data technologies, the various stages of their maturity is represented in the following figure:

Levels of Big Data Maturity	
Level 5 **Data & Analytics as a Service**	Operating as a "data service provider"
	Self-Service data
	Collaboration and sharing analytics across the enterprise
Level 4 **Enterprise Adoption**	Leveraging use cases for multiple LOBs
	Integrated metadata, quality and governance across Big Data
	Predictive insights integrated into business operations
Level 3 **Business Adoption**	Leveraging discrete LOB use cases
	Structured and unstructured analysis
	Predictive analytics applied to Big Data
Level 2 **Technical Adoption**	Using Big Data mostly for storage / transform
	Usage primarily by IT
	Some Big Data exploratory analytics
Level 1 **Infancy**	Thinking about it
	Initial Big Data environment in place
	Proof-Of-Concept / Pilot

Big Data- Problem or Opportunity?

While the potential of Big Data has been harnessed by many giant companies, the acquisition and storage of the data pertaining to many entities and individuals brings in enormous amounts of responsibility. The threat of Malware and leakages threatens to undermine the existence of many companies that could be exposed to legal issues and enormous amounts of fine, further underlined with the implementation of Global Data Protection Regulations by the European Union from May 2018.

Big Data Use cases

The Facilitation of Big Data Management technologies has opened up the world to the power of Artificial Intelligence, which has been around for a while, but has not been able to make much business impact.

CHAPTER 8

Machine Learning and Artificial Inteligence

Artificial Intelligence, is a branch of computer science that deals with the simulation of intelligent behavior in computers and aims to improve their faculties of reasoning, knowledge, planning, learning, natural language processing, perception, decision making, and the ability to move and manipulate objects (Robotics).

Artificial intelligence that has been touted for long as the killer application that will enable machines to think like Human beings resulting in unbelievable productivity had many unsuccessful stints leading to a number of starts and stops in the past.

The activity in Artificial intelligence, a term adopted at Dartmouth in 1956, experienced many periods of disinterest and disinvestment especially during 1974-80 & 1987-93 due to the inability to generate impressionable results leading to frustration of the investors.

The advances in numerous technologies like Big Data, Cloud, New generation Programming knowledge, development of Business Intelligence tools and the yeoman work of companies like Microsoft, IBM & Google along with open source tools like Hadoop, Golang, Python, R etc. have now given a huge boost to the Algorithm led movement of Artificial intelligence coupled with Machine learning. At its core, Machine learning is simply a way of achieving AI.

The availability of large amounts of data through various initiatives discussed earlier and with vast amount of data generated by the users while interacting with the various portals has offered the companies the opportunity to train machine learning models to rapidly simulate discovered patterns and predict the human behavior using appropriate mathematical models. Techniques like Alternate Least Squares, Matrix reduction models enable analysis of large amounts of data and create appropriate models that close in the gap with actual observations leading to accurate predictions for the future. The marketers now have the data not only about the behavior of their subjects, their likes, dislikes and online search patterns, but also have the mapping of behavior with others with similar demographics and psychographics. By correlating them, they are able to predict the behaviors of any of their observed subjects well into the future. Thus AI/ML have been instrumental in assisting & augmenting the efforts of human in their activities and also in automating a large number of repetitive tasks, freeing up human time for more strategic pursuits.

Some of the notable exponents of AI/ML are given below:

- Google's Deepmind and Rankbrain machine learning-artificial Intelligence systems are used to accurately predict the human behavior while searching online and also process the search results. Google uses Deepmind AI algorithms to dramatically improve energy efficiency of its operations.

- Fluid AI uses AI/ML powered customer service bots to make banking fun for customers by mimicking human interactions with customers, vastly reducing operational costs.

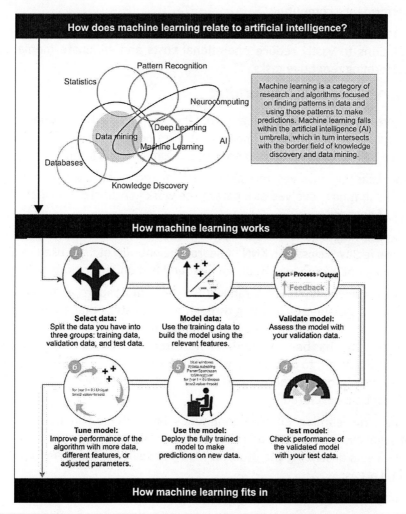

Source: import.io As the largest data source on earth and growing, web data provides incredible value. Import.io enables any organization to gain intelligence, efficiencies, and competitive advantages from the vast amount of data on the web.

- Niki, an AI/ML company offers chatbots that use Natural Language User interfaces offering their clients of their customers to interact in their natural language.

- ShopR360 offers AI/ML powered solutions to malls and large retailers to differentiate their customers and employees etc. by integrating with the CCTV infrastructure.

- Baidu, the Chinese search engine giant uses AI/ML for image processing, speech recognition, natural language processing, deep learning and high-performance computing.

- IBM offers Robotic Process Automation Powered Business management solutions to vastly reduce operational costs and eliminate menial labour performing repetitive tasks.

The rise of Machine Learning

A computer program is said to learn from its experience E with respect to some task T and some performance measure P, if its performance measure on T, as measured by P, improves with experience E. - Tom Mitchell (1998).

Machine Learning involves modelling real life behavior using computational algorithms that have evolved as a part of the work in Artificial Intelligence over a number of decades.

Machine Learning algorithms such as SVM (Support Vector Machine), Random Forest, Naïve Bayes classifier, KNN (K nearest neighbour) etc. are used to discover patterns present in data which cannot be found by humans in normal course.

The tools enable the system to iteratively evolve the most appropriate combination of dependent variables by learning through multiple steps that are implemented over large test data. Once the most appropriate model that explains the patterns found in test data has been evolved, the next step is to reduce the dimensionality of the data drastically to discover & weed out un-connected variables. This process is then repeated for a further refined model that closely explains the behavior of the subject being explored.

Thus machine learning enables continuous improvisation in performance of systems that evolve with time and experience explained through the availability of more data sets describing the process. **Machine Learning has found application in several areas:**

- Analysis of consumer behavior.

- Fraud detection in financial products and services consumption.

- Recommendation Engines in media and ecommerce.

- Stock market trading to predict the movement of share prices.

- In the field of Digital marketing: Email, Social media & Search engines for automatic. response generation, targeted promotions and advertisements.

- Social media such as Facebook, LinkedIn for accurate feeds, facial recognition etc.

- Healthcare (ex: Cancer cell discovery).

- Gene discovery and their classification and a numerous other applications in researching and analyzing consumer behavior.

The various aspects of Machine Learning are depicted in the following picture in a simple manner.

Machine Learning (Types)

Machine Learning

Supervised Learning (Labeled data, Direct feedback, predict outcome)	Unsupervised Learning (No Labels, No feedback, Discover pattern)	Reinforcement (Learn through series of actions, with rewards loading to correct decision)
Classification	**Regression**	Clustering, Dimensionality reduction, Density Estimation	**MaxQ-Q Learning**
Support Vector machines	Linear Regression, GLM	K-Means, K-Medoids Fuzzy C-Means	Markow Decision Process
Discriminant analysis	SVR, GPR	Hierarchial	Tabulat TD
Naive Bayes	Ensamble Methods	Govssion Mixture	Monte-Carlo
Nearest Neighbour	Decision Tyres	Neural Network	Least-Squares Methods

While traditional analytics is more inclined towards statistics and data analysis, Machine learning involves an overlay of many dimensions of human behavior like Philosophy, Biology, Psychology, Neuroscience and Analytical behavior expressed through the field of Probability and Statistics. This is expected to lead the computer's march towards the approximation of human faculties in Behavior & Thinking. Thus Machine learning is a branch of Artificial Intelligence which catalyzes this approximation through an iterative and automated process.

Machine learning consists of various phases that involve: Data collection and cleansing, organizing data, building training sets for continuous improvement of performance, mining the data, refining the model, feeding

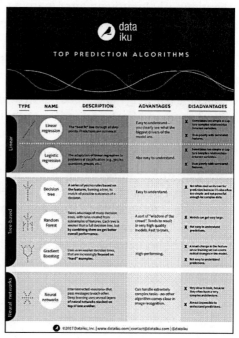

the results obtained for comparison with actual results and further refinement of the model with a recursive approach.

Machine learning involves extensive use of algorithms to re-engineer business processes across various domains of an organization including Sales & Marketing, Finance, HR, Manufacturing, Customer service and the like.

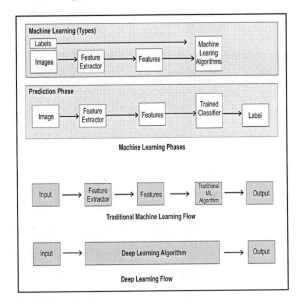

The iterative nature of the algorithms, which refers to probing, learning and continuously improving after learning from every error and a previous iteration, enables them to correct themselves. Hence, moving closer to reality and expected outcomes. The various steps involved in this process happen in a fraction of a second, enabling the decision making process to be efficient, objective, accurate and predictive.

Machine learning makes it easier to devise sophisticated software systems without much human effort. Instead of spending years coding features or fine tuning a system with a lot of parameters, we can use machine learning to get things done in a much shorter time span. Don't be surprised if you soon begin to see and use technology and gadgets, which are currently seen in science fiction movies.

Machine Learning flourishes in the environment in which large data sets are continuously available to train and improve the outcome of the algorithms to the real life. The advent of Big Data technology thus provided the necessary fillip to the Machine Learning outcomes, which further gave a boost to the movement of Artificial Intelligence.

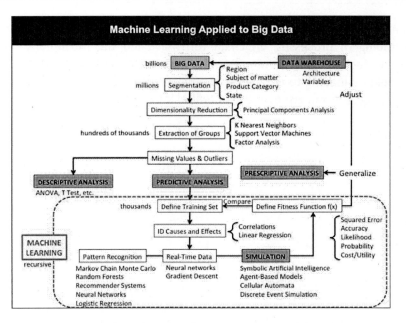

As per a PWC report, Machine learning has a great potential impact across various industries as depicted in the following diagram.

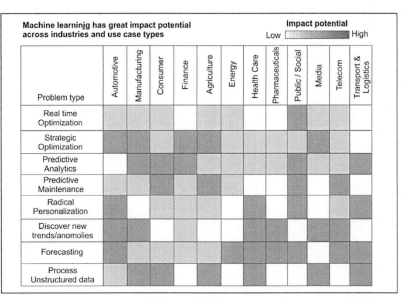

A more detailed analysis of AI & Analytics and their impact across organizations and contexts can be found in the book- AI & Analytics by Sameer Dhanrajani.

Resources for learning Data science

https://www.edx.org/professional-certificate/berkeleyx-foundations-of-data-science#courses

The combination of big data and advent of the Machine Learning led to accuracies & fine tuning of processes, which in turn have led the movement towards automation technologies. Automation of repeated processes and tasks across various fields is leading to unbelievable efficiencies to those who use them, but also is leading to a concern over the potential loss of jobs across industries in the future.

CHAPTER 9

Internet of things - the Booming Penetration

The advent of big data also synchronized with the proliferation and another important aspect of technology, namely Internet of Things (IoT). While the birth of Internet can be traced back to 1969, 1990 marked the official birth year of the Internet of Things (IoT). IoT facilitated connection of things other than human beings through embedded sensors that could be connected to the internet and communicated over the internet with other machines, things and to human beings.

Creating an M2M Protocol, Andy Stanford-Clark of IBM and Arlen Nipper of Arcom (now Eurotech) introduced the first machine-to-machine protocol for connected devices: MQ Telemetry Transport (MQTT). The year 2010 marked a new milestone in the field of Internet of things with the announcement of connected cars by Google.

UNECE (United Nations Economic commission for Europe) has declared IoT generated data as one of the key sources of Big Data.

(https://statswiki.unece.org/display/bigdata/Classification+of+Types+of+Big+Data)

Internet of Things (machine-generated data): derived from the phenomenal growth in the number of sensors and machines used to measure and record the events and situations in the physical world. The output of these sensors is machine- generated data, and from simple sensor records to complex computer logs, it is well structured. As sensors proliferate and data volumes grow, it is becoming an increasingly important component of the information stored and processed by many businesses. Its well-structured nature is suitable for computer processing, but its size and speed are beyond traditional approaches.

Data from sensors

A. Fixed sensors

- Home automation
- Weather/pollution sensors
- Traffic sensors/webcam
- Scientific sensors

- Security/surveillance videos/images B. Mobile sensors (tracking)
- Mobile phone location
- Cars
- Satellite images

C. Data from computer systems

- Logs
- Web logs

The amount of data transacted through the internet grows manifold as the communication between the devices and their principals does.

Technology Roadmap: The Internet of Things

Starting with RFID (Radio frequency identification) chips in the Year 2000, the advances in the field of Internet of Things is expected to permeate to the entire world connecting humongous number of devices with sensor that are then hooked up to the internet through advanced communication platforms and technologies.

By 2020, the number of interconnected devices and the associated business opportunity is expected to grow manifold to over 30 Billion connected objects and 50 Trillion US Dollars in revenue opportunity.

By 2020, the IoT Business, with the help of cost-effective sensors, made possible due to the increased economies of scale and also the cumulative advances in all the interconnected technologies of hardware, middleware, software and storage technologies, would be in a position to create a humongous value of over 50 Trillion US Dollars as per current estimates. The collective intelligence and processing power of all these devices offers enormous benefits to the mankind, but not without the associated threats due to the increased dependence and the corresponding tilt of incentive in favor of cyber attackers and terrorists.

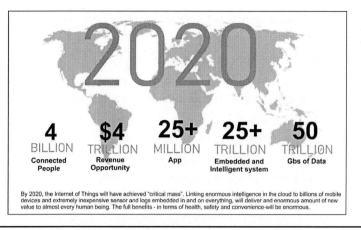

Source: https://gigaom.com/2016/07/15/review-smartdraw-helps-to-tame-wild-iot-networks/

IoT will impact all areas cutting across consumer and industrial usage. While smart home, wearables and personal trackers are good use cases for Consumers, IoT can be leveraged across all areas of design, manufacturing, storage , transportation, maintenance and live performance tracking through the value addition cycle of products and services to dramatically enhance the productivity and profitability of organizations.

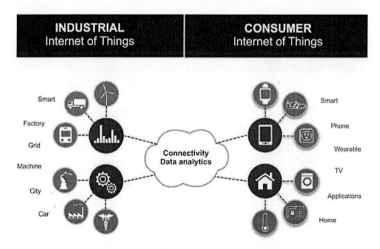

As of now, IoT is extensively used in the following areas:

- Tagging and monitoring the movements and performance parameters of automobiles, animals, accessories and dependents.

- Information collection and dissemination for optimum agricultural output.

- Automatic meter reading and energy utilization management for all electrical devices.

- Security and Surveillance systems for a wide variety of establishments and connected homes

- Building automation and maintenance services.

- Machine to Machine connectivity offering communication, ecommerce and collaboration opportunity through high levels of Automation.

- Smart cities to effectively manage delivery of efficient products and service across every area that touches a citizen's life.

- Telemedicine and healthcare for remotely measuring and tracking the health parameters to offer quick resolution to patients in remote areas.

The paper, Blockchain Technologies for the Internet of Things: Research Issues and Challenges, Mohamed Amine Ferrag, Makhlouf Derdour, Mithun Mukherjee, Member, IEEE, Abdelouahid Derhab, Leandros Maglaras, Senior Member, IEEE, Helge Janicke highlights the various studies undertaken across a number of IoT related domains that are impacted by Blockchain implementation

Centralized platforms can offer innumerable services through cloud-based platforms by converting every dumb object into intelligent and communicable systems. Governments across the world have realized the potential of IoT and are implementing various projects under the category of 'Smart Cities', while service, technology and infrastructure providers are leveraging advanced technologies and innovation to dramatically optimize and enhance the capability and productivity of systems across every field we can think of.

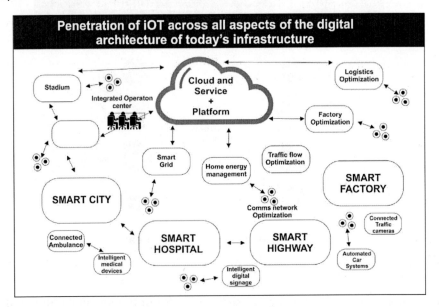

The Internet of Things is a new paradigm that is expected to make life much more

convenient for citizens across the world. With things connected to the internet, their users can access and control it from anywhere. This dramatically increases the productivity of human beings while creating huge opportunity for Data collection, analysis, monitoring, track ability, market opportunity.

Thereby IoT can create value for proactive organizations, by giving them a huge competitive advantage. This could also be a source of risk due to the vulnerability of these devices to malicious attacks by cyber terrorists.

Big Data technologies could play a crucial role in managing the humongous amount of information generated by the sensors deployed on all things that need to be monitored and managed.

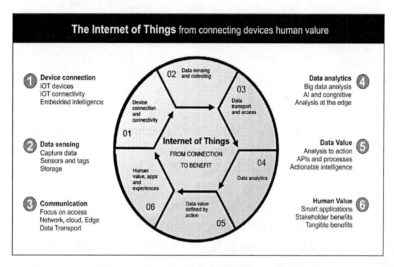

Companies like General Electric, Rolls Royce, Shell and many more are proactively using the IoT technology to dramatically improve their efficiency as well as reduce the chance of failures and defects by combining the technology with cutting edge tools facilitated by Analytics, Artificial Intelligence and Machine Learning, as depicted in the table enumerating the case studies on Big Data Analytics.

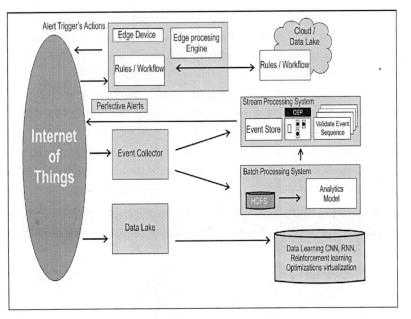

As we take advantage of the connectivity revolution, we are also exposing ourselves to the unforeseen attacks on the IoT systems across the world through cyber-attacks like the October 2016, DDOS attack that paralyzed systems across the world.

https://www.cnbc.com/2016/10/22/ddos-attack-sophisticated-highly-distributed-involved-millions-of-ip-addresses-dyn.html

Massive cyber-attack 'sophisticated, highly distributed', involving millions of IP addresses

Javier E. David | @TeflonGeek Published 5:12 PM ET Sat, 22 Oct 2016 Updated 8:45 AM ET Mon, 24 Oct 2016CNBC.com

We will address this issue later.

DATA MANAGEMENT IN A TYPICAL ENTERPRISE AND THE THREAT OF SINGLE POINT OF FAILURE The increasing competition and the need for outsmarting the competitors, are forcing the organizations to rethink and modify their approaches to Data Management. This scenario is witnessed even in the small organizations.

The typical schema in an organization that spans multiple functions and activities is given below:

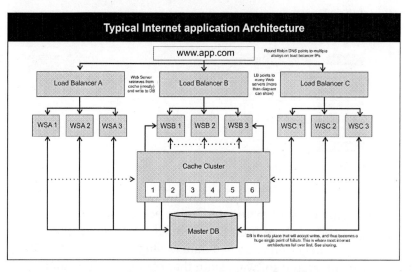

However, in organizations that have advanced data measurement practices due to the availability of large amounts of data, as these organisations are higher up in the evolution of data management practices they use a combination of structured and un-structured databases as presented in the following figure:

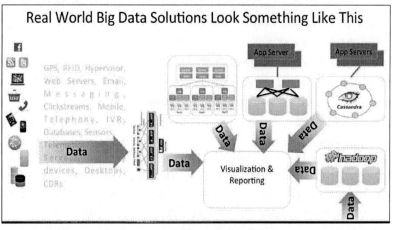

Large companies implement Data lake solutions. The data management in such cases can be visualized as:

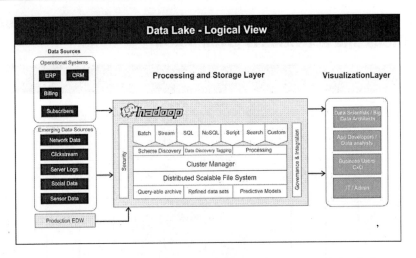

While large companies have the resources to invest in Data Lakes, smaller companies can still combine their Data Storage, Data Processing and Analytical activities in to an integrated or unified Data Management Platform (DMP). A high-end DMP is an integrated software suite that combines Data storage, processing and analytics and offers an intuitive and easy-to-navigate executive dashboard. The role of a DMP is to

- Collect structured and unstructured data from all sources: internal and external, covering an organization's own applications, systems, websites and products, data from partners and other associates and any other third-party data used by the company.

- Integrate and store all the data collected.

- Apply analytical tool and provide appropriate insights to the top management and all the other data driven parts of business.

Some of the key DMP offerings include Adform DMP, Adobe Audience Manager, KBM Group's Zipline, Lotame, MediaMath DMP, Neustar Identity DMP, Nielsen exelate, Oracle BlueKai, Salesforce DMP (formerly Krux) and Turn Digital Hub for Marketers. Platforms like IBM Insights, SAS Data Management, offer the capability to access data on legacy systems and Hadoop. These platforms offer enterprise capabilities to enable, manage and analyses large volumes of structured and unstructured data by performing activities to integrate, cleanse, transform and govern data on premises and in the cloud.

With the proliferation of Internet of Things, the amount of data that needs to be handled across all segments of organization in private, public and government domains is going to be huge. Use of DMPs can also allow organization to leverage the technologies like Artificial Intelligence and Machine Learning for significant competitive advantage. DMPs can also offer the organizations to manage the regime of GDPR in a comprehensive manner. However, in all these cases, there is the risk of failure of varying stages due to probability of failure at a single point of control due to centralization of management. A change in the management or a corruption of a major source of storage or processing could lend its way to a shutdown of access of considerable portion of organizational operation.

CHAPTER 10

Malware Attacks and the Cyberthreats

The Rapidly Growing Threat of Cyberwars and Malware Attacks Threatening the Existence of Organizations

As we have become more and more dependent on technology and as the life gets more and more automated, we are faced with severe threats from all sides and have never been more vulnerable. Imagine waking up in the morning one day and not being able to log into your online bank account as it

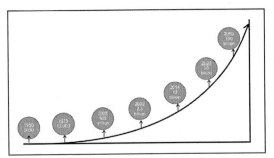

has been compromised or the data of the banking system and its records have withered or have been corrupted or destroyed. This is indeed not an improbable event as many global leading organizations have been attacked by Malware with severe repercussions in the recent past. The digital citizens of today are faced with many life changing threats like:

- Viruses,
- Malware,
- Spyware,
- Worms,
- Trojans,
- Phishing attacks
- Botnets,
- Data Leakages
- Identity thefts
- Corporate Espionage and many more...

All these are in some way or the other linked to the data and associated information the perpetrators are trying to usurp and immobilize the targets to gain unfair advantage. Hence it is imperative for everyone to recognize this and work towards associated risk mitigation and management.

With the increasing use of Internet by all things, human and non-human, there is a huge traffic of data flow across organizations, between the devices connected to the corporate networks and also the other departments and officials in the organization. This could be a huge source of vulnerability as the hackers could use the loop holes in the security management of the IoT devices and other connected tools of automation. For example, robots ca be used to gain access to and launch malware attacks leading to information leakages, operational disruptions and sometimes leading to standstill of operations and huge losses.

There were several cases of hackers gaining access to the loosely secured IOT devices used in the smart home context and use their processing power for mining of cryptocurrency, while the owners of the devices are blissfully aware of the same. Here is where the concept of Blockchain could act as a deterrent and as a risk management tool. The same is explored in a later section in the book.

A case in point is the massive outage of internet witnessed due to the DDOS attack of October 2016. The 2016 DYN cyberattack took place on October 21, 2016 and involved multiple distributed denial-of-service attacks (DDoS attacks) targeting systems operated by Domain Name System (DNS) provider Dyn, which caused major Internet platforms and services to be unavailable to large swathes of users in Europe and North America. The groups Anonymous and New World Hackers claimed responsibility for the attack, but scant evidence was provided. https://en.wikipedia.org/wiki/2016_Dyn_cyberattack

CHAPTER 11

Risks of Centralisation & Single Points of Failure

As the world is reeling under the outrage due to the data leakage of over 87 million Facebook users in the US, wrongly leveraged by a company called Cambridge Analytica, it is indeed worthwhile to recount some of the recent significant cases of cyber security breaches.

As can be seen, the cyber-attacks did not spare the companies which are expected to possess the most secure of the systems. Companies like Google, Nortel networks, Target, Yahoo and many more have fallen victims of the cyber terrorism jeopardizing the security of their consumer and the data that they were supposed to guard. Aramco, the world's largest company by market capitalization once, was crippled by the attack on its computers and network

systems, an attack which was supposedly meant to cripple its oil production output that could have disturbed the economics of the world.

While in many cases the motives behind the cyber warfare and attacks are economical (for example, Ransomware attacks), in many cases, the motives and the identity of attackers is unknown even today.

The increasing risk due to the 'Single Points of Failure' at Centralized organizations, the growing threat of Cyber terrorism and the increasing mistrust between the Organizations and the subjects warrants drastic solutions.

Blockchain, a new paradigm for managing the growing risks through a variety of features that promote security and GDPR (General Data Protection Regulations) by European Union expected to come into force in May 2018 to protect the rights of European Union Citizens (That impacts companies globally and could be followed across the world in due course) are discussed in the subsequent chapters.

CHAPTER 12

General Data Protection Regulations and the Organizational Imperatives

Risks to corporates arising out of customer outrage and activism on account of data leakages and alleged corporate impropriety is nothing new. In 2015, LinkedIn paid over 13 million US Dollar to settle a class action suit on account of email spamming to members' contacts while the outrage on account of Facebook's data leakage of over 87 million US members to Cambridge Analytica for unauthorized exploitation is a landmark in the history of mankind.

With the increasing amounts of data being stored, accessed and acted upon by the organizations and the proliferation of risks associated with the single point of failure, malware attacks and indiscriminate practices towards management of data, European Union has enacted the General Data Protection Regulations effective from May 2018. This act is applicable to all companies situated anywhere in the globe, dealing with personal data of citizen of any European Union member country. Failure to adhere to the stringent rules will result in a fine of a higher of 4% of global revenues or 20 Million Euros of defaulting organizations.

Organizations tend to accumulate:

- structured,
- semi-structured and
- unstructured data

In a number of ways depending on their interactions, goals, short term & long term strategies and business models.

Personal data of subjects could be in the form of:

- Personal details like Name, Date of Birth, Email id, address, region, religious and sexual orientations, passport details,
- Financial details like bank records, salary trends, investments,
- Social information like photographs, videos, political and religious opinions etc.

These information are collected through:

- CRM activities,
- Web site interactions & marketing responses,
- Business transactions and Purchase activities,

- Email & opinion surveys,
- Interview processes while evaluating for hiring,
- Visitor, enquiry and feedback tackers
- App and event interactions
- Employee information systems

This data is splattered over various internal data storage and processing systems, Enterprise data warehouses and Data lakes.

This information accumulated over the period of a number of years and added into the future, now under GDPA , offers rights to the individuals to restrict the usage by the holders of the information as per the agreed upon terms and for the duration of the same.

Individuals have the right to request the holders regarding information on:

- Usage of the data,
- Modify the data,
- Transfer of data to other entities,
- Access to data,
- Right to erase the data from the records,
- Right to know about any data breaches pertaining to their information within 72 hours of any such action etc.

Being implemented statutorily and also in Principal, the GDPR expects all the organizations to act in a responsible and accountable manner with respect to the management of data of their subjects. It becomes imperative on the Processors of data to expressly and unequivocally seek the permission of their subjects for usage of any information pertaining to them and in case of children below 16 years of age, their parental/ guardian's content becomes a must.

Use of Pseudonyms instead of actual names reduces the risk of data breaches and associated damages a lot. Coupled with stringent security measures and adoption of best practices including certifications like ISO 27001 gain a huge importance in the current paradigm.

Companies have to review their policies and procedures, owners & categories of data collected for personal or non-personal uses and put in place appropriate control mechanisms in a demonstrable manner.

A single point of contact with a designation of Chief Data Officer becomes a critical role to be designated and maintained by organization. He needs to be singularly accountable for all things connected with Data within the organization. He should be able to have a full view of the sources, paths, destinations and storage containers of data across his/her organization and should continuously & proactively take appropriate measures by adopting right means and technologies to safeguard his organization for any data breaches. Organizations like Informatica, an IT organization focused on Data Management and Analytics offer excellent tools to stay on top of the challenge offered by GDPR.

Adopting the best practices in a demonstrable manner can also act as a great opportunity to organizations to clean up their acts, minimize the risks to their clients, customers and their partners, while gaining the Trust of all concerned that can strengthen their market position & performance.

Organizations need to use a number of strategies and tactics while leveraging the technology to the fullest extent.

A systematic and focused approach rooted in the best practices espoused some of the finest Japanese Management Paradigms like Six Sigma approaches like , Poka Yoke, DMAIC, DMADV can help organizations to implement best possible processes and systems with long lasting impact.

It is imperative that the end result should be to have a single view of customer's information across all division of organization, adopt best practices to leverage the data within the boundaries of the propriety, ethics and legality while optimizing the business value.

Techniques to address GDPR and strengthen organization:

Six Sigma is a set of tools and techniques for process improvement that minimizes the chances of any defects that can offer while carrying out the processes. Any operation that is operating at the level of six sigma is supposed to produce fewer than 3.4 defects per million opportunities or operate at an accuracy level of 99.99966% accuracy.

It involves using a variety of approaches like DMAIC (Define, Measure, Analyze, Improve and Control) for improving existing processes of an organization, while DMADV (Define, Measure, Analyze, Design and Validate) is a systematic approach to developing new businesses and processes that could be disruptive.

While DMAIC is a process that can be used in response to deteriorating Voice of Customer, Voice of Business or Cost of Poor Quality, the appropriate tools that can be used for managing the march towards GDPR compliance for organizations can be outlined as follows:

5S methodology for GDPR compliance:

- **Set** - Take stock of all existing, data sets and data management practices
- **Sort**- Arrange the data sets across different functions cutting across Marketing, Human Resources, Sales & CRM, ERP, IT, Third party associates and any others, port them into a common platform for an integrated view that can be further analyzed and taken stock of. If possible, consider using Data lakes and Enterprise data warehouses, common repositories.
- **Shine** – Clean up the data, eliminate redundancies and potential sources of risk, optimize interactions across IT, Business and Accounting teams & Third

party associates and outline appropriate processes and systems to manage risk going forward.

- **Standardize**- Once the best practices are outlined, standardize policies, processes and systems and outline the interactions amongst the various divisions with clearly defined responsibilities and monitoring formats.

- **Sustain**- The responsibility should be fixed and a clear champion in the rank of a Data Protection Officer should be firmly put in place to sustain the efforts and continuously improvise the same for future proof operations.

It is an excellent methodology that can be used by organizations to get a 360-degree view on the data of their subjects and how it is used while implementing & standardizing the best practices.

Poka Yoke is an approach that aims at mistake proofing an organizational effort and limits the chances of failure. This involves putting in place adequate precautionary measures in place to:

(a) Warning signs to be triggered when the system is likely to go out of control,

(b) Stop the system and limit damage in case an unforeseen mistake happens and

(c) Launch an automated fall back response to limit the loss of stoppages with a feedback loop in place to prevent such mishaps in the future.

Organisations that adopt such best practices proactively manage the risk and gain the trust of their consumers while minimizing cost of compliances if any. This gives them immense competitive advantage and a sound market position.

One interesting offshoot of the GDPR act and the impact on the organization and attitude of citizens across the world is, to see what will happen to the huge amount of data and information carried by the different organizations and how they will manage the same. The areas that could be drastically affected are:

- Social media platforms.
- Employment portals.
- Classified services portals.
- Email service providers.
- Market places spanning various products and service globally.
- Ecommerce players cutting across categories and geographies and many more!

It is imperative that centrally run organisations operating in all these areas look seriously at altering their approaches and business models to be able to compete with the Blockchain based organisations which provide far higher levels of transparency, empowerment, identity protection and financial rewards to their platform users.

CHAPTER 13

Blockchain - An Introduction

The Tilting Balance of Risk Versus Rewards

As has been observed in the earlier pages, the rewards of using cutting edge technologies for the organizations are increasingly outweighed by the risks arising due to

(A) Cyber-attacks and data leakages,

(B) Increased vigilance of Global regulatory authorities to protect the rights of the citizens

(C) Increased consumer activism to protect their rights against misuse of their personal data

(D) Mistrust among the players as the transactions increased with opportunities to defraud

(E) Mistrust of the citizens and consumers with any authority including Governments holding their information

The following are some of the cases that explain the lack of trust among counter parties to a transaction:

(I) When one buys any product or service, including lifesaving medicines, one is not sure about genuinity of the product.

(II) Automobile spare parts business is prone to use of massive amount of duplicates leading to mistrust among the consumers regarding the originality of the spare parts.

(III) Art lovers are not sure regarding the authenticity of the art they are buying.

(IV) Artists are not sure whether their art is going to be replicated and monetized in an Unauthorized manner.

(V) Employees are not sure whether their organizations will misuse their personal information and compromise their privacy during or after their tenure.

(VI) Candidates are not sure whether the data they are posting on various classified portals will be exploited by the employment portals, educational platforms, organizations they interview with and the like.

(VII) Social media platform users are not sure about the privacy of their information, thanks to the proliferation of third-party applications and plug-ins.

(VIII) Clients and consumers of Financial Services' companies and products are not sure of the way the vast amount of data collected by them will be protected.

(IX) The numerous applications and platforms that provide any amount of entertainment and services to the clients possess huge amount of information which is now churned and mined for a phenomenal perspective of the consumer, so that the companies know more about their consumers than they know about themselves.

(X) The Machine to machine interactions can totally go out of control without a proper central command or a protection mechanism.

This has led the world to the new paradigm of 'Blockchain' which possesses a number of risk mitigating properties.

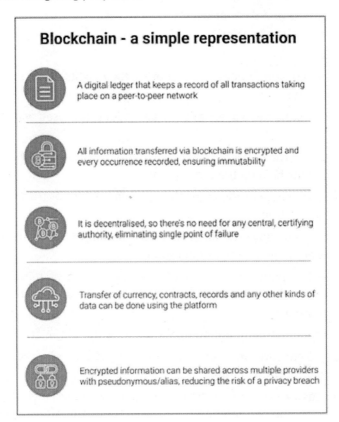

Blockchain - a simple representation

A digital ledger that keeps a record of all transactions taking place on a peer-to-peer network

All information transferred via blockchain is encrypted and every occurrence recorded, ensuring immutability

It is decentralised, so there's no need for any central, certifying authority, eliminating single point of failure

Transfer of currency, contracts, records and any other kinds of data can be done using the platform

Encrypted information can be shared across multiple providers with pseudonymous/alias, reducing the risk of a privacy breach

Blockchain

All of us know Bitcoin as a digital currency unit with which we can transfer money from a place anywhere in the world to anywhere else, provided you have an internet connection. Just like how, one can make call over internet without the intervention of any third party.

It sounds great but, is it so easy?

What if you have 5 bitcoins in your account and execute a spend transaction simultaneously over the internet for 5 bitcoins to 5 different accounts at the same time? Since there is no central party or mediator like in the case of a banking transaction in which the accounts are tallied on a live basis, it could well be possible that all the 5 people would perhaps receive the transaction at the same time and account for it! This is the classic problem called 'Double spending', which many Technologists and digital evangelists have not been able to solve for decades, as **Consensus for transactions done between unknown parties on the internet, eluded the world for ages.**

In computer science, this problem was formulated as Byzantine General's Problem in 1982 by Leslie Lamport, Robert Shostak and Marshall Pease in their 1982 paper. Byzantine refers to the Byzantine Generals' Problem refers to a situation faced by a group of generals encircling and attacking a city without any reliable communication path among themselves. The challenge is to come to the right consensus of going with the right majority decision in the face of lack of trust amongst themselves due to the possible infiltration of their camp by the rival kingdom.

Byzantine fault tolerance (BFT) is the dependability of a fault-tolerant computer system, particularly distributed computing systems, where components may fail and there is imperfect information on whether a component has failed & why. In a "Byzantine failure", a component such as a server can inconsistently appear both failed and functioning to failure-detection systems, presenting different symptoms to different observers.

It is difficult for the other components to declare it failed and shut it out of the network, because they need to first reach a consensus regarding which component has failed in the first place. The solution for this problem has the capability to address the issue of 'Double spending' described earlier.

While many attempts have been made to solve this problem, it is only in October 2008, that a person or a group of people in the name of 'Satoshi Nakamoto' presented a fool proof solution to facilitate creation and transfer of digital assets online, through a white paper, offering Byzantine fault tolerance for online transactions.

The term is derived from the Byzantine Generals' Problem, where actors must agree on a concerted strategy to avoid catastrophic system failure, but some of the actors are unreliable. Byzantine fault tolerance has been also referred by the phrases **interactive consistency** or **source congruency, error avalanche, Byzantine agreement problem, Byzantine general's problem,** and **Byzantine failure**. Source: Wikipedia

In 2008, a whitepaper 'Bitcoin: A Peer-to-Peer Electronic Cash System' available at https://bitcoin.org/bitcoin.pdf , purportedly written by 'Satoshi Nakamoto' presented the first fail proof solution to the Byzantine General Problem through a brilliant synthesis of Programming, Mathematics, Cryptography and a high level economic far sightedness.

This was manifested in the form of an algorithm named 'Proof of Work', which is based on Consensus mechanism. This definitely solved the problem of 'Double Spending' that allowed netizens to spend their online assets more than once and many times over.

This coupled with the replication of the ledger among transacting parties through an automated process of interparty dealings and a self-sustained, gaming theory based reward mechanism to incentivize those involved in the maintenance of network sanctity led to the launch of the crypto currency, 'bitcoin' on 3rd January, 2008.

The POW (Proof of Work) based consensus mechanism makes it improbable for any party or a group of parties in the system, to rewrite the shared ledger as it involves disproportionately large resources for doing so, in the process of convincing the majority of the participants to agree to the new source of truth.

The technology paradigm, behind the 'bitcoin' is now known as Blockchain that has taken the world by storm, ever since.

So what is a Bitcoin and what is Blockchain?

Before we understand how Bitcoin works, let us look at an interesting situation. We have a group of 100 businessmen maintaining their ledger in a book.

Every day, they are grouping all their transactions into a page and adding a page to the book.

All of them verify each transaction and approve on reaching majority and finally reach a consensus to add the page. So now they have added 100 pages and things are going fine.

One day, they realize that some of the members of the group are trying to push wrong transactions deliberately and this has led to a lot of mistrust. Over and above that, once someone misplaces the book and one has a nightmare fearing the loss of all their transactions.

This is the classic problem due to a 'Single Point of Failure' which if attacked by an adversary, the whole system could collapse.

So they decided that every one of the members should hold a copy of the book so that they are not only able to verify all the transactions, but also able to update the rest, in case any of the pages is torn or if any of the books is spoiled due to any problem.

All the Members were having a Copy of all the Transactions Grounded in Serially Linked Pages and to Change any Transaction on any Page, Majority have to Agree to Facilitate the Change

So it was working fine and everyone was happy about the past data.

In case any new page had to be added, all of them would vote for the transactions and the majority approved transaction could get added. So, in order to change any transactions and push through one's view of a different set of transactions, they needed to get the approval of over 50 other people.

Over a period, the number of people undertaking the transactions started growing by leaps and bounds and so were the number of transactions. They had to find some way to ensure that they were able to handle the volume as the number of people who were on board to approve the transactions were far less than the number of people who were conducting the transactions that needed to be approved and grouped.

They devised a new system.

Each board member can catch around 100 transactions (fixed as per the number that can fit in a page) from among the transactions that needed to be approved or disapproved, grouped them into a page and put them up for voting. All the members will view that page holistically, verify each transaction once again and add them to the book. When more than 50% of the board members approve the transaction, the page is considered final and the race for the next page is on. The member whose page was added to the book was given a reward of INR. 25/- and he could also earn some money out of the money offered by the users whose transactions he chose to verify.

Verification of each transaction involved checking out whether the transacting parties are genuine, and the sender had the necessary balances to conduct the transaction. This multiple verification process and the serial number based adding of the transactions in an immutable manner was able to by far, solve the problem of 'Double spending' or multiple entries for the same transaction.

But another problem remained. The huge number of transactions and the speed at which they were being generated resulted in multiple pages being created at the same time and there was utter confusion as to whose page had to be added to the book!

To overcome this they decided to add on more layers for selecting the page from among pages created by people involved. They decided to make the page creators play a game and whoever wins, their page would be selected, and they would be rewarded for creating the page.

Everyone had to guess a random number, The number called 'Nonce' (Number used only once) was paired with the transactions and a number derived out of the latest page number and a new number was derived using a standard calculation. This was done by taking into account all the transactions included for the page + the unique number Nonce+ a Single representative element for all the transactions and a representation of the previous page.

For example - if x was the previous page number, a function $f(x)$ was created to represent all the details up to the previous page. The winner member had to create a new number which represented the following:

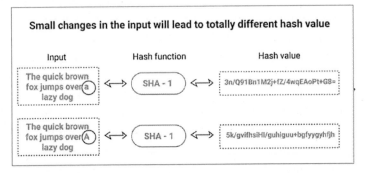

f [f(x)+representation of all transactions on the page +all transactions grouped for the new page + NONCE]

The function f(x) is termed as the Hash of x. While element which represented all the transactions as a unique number is called the Merkle root.

Merkle Root also known as the Root hash, is derived by hashing together pairs of transactions in each block and hashing pairs of hashes together till there is only one element left to hash.

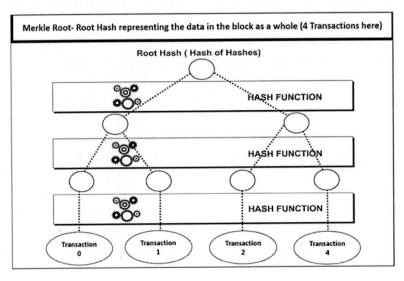

Hashing

While hash is a unique number derived out of the base number, the Merkle root is derived out of hashing pairs of transactions together till only one element is left.

Since the hash was unique, change in any transaction would result in the change in the Merkle root and hence it would be easily caught in case anyone tried to tamper even with one transaction at a later date.

A challenge was then thrown at the board members also called the Mining pool of members, in the form of a targeted function value below which the creator of the page would be considered winner and his page of transactions could be added to the book and reward offered. For this, the member had to use NONCE a number of times before he could meet the target and this took a lot of effort.

All the board members have been playing this game ever since and new pages are being created every 10 minutes (or any interval as prescribed by the group based on which the challenge was chosen).

There have also been some issues with different pages added to the book a few times, but the group was able to successfully resolve this by ensuring that at any time, the book with the largest serial number of approved pages with the majority of the group members prevails and the rest of the pages are torn off and the transactions on those pages have to be taken into new pages in the future, albeit as per the same process.

The system has been going well and there have so far been no issues of double spending or any member trying to override the transactions through brute force or by any other means.

It is now doubly difficult for any member wanting to change the transaction as he not only has to get his page entered into the consideration set for approval through a tedious process, but also has to get the majority onto his side, a task which is almost impossible.

In the case of bitcoin, the members are called miners and those who are creating transactions are the account holders submitting their transactions through their wallets. The pages are represented by blocks and the transactions are the transfer details of the digital currency unit from one account to another.

Bitcoin also provides for one level of identity protection for the users by delinking the real names of the account holders with the transaction and also by ensuring that only authorized persons are able to create and verify transactions and check balances.

History of Blockchain

The Blockchain concept first came into existence with the launch of Bitcoin on 3rd January 2009, by a person claimed as Satoshi Nakamoto who published a whitepaper in October 2008, explaining the concept. The Bitcoin is also known as the first Cryptocurrency that facilitated transfer of value across its holders, without any involvement of central authority like a Government or Central Bank. The platform solved the problem of 'Double Spending' on internet, which involves spending a digitally owned asset, more than once at the same time.

This was done through an amazing combination of advanced technological concepts involving Cryptography, Mathematics, Programming, IT Architecture concepts, Economic foresight while also overlaying with tremendous execution and marketing strengths.

While the addressing linked to the owners, whose identity is not still known contains over 9 lakh bitcoins amounting over 7 billion US Dollars as of end March 2018. The network continues its faultless operation into the 10th year of its existence without any semblance of governance at the helm. This is indeed deemed as one of the biggest wonders of our times and has also given rise to whole new paradigms on running autonomous and unregulated entities working together to create value.

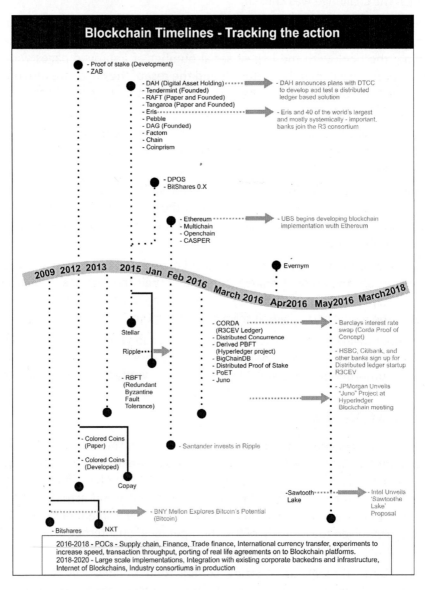

Blockchain Timelines - Tracking the action

2016-2018 - POCs - Supply chain, Finance, Trade finance, International currency transfer, experiments to increase speed, transaction throughput, porting of real life agreements on to Blockchain platforms.
2018-2020 - Large scale implementations, Integration with existing corporate backedns and infrastructure, Internet of Blockchains, Industry consortiums in production

CHAPTER 14

Bitcoin & the Blockchain - the Inception of the 'Bigbang'

Bitcoin and the Blockchain

Bitcoin, launched in January 2009, successfully implemented the concept of cryptocurrency, implying a unit of money that has been created on the net and can be distributed without the fear of double spending

To own a bitcoin, all one needed was a computer with an operating system and fiat currency to convert into 'bitcoins'.

"Bitcoin is a remarkable cryptographic achievement and the ability to create something that is not duplicable in the digital world has enormous value" – Eric Schmidt, Ex-Chairman & CEO-Google Inc. (2001-11))

Bitcoin is the first implementation of Blockchain Technology consisting of six primary elements:

(A) An updated distributed ledger replicated across all the peers undertaking transactions through the platform, consisting of the updated status of Unspent Outputs (UTXO) in chronological order.

(B) A Network of nodes undertaking to verify and propagate the transactions generated by the participants.

(C) A group of miners dispersed across the world to mine the transactions to ensure authenticity of the same, maintaining the integrity of the Blockchain for all times to come, using an automated execution of the protocol defined by the consensus algorithm called Proof of Work. Proof of Work represents the amount of work that the miners undertake by utilizing their computing power and electricity spent, to be eligible for block rewards in the form of newly minted coins as per a predefined formula.

How does Bitcoin Blockchain work?

(A) Blockchain wallets used by the participants to initiate transactions and store the value in the form of UTXOs or Unspent units.

(B) The Value that is exchanged across the platform, namely the 'Bitcoin' which is treated as a crypto currency with all the properties that we associate with the fiat currency in the real world, except the unitized physical representation and regulatory approvals.

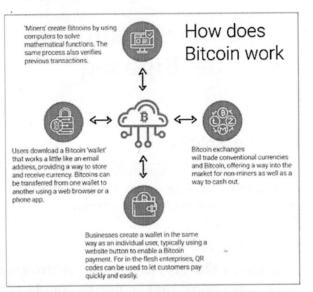

(C) Exchanges that facilitate buying and selling of crypto currencies and derived products known as tokens amongst themselves and using fiat currencies & conversion of the same into fiat currencies in a dynamic fashion.

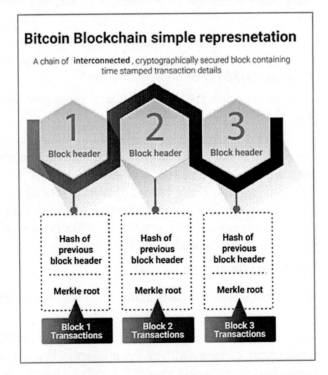

Now let us examine, what information is contained in the blocks in the bitcoin

Blockchain. The information in the blocks is readable by public through the bitcoin explorer and contains details of the transaction between entities represented by their respective public keys.

What's in a "Block"?

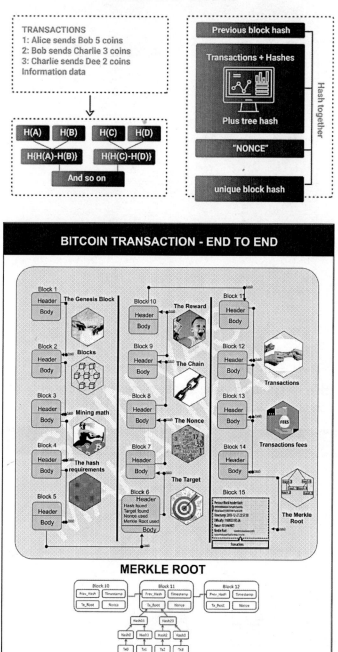

- To buy and use a Bitcoin one has to do download a bitcoin wallet from any of the providers like Coinbase, Bitcoin-Qt etc., and create an account. Some of the top Bitcoin wallet programs and their comparison is given below:

Features	Coinbase	Bitcoin-Qt	Bitcoin Wallet
Send and Receive	Yes	Yes	Yes
Buy and Sell	Yes	X	X
Link Bank Account	Yes	X	X
Pay by Email	Yes	X	X
Merchant Services	Yes	X	X
Web	Yes	X	X
Desktop	X	Yes	X
Smartphone	Yes	X	Yes
You Control private Key	X	Yes	Yes
They Control private Key	Yes	X	X

There are different types of wallets that allow the participants to create their accounts which provide varied levels of safety and facilities.

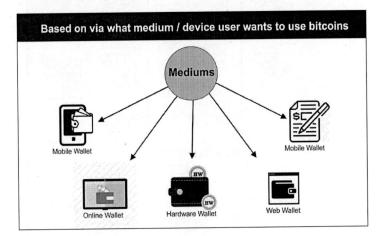

They are further classified into Hot wallets and Cold wallets.

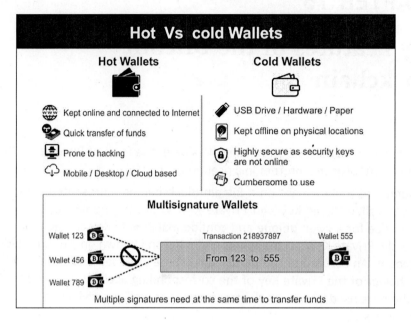

CHAPTER 15

Key Features of the Bitcoin Blockchain

Bitcoin allows pseudonymous transfer of value in the form of Bitcoins (BTC) or a fraction of BTC over the internet in a pseudonymous fashion

The identity of a participant on a Bitcoin Blockchain is represented using a key value pair called Public Key and Private Key. While the Public key, a uniquely derived value for a given unique and confidential Private Key can be revealed to anyone, the Private Key is extremely confidential and known only to the holder of the account. An account of the participant can be accessed and transacted only by the holder of the Private Key of the corresponding account. Secured Hashing Algorithms are used to encrypt the transactions as well as arrive at the addresses of the holders.

Bitcoin Core – Inside an Autonomous Organization & its Interactions with External Participants

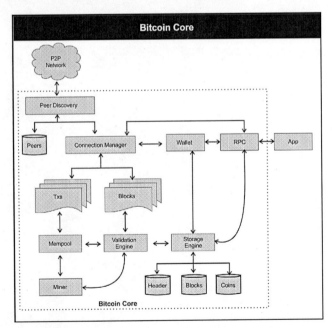

P2P network of participants and external applications like explorers, payment gateways etc., interacting with the Blockchain through wallets that continuously

interact with storage & connection manager to know pending transactions for providing updated status of UTXOs to holders.

Transactions created by peers & propagated to the network through nodes, selected from the pool by miners creating blocks that update the Blockchain as per validation protocol.

The raw blocks files along with details of peers (Public Keys) are stored in the .dat files in the hard disk along with index of transactions and block headers stored in Level DB databases.

Blockchain Hash Function

A hash function is a unique way function that produces a unique output for a given input that cannot be replicated. Hash of any information is treated as the unique and indisputable representation of the information. Hashes form the heart of Blockchain as the blocks are represented by the hash of the information and are chained together as a linked list of chronologically mined and validated blocks.

The Private Key and the Public key are used to encrypt information using mathematical algorithms rendering decryption virtually impossible without these keys. Computationally, it is similar to the factoring of prime numbers, which is a simple, mathematical procedure. However, decomposing the result is difficult without prior knowledge of its factors.

The process of encryption and decryption using the keys is depicted in the following picture:

All participants are provided unique addresses by their wallets which are secured by strong password based encryption. The relationship between the Private keys, Public keys and their respective addresses is depicted as follows:

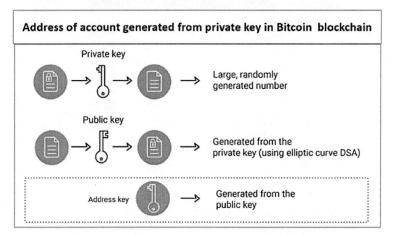

The wallets allow their holders to generate multiple addresses represented by their respective Private keys and unique Private keys. While Private Key is a random generated alpha numeric number, the public key is derived from the private key and the address is further derived from the public key.

The Public key or the address is used to identify the participant on the Bitcoin Blockchain network and can be used to transfer or receive funds.

Any transaction on the Bitcoin Blockchain is encrypted by Digital Signatures that are generated by the Public key of the recipients, transaction details and the private key of the sender.

Digital Signatures

Blockchain digital signatures rely on the concept of *asymmetric encryption*.

The combination of the Public key of the recipient and the Private Key of the recipient along with unique information pertaining to the transaction can be used to encrypt the transaction to be transmitted through the Blockchain network. This can be further used by the network constituent.

Bitcoin		
mBTC 477.06		
⁺USD 112.44		
● 21 Apr Donation for Bitcoi....	+ 6.26	
● 19:29, 17 April.... Donation for Bitcoin Wallet	+ 13.09	
● 17 Apr Donation for Bitcoi....	+ 1.00	
● 15 Apr 13th VECF HS&D A....	+ 0.97	
● 15 Apr 18th VEKNF HS&D A....	+1.00	
◀ REQUEST COINS SEND COINS ▶		◎

Data encrypted with a public key can be decrypted by the Private Key of the holder, while information encrypted by Private Key can be decrypted by using a public key of the recipient.

The Digital Signatures are a unique aspect of Blockchain transactions and provide a layer of security for carrying out & validating genuine transactions.

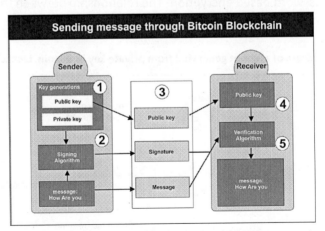

The bitcoin transactions are transmitted to the Bitcoin Blockchain through a Node that is associated with the exchange through which the transaction is undertaken.

A snap shot of a cryptocurrency exchange is given below:

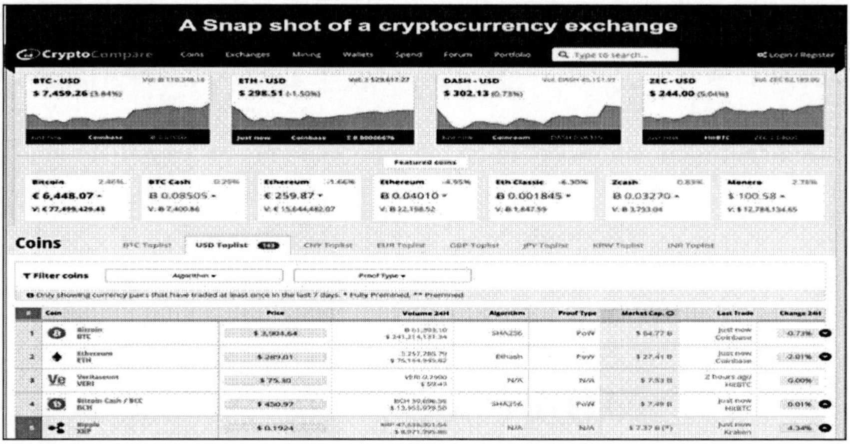

A Snap shot of a cryptocurrency exchange

Bitcoin mining is the process by which transactions are verified and added to the public ledger, known as the Blockchain, and also the means through which new bitcoin are released. The mining process involves compiling recent transactions into blocks and trying to solve a computationally difficult puzzle.

Network nodes must process any new block before its official inclusion in a Blockchain's publicly accessible ledger. The transactions & their blocks should be validated and approved by all concerned before adding to the chain of existing blocks. This process is called Mining. Depending on the type of Blockchain and the purpose of their existence, different Blockchains use different types of consensus mechanisms to arrive at a conclusion regarding the validity of the transactions.

The transactions are then confirmed by the network through a process called Bitcoin Mining defined by the consensus mechanism known as 'Proof of Work'.

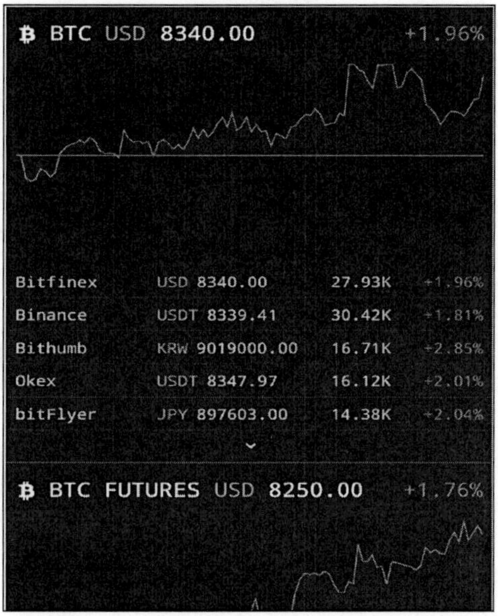

Once the transactions are confirmed, the block containing the transaction is published and added to the chain of existing blocks. A historic pricing chart of Bitcoin is given below, depicting its price movement from almost nil in 2009 to over 8000 USD in 2018.

The transactions can then be queried on the Blockchain and explored by anyone who possesses the information of the Public key or the Transaction hash that is provided by the system.

A snapshot of the Blockchain explorer is depicted in the following picture:

Block #519089

Summary		Hashes	
Number Of Transactions	1231	Hash	0000000000000000005f5b195012937fab11ca591fbafef66f78fb30536e
Output Total	7,382.77569363 BTC	Previous Block	0000000000000000012af725feebf7fe513d963678f442a52f29a666e7c2bf
Estimated Transaction Volume	744.62724685 BTC	Next Block(s)	
Transaction Fees	0.21664571 BTC	Merkle Root	ac39eb74e0ad1da27ba3bd44809a3e62b9bc005e089d1e29358ae72eb06ec15
Height	519089 (Main Chain)		
Timestamp	2018-04-20 07:52:20		
Received Time	2018-04-20 07:52:20		
Relayed By	BTC.com		
Difficulty	3,839,316,899,020.67		
Bits	390660589		
Size	670.958 kB		
Weight	2397.002 kWU		
Version	0x20000000		
Nonce	2153285528		
Block Reward	12.5 BTC		

Transactions

			2018-04-20 07:52:20
No Inputs (Newly Generated Coins)	➡	1C1mCxRukix1K9sgAY5nQQJV7samAcZpv	12.71664571 BTC
		Unable to decode output address	0 BTC
			12.71664571 BTC

Strengths and Limitations of Bitcoin Blockchain platform

While the Bitcoin Blockchain platform has revolutionized the alternate currency markets and has stood the test of time for over nine years without any compromise and malware attack on its platform integrity, the consensus process suffers from the severe limitation of scalability and excessive energy consumption. A snapshot of a typical mining pool carrying out the mining on Bitcoin Blockchain is given in the following page.

The enormous amounts of energy and the computer processing power consumed by many such pools globally leads to a furor about the sustainability of such activities thus questioning the future of Bitcoin Blockchain.

Further the concentration of mining in the hands of select miners globally, puts the Blockchain at the risk of a 51% attack that happens when the miners with a collective mining capacity of a majority can collude together to undermine the sanctity of the Blockchain.

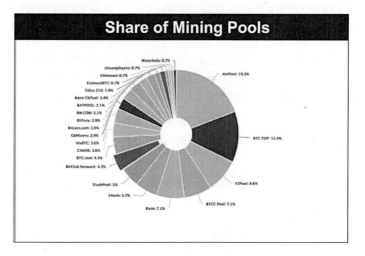

Mining pool concentration in the hands of a handful of miners.

However, the economic reasons have acted as a deterrent to such a possibility as envisaged by 'Satoshi Nakomoto' in his white paper of October 2008.

The success of bitcoin, has resulted in an enormous interest in the cryptocurrency market with a number of entrepreneurs coming out with different versions of Bitcoin through hard fork (program upgrades resulting in new chains) and also those with altogether a new logic that offers far more secure and scalable solutions with additional features like anonymity.

Monero and Z-Cash are 2 such improvised Cryptocurrencies offering anonymity to those conducting transactions over their platforms.

Though, in principle, it is not possible to identify the participants in the transactions in the Bitcoin Blockchain, it is technically possible to trace back the identity of the transaction generators in a deductive manner, leading to the IP address used by them.

A number of improvement proposals have been under implementation over the Bitcoin protocols that are expected to increase the speed of transaction processing.

Interestingly, Bitcoin offered another opportunity for entrepreneurs to offer the 'Proof of Ownership' service to content creators and Intellectual property owners.

Bitcoin program allows for an immutable record of its transactions that includes confirmation of any information that has been updated on the Blockchain and confirmed.

An example of such a service is https://www.po.et/ . Po.et uses cryptography to give both publishers and content creators the tools to automate the licensing process without relying on third parties, namely, Proof of Existence.

Po.et is a shared, open, universal ledger designed to record metadata and ownership information for digital creative assets. Po.et is a continuation of Proof of Existence, the first non-financial application of the Blockchain. By creating an open platform on the Bitcoin Blockchain, Po.et aims to create the most institutional, globally-verifiable record of digital media assets. This record will be a framework for building smart, interoperable media applications using a shared, standard and extensible metadata format.

Source: https://www.po.et **A look at the list of top cryptocurrencies being used globally as of May 2018, is given below:**

To summarize, let us recount the key aspects of Blockchain technology:

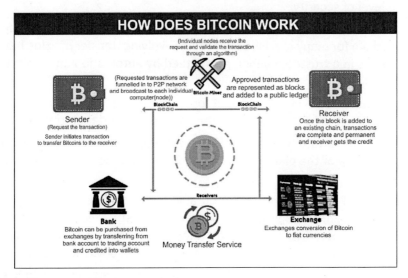

Blockchain involves:

(A)   A set of computers or Nodes, trusted or untrusted, acting as a part of a system, collaborating with each other in a programmatic manner to accept and verify transactions presented to the system.

(B)   A distributed ledger shared across all the relevant nodes and participants after recording all the approved transactions in a chronological manner to serve as a single source of truth.

(C)   Grouping of the transactions into unique blocks that are chained together in such a manner that allows one to trace a transaction to the respective block for all times to come, thus resulting in immutability of the transaction log.

(D)   A number of participants interacting with each other in a Peer to Peer manner through a front-end application, through the nodes and submitting transactions financial or non-financial for verification, confirmation and recording into blocks.

(E)   A mechanism to query the transaction to know the details of the same through an explorer.

(F)   A system of identity to allow the participants to disclose, keep confidential or operate in a pseudonymous manner (alias name) depending on the characteristics of the platform.

(G)   A cryptographically generated identity representing the participant in a unique manner through a Public Key and Private Key pair to be identified by the Blockchain to allow transactions by them.

(H)   A system of encoding and decoding the transactions to be viewable by the authorized members internal or external as the case may be, providing a high level of security.

(I) A smart contract or an application that allows the participants to leverage the Blockchain for many real life applications involving transfer of value between the peers in a trusted manner, guaranteed by automation and indisputable recording.

J() Autonomous and highly efficient operations that can be verified while maintaining the confidentiality of the participants and their transactions.

(K) A system of reward for all participants working together to perpetuate the performance of the platform in a fool proof manner to ensure sanctity of its operation.

(L) A fool proof mechanism to ward off any threats for sabotaging integrity of the Blockchain, through an appropriate consensus mechanism depending on the use case. This provides the tolerance of the Blockchain against any significant faults that may arise from known or unknown sources.

(M) A systematic program to continually improve the performance to keep up the platform in tune with the current technological paradigms, that may undermine its performance or its ability to keep its participants, rewarded.

Consensus Mechanisms (POW, POS, DPOS, PBFT, etc.)

The mechanism by which the members come to an agreement about the authenticity of the transaction is referred to as the 'Consensus Mechanism'.

Consensus formation ensures the involvement of multiple validators in a systematic and predetermined manner ensuring decentralization and objectivity of decision making. It ensures the implementation of the key features of the Blockchain platform like 'Increased trust, immutability of the transactions and the maintenance of integrity of the platform.

Consensus mechanism is the soul of the Blockchain platform and it has to help the members in reaching the right decision 100% of the time. The sanctity of the Blockchain application depends on the strength and reliability of is consensus mechanism. The consensus mechanism followed by Bitcoin and the earlier version of the public Ethereum client is known as Proof of Work (POW) where, the miners or validators are competing with each other and burning invaluable resources like computing power and enormous amounts of electricity to guess the right Nonce and create the targeted hash and win the race to create the block.

While this provides huge security for the network from hostile miners wanting to create and approve wrong transactions, this also creates a huge issue with scalability of the platform and huge concerns with respect to environmental damage caused due to expending huge amounts of valuable resources, though this method successfully prevents double spending and also dis-incentivizes creation of undesirable and unplanned forks (causing alternate chains of blocks in run time due to more than one chain of blocks being formed from a given block number).

To address this, Ethereum and a number of Blockchain platforms that run applications in the form of smart contracts, decided to adopt Proof of Stake (POS) where the chance of creating a new block is directly proportional to the share of the coins/ currency at stake.

POS mechanism ensures that there is no wastage of resources like in the case of POW mechanism and hence there is no creation of new coins during the consensus process. However the miners are incentivized for confirming the transaction and maintaining the integrity of the platform. However, a drawback for the POS mechanism is that it is susceptible to 'Nothing at Stake' problem. This involves the miners to process more than one block at the same block without possessing any additional stake and causes forks while earning the transaction fees in multiple

ways for the same block. Hence the POS has been modified to include 'Staking' by the Blockchain platforms to prevent this problem. Staking involves pledging one's stake or a borrowed stake to be able to participate in the mining process with a risk of losing the pledged stake in case of any wrong doing by the miner like acting like a byzantine node, approving wrong transaction or participating in fork creating transaction. Ethereum uses this modified version of POS namely Casper in its upcoming version of its Public Blockchain platform.

Another modified version of the POS consensus mechanism is DPOS, namely, Delegated Proof of Stake. Delegated proof of stake involves selection of a representative group of miners as a subset of the entire eligible group of miners and allowing them to create the block in a pre-designated manner, for example, round robin based system etc. DPOS enables a rapid scale up of the platform applications as it can handle a number of transactions in parallel at the same time with different group of delegates working on different transactions at the same time. EOS, ARK etc. are some new age platforms that use DPOS consensus mechanism and offer very high transaction throughputs that can compete with the traditional financial system.

PoET or Proof of Elapsed time is another very interesting consensus mechanism offered by Intel to the Blockchain world. PoET involves the miners who forming the block to randomly guess a minimum waiting time for the creation of the block. The miner whose wait time is the lowest and hence the fastest to create a new block is considered the winner. No miner can win the opportunity to create two consecutive blocks and hence, the chance of any miner dominating by creating a parallel chain of blocks that can cause forks is minimized. PoET is considered an ideal option for Public Blockchain without the need for an expensive mining algorithm like that of POW. Hyperledger Sawtooth uses PoET consensus mechanism.

BFT and variants like PBFT- Practical Byzantine Fault Tolerant consensus mechanism are used when the transaction involves trusted parties and hence a smaller well defined quorum is considered sufficient to approve transactions to reach a definitive finality of transaction outcomes.

In general when the participants are well identified and their credentials are known, the consensus mechanism can be less or nil resource coming as the actors involved in wrong decision making can be immediately taken care in case they act against the spirit of the propriety of the interactions. PBFT is best suited for enterprise Blockchain platforms. POW (Proof of Work), POS (Proof of Stake), DPOS (Delegated Proof of Stake) & PBFT (Practical Byzantine Fault Tolerance) algorithms are the most frequently used Consensus Mechanisms that have stood the test of time.

CHAPTER 16

Ethereum - The State Machine

The Birth of Ethereum

Ethereum: The new generation Killer application to catalyze innovation and entrepreneurship globally.

The next major development in the history of Blockchain happened with launch of the Public Blockchain, Ethereum that allowed Turing-Complete programs to be run on its Blockchain, while also having all the salient features of the Bitcoin Blockchain

Ethereum was proposed in late 2013 by Vitalik Buterin, a cryptocurrency researcher and programmer. Development was funded by an online crowd sale that took place between July and August 2014. The system went live on 30 July 2015, with 11.9 million coins "premined" for the crowd sale at a price of 35 cents.

Vitalik Buterin
2013

- Bitcoin script language allows some sophisticated calculations (verifying conditions) though it is **not Turing-Complete**...

- Blockchain system with embedded **Turing-Complete** language would allow to verify *any [computable] condition!*

Ethereum facilitated the launch of many P2P organizations that can conduct their operations over the net without the fear of counterparty trust issues through the use of applications named 'Smart Contracts'.

The vision of Vitalik Buterin was to create a powerful Blockchain platform to launch any type of Blockchain application using smart contracts.

Ethereum revolutionized the concept of Blockchain by allowing the use of high-level programming languages like Solidity to create applications to automate the business processes and record them on the Blockchain. This allowed a large scale innovation to be triggered where all the centralized organizations conducting businesses offering a variety of services to end consumers could be modelled without a centralized control structure and aggregation, through applications called 'Smart contracts'. End users can now conduct businesses among themselves in a peer to peer manner without any human intervention.

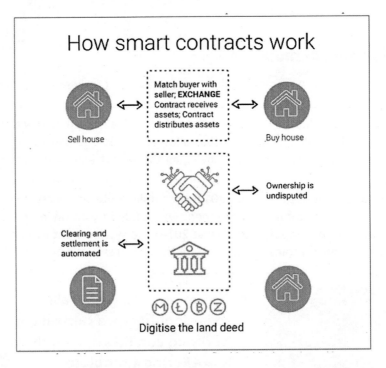

Real life agreements to record buy and sell assets can now be totally automated.

The assets are digitised and the ownership transfer of the assets is captured through a smart contract and the transaction is recorded for good on the Blockchain.

Ethereum thus, allowed not only the recording of the ledger, but also the recording of the transactions conducting through a complex logic mirroring the real life execution of agreements.

When the smart contracts are programmed, compiled and migrated on to the Ethereum Blockchain, the smart contracts are provided an address depicting the location of the contract on the Blockchain and the application is recorded in a block and distributed across all the nodes. Hence these applications are called Decentralized applications. Decentralized applications interact with the external users through a web browser as depicted in the following diagram.

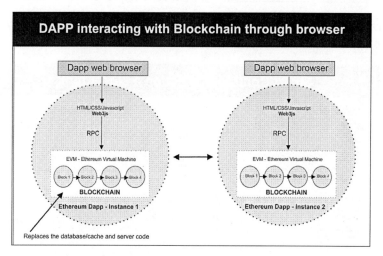

How do the smart contracts work?

In addition to the transactions caused by the exchange of UTXOs in Bitcoin Blockchain, the transactions in the Ethereum Blockchain are undertaken though complex applications called Smart contracts that are triggered by data and inputs from external accounts in an automatic manner. The list of all transactions and their Merkle root are then stored in all the blocks. A high-level representation of the same, focusing on the smart contract triggered change of state is depicted as follows:

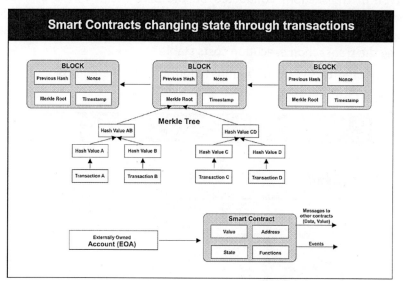

When the smart contracts when triggered through an external account, the business logic embedded in the contract automatically gets executed and the state of the ledger balances all the corresponding accounts gets updated and is written on all the nodes of the Blockchain.

While reading any date from the Blockchain, the data can be read only from the nearest node, but while writing, the data is written onto all the nodes.

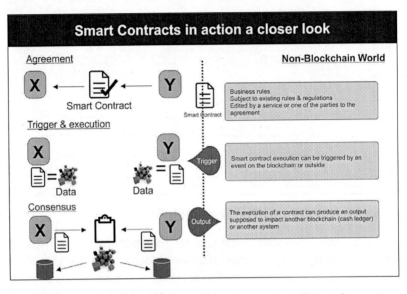

Hence it takes more effort and resources to write and update information on the Ethereum Blockchain. To incentivize this, Ethereum Blockchain uses the concept called Gas that is used by the users to pay for the effort undertaken to execute any type of transactions conducted on the Blockchain. Gas is expressed as a conversion unit of the native currency of the Ethereum Blockchain namely, ether and keeps varying in time to adjust for the variation of the price of ether, thus keeping the transaction execution costs stable.

A step by step execution of a transaction in the Ethereum Blockchain can be visualized in the following manner:

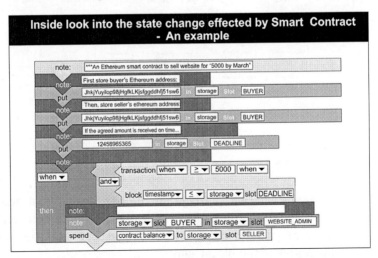

A close look at the information stored in the Ethereum block is given in the following diagram:

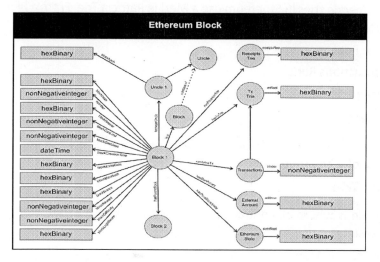

Some key definitions:

- **Ommer/ Uncle:** a child of a parent of a parent of a block that is not the parent, or more generally a child of an ancestor that is not itself an ancestor. If A is an ommer of B, B is a **nibling**(niece/nephew) of A. Ethereum has a mechanism where a block may include its uncles; this ensures that miners that create blocks that do not quite get included into the main chain can still get rewarded

- **Block nonce:** a meaningless value in a block which can be adjusted in order to try to satisfy the proof of work condition

- **Externally owned account:** an account controlled by a private key. Externally owned accounts cannot contain EVM code

- **Difficulty** is a measure of how **difficult** it is to find a hash below a given target.

- **Gas:** a measurement roughly equivalent to computational steps. Every transaction is required to include a gas limit and a fee that it is willing to pay per gas; miners have the choice of including the transaction and collecting the fee or not. If the total number of gas used by the computation spawned by the transaction, including the original message and any sub- messages that may be triggered, is less than or equal to the gas limit, then the transaction processes. If the total gas exceeds the gas limit, then all changes are reverted, except that the transaction is still valid and the fee can still be collected by the miner. Every operation has gas expenditure; for most operations it is ~3-10, although some expensive operations have expenditures up to 700 and a transaction itself has an expenditure of 21000.

Tries in Ethereum

All of the merkle tries in Ethereum use a Merkle Patricia Trie. From a block header there are 3 roots from 3 of these tries.

1.   State Root
2.   Transactions Root
3.   Receipts Root

State Trie

There is one global state trie, and it updates over time. It's worth noting that this storage Root Is the root of another Patricia trie:

Storage Trie

Storage trie is where all contract data lives. There is a separate storage trie for each account.

Transactions Trie

There is a separate transactions trie for every block.

The ordering is mostly decided by a miner, so this data is unknown until mined. After a block is mined, the transaction trie never updates.

Receipts Trie

Every block has its own Receipts trie.

- **Source:** https://github.com/ethereum/wiki/wiki/Patricia-Tree.

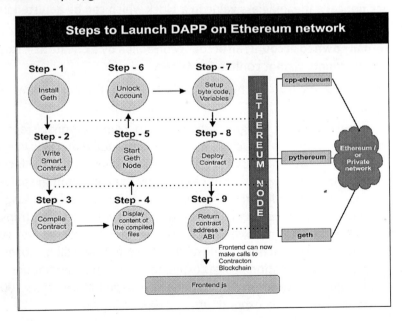

The above diagram gives a step by step description of the process to launch the smart contract on an Ethereum Blockchain.

Ethereum project offers a number of tools and techniques to program smart contracts and deploy them on the main Ethereum Blockchain.

Remix IDE is the most popular development framework that allows programmers to develop, test and deploy the smart contracts on to the Ethereum test network. After successfully testing the same, the same can be migrated on the local node and then deployed on the main network.

A sample use case of a Smart contract development project looks as follows:

CREATE AND DEPLOY A FULLY DECENTRALIZED DAPP IN EHTEREUM

The steps involve the following activities:

(A)   Create a Smart Contract from scratch using Solidity program.

(B)   Deploy Smart Contracts on ropsten test network

(C)   Create the frontend of the DAPP (Decentralized application)

(D)   Connect the deployed contract with your application

(E)   Deploy the final DAPP on the decentralized hosting of IPFS

(F)   Use your custom domain with IPFS

IPFS, namely Inter planetary file system, described in more detail at a later stage is the file storage system used along with Blockchain applications as a decentralized external storage of Blockchain related information. This is because, Blockchains like Ethereum are basically excellent for transaction processing and terrible expensive for data storage. Hence data is stored externally and referenced through IPFS hash links as required.

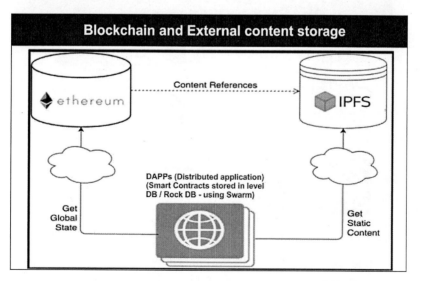

The technology used is given below:

- **Database:** The Ethereum's Testnet Ropsten Blockchain.
- **Hosting:** IPFS to get free hosting forever in a decentralized platform.
- **Frontend:** React.js with webpack or plain JavaScript.
- **Domain name:** Godaddy or any other domain registrar.
- **Contract's programming language:** Solidity 0.4.11, right now the most famous language for developing Smart Contracts.
- **Frontend contracts:** web3.js to (JavaScript library for Ethereum) uses those contracts in your web user interface.
- **Frameworks:** Truffle to deploy, test and compile our contracts.
- **Development server:** Node.js to use the app while developing locally along with testrpc.
- **Metamask:** Metamask browser is a google chrome plugin with a built in node use the final application like the end user would.

The steps that are followed in developing the DAPP and deploying the front end application and the Smart Contract are as follows:

Setup the project

- Program the Solidity contracts
- Create the frontend application
- Deploy the application online with IPFS

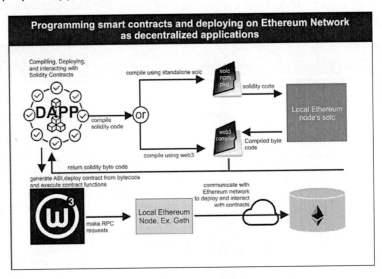

The killer application of Ethereum was in allowing for the Crowd funding of projects through sale of Tokens linked to Ether, the native currency of Ethereum platform.

A real life use case of a smart contract is given below:

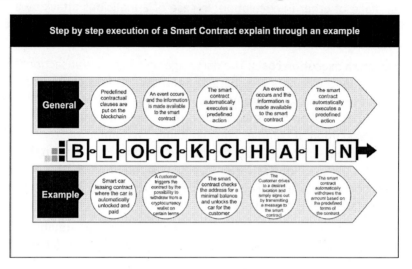

The car leasing company, which operates through a 'Smart contract', holds the funds in the form of cryptocurrency (ether denominated) in the case of Ethereum in the smart contract address. The customer pays through the same medium through his funds held in a wallet corresponding to the Blockchain to avail the services of the smart contract.

Transaction costs, Value creation and exchange on Public Blockchain Platforms:

The value in Public Blockchains like Bitcoin, Ethereum etc., is created and exchanged in the following ways:

(i) **Mining Reward:** Mining Reward is the number of units of cryptocurrency given to the miners taking part in approving transactions and upkeep of Platform sanctity. This is reflected in the generation of the numeric value called Nonce (Number used only once) generated by the miners, that helps in the uniqueness of the block created.

This is created and issues to the Miners at the time of a new block creation. For example in Bitcoin it is 12.5 Bitcoin and Ethereum it is 3 ether (being dropped to 0.6 ether with the adoption of Hybrid POW/POS mining at the time of launch of POS based Casper platform by Ethereum). This is used to compensate for the amount of resources like electricity and computer processing power expended by the miners for block creation in the POW consensus process. This value varies from platform to platform and changes across time periods (In Bitcoin, it is halved every four years) and in non POW consensus it is mostly nil.

When Ethereum Blockchain shifts from POW to POS fully (expected by end of year 2018) , the mining method changes to staking method with nil mining rewards and the miners get voting power to approve transactions based on their stake of ether in circulation. In case of a malicious attack by a staker, they stand to lose 3 times the value of their ether staked. (Source https:// www.finder.com.au/ ethereum-mining-rewards-set-to-drop-by-80).

(ii) **Transaction execution costs:** The parties generating the transactions that are approved by the miners are charged a transaction fees expressed in terms of the base currency. In case of Bitcoin, the smallest base unit is Satoshi (1 Bitcoin is 100million Satoshis) In case of ethereum , the transactions also contain execution of complex code containing a number of steps. Each step in the program will have a specific transaction fees expressed in the form of Gas units. The price of Gas varies inversely to the price of ether to keep the transaction prices stable. The Gas price in ethereum on 31st of July 2018 is approximately 1.1 Gwei (Giga wei).

The following table gives the conversion of ether into multiples of the smallest value unit in ethereum Blockchain, namely, wei. (source http:// ethdocs.org)

Unit	Wei Value	Wei
wei	1 wei	1
Kwei (babbage)	1e3 wei	1,000
Mwei (lovelace)	1e6 wei	1,000,000
Gwei (shannon)	1e9 wei	1,000,000,000
microether (szabo)	1e12 wei	1,000,000,000,000
milliether (finney)	1e15 wei	1,000,000,000,000,000
ether	1e18 wei	1,000,000,000,000,000,000

(iii) **Tokens:** While Bitcoin is suitable only for exchanging Cryptocurency (BTC) on its network, a number of public platforms like Ethereum involve running of complex code through a sandboxed Turing complete virtual machine. In case of Ethereum, It is called EVM (Ethereum Virtual Machine) that runs on every node of its network. This allows for creation of multiple organisations with their own Smart Contracts running on the network with their unique logic, each allowing multiple parties to engage in peer to peer transactions, exchanging and creating value for their respective organisations. Each organisations is allowed to create its own unique token which is compliant with the respective Blockchain platform on which it is launched and is functioning.

Ethereum Blockchain allows for mainly two types of tokens ERC 20 and ERC

721 which are compliant with its Blockchain platform. While ERC 20 tokens are fungible and are interchangeable, ERC 721 is a unique innovation that allows for each asset on its Blockchain application to have its own unique value. ERC 721 tokens were originally created for an application called Cryptokitties (https://www.cryptokitties.co/) on Ethereum platform to create unique non-fungible assets with varying prices as a Proof of Concept, that proved a success.

Thus ERC 20 tokens are more like money, ERC 721 token is like a thing or an entity that is unique and different in value from each other.

ERC 20 tokens are expected to be replaced by ERC 223 tokens in due course. ERC 223 standard is put in place to rectify a defect in the ERC 20 standard that allows a token to be sent to a contract that does not allow withdrawal & freezed from where, you cannot retrieve your tokens in case of wrong transfer.

Summarizing the properties of Blockchain:

A. **Peer to Peer:** Blockchain enables Peer to peer transactions across parties hitherto unknown to each trusted without any intermediaries or central authorities, through an automated program that guarantees correct transactions in a decentralized manner. Thus, role of non-value adding middlemen and associated cost is minimized.

B. **Secure Transactions:** The transactions on the Blockchain take place between parties verified and authenticated through cryptographically secured keys and digital signatures, approved and authorized by a tested democratic process known as Consensus Mechanism.

C. **Immutable Data:** Once a transaction is approved and data recorded, it is considered immutable. All the changes thus become identifiable in the form of the updating transactions and their corresponding track record. Thus, any tampering of data in the Blockchain becomes evident. Hence the data is the Blockchain is considered Tamper evident.

D. **Auditability:** In case any data is changed after a record of the data is obtained at a given point in time, the hash of the data and that of the overall set of data (stored in the form of a Merkle root or combined hash of hashes) changes. Hence Blockchain can be used for auditing of data to throw out any unapproved tampering at a later date.

E. **Paperless:** Automated and efficient processed, result in paperless transactions resulting in increase in the speed of execution, increase in operational efficiency and reduction in costs.

CHAPTER 17

DAOS & ICOS- Facilitating Enterpreneurship

The rise of DAO- Decentralized Autonomous Organization.

DAOs are offshoot of the Blockchain platform launched by Vitalik Buterin in the year 2014. The functioning of the Ethereum platform is well explained in the yellow paper at the link, http://gavwood.com/paper.pdf

The convergence of the different themes that have made Blockchain a reality has resulted in the ability of the entrepreneurs to launch autonomously run organizations. The facilitation of

- Peer to peer transactions in a trusted & pseudonymous environment
- Program driven consensus
- Decentralized and democratic approach to organizational functioning Platform supported indisputable consensus that imbibes trust into all transactions
- Open source movement to collaborative development
- Disruptive urge of the entrepreneurial community that got a vent to launch their ideas into action without being burdened by regulation, through the launch of tokens through ICOs in a speedy manner, resulted in the creation and proliferation of the Decentralized Autonomous Organizations catering to different needs, different markets and different customer groups, aimed at 'Disrupting' the traditional approach by the way organizations always worked.

Different types of Decentralized entities can be summarized in the following chart:

Dapps, DAOs, DACs, DASs

Decentralized applications (Dapps)
- Is an application that runs on a network in a distributed fashion with participant information securely protected and operation execution decentralized across network nodes.

Decentralized Autonomous Organizations & Corporations (DAOs & DACs)
- In a DAO/DAC, there are smart contracts as agents running on Blockchains that execute ranges of prespecified or preapproved tasks based on events and changing condition.
- Storj, Smart Contracts operated, decentralized file storage

Decentralized Autonomous Societies (DASs)
- For in the future this can be a DAS where a fleet of smart contracts, or entire ecosystems of Dapps, DAOs, DACs operating autonomously

Decentralized autonomous organizations are run through Smart contracts with minimal intervention of humans. The entire business logic on which the decisions are made in the DAO are encoded into a smart contract or a set of interconnected smart contracts that are then migrated on to the Blockchain Node, from where they are appended to the database of every node, following a confirmation. They are identified by an 'Address' which is auto generated and is used whenever the application has to be invoked by their interface or a program.

Except for a small portion of the logic that is considered the secret sauce of the promoters launching the DAO, the rest of the logic is included in the front-end user interface. The source code of the DAO is generally available in the public domain like GitHub and the entire community of Blockchain developers is allowed to use it albeit at times, with a small royalty to the actual developers.

The website https://www.stateofthedapps.com/ provides the details of all the DAPPS that have been created or the ones in the process of being launched in the future.

The various aspects of the Decentralized Application eco system are summarized well in the following diagram:

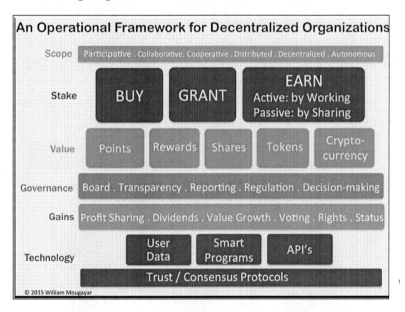

The DAOs which are run by the Distributed Applications, namely DAPPS are governed by a programmatic consensus driven approach while interacting with the external world of contractors, customers and any members or other programs interacting with the application.

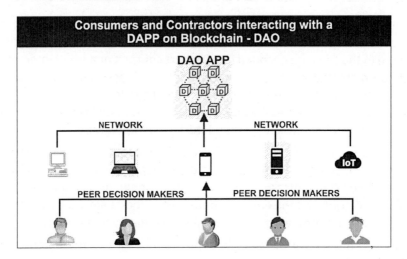

The Decentralized Autonomous Organization has the following main features:

- It offers cryptographically secured confidentiality to the identity of the users of its programs.

- Decisions are taken as per the programmed business logic which is intractable. Hence the organization is considered incorruptible.

- The creators of the smart contract do not have any say in the running of the organization. They can receive their share of the proceedings as per the policies encoded into the business logic.

- The management and the shareholders are represented by the token holders in proportion to their holdings.

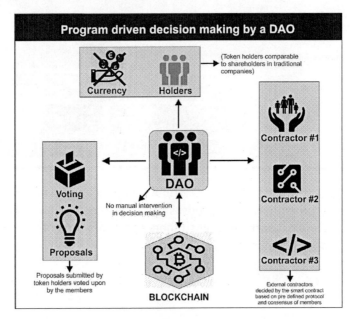

- While transactions are encoded into the smart contracts, the governance of the DAOs is done as per a set of rules and policies explained in the 'White Paper' explaining the business model and the rationale behind the launch of the same, based on which the investors invest in the tokens through contributions at the time of the launch.

- DAO can hold its own resources in the form of cryptocurrency/ token balance which it uses to incentivize participants that enable the organization further the progress of the organization or remunerate those that worked for it.

- The DAO will have a democratic process of selecting the appropriate proposals for investment.

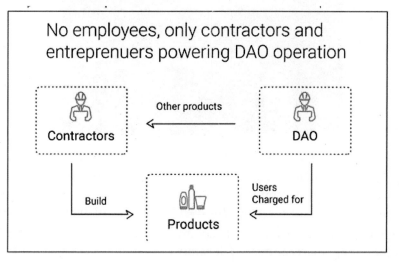

- All the transactions are conducted in an absolute trustworthy manner amongst the peers catered to by the DAO.

- While it is possible that DAO is interacting with a variety of parties in the external world through a web interface, there are no human employees on its roles.

- The promoter group which also possess a good percentage of the tokens issued could be overseeing the functioning of the smart contract and could be on the stand by in case of unforeseen situations.

- In unforeseen situations the contract can be programmed to shut down and the entire balance of the crypto assets held by its address can be offloaded into the address of the contract creator which can then be taken care of. But the business logic encoded into the contract cannot be changed.

Thus, it can be seen that DAOs by operating in a trusted and automated manner result in triggering a wave of innovation and value creation without the expenses associated with carrying a lot of physical assets and employees on role.

Some examples of Decentralized organizations in front of us:

- The solar system, the galaxy and the universe.
- The Bitcoin core Blockchain which transacts currency worth of billions of US Dollar worth without the intervention of any centralized regulatory authority.

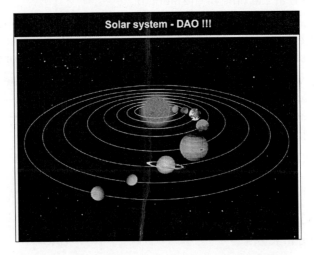

The concept of DAOs has led to the launch of organizations which are totally out of the purview of the regulators and are governed by computer applications named DAPPS made up of Smart contracts. Incentivized with their own community based crypto assets namely, Tokens issued through the process of Initial coin offerings.

Any organization can now build communities by creating Decentralized applications using smart contracts by leveraging Ethereum Blockchain for verifying the transactions and offering trust in an automated manner.

To do this, the companies running the smart contracts can use their own currency linked to their business which is used by all their customers and which is used for rewarding all their partners and shareholders.

Traditional fund raising approach	Blockchain enabled crowd funding
Business plan	Whitepaper
Elevator pitch & personal intro	Website, Slack, Reddit, Twitter, etc.
Institutions	Everyone
VC	ICO

Ethereum facilitated this process by allowing standardized protocols in the form of ERC 20, ERC 223 and ERC 721 for launching smart contracts that implement token through Ethereum Blockchain.

The tokens are launched to fund the decentralized autonomous organizations developed using the DAPPs created by the cryptopreneurs.

The tokens are a means of incentivising the promoters, employees and all those working to further the viability of the platform and also used by those conducting transactions. This in turn leads to the demand of tokens and increases their value in fiat currency that can be traded in crypto currency exchanges across the world.

Public Blockchain platforms like Ethereum, EOS etc., have facilitated unique opportunities for monetizing previously unthinkable types of assets like data generated from various IoT devices and from various other sources.

A high level diagram of such a DAPP namely Databroker is depicted below.

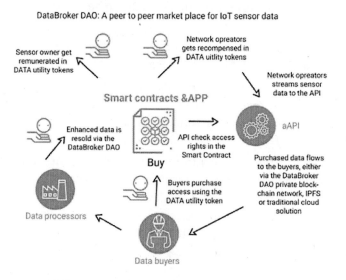

DataBroker DAO: A peer to peer market place for IoT sensor data

What are the different types of Tokens?

The money from the entrepreneurs is collected in the form of the platform currency like Bitcoin and Ethereum and the corresponding numbers of tokens are then transferred from the initial pool created by the contract creator to the participants of the DAPP.

A token over the Ethereum platform is considered as a digital asset that is initially convertible to Ethereum, but in due course can find its own value in the external world depending on the demand created for its use and traded through the crypto exchanges.

Token Types		
Token Type	**Examples**	**Description**
Coin / Currency	Ethereum, Bitcoin, Litecoin	Digital currencies like Bitcoin in which encryption techniques are used to regulate the generation of units of currency and verify the transfer of funds. They are operating independently of a central bank.
Utility Token	Steem, BAT, Siacon	The utility tokens are service or units of services that can be purchased. ICO of an utility token can be compared to a Kickstarter campaign to purchase products or services in advance.
Tokenized Securities	Trust Token	Tokens are representing shares of a business. Utility Tokens that can appreciate in value without the work of the Token holder based on value created by others are classified as Tokenized Securities. ICO of a Tokenized Security has to follow the rules of financial regulators.

The tokens created by adhering to these protocols, can be used as currency by the respective smart contracts on the Ethereum Blockchain and are fully trackable on the same

While Bitcoin disrupted the global 'Currency' markets, Ethereum disrupted any and every market by facilitating 'Crowd Funding' of ideas.

Crowd funding grew rapidly as an alternate to early stage venture financing across the world and led to over US Dollar 1.3 Billion worth of investments pouring into Blockchain based projects funded though Cryptocurrency denominated instruments, namely 'Tokens'.

The projects over Ethereum platform are funded by the 'Tokens', which are equivalent to the real life 'shares'. As the money was collected using smart contracts launched over the Ethereum network, all one needed to launch a company, raise money and create value, is an Ethereum linked wallet, a well selected use case with a program and a POC along with a white paper describing the project.

How do you acquire a token?

Tokens are launched through a Crowd funding process called ICO (Or Initial coin offering).

Thus the wave of crowd funded Blockchain based peer to peer businesses through the launch of Initial Coin Offerings (ICO) which also stands for Idea & Community on One platform took off and picked up acceleration in the year 2017.

Some of the prominent ICOs that have raised money from the investors in the form of BTC or Ether are given below (The value is represented in US Dollar equivalent at the time of the launch).

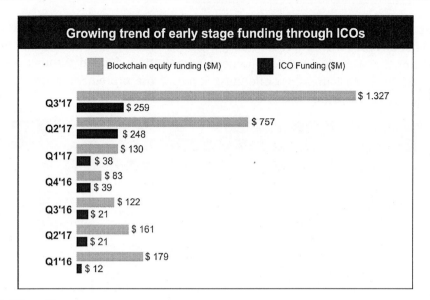

ICO Timelines:

Name	DAO/ Platform	Year	Amount Raised (US $Mill)
Ethereum	Blockchain Platform	Jul-14	18
The DAO	Failed DAPP	Apr-16	150
WAVES	Blockchain Platform	Jun-16	16
Qtum	Blockchain Platform	Mar-17	15
Gnosis	DAPP- Prediction market	Apr-17	13
Status	DAPP interface platform	Jun-17	100
Bancor	Decentralized Liquidity network	Jun-17	156
Tezos	Blockchain Platform	Jul-17	232
EOS	Blockchain Platform	Ongoing	185

It is interesting to see that some of the ICOs are aimed at building competing platforms while the tokens are issued on existing prominent platforms. For example Ethereum's ICO investment was raised in Bitcoins while the EOS which is proposing to disrupt Ethereum's approach to Blockchain application development is raising money in Ether using a Token contract launched on Ethereum Blockchain.

The planning, launch and management of the ICOs to raise resources in the form of tokens maps closely to the launch of capital market securities in the real world. Only thing is that, the process is much simpler and attracts investors through the novelty of the process, promise of disruption, invitation to create and be a part of a community and is targeted at small & big investors at the same time.

Apart from Ethereum, there are a number of other types of platforms that can offer options to launch smart contracts and Decentralized applications that form a part of the Decentralized Autonomous organizations funded through tokens launched through Initial Coin offerings: Some of the prominent platforms are outlined in the following figure:

Smart Contract platform comparison						
	Smart Contracts			Protocol Details		Other
	Turing Complete	Verifiable	Consensus Process	Interoperability	Scalability	Governance
DFINITY	Yes	No	Threshold Relay PoW/PoS	Interoperable with Ethereum	Paralell mining networks	Self amending protocol informed by Futacratic DAO
Qtum	Yes	No	UTXO PoS	Interoperable with Ethereum & Bitcoin heritage networks	Contract code executed off chain	Foundation informed by DAO
COSMOS	No (Can trigger contracts on other chains)	No	Federated PoS	Interoperable with all networks connected through a hub chain	Paralell side chains & interconnected blockchains	DAO
BOScoin	No	No	Federated PoS	Minimal Interoperabiltiy	Small cohort of semitrusted nodes quickly reach consensus	DAO
ethereum	Yes	In development	PoW (Transitioning to Casper)	Minimal Interoperabiltiy	Sharding & possible implementation of Raiden Network	Foundation
tezos	Yes	Yes	Delegated PoS	Interoperable with Ethereum	Contract code executed off chain & paralell consensus networks	Self amending protocol informed by a DAO (possible shift to futacratic governancee later)
	Yes	No	PoS/PoW	Interoperable with Ethereum	State channels	Futacratic DAO

Source: Smith + Crown table compiled DFINITY, Qtum, Cosmos, BOScoin, Ethereum, Tezos and Aeternity whitepapers and other official soruces

What is an ICO?

ICO is termed as,

- Issue of new, unique crypto asset units known as tokens
- Exchanged against existing crypto currency units like Ether, Bitcoin, NEM etc. depending on the platform
- To fund new projects based on Blockchain technology.

It is important to understand that though the requirements for launching the ICO are much simpler with respect to Fund Raising through the conventional process for early stage start-ups, the responsibility for the funds raised is much more than the normal process. The funds raised in the crypto currency form are to be deployed as per the utilization plan presented in the white paper.

Since the coins are not regulated in most of the countries, it is generally considered as an advance for the use of the platform and its products and services and not as tradable financial securities that are heavily regulated.

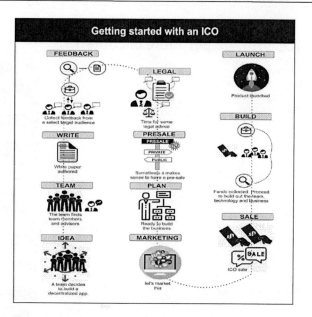

The various stages of the ICO process are given below:

Idea and Planning:

The following questions should be answered in a convincing manner:

- Why do you want to launch the DAO?
- What is the DAO proposing to achieve?
- How is the DAO proposing to go about its business?
- Target customers
- Value proposition
- Business planning
- Business case and Business model canvas should be drawn up.

The promoters should not only to be able to convince the investors and stakeholders about the idea, but also ensure focus that can be projected to the external world of investors in a convincing manner.

Analyze similar DAOs available in the public domain and their respective Whitepapers. Create a technical and functional architecture for the project and get it vetted by functional and technical experts.

These should be represented in a Whitepaper (Version 1) explaining the rationale, solution, technical and management bandwidth to execute the project and a three page high level summary to be able to explain the concept in a simple manner too.

Create a sample contract and test it on the Test network.

An example of a typical ICO (Databroker) white paper's contents is depicted in the following figure.

ICO Whitepaper Table of contents

CONTENTS

Credits- Databroker ICO

The management team behind the DAO, launches a whitepaper explaining the activities proposed to be conducted by the DAO along with an investment pitch through a website announcing the launch of the DAO.

The contents of sample Whitepaper are presented below:

In the whitepaper the management team outlines the state of the project, timelines of the project and the road map as it sees etc. This information is clearly outlined giving a clear picture about the community and activities to the investors.

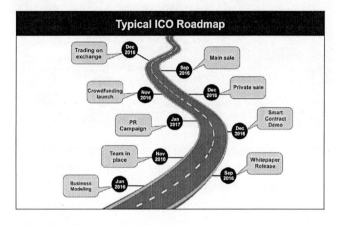

The management outlines the details of the number of tokens it has proposed to issue over the life time of the contract and the rate at which the new tokens would be issued if any, the distribution methodology of the token, indication of the share of tokens allotted to the promoters which will be used for business development, generating incentives for early platform adopters, marketing etc.

Token Details		
Presale 17th of November / 5pm UTC to 5th of March 2018 / 8pm UTC	**Token Sale** 6th of March 2018 / 2pm UTC to 5th of April 2018	**Token Distribution**
Supply 500,000,000 REPUX	**Accepted Currencies** ETH, BTC and Wire Transfer	● Presale ● Sold During Token sale
Price 1 REPUX = 0.20 usd	**Token Distribution Date** 5th of April 2018	● Rewards Pool ● Sold on platform ● Founding Team
Maximum Goal Hard cap: 33,100,000 USD Soft cap : 1,000,000 USD	**Emission Rate** No new tokens will be created	● Ambassadors ● Token sale bounties

Execution phase:

The team consisting of founders, core team of employees including a development team and advisors who are convinced about the concept and ready to be a firm part of the 'Community' has to be in place at-least at on paper with firm time and mind shares committed to the project.

The smart contract must be developed for launching and distribution of the Token created for the project and launched on the corresponding Blockchain platform. The same must be showcased through a website landing page with a crisp, attractive, informative and convincing manner, providing the details of the contract address to which the investors need to send their crypto currencies.

Example of a DAO (courtesy, Storiqa , a decentralized market place) announcing the proceedings of a crowd sale through its website is given below:

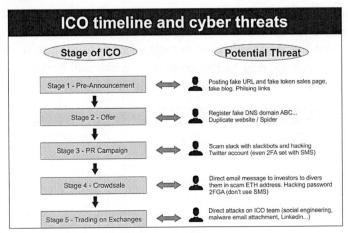

Develop, test, conduct a code review and launch the smart contract corresponding to the project corresponding to the staging presented in the white paper as a MVP to present to potential investors.

Raise Funds:

It is important for the ICO managers to keep an eye on the various types of cyber threats that can endanger the amounts raised from the investors. Hence sufficient steps need to be taken to ensure that a hacker proof process is followed with appropriate safeguarding measures.

The management then requests the investors to chip in for investing their funds by sending Ethers/ bitcoins (base currency) from their address on the Ethereum or the corresponding Blockchain created using a compatible wallet.

This is done in various stages:

(A) **Private sale stage:** The founders should raise a few resources for serious and knowledgeable investors by approaching investors, HNIs, PE funds etc., by convincing them of their idea and vision. The purpose of this is to get the idea scrutinized and approved by credible investors and get their buy in. This could bring in strategic partners and also offer credibility for future investors.

(B) **Pre-sale stage:** This stage consists of short window of 2-3 weeks and involves targeting a limited group of people, investors and project backers with an exclusive offer that offers committed allotment, generally at a discounted price. The money raised in the Pre-ICO stage is used toward the development of the smart contract to a robust level and also to generate funds for marketing during the Main ICO stage.

During this time, the founding team should actively look for opportunities and proactively participate in various events to meet up with potential project backers and community participants to test, improve and spread the word about the project.

(C) **Main sale stage:** This stage involves aggressive marketing through targeted digital marketing activities, participation in several social media platforms like LinkedIn, Facebook, Twitter, WhatsApp, Telegram etc., and also aggressive participation in community and industry related events to increase the awareness and interest levels for garnering maximum sale of the tokens.

During this stage, the DAO promoters generally also adopt the strategy of offering 'Airdrops', where free tokens are given to targeted potential investors active on LinkedIn, Twitter and Telegraph accounts, so that they can spread a positive word about the ICO and generate more demand for the tokens.

Upon successful completion of the crowd sale proceedings, appropriate number of tokens corresponding to the amount of Ether sent will be transferred to the investor's address and will be reflected in his/her wallet.

Once the tokens are listed on the crypto exchanges, the investor is free to trade and convert into ether or any other crypto assets as per his choice.

For more information and detailed working of Medical record Blockchain, please refer, https://medicalchain.com/en/whitepaper

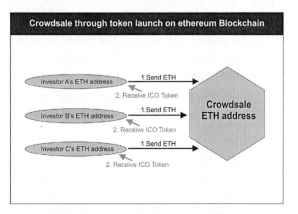

Augur (Ethereum base), Golem (Ethereum base), Factom (Bitcoin base) are some of the top tokens in demand from the investors.

The activity of the token contracts on the exchanges can be seen in the following diagram (https://ethplorer.io/top):

Post ICO stage:

All steps should be taken to support and ensure the safety and security of the wallets of the investors and the holding of the tokens. Smart contracts should be continuously monitored to ensure that there is no unusual activity or unexpected transactions due to faulty logic.

Top Ethereum Tokens Activity

by Capitalization		by Trade Volume		by Operations		

Tokens Cap: $ 24 B (2.8 %) for 465 Tokens. Trade Vol (24h): $ 1,178 M (-8.7 %)

#	Token	Cap	Price	24h	7d	30d
	Ethereum (ETH)	$ 51,099 M	$ 520.05	-13.3 %	-24.5 %	-44.6 %
1	EOS (EOS)	$ 3,187 M	$ 4.34	-13.9 %	-25.2 %	-56.8 %
2	Tronix (TRX)	$ 1,738 M	$ 0.03	-11.2 %	-23.7 %	-47.0 %
3	VeChain Token (VEN)	$ 1,734 M	$ 3.46	-12.5 %	-0.8 %	-39.3 %
4	OMGToken (OMG)	$ 953 M	$ 9.34	-15.4 %	-30.3 %	-43.7 %
5	BNB (BNB)	$ 838 M	$ 8.47	-7.8 %	11.3 %	-21.0 %
6	ICON (ICX)	$ 724 M	$ 1.87	-14.1 %	-24.6 %	-61.3 %
7	Digix DAO (DGD)	$ 671 M	$ 335.42	-17.0 %	-0.8 %	38.8 %
8	Populous Platform (PPT)	$ 484 M	$ 13.09	-13.4 %	-14.6 %	-56.1 %
9	Maker (MKR)	$ 391 M	$ 631.65	-11.1 %	-20.1 %	-44.4 %
10	RHOC (RHOC)	$ 355 M	$ 0.99	-13.3 %	-24.8 %	-56.0 %

In case of any unexpected transaction, the promoters generally have the option of killing the smart contract and getting the token/ currency balances transferred to the account of the contract owner which then should be taken care in an appropriate manner in the interests of all the stake holders.

The investors will be happy when the project is going as per plan and the price of the token is increasing thus improving the value of the investments.

While the DAO performs as per the business logic embedded in the smart contract, the following parameters affect the price of the token:

- The demand supply gap of the tokens that is dependent on the number of tokens in circulation and also the time that the tokens are held by the holders. Higher is the holding period, the higher is the demand supply gap.

- Velocity of the token movement: Increased traction and volumes reflect the interest in the token purchase and hence increases the price of the token.

- Increased demand for the products and services offered by the platform, which need the utilization of token.

- The success of the DAO depends on a good marketing effort and delivery of high quality of services. The dominant share holder team should keep an eye and ensure that all efforts are taken to scale the demand for the usage of the products and services of DAO.

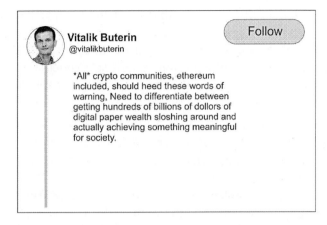

Vitalik Buterin
@vitalikbuterin

Follow

All crypto communities, ethereum included, should heed these words of warning, Need to differentiate between getting hundreds of billions of dollors of digital paper wealth sloshing around and actually achieving something meaningful for society.

In recent times, there have been a number of situations where the security of the Blockchain platforms and DAPPs are compromised. Hence utmost care must be taken to ensure that the testing of the platforms is done perfectly. A continuous vigil and monitoring system should be in place to ensure that cybercriminals do not end up usurping valuable assets of the investors through fraudulent means. It is indeed an irony that, though the Blockchain is supposed to protect the world against the malware attacks and cybercriminals, these applications also can be attacked by sophisticated criminals and should be guarded against. Some of these attacks are listed below:

Top Blockchain attacks & controversies:

Cryptos for dark web activities on Silk Road: Silk Road was an online black market, and the first modern darknet market, best known as a platform to sell illegal drugs. In October 2013, the US Federal Bureau of Investigation (FBI) shut down the website, and arrested Ross Ulbricht on charges of being the site's pseudonymous founder "Dread Pirate Roberts", and recovered 1.44 lakh bitcoins that were allegedly used to conduct transactions on the website. This exposed the utility of unregulated cryptocurrencies for criminal activities.

Fall of the largest crypto exchange Mount Gox: In February 2014, Mt Gox, the then largest exchange trading bitcoins, filed for bankruptcy, claiming that over $450 million worth of bitcoins were lost from its servers. Though around $100 million worth of bitcoins were later found, the rest have not been traced and have been either stolen or are lost forever.

NEM Coincheck exchange hack: In January 2018, one of the largest cryptocurrency exchanges, Vancouver-based Coincheck, reported that over $534 million worth of NEM coins were stolen. Though a part of the stolen NEM was later traced to trades conducted in Canada and Japan, the company declared there is little hope of tracking most of the coins.

Parity wallet freeze: On November 8, 2017, UK-based Parity Technologies Ltd, a leading provider of Blockchain technology platforms and applications announced a user had exploited a software vulnerability in its multi-sig wallets, resulting in a freeze of over 500 multi-sig wallets containing over $150 million worth of ether, some of it belonging to startups that had raised funds through ICOs. This led to the $150 million worth of ether being indefinitely suspended. On July 19, hackers exploited another software bug in the Parity wallet to steal over $30 million in ether.

The DAO Smart contract bug: On June 17, 2016, the DAO was subjected to an attack that exploited a combination of vulnerabilities, including the one concerning recursive calls, and the user gained control of 3.6 million ether, around a third of the 11.5 million ether that had been committed to the DAO. The 3.6 million ether had a value of about $50 million at the time of the attack. The lost ether were later recovered by hard forking the Ethereum platform, which split the Ethereum community into two, and by moving the diverted ether to a recovery address. This, however, exposed the vulnerability of smart contracts to programming bugs. This is done through a Reentrancy attack that is like a recursive call to exploit vulnerability due to smart contract logic does not consider state change stage in Ethereum Blockchain.

The Bitcoin hack: On August 15, 2010, two bitcoin addresses received 92.2 billion addresses as recorded in the block #74638 along with 0.01 BTC for the miner. This happened due to the error called 'Integer Overflow' which does not let the system take cognizance of too high values (> 21.1 million in case of Bitcoin). The problem was solved by a soft fork and deletion of the block, treating it as a case of programming error. The resultant 'good Blockchain' overtook the mistake infested Blockchain at block # 74691 as th authoritative source of bitcoin transaction history.

Malicious Smart contract attack: Qihoo 360 Technology Co. Ltd., is a Chinese internet security company known for its antivirus software demonstrated on EOS platform, how a malicious smart contract can bypass Address Space Layout Randomization (ASLR) to attack a node, leading to a subsequent compromise all the nodes in the network.

Pigeoncoin Hack: A vulnerability was discovered in Bitcoin core platform that resulted in attackers being able to double print 235 million Pigeoncoin, that amounted to over 25% of the overall coins in circulations. This shows the importance of the forked blockchains to continuously track their base platforms & update their software

51% attack : Some of the cryptocurrencies like Electroneum, Monacoin, Verge, Bitcoin gold, Litecoin cash, Zencash have been subjected tot 51% attack that undermine the decentralization aspect of the Blockchain operation.

ICO account hack: CoinDash a crypto startup raised $7.3 million before a hacker changed the address, causing donations to go to an unknown party. The company shut down the ICO, but promised to send its native token award, CDT, to those who attempted to donate, but not before the hacker made over $10 million worth of receipts to the wrong address.

Cross function race condition: This happens when functions share same state (this is very common problem within developer community as it leads to non-deterministic issue in production which cannot be reproducible easily.

Reentrancy attack: It is like a recursive call to exploit vulnerability due to smart contract logic does not consider state change stage in ethereum Blockchain

Illicit cryptomining: This happens when cryptominers surreptitiously install mining programs on their behalf on unsuspecting machines connected to the internet like windows servers, laptops, android devices and IoT endpoints. These mining programs end up making money to these criminals while the owners of these end up getting high electricity bills for their usage.

The above cases expose various shortcomings of unregulated cryptoasset markets like:

- Utility of cryptocurrencies for criminal activities
- Inability to take a legal recourse in case of loss of cryptoassets
- Vulnerability of cryptoasset accounts to hacking of exchanges and wallets
- Vulnerability of cryptocurrencies in case accounts are rendered unusable due to a freeze caused by a software bug or loss of the private key

  There are many cases where cryptocurrency owners have lost huge amounts of cryptocurrencies when their private keys were forgotten, stolen, or lost, or the computers in which they were stored were rendered unusable. A lot of precautions have to thus be taken while launching smart contracts to ensure they are free of bugs, and also by holders of cryptocurrencies to safeguard their private key.

As these are known attacks in the past, developers or testers need to think beyond what else can be exploited and upgrade their skills to ward off such attacks in the future.

Smart contracts are fully functional powerful programs manipulating sensitive and valuable data, storing & altering value on the Blockchain while interacting with external world through various interfaces & Oracles. Hence, smart contracts offer a lucrative targets for malicious attackersas they can store enormous value. Being a relatively new field implies a limited number of trained experts are available for best in class development & testing. Hence, auditing the smart contracts is a must before launching the corresponding DAPPS on the Mainnet. Tools like Mythril, Oyente, Solgraph, Manticore etc., offer a lot of options for undertaking fool proof audits and vulnerability scanning of smart contracts. https://securify. chainsecurity.com/ is an interesting platform for scanning Ethereum smart contracts for vulnerabilities. For best practices in smart contract security, one may refer https://consensys.github.io/smart-contract-best-practices/bibliography/

CHAPTER 18

Blockchain Certified LLPS to Boost Entrepreneurship

The success of the ICOs and the explosion of the DAO led business models bring forth an interesting observation.

Bitcoin, which is nothing but a DAO, an entity that has created an immense value to its holders, is not owned by any physical entity or a registered individual or a group.

The value to the founders is the value of the underlying tokens aka shares without any legal representation.

In future it is possible to create an entity without any legal position.

ICOs and Tokens are Proxies for Unregulated Fund raises & Shares to sidestep the rigor of Regulation & Scrutiny- They end up using expensive methods of using public Blockchains with high transaction costs, risk of fraud & confusing systems of multiple tokens, exchanges, conversions etc.

But the need of burgeoning Startup landscape of promoters to come together, contribute time and resources , track shares , account for changes in shares, value of contributions put in etc. are increasing day by day. But the current regulatory environment of creating companies, closing companies, increasing shares & share capital does not aid this process.

Single points of failure, trust based agreements & dealings are a bane for any organization. The Proposer, Endorser, Orderer, Committer and Scanner (Wallet, valuer, auditor, notary, exchanger, recorder, and communicator & transaction finder) services are a part and parcel of every service.

A Startup Recordkeeping service without any associated tokens

with following aspects can be of immense value:

(A) Individuals can come together to form LLPs with simple agreements.

(B) Startup record keeper will provide complete support in

    o   Valuation through an advisory,

    o   Record auditing & authentication through a Notary,

    o   Record keeping of the shareholding track through a Minimal cost, Distributor Ledger Technology based Pvt Blockchain with Zero Faults & Minimal Transaction costs through Filtered & Trusted Authentic nodes selected through a qualification criterion that minimizes chance of

Fraudulent or Rogue node interventions thus Eliminating Mining costs.

o   In fact, Hyper ledger Sawtooth with its Public version and a PoET consensus serves this requirement excellently if only the nodes are compensated in some form with a Fiat currency or any other value based on the transactions conducted and recorded. Hyperledger Sawtooth has many more interesting features that allow the creation and trade of platform assets as well, if need be!

Startups can then quickly come together, access a streamlined process of share& effort valuation access perfect Record keeping & tracking without any headaches of keeping track of their shares till they exit.

All the promoters & share-holders will be provided a live share tracking wallet along with a periodically reviewed value per unit. This could be exposed among various entities providing a platform for exchange. There could be a common internal platform value unit that could represent a business share unit with corresponding value conversion rate. For example Business1 could have 1 lakh shares issued @ 10/each, shares being denoted by a Platform unit. Accounting for share allotments & accounting in LLPs is much simpler unlike in a private ltd company. This then, can eliminate the major need for the ICOs and the tokens which are perhaps one way of recording the value creation process but with the added risk of not being recognised legally, ever!

CHAPTER 19

Blockchain Platforms for Web 2.0 Applications

While Ethereum has been the most popular and proven platform for developing Consumer oriented peer to peer decentralized autonomous organizations, there are a number of options now available to the entrepreneurs to develop their platforms depending on their area of operation and the use case.

Some of the interesting applications developed using Public Blockchain platforms as an alternative to the existing popular centralized applications are given below:

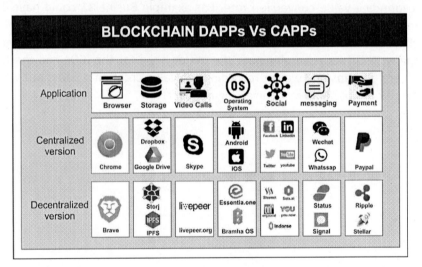

The Blockchain platforms need to be assessed on the following parameters:

- The Blockchain platform must provide for smart contract and application development functionality to match the functional and technical requirements.

- The platform should provide for transfer of value among the participants either through a platform specific digital asset representation or through the digital transfer and proper accounting of fiat currency like US Dollar etc., through a payment gateway.

- The platform should be scalable with proven stability.

- The consensus mechanism should be fool proof with no chance of double spending.

- The platform should offer adequate tools and support systems to enable the development, testing, migration and management of smart contracts.

- The platform should offer low latency, sufficient throughput and transaction processing capability to be able to scale operations without any limitations and also offer excellent customer experience.

- The platform's value representing unit should be freely convertible into fiat currency and help in realising the value in the real world. Hence it should be adequately traded in the corresponding exchanges that permit the same.

Platform Options to build Decentralized Applications

Ethereum

(https://www.ethereum.org/)

Developed by the Swiss based Ethereum Foundation led by Vitalik Buterin and first released in July 2015, Ethereum is an open-source, public, Blockchain-based distributed computing platform and operating system featuring smart contract functionality. It supports a modified version of Nakamoto consensus via transaction based state transition. Ethereum clients available for Linux, Windows, mac OS, POSIX, Raspbian. Ethereum allows programming in Solidity and offers extensive support to developers through excellent documentation and ability to develop the application on localised test environments that can be launched in Main network once ready.

Ethereum offers a decentralized platform that runs smart contracts: applications to conduct peer to peer operations in a programmable manner and verified by the Public Blockchain platform, thus offering trust through system.

- Ethereum offers Token functionality that allows the developers to operationalise their ideas and create new autonomous organizations called DAOs (Decentralized Autonomous Organizations) that can reflect the Peer to Peer versions of many centralized corporations today. DAOs comprise of applications running on the custom built front ends with powerful platform shared globally that can move value represented by tokenised assets without the fear of a middle man and censorship.

- Ethereum offers three versions for development of smart contract:

- Ethereum Homestead, that uses Proof of Work Consensus Algorithm that is most suited for building public and open source applications. Ethereum Casper, that uses Proof of Stake consensus algorithm and an enterprise version that that works with Proof of Authority consensus algorithm.

There are various client software that have been created for this platform. It does not have high data storage capabilities. Storing and retrieval of complex data have limitations.

To overcome this, we need to store the data off chain and manage them through

Blockchain compatible data bases and technologies.

IPFS (Inter planetary File server) and Swarm are two protocols that help us in managing large amounts of data off the chain in a way, referenceable across the Ethereum network in a decentralized manner.

IPFS (https://ipfs.io/)

We can now address large amounts of data with IPFS, and place the immutable, permanent IPFS links into a Blockchain transaction. This timestamps and secures your content, without having to put the data on the chain itself.

The Inter Planetary File System (IPFS) is a peer-to-peer distributed file system that seeks to connect all computing devices with the same system of files. In some ways, IPFS.

Each file and the blocks within it are given a unique fingerprint called a cryptographic hash.

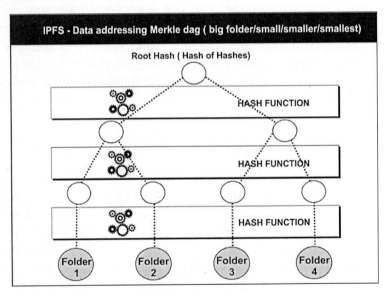

When looking up files, you're asking the network to find nodes storing the content behind a unique hash. By inserting the hash of the data pointing to the file on the nodes, instead of large files through the Smart contract, we can dramatically enhance the capability of the Blockchain platform at a very nominal cost.

How do the files located in IPFS in the contract owner's computer interact with the Ethereum network?

The developer of the smart contract will allow the files of its users to be stored in IPFS enabled system. The metadata of the files are stored across all the nodes in the Blockchain. When a user queries for the metadata, the Blockchain returns the corresponding files required by querying the same by referencing the corresponding IPFS hash link embedded in the smart contract.

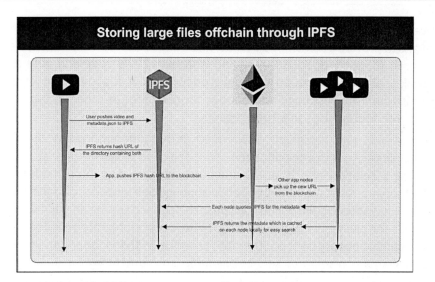

The user will interface with Blockchain through a web interface, interacting with the Blockchain through an API.

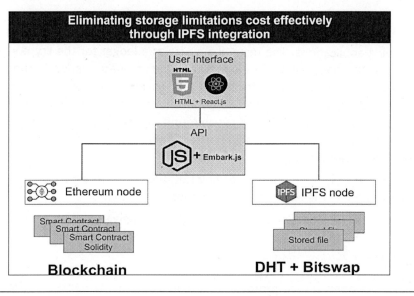

Source: Twitter.com

Ethereum also supports SWARM, a decentralized file system platform similar to IPFS, which comes integrated with the Blockchain platform to manage large files off its main chain. While it is similar to IPFS in many ways, transactions involving storing files in Swarm need to be paid in Ether thus increasing the cost of participation marginally. (https://github.com/ethersphere/swarm)

Swarm is a distributed storage platform and content distribution service. It is a native base layer service of the Ethereum web 3 stacks. The primary objective of Swarm is to provide a sufficiently decentralized and redundant store of Ethereum's public record, in particular to store and distribute DAPP code and data as well as block chain data. From an economic point of view, it allows participants to efficiently pool their storage and bandwidth resources in order to provide the aforementioned services to all participants.

From the end user's perspective, Swarm is not that different from WWW, except that uploads are not to a specific server. The objective is peer-to-peer storage and providing a solution that is DDOS-resistant with zero-downtime, fault-tolerant and censorship-resistant as well as self-sustaining. Self-sustenance is achieved by a built-in incentive system which uses peer to peer accounting and allows trading resources for payment. Swarm is designed to deeply integrate with the devp2p multiprotocol network layer of Ethereum as well as with the Ethereum Blockchain for domain name resolution, service payments and content availability insurance.

Some of the promising platforms and their unique features are listed below:

LISK

Lisk is an Open source Blockchain platform that supports JavaScript language for developing applications. The main chain acts as a ledger for the cryptocurrency Lisk while sidechains allow developers to launch any application in the domain of Consumer applications, Gaming, IOT and Social networking. List uses DPOS (Delegated Proof of Stake) based consensus mechanism in which 101 delegates are selected by the stakeholders in each round to forge one block at a time as per the selected order. Lisk offers a high transaction throughput of 25 transactions per second and a block timing of 10 seconds.

List offers an easy web interface to buy LSK, the platform based cryptocurrency and participate in the applications developed on the platform.

The details of the blocks on Lisk Blockchain can be viewed at https://explorer.lisk. io/ .

STELLAR

Stellar is an open-source protocol for exchanging money backed by Non-profit Stellar foundation.

Stellar allows for transfer of value across the world over internet through servers that run software implementation of the protocol, forming a global value exchange network. Each server stores a record of all "accounts" on the network in a "ledger". The transactions submitted through the clients are approving as per a consensus protocol and the ledgers are synchronized every 3-4 seconds.

Stellar offers Smart contract functionality with applications written in JavaScript, Java and Go. It uses a proprietary consensus mechanism SCP that is a significant improvement over Proof of Work that result in no cost of mining and high throughput of 1000 transactions per second with an average block time of 3.5 seconds.

Stellar ideally suited for financial transactions that involve transfer of money across countries. Non-profit and microfinance companies use Stellar to move funds across the word.

Crowd funding through ICO linked to its currency XLM, is one of the prominent use cases of stellar protocol.

In 2018, Stellar announced their affiliation with Keybase to eliminate the need of extended cryptographic addresses for international transactions

NEM

Malaysia based NEM, uses a cryptocurrency XEM as a native token.

It uses a unique Consensus mechanism called POI (Proof of importance) that gives weightage to the miners in proportion to the number of tokens held in conjunction with the average duration of holding. Their miners who hold over 10000 token have a chance of earning additional rewards.

NEM is built from scratch as a powerful and streamlined platform for application developers of all kinds, not just as a digital currency. Using NEM in your application is as simple as making RESTful JSON API calls allowing you to configure your own "Smart Assets" and make use of NEM's powerful Blockchain platform as you're fast, secure and scalable solution.

Configured for your use, NEM is suitable for an amazing variety of solution classes, such as direct public transactions via streamlined smartphone app, efficient cloud services that connect client or web applications.

NEM offers an enterprise version useful for extensive enterprise level use cases with secure functionality like, Digital identity, Crowd funding, Token launch through ICOs, Educational records management system etc.

NEM offers additional security for users through multi-signature wallet implementation.

NEM smart contracts can be coded in Java. NEM offers customised templates that ease the task of development of smart contracts.

Malaysian government announced that its universities will offer their educational certificates anchored on NEM platform.

NEO

Neo is a China based Public Blockchain platform that offers a number of advantages over Ethereum.

Neo claims to combine the power of Blockchain technology and uniquely created high security identities of users to create smart assets than can be operated upon by smart contracts for a new generation of transactional activities.

Digital assets are programmable assets that exist in the form of electronic data. The use of Blockchain technology to realize asset digitization has features such as decentralization, mediation, trust less, traceability, and high transparency. NEO supports multiple digital assets at the bottom level. Users can register assets on NEO, freely trade & transfer, and resolve the mapping relationship with physical assets through digital identities. The assets registered by users through a compliant digital identity are protected by law.

Digital identity refers to the identity information of individuals, organizations, and things that exist in the form of electronic data. The current mature digital identity system is based on the PKI's X.509 standard. In NEO, we will implement a set of X.509-compliant digital identity standards. This set of digital identity standards, in addition to the X.509-compliant hierarchical certificate issuance model, will also support the Web of Trust peer-to-peer certificate issuance model.

The biggest feature of the NeoContract smart contract system is the seamless integration with the existing developer ecosystem. Developers can use C#, Java, and other mainstream programming languages to develop, debug, and compile smart contracts in familiar IDE environments (Visual Studio, Eclipse, etc.) without learning a new programming language.

NEO's universal lightweight virtual machine NeoVM is highly deterministic, highly concurrent, and highly scalable. The NeoContract smart contract system enables millions of developers worldwide to quickly develop smart contracts. NeoContract will have a separate white paper describing the implementation details.

CARDANO (ADA)

Originally known as the Ethereum of Japan, ADA offers a number of versatile features to its platform adaptors. Founded by an Ethereum developer, Charles Hoskinson, ADA is supposed to possess advanced quantum resistant features against malware attacks. The Blockchain platform offers smart contract functionality as well as a strong Digital identity system of regulatory standards.

Smart contracts on Cardano are programmed in Haskell and it uses Aurobro's Proof of Stake consensus algorithm with a high resistance or DDOS attacks due to higher transaction fees with no remuneration for mining.

Using an approach known as side chains, Cardano SL, a general purpose cryptocurrency enables domain specific cryptocurrencies, such as Ethereum Classic. This way, any innovation developed via domain specific cryptocurrency can have participants who hold value in a general purpose cryptocurrency. Examples of such applications are identity management, gaming and gambling, and verifiable computations.

The unique feature of Cardano is its wallet which allows interoperability between a variety of cryptocurrencies and in future aims to offer interoperability with fiat currencies making it easy for any entrepreneur in the world to launch their DAO even if the cryptocurrency is not allowed in their region by the respective governments.

Block time in Cardano Blockchain is 20 seconds and the through put is around 10-15 transactions per second.

ARDOR/NXT

Ardor is a new generation Java programmable platform which enables a seamlessly scalable Blockchain eco-system to enterprises through the concept of Sidechains linked to the main chain. It offers IGINIS as the fuel token for transactions. Using a POS consensus algorithm, it offers 1000 transactions per second throughput with an average block time of around 1 minute. Ardor comes with its own decentralized exchange offering multi-chain interoperability, versatile support for ICOs with an excellently packaged client to manage asset exchanges with cross chain functionality.

ARK

Originating in Germany, it offers a unique 'Smart Bridge Technology' that offers push button cloneable Blockchain platform that enables to link various ecosystems and Blockchain platforms to create a web of interconnected Blockchain and ecommerce entities seamlessly interacting with each other. Ark uses 'Delegated Proof of Stake (DPoS) consensus mechanism which enables a highly secure and scalable operation at the same time, for the benefit of mass consumers and developers.

Smart contracts in Ark are developed in JavaScript. Average Block time is around 8 seconds with a transaction throughput of 10 transactions per second.

Ark proposes to offer several unique features to connect different Blockchains.

- A strong 27-member core team to oversee the development and maintenance of Blockchain while keep up with the sanctity of autonomy of the Blockchain operations

- Physical card and transfer equipment facilitating off chain and on chain transactions across merchants with the help of point of sale and near field communication (NFC) enabled terminals.

- Optional privacy transactions to extend the applicability of Blockchain ecosystem to all types of requirements that need confidentiality

- Bridge between Blockchain not limiting to major platforms like Bitcoin, Ethereum, Lisk etc.

- Integration with Inter Planetary File System (IPFS) to address Blockchain bloat due to transaction sizes and volumes accumulating over a period of time

- High level of data storage capability through Inter Planetary Data Base (IPDB) integration.

COSMOS (Internet of Blockchains)

Supported by Interchain foundation (ICF), Cosmos offers to connect multiple Blockchain to form the Internet of Blockchains.

Cosmos offers Cosmos SDK to develop custom Blockchains with plug and play models based on a Byzantine Fault Tolerant consensus model which is a variation of Proof of Stake model, Tendermint core.

Cosmos enables creation of a network of Blockchains that are interoperable amongst themselves and any other Blockchain applications developed on other public platforms as well.

The first Blockchain in Cosmos network is Cosmos Hub with a native token, Atom. Cosmos follows a hub and spoke model, Cosmos offers a decentralised exchange linking many Blockchains, unlike the conventional exchanges that are vulnerable to malware attacks due to Single points of failure.

Cosmos core follows Tendermint consensus mechanism that is a Byzantine fault tolerant version of Proof of Stake mechanism, offering high speed and high throughput of over 10000 transactions per second for 250 byte transactions.

On October 22nd 2018, world's leading technology consulting firm, Accenture, demonstrated a solution that enabled two or more Blockchain enabled ecosystems to integrate, solving a critical challenge for broad adoption of Blockchain technology by achieving process synchronization between business process synchronization between Digital Asset, R3 Corda, Hyperledger Fabric and Quorum distributed ledger platforms.

CHAPTER 20

The Birth of Enterprise Blockchain

The disruption unleashed by bitcoin in the currency space led to the launch of a number of Altcoins arising out of the hard fork (substantial upgradation of platform functionality), while Ethereum functionality threatened to disturb every business that catered to customers through a centralized model.

The evolution of the Blockchain paradigm reached the next stage with the launch of a number of platforms focusing on enterprise applications. These applications do not involve any internal currencies but could facilitate launch of internal assets that could be tracked through a pre-determined governance mechanism.

Some of them are described below:

Hyperledger Project

Hyperledger Project is promoted by a consortium of organizations led by IBM and Linux foundation.

This project comprises of many sub projects contributed by many leading global organizations.

Hyperledger is an open source cross industry collaboration attempt that plans to promote the adoption of Blockchain across different industries.

Blockchain is well described by IBM as 'Peer to Peer' Distributed ledger for a new generation of transactional applications that vastly improve dependability, security, accountability and transparency while streamlining business processes.

In Enterprises the stress is more on accountability, identity, scalability and economy of operations as corporates are more bothered about their return on investments. Hence the consensus mechanisms like that of the cryptocurrencies are not relevant.

FAQs to be answered while implementing Enterprise Blockchain applications

Differences between Permissioned Blockchain along with Integration, Interoperability & Implementation challenges...

Police department of Q state, a state is India has decided to implement a Blockchain based solution (QPBC Q Police Blockchain certificate) for automating the process of issue of some of its citizen certificates. What are the issues it needs to consider? Some of them are given below:

Is QPBC a Permissioned Blockchain or Permissionless Blockchain?

It will be a Permissioned Blockchain with a Founder/Admin node with the Technology/Networking head of Q State Police Department. Police and law enforcement authorities need to have clear control and visibility on who is complaining and who is tracking. There will be a lot of confidential elements involved in case records. For example, they would not like to reveal the status of investigations in most cases till the case is solved etc. All these confidentialities and private matters cannot be guarded secretly on a Public Permissionless Blockchain; hence access control have to be selectively & strictly enforced, possible only through Permissioned Private Blockchain. If there any items that can be exposed to general public, those things can be opened up for public view.

What are the workflow difference between these above two options?

Permisisonless Blockchains are used when there is open access for read/write/ access and hence the data in them is most trustworthy and Permissioned Blockchains are extensions of Private environments with more decentralization and simplified workflows for data sharing across parties. In case of Permissionless Blockchain based DAPPs, it is easier to create smart contracts, but they have other issues like scalability, public data, lack of control (which makes them suitable for highly scalable consumer applications with no parties trusting each other. The best combination is to have a Hybrid, Permissioned (for customisation, control, Privacy) + Public (to store the hashes for transaction immutability & hence highest transparency). Most of the applications around the world today are 'Hybrid'.

Permissioned blockchains offer 'Channel' or 'Node to Node Flows' feature which allows that the workflows between parties in the same network to be customised to answer Privacy & control issues. In Permissionless, there is a single DAPP with replication across the Distributed' with a standard consensus mechanism.

How can we move the Blockchain servers from on on-premise servers to cloud or vice versa?

Blockchain nodes in the same network will be having some nodes in the premises and some nodes across various Cloud platforms. They operate and communicate through SDKs/ APIs etc. The same chaincode written for the on-premise node can be shifted to the Cloud in minutes without any change. Cloud based nodes offer easy installation, management and security as they abstract a lot of issues that we need to take care in the on-premise applications. On-premise applications will take a lot more effort, care as the administrator needs to do a lot of activities like installation, security, API management, network availability, perpetual maintenance with high service levels etc., unlike in the Cloud based applications, which are very convenient & offer a lot of integrated solutions to manage the network, but can be operationally costly to maintain.

How can we move the Blockchain program code from one platform to another? Will there be any issues and challenges?

Moving code from one platform to the other depends on a number of platform specific issues like the Programming languages issued, Consensus mechanisms adopted etc. It is better to consider all the things in the beginning and take a call on Platform.

What is the data structure and scheme for storing the data on an Enterprise Blockchain?

Blockchains best understand JSON objects and hashes for storing data and information & also for retrieving & comparing. The Private data can be stored in the databases. Let us consider the case of Hyperledger Fabric. World state (The updated state of assets after execution of the transactions at any point of time) will be stored in the peer nodes in a Couch DB & Ledger will be stored across all nodes. The ledger consists of chained list of hashes of blocks. This is maintained by all the peers and some orderers as well. Hyperledger uses Level DB / Couch DB for storing these as per the Fabric version used. The private data can be stored on Premise with the respective department as per confidentiality issues and preferably in Mongo DB. All these will be stored in the respective Node's hardware and networking environment. MySQL also can be used with the latest upgrades of the enterprise platforms, with proper APIs/ middle layers to convert the data into the format required by the respective Blockchain platforms. In the open sourced edition, Couch DB is used mostly as it is suitable for Key Value Store with querying flexibility. The cloud platforms use their own different type of compatible databases for both the Data structures.

Can Blockchain data be used by different platforms?

Blockchain nodes are programmed to expose their nodes to outside clients through APIs. There is absolutely no issue for the data put on Blockchain to be queried and needed data taken out through these APIs for analytical purposes, as long as the user has the Access Control rights. Blockchain APIs and related SDKs help in configuring the overall architecture of a Blockchain based solution and help in integrating with internal systems as well as interoperability with other Blockchain platforms.

What are the factors affecting performance and throughput?

In Private Blockchains, the transactions are almost instantaneous. The issue comes when there is a delay in approval by one the authorising/ decision making nodes in sending its approval to the transaction by appending its Digital signature. Hence in the program for every transaction there will be a upper limit specified for the approval process to be completed, failing which the transaction will be cancelled and process restarted.

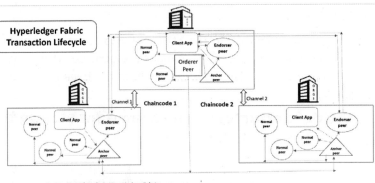

Transaction Lifecycle in Hyperledger Fabric:
1.   Client generates a transaction and sends it to the endorser peers.
2.   Endorser peers run the chain code and send the affirmations to the respective clients through the connecting peer
3.   The client sends transactions along with the endorsements to the Orderer peer
4.   Orderer peer includes the transactions in a block & sends the same to the anchor peers of the respective organisation
5.   Anchor peers distributes the block to the concerned approved normal peers authorised as per chain code
6.   All the peers validate the transactions and commit the block to their respective ledgers and updates their Blockchain

Case study: Golang Chaincode in Hyperledger

What is chaincode?

Chaincode is the programmatic implementation of business logic in Blockchain in the form of smart contract to effect transactions and update asset records of the participants. Following languages are used to write chain code in enterprise Blockchains (ex: Hyperledger Fabric).

GO, Solidity, Node.js, Java Script, Java, Kotlin. Rholang, C++ are generally the languages used to create Chain code in different platforms.

Chaincode sample

Let us examine a sample code, taken from Hyperledger Fabric documentation in Go language and understand, how it creates and effects the change in their values in the shared/ distributed ledger of the respective platforms.

```
package main
import (
    "fmt"
    "github.com/hyperledger/fabric/core/chaincode/shim"
    "github.com/hyperledger/fabric/protos/peer"
)
// SimpleAsset implements a simple chaincode to manage an
asset
type SimpleAsset struct {
}
```

```go
// Init is called during chaincode instantiation to initialize any
// data. Note that chaincode upgrade also calls this function to reset
// or to migrate data.
func (t *SimpleAsset) Init(stub shim.ChaincodeStubInterface) peer.Response {
    // Get the args from the transaction proposal
    args := stub.GetStringArgs()
    if len(args) != 2 {
        return shim.Error("Incorrect arguments. Expecting a
        key and a value")
    }
    // Set up any variables or assets here by calling stub.
    PutState()
    // We store the key and the value on the ledger
    err := stub.PutState(args[0], []byte(args[1]))
    if err != nil {
        return shim.Error(fmt.Sprintf("Failed to create
        asset: %s", args[0]))
    }
    return shim.Success(nil)
}
// Invoke is called per transaction on the chaincode. Each transaction is
// either a 'get' or a 'set' on the asset created by Init function. The Set
// method may create a new asset by specifying a new key-value pair.
func (t *SimpleAsset) Invoke(stub shim.ChaincodeStubInterface) peer.Response {
    // Extract the function and args from the transaction
    proposal
    fn, args := stub.GetFunctionAndParameters()
    var result string
    var err error
    if fn == "set" {
        result, err = set(stub, args)
    } else { // assume 'get' even if fn is nil
        result, err = get(stub, args)
    }
    if err != nil {
        return shim.Error(err.Error())
    }

    // Return the result as success payload
    return shim.Success([]byte(result))
}
```

```
// Set stores the asset (both key and value) on the ledger.
If the key exists,
// it will override the value with the new one
func set (stub shim.ChaincodeStubInterface, args []string)
(string, error) {
    if len(args) != 2 {
        return "", fmt.Errorf("Incorrect arguments.
        Expecting a key and a value")
    }
    err := stub.PutState(args[0], []byte(args[1]))
    if err != nil {
        return "", fmt.Errorf("Failed to set asset: %s",
        args[0])
    }
    return args[1], nil
}
// Get returns the value of the specified asset key
func get(stub shim.ChaincodeStubInterface, args []string)
(string, error) {
    if len(args) != 1 {
        return "", fmt.Errorf("Incorrect arguments.
        Expecting a key")
    }
    value, err := stub.GetState(args[0])
    if err != nil {
        return "", fmt.Errorf("Failed to get asset: %s with
        error: %s", args[0], err)
    }
    if value == nil {
        return "", fmt.Errorf("Asset not found: %s", args[0])
    }
    return string(value), nil
}
// main function starts up the chaincode in the container
during instantiate
func main() {
    if err := shim.Start(new(SimpleAsset)); err != nil {
        fmt.Printf("Error starting SimpleAsset chaincode:
        %s", err)
    }
}
```

This is the whole code. Let's see how it works.

There are 4 functions

1. Init function to instantiate and create asset

2. Invoke function to enable transaction when the proposal is submitted

3.   Get function to get asset data from ledger

4.   Set function to set asset data to the ledger

Algorithm Chain code sample

Steps:

1.   Create structure data from data type Simple Asset

2.   Create init function to instantiate and set initiate asset values

    a.   Check the arguments is correct if not return error message

    b.   Set up asset if failed return failed message

3.   Create invoke function to enable each transaction

    a.   Check what kind of operation needed get ot set

    b.   If set operation is needed, then call set function

    c.   If nil value or get received, then call get function

    d.   If any error has returned display error

    e.   If operation was successful display success message

4.   Create set function to set asset values

    a.   Check parameters and if any issues return error message

    b.   Set asset values if doesn't happen return error message

    c.   Otherwise return nil and args

5.   Create set function to get asset values

    a.   Check parameters and if any issues return error message

    b.   Get values from asset

    c.   If fetching asset failed return error message

    d.   If asset not found return message accordingly

    e.   Otherwise return values

6.   Create main function

    a.   Create a new struct and if not created print error message

7.   stop

So, let's see how it is coded?

Housekeeping

Package main declares that this is an executable file & not a shared library. So we import basic libraries to program

```
package main
import (
     "fmt"
```

```
"github.com/hyperledger/fabric/core/chaincode/shim"
"github.com/hyperledger/fabric/protos/peer"
)
```

Step 1: Create structure data from data type Simple Asset

```go
type SimpleAsset struct {
}
```

Step 2: Create init function to instantiate and set initiate asset values

```go
func (t *SimpleAsset) Init (stub shim.ChaincodeStubInterface)
peer.Response {
    // Get the args from the transaction proposal
    args:= stub.GetStringArgs()
    if len(args) != 2 {
        return shim.Error("Incorrect arguments. Expecting a
        key and a value")
    }
    // Set up any variables or assets here by calling stub.
    PutState()
    // We store the key and the value on the ledger
    err := stub.PutState(args[0], []byte(args[1]))
    if err != nil {
        return shim.Error(fmt.Sprintf("Failed to create
        asset: %s", args[0]))
    }
    return shim.Success(nil)
}
```

Step 3: Create invoke function to enable each transaction

```go
func (t *SimpleAsset) Invoke(stub shim.ChaincodeStubInterface)
peer.Response {
    // Extract the function and args from the transaction
    proposal
    fn, args := stub.GetFunctionAndParameters()
    var result string
    var err error
    if fn == "set" {
        result, err = set(stub, args)
    } else { // assume 'get' even if fn is nil
        result, err = get(stub, args)
    }
    if err != nil {
        return shim.Error(err.Error())
    }
    // Return the result as success payload
    return shim.Success([]byte(result))
}
```

Step 4: Create set function to set asset values

```
func set (stub shim.ChaincodeStubInterface, args []string)
(string, error) {
    if len(args) != 2 {
        return "", fmt.Errorf("Incorrect arguments.
        Expecting a key and a value")
    }
    err := stub.PutState(args[0], []byte(args[1]))
    if err != nil {
        return "", fmt.Errorf("Failed to set asset:
        %s", args[0])
    }
    return args[1], nil
}
```

Step 5: Create set function to get asset values

```
func get (stub shim.ChaincodeStubInterface, args []string)
(string, error) {
    if len(args) != 1 {
        return "", fmt.Errorf("Incorrect arguments.
        Expecting a key")
    }
    value, err := stub.GetState(args[0])
    if err != nil {
        return "", fmt.Errorf("Failed to get asset: %s with
        error: %s", args[0], err)
    }
    if value == nil {
        return "", fmt.Errorf("Asset not found: %s", args[0])
    }
    return string(value), nil
}
```

Step 6: Create main function

```
func main () {
    if err := shim.Start(new(SimpleAsset)); err != nil {
        fmt.Printf("Error starting SimpleAsset chaincode:
        %s", err)
    }
}
```

Since you have gone through the explanation, you can now understand what is happening.

> **Source:** Hyperledger fabric documentation.

Comparison of Centralised & Blockchain approaches			
Feature	Centralised Database	Public Blockchain	Enterprise Blockchain
Ledger	Centralised in one location with replicaition	Distributed across all nodes. However nodes have the option to carry the entire ledger or part ledgers & select their clients accordingly.	Shared between transacitng parties on a need to know basis
Confidentiality	Highest level of confidentiality possible	Information on transactions, open to all	Access control on a need to know basis
Identities	As per organisational rules can be linked to normal identities & hence if data is leaked, there is a threat of loss of highly valuable customer information & confidence	Algorithmically linked Public & Private keys of pseudonymous or anonymous identities, protecting the link between transactions and actual identities	Generally linked to roles and operated through secure identities, with Publlic & Private keys normally based on X.509 certificates
Immutability of ledger data	Can be changed by any authorised party anytime	Considered immutable unless a massive 51% attack takes over the Blockchain and rewrites dat. Hence, considered improbable	Changes of ledger contents can be modified by appending new contracts & trail of same is recorded ensuring transparency. Data can however be erased permanently through appropriate programming of smart contracts.
Smart Contracts	Not applicable. Data is uploaded and appended s per interactions with normal applications within the organisation	Smart contracts or new generation applications that reflect real life agreements, executed by external accounts or invoked when certain conditions are met, help in autonomous functioning of Decentralised applications (DAPPs) that enable DAOs (Decentralised autonomous organsiations)	Processes across organisations or real life entities are automated & agreements enforced through 'Smart Contract' or 'Chain code' , a new generation application that enable elimination, of intermediaries, corruption, fraud, wastage of resources like time, money & paper. Shared ledgers are updated as a consequence.
Provenance	Not a feature, as there is no chain of data structures stored with time stamps	Provenance of the data recorded is available as every tranaction and appended blocks are timestamped before commiting. Every item can be traced back to its origin	Provenance of the data recorded is available as every transaction and appended blocks are timestamped before commiting. Every item can be traced back to its origin
Speed of Transaction processing	Instantaneous with no limits. Since an organisation trusts itself maximum and the databases are operated by responsible officials, instantaneous updations happen.	Slow as all participants are considered potential attackers with lowest level of trust and hence highest effort is needed to confirm traansactions.	High Transactions speeds are possible as the participants are trusted and traceable & hance not prone to mischief.
Vulnerability to Malware & Cyberattacks	Highly risky as it provides highest incentive to attack Centralised databases for ransomware or disruption. Best of the global leaders having highest level of cybersecurity have been attacked.	Highly resilient. However, smart contracts and associated infrastructure like wallets, exchanges etc., are prone to malware attacks if they are centralised entities. 515 attacks are possible on smaller & newer Blockchains.	Highest level of security as the data and applications are protected through multiple layers of security mechansims as the identities and tranactions are undertaken after ta thorough validation. Secured cloud service providers provide an added layer of safety to Blockchain infrastructure.

CHAPTER 21

Hyperledger Projects - Fabric, Sawtooth - Versatile and Empowering

The following are some of the major platforms used to develop Blockchain applications for enterprises:

1. Hyperledger Fabric

Hyperledger Fabric (https://www.hyperledger.org/projects/fabric) is a modular enterprise Blockchain framework developed by IBM for enabling organizations across industries to adapt quickly to the paradigm of Blockchain development. 159 engineers from 28 organizations contributed to project to advance open Blockchain products and services

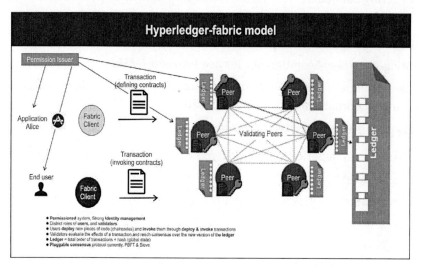

Hyperledger Fabric allows components, such as consensus and membership services, to be plug-and-play. Hyperledger Fabric leverages container technology to host smart contracts called "chaincode" that comprise the application logic of the system. Hyperledger Fabric was initially contributed by Digital Asset and IBM, as a result of the first hackathon.

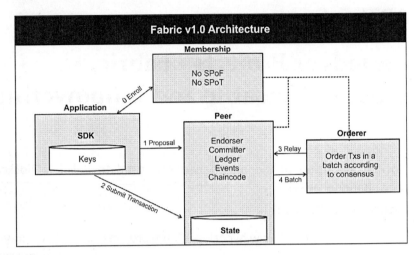

Key Features

- Channels for sharing confidential information
- Ordering Service delivers transactions consistently to peers in the network
- Endorsement policies for transactions
- CouchDB world state supports wide range of queries
- Bring-your-own Membership Service Provider (MSP)

Extensive documentation of Hyperledger along with use cases across supply chain and financing domains are available in GitHub.

2. Hyperledger Sawtooth Lake

https://sawtooth.hyperledger.org/docs/core/releases/0.7/introduction.html

- It is an open source platform.
- Contributed by Linux foundation & supported extensively by Intel.

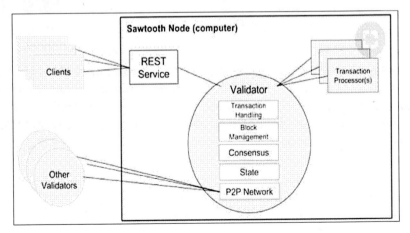

- Sawtooth supports a revolutionary consensus algorithm, Proof of Elapsed Time (PoET) that allows for versatility and scalability suited for a variety of solutions.
- Useful for both Private and Public Blockchain applications.
- Many languages for transaction logic like Java, Java script, GO, Python etc.

Features

1. "Sawtooth Lake" is a highly modular platform for building, deploying and running distributed ledgers.

2. Distributed ledgers provide a digital record (such as asset ownership) that is maintained without a central authority or implementation. Instead of a single, centralized database, participants in the ledger contribute resources to shared computation that ensures universal agreement on the state of the ledger.

3. The technology has been proposed for many different applications ranging from international remittance, insurance claim processing, supply chain management and the Internet of Things (IoT).

4. Distributed ledgers generally consist of three basic components:

   o A data model that captures the current state of the ledger

   o A language of transactions that change the ledger state

   o A protocol used to build consensus among participants around which transactions will be accepted by the ledger.

   In Sawtooth Lake the data model and transaction language are implemented in a "transaction family"

   o Endpoint Registry - A transaction family for registering ledger services.

   o Integer Key - A transaction family used for testing deployed ledgers.

   o Marketplace - A transaction family for buying, selling and trading digital assets.

This set of transaction families provides an "out of the box" ledger that implements a fully functional marketplace for digital assets.

With a scalable Public Blockchain framework without any need for a token and a versatile Smart contract feature support, Sawtooth offers the best of both worlds and the silver bullet the Blockchain technology is looking for.

Every Blockchain platform has its own design motivation, the below are Sawtooth's design motivations:

- **Designed to use at scale**
- **Keep the ledgers, distributed**
- **Keep smart contracts safe, secure to use**

- Parallel transaction execution to increase transaction through put.
- Multi language support for smart contract development
- Well suited for supply chain, identity management, financial and asset management scenarios & can be adapted for other industries as well.

Primary functionalities of Sawtooth are,

1. On-chain governance: Use smart contract programs to handle the configuration settings

2. **Advanced transaction execution engine:** Other Blockchain platforms execute the transactions in sequential order, resulting in slow transaction throughput. Sawtooth can execute the transactions in parallel to increase the transaction throughput. This is a big advantage because in enterprise applications, we can't wait for mining process to complete to take action and timeliness of process is critical.

3. **Support for Ethereum:** Ethereum platform has a strong developer community and tooling. Since most of the developers started learning the Blockchain platform with Ethereum, it would be easy to start developing Sawtooth applications if you have experience with Ethereum application development.

4. **Dynamic consensus:** The Blockchain ecosystem has various ways to bring about the agreement on changes in the data in the system. The agreement process is called Consensus Protocol like PoS, PoW, PoA , PBFT, BFT etc. Hyperledger framework allows us to change to any Consensus on the fly by allowing pluggable Consensus framework.

In future Sawtooth team plans to:

- Streamline the performance,
- Enhance more privacy,
- Include 'Zero Knowledge Proof' for the transaction validation

Interoperability between Blockchain platforms

Since we are seeing large number of new Blockchain platforms and each platform provides unique features. There is question always lying in front of the team

is about how to integrate one Blockchain platform application with another application. For example, Ethereum DAPP integration with Hyperledger's application as, each company will have their own unique needs that lead them to their choice of the platform.

Sawtooth promises for some form of interoperability between Blockchain platforms.

"The recent experiment by the sawtooth team was, integrating Hyperledger Burrow with sawtooth, was a successful one."

What makes Sawtooth special ?

- **PoET:** Proof of Elapsed Time Consensus Protocol
- **Transaction families:** Running smart contracts in different languages

Understanding Sawtooth Blockchain network:

- Since it is a permissioned network, every participant must identify themselves with others in the network.
- Network decides whether to let them in.

Understanding Proof of Elapsed Time:

- Each participant in the Blockchain network, waits for a random amount of time to become the next block creator.
- First person to finish the waiting gets to become the leader with an opportunity to create the new block.

In order for this to work, two major requirements need to be verified:

- Did the lottery winner actually choose random time in the right way?
- Did the lottery winner actually wait for the time chosen by them?

  "PoET works with special hardware integration, to provide special security to the code executing"- It is named as Trusted execution.

PoET comes from Intel with special CPU instruction set called Intel Software Guard Extensions (SGX), the code which is responsible for selecting the random number to be executed apart from the transaction execution and independently.

How does PoET work?

- A new participant starts the node, downloads the trusted code's from the Blockchain network
- On initialization, trusted code creates a public, private key pair
- Participant sends a SGX attestation which includes the trusted code's public key to the rest of the network as a part of join request.
- Once approved it is added to the network.

Participating in block creation

- Participant gets a signed timer object from the trusted code.
- Participant waits for the time specified in the timer object
- Participant obtains the certificate/approval (signed by the private key of trust code) that the participant wait time has completed.
- Participant sends the certificate and new block from the pending transactions to the other peers/participants.

- Others will validate the certificate and execute the application with new block of transactions.
- Then new round starts again.

Sawtooth contains other protections on top of SGX. How often a participant wins the lottery, is monitored by the system to remove/blacklist the bad actors in the system.

CHAPTER 22

Enterprise Blockchain Platforms - A Brief Look at Options

R3-Corda

https://www.corda.net/

- It is open source. Network is owned by R3.
- It was initially designed for Finance industry, but it can be applied to other industries like Insurance, Retail etc.
- It is using the term DLT (Distributed Ledger technologies) instead of Blockchain.
- It allows organizations to combine the best of Blockchain technology with the convenience of leveraging their existing databases, thus easing a lot of pains associated with the migration to the new technology paradigm,

Features

1. It is similar to traditional application development in many ways and uses Java and Kotlin languages.
2. It has the permissioned network ability.
3. Any digital asset can be created and transferred.
4. It used the term called state, which has the current data. It has all the history of transaction with query feature.
5. It is having the "Notary" to validate the transaction for uniqueness.

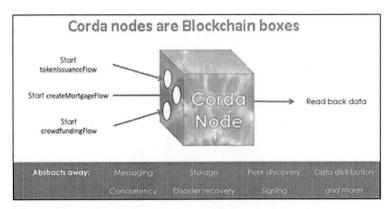

6. It provides the capability to integrate the RDBMS database to store and retrieve data.

7. It has RPC protocols to interact with, then it has concept called flow which is responsible for create and commit transactions.

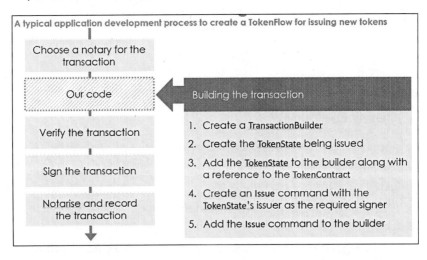

A typical application development process to create a TokenFlow for issuing new tokens

Choose a notary for the transaction

Our code ← Building the transaction

Verify the transaction

Sign the transaction

Notarise and record the transaction

1. Create a TransactionBuilder
2. Create the TokenState being issued
3. Add the TokenState to the builder along with a reference to the TokenContract
4. Create an Issue command with the TokenState's issuer as the required signer
5. Add the Issue command to the builder

An end to end flow can be represented as in the following figure.

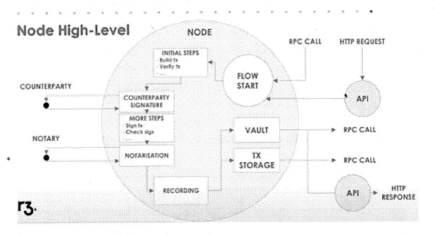

8. Smart contracts are written using Kotlin or Java. Smart contracts in Corda are known as Cordapps

    A typical Cordapp is represented in the following diagram.

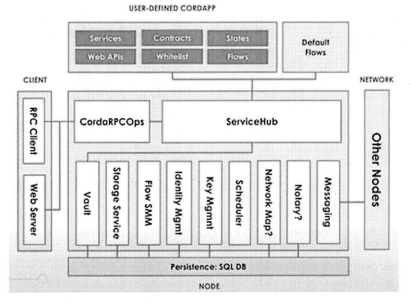

9. It can be scaled easily and new nodes can be provided.

10. It is having the template for projects explaining the functionality and good documentation.

11. Partners: R3 leads a consortium of more than 200 firms in research and development of distributed ledger usage in the financial system and other areas of commerce

It is pertinent to note that, R3 Corda a leading private permissioned Blockchain based application for distributed ledger applications is expanding its utility across a variety of use cases beyond the financial applications, which it was originally deemed to cater to. R3 is emerging as a versatile platform with a high level of compliance to GDPR norms of the European Union

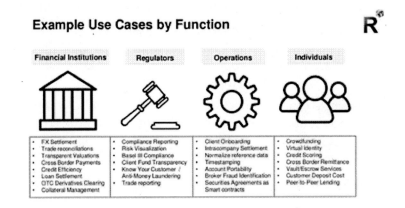

In December 2018, R3, launched its new Corda Settler, an application purpose-built to allow for payment obligations raised on the Corda blockchain platform to be made through any of the world's payment systems, both traditional and blockchain-based in close alignment with the cryptocurrency XRP.

The Corda Settler is an open source CorDapp that allows payment obligations arising on the Corda Network to be settled via any parallel rail supporting cryptocurrencies or other crypto assets, and any traditional rail capable of providing cryptographic proof of settlement. Uniquely, the Corda Settler will verify that the beneficiary's account was credited with the expected payment, automatically updating the Corda ledger.

In future, the Settler proposes to support domestic deferred net settlement and real-time gross settlement payments.

Source: https://www.r3.com

Source: R3 - for more information or R3 Corda key concepts refer Annexure 6

Quorum: (https://www.jpmorgan.com/global/Quorum.)

- Quorum - is an enterprise-focused version of Ethereum
- It provides permissioned network, transaction abilities specially designed for financial use cases.
- Developed by JP Morgan.
    1. It contains all the same features as Ethereum.
    2. It adds privacy to transaction using Concept called constellation network.
    3. It is secured and any dapps can be developed using Solidity.
    4. It has its own consensus mechanism called Quorum consensus to increase through put of the transaction, which is poor in Ethereum.

Quorum Chain is a time-based, majority-voting algorithm that utilizes smart contract to govern consensus and manage who can partake in consensus. Transactions propagate votes through the network and Ethereum's signature validates signatures received from Maker and Voter nodes.

Quorum offers single chain architecture with the entire node carrying the same ledger but with access only the information relevant to them. This is done through a unique architecture that encrypts the information from being visible to the non-relevant nodes.

Chain: (https://chain.com)

- It is an open source platform.

- Mainly for financial institutions.
- Any financial assets can be transferred, peer to peer.
- It is scalable, secure, and robust.

Protocol Used: Chain Protocol, for asset registration and transferring seamlessly and scalable network of Blockchain

Features

1. Native digital assets - Currencies, Securities
2. Permissioned network - Role based permissioning inside network
3. An immutable ledger
4. Multi signature accounts - Business, Institutions
5. Full Stack Security - HSM Integration, Cryptographic, Auditable
6. Smart contracts - Programmed business rules
7. Transaction privacy - Only involved parties get to share the data.
8. Reference data - Asset definitions, compliance data and annotations. It is having chain core to build network.

Multichain: (https://www.multichain.com/)

- It is open source platform for developing Private Blockchains for creating and tracking assets on a Blockchain platform. Its main aim is to help the organizations to launch their own Blockchain based asset tracking solutions in a fast manner.

Features

1. Rapid development - 2 steps to launch network, 3 to connect with existing one.
2. Unlimited assets - Create assets in platform level, atomic, multi-party, multi asset transactions possible
3. Create multiple key value to share data securely
4. Permissioned - Who can connect, send and receive transactions.
5. Developer friendly.

It is having the multichain node to start the network.

Currently Multichain is one of the most popular Blockchain platforms in the world for developing Private Blockchains. Its clientele include Visa, NASDAQ, Citibank, First Capital, Fiserv, MUFG, State Street, Fidelity etc.

Open Chain: (https://www.openchain.org/)

Open chain is an open source distributed ledger technology. It is suited for organizations wishing to issue and manage digital assets in a robust, secure and scalable way.

Features

1. Instant confirmation of transactions.

2. No mining fees.

3. Extremely high scalability.

4. Secured through digital signatures.

5. **Immutability:** Commit an anchor in the Bitcoin Blockchain to benefit from the irreversibility of its Proof of Work.

6. Assign aliases to users instead of using base-58 addresses.

7. Multiple levels of control.

    Fully open ledger that can be joined anonymously. Closed-loop ledger where participants must be approved by the administrator.

    o   A mix of the above where approved users enjoy more rights than anonymous user.

8. Hierarchical account system allowing to set permissions at any level.

9. Transparency and auditability of transactions.

10. Handle loss or theft of private keys without any loss to the end users.

11. Ability to have multiple Open chain instances replicating from each other.

Openchain allows Private organizations to

*   leverage its existing Database and migrate onto Blockchain

*   Set up its own Blockchain on one node, become an administrator and add participants in due course.

*   Allows Publisher/ subscriber model with one validating cluster and many participating cluster.

*   Openchain works well with No SQL database, Cassandra, which works well across a wide variety of situations in a given organization.

Ethereum for Enterprise

Ethereum has collaborated with Microsoft to enter the Private Blockchain space through Blockchain as a Service, offered by Microsoft (https://azure.microsoft. com/en-in/solutions/Blockchain/).

*   Microsoft and ConsenSys are partnering to offer Ethereum Blockchain as a Service (EBaaS) on Microsoft Azure so Enterprise clients and developers can have a single click cloud based Blockchain developer environment. The initial offering contains two tools that allow for rapid development of Smart Contract based applications: Ether. Camp - An integrated developer environment, and BlockApps - a private, semi-private Ethereum Blockchain

environment, can deploy into the public Ethereum environment.

- Start-ups in energy, supply chain, wealth management and document archiving are finding it useful to start working on Openchain quickly and develop POCs.

There are a number of other developer friendly platforms for interconnecting the Blockchains, for specialized applications like IOT and also for handling large scale data for enterprise Blockchain applications based on Blockchainified NoSQL databases like Cassandra, RethinkDB etc. Some of them are given below.

1. BigChainDB: (https://www.bigchaindb.com/about/)

With the datasets across the Blockchain universe growing rapidly due to the replication of the data stored across all the nodes, it becomes increasingly difficult for organizations to carry out their transactions across the various use cases and the numerous Decentralised organization in a scalable and efficient manner. To ensure integrity of the data, while a lot of transactions are done, off chain, BigchainDB has come out with a solution which allows huge throughput for transactions of the scale of Big Data magnitude. The promoters who grappled this problem while running Ascribe.io, a Blockchain enabled Proof of ownership & market place service for artists and creators globally, felt the need for such a platform and found the solution in the form of BigChainDB built on a NoSQL database platform, namely, Rethink DB.

BigchainDB is a Blockchain database offering decentralization, immutability and native assets for offering services to its users in a cost effective and sustainable manner, It liberates the developers and organizations cutting across the fields of IoT, Artificial intelligence, supply chain and intellectual property to build and deploy large scale use cases, while leveraging the benefits associated with Blockchain technology.

Some of the features offered by BigchainDB are:

Decentralization

No single point of control. No single point of failure. Decentralized control via a federation of voting nodes makes for a P2P network.

Query

Write andrun any MongoDB query to search the contents of all stored transactions, assets, metadata and blocks. Powered by MongoDB itself.

Immutability

More than just tamper-resistant. Once stored, data can't be changed or deleted.

Native Support of Multi assets

With no native currency on BigchainDB, any asset, token or currency can be issued.

Byzantine Fault Tolerant (BFT)

Up to one third of the nodes in the network can be experiencing arbitrary faults and the rest of the network will still come to consensus on the next block.

Low Latency

A global network takes about a second to come to consensus on a new block. In other words, transaction finality happens fast.

Source: R3-4 more on R3 Corda platform, refer annexure 6.

2. Fluree: (https://flur.ee/)

Fluree is another remarkable companion for the organizations wanting to migrate to the Blockchain ecosystem. Fluree allows organization working on different types of structured, unstructured data cutting across a number of centralized and decentralised applications to seamlessly migrate the data to its Blockchain enabled data base and have a singly query option for the same.

FlureeDB supports a variety of Blockchain consensus according to desired transaction characteristics. Low-consensus needs (internal transactions) transact very rapidly, while high-consensus needs leverage the benefits of decentralized, public record and verification. FlureeDB's query allows joins across multiple DBs, so multiple consensus DBs can be queried as a single DB system.

Fluree's internal, permissioned database allows for complete privacy with single-digit millisecond queries and immutable blocks of transaction data. This level of consensus allows for complete control. Soon, organizations can elect to pre-define a network to verify transactions in a shared database ledger. This allows trust and transparency within a cluster of entities without risking public exposure.

In future, FlureeDB plans to upgrade their platform to allow applications perform transparent but safe transactions by taking complete advantage of the public Blockchain. The public database ledger allows for decentralized, immutable, and transparent records.

3. Factom

https://www.factom.com/ Factom is an interesting project that offers a safe digital storage and auditing platform for all manuscripts and all other documents in an organization.

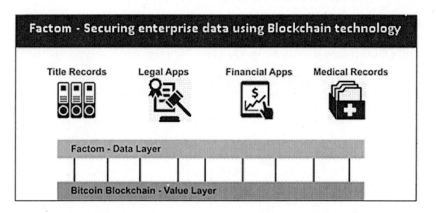

All the data that needs to be secured and tracked in an organization, is uploaded on the Factom data layer in a secure and easily retrievable manner through appropriate sharing and indexing of files.

Factom periodically anchors the entire data on its platform and stores the hash of the same on to both Bitcoin and Ethereum Blockchain to be resilient against single point of failure.

The data store then becomes a powerful service to retrieve, audit and maintain large sets & streams of data thus securing the same with the help of Blockchain Technology. Factom is finding powerful use cases in the field of IOT, Finance, Academy, Art and many more.

4. IBM ADEPT

IBM in collaboration with Samsung and Ethereum is implementing the ADEPT project to secure IOT devices from being manipulated by malicious software leading to DDOS attacks and other misuse of the devices. ADEPT (Autonomous Decentralised Peer to Peer Telemetry) is now an open source project enthusiastically participated by a number of companies covering the entire landscape of IOT devices.

IBM provides the technology platforms for connecting the devices to the Blockchain over the cloud and also provides the necessary authentication, analytical support and intelligence for the devices. The project is executed over Ethereum Blockchain that provides the smart contract functionality to enable the devices to safely transact with each other in a peer to peer manner.

IBM and Samsung demonstrated a Proof of Concept of the project to demonstrate how a Samsung washer is able to buy washing powder over the net from Amazon site.

Once successful, this technology coupled with the device near analytics from edge & fog computing technologies will enable the devices to identify, thwart and refute any malicious cyber-attacks, offering the solution against DDOS type attacks in the future.

5. Microsoft COCO framework

Microsoft COCO frame is in many ways, a solution, the world is looking forward to.

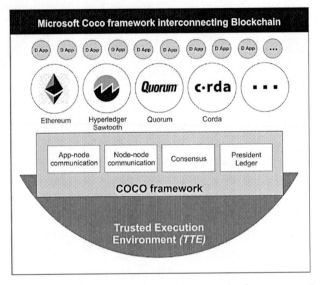

In normal case, as we see in the use case matrix for enterprise Blockchain applications, enterprises today operate in a complex environment. They can be a part of a Private Blockchain Network like Openchain for internal use, a Private consortium like a Hyperledger Fabric for supply chain management, promote a few DAOs on Public networks like Ethereum and also be a part of a Peer to Peer Financial exchange through R3 Cords. Apart from this, they may be having their own database for maintaining confidential and internal information. If this is the case, how can such complexity be managed?

Microsoft COCO offers them a platform for seamlessly interconnecting all parts of their organization across all the chains and managing the same in synergistic manner. This coupled with use of data based like FlureeDB and other SQL and NoSQL databases for a seamless query across all the platforms, enterprises will be best positioned to bring in 'Trust' into their dealings with all their customers, employees, vendors, shareholders and their partners, while automating most processes for an increased profitability with minimum risk.

Though there are a number of exciting projects like Storj (to act as a decentralised cloud storage), Maidsafe (For safe and secure DNS servers indexing developer friendly platforms like Lisk, Ark , Cosmos etc.) , we need to stress that some of them are still in idea execution stag and may have a long way to go.

CHAPTER 23

DMADV: Lean Six Sigma Inspired Approach to Architect A BCT Solution

Blockchain – An Impending Opportunity or A Necessity For Organizations to Adopt

To mitigate risks in an increasingly complex world characterized by competition, technological disruption, redundancy of existing skills due to automation, increasing dependency on third party device, robots and other interconnected objects which could lead to new layer of vulnerabilities, Blockchain is imperative for today's organization to redefine itself and remodel its operations for a new paradigm.

How does Blockchain facilitate Risk Management?

(A) The peer to peer nature of transactions with a shared distributed ledger as a single source of truth approved, removes the dependence from a central authority that can either influence unfairly or be a single source of failure.

(B) Anonymization/ Pseudonymization of identity leads to protection against leakages of personal information

(C) Authorization protocol for undertaking transaction will ensure that there is an audit trial for every transaction with time stamp in an immutable manner

(D) Consensus implementation for transaction approval ensures that for overwriting genuine transactions and undertaking fraudulent transactions, enormous amount of resources bordering on the verge of impossibility need to be spent.

(E) Automated transaction handling through Smart Contracts ensures that there is no error due to manual intervention or fallibility. The smart contract be architected to ensure that proper process automation is undertaken and tested for failure and wrong results.

(F) Shared distributed ledger amongst transacting participants ensures that, no single party can change the transaction record and also offers tremendous resiliency against a number of fault inducing scenarios.

(G) Following appropriate strategy to ensure outlining the right processes as well as automation of the same through adoption of best practices like Six Sigma and DMADV approach ensures that the organization streamlines in processes for maximum productivity.

DESIGNING A NEW FUTURE WITH DMADV APPROACH - [Define Map Analyze Design Validate] and Scale

Define Your Goals & Key Parameters

What are the problems in your existing system or opportunities for improvements you fore-see? Lean Six Sigma approach provides a structured approach to defining the problems that need to be addressed by a given project or a solution.

Voice of Customer, Voice of business, Cost of product and Service quality need to be monitored and assessed to get an understanding of the areas of significant impact. Are your customers demanding anonymity of their transactions?

- Is your competitor providing a better solution that offers no centralized access to customer's details?
- Are you faced with significant delays in your supply chain or process flows?
- Is your business dependent on a significant trust between a number of partners, vendors, contractors, associates and employees that impact your working capital cycle?

There could be many more such issues.

- Blockchain approach is also capable of significantly crashing all types of wastes in the system by streamlining and automating processes.
- The wastes are summarized in the acronyms, WORMPIT or TIMWOOD.

WORMPIT

- Waiting
- Over production
- Rejects
- Motion (Excess)
- Processing (Over)
- Inventory
- Transportation

TIMWOOD

Others use a different acronym to remember the 7 wastes of lean TIMWOOD. In this case the term rejects is replaced with defects:

- Transportation
- Inventory
- Motion (Excess)
- Waiting
- Over production

- Over processing

- Defects

It is important to remember that the Lean Methodology can be applied to identify and eliminate the wastes, which can lead to significant improvement in Process flows that are automated while developing a smart contract or an application for Blockchain implementation.

Is Blockchain an appropriate solution? What are the alternate solutions you have? If Blockchain is the right solution, define the results expected and create a project charter for implementation.

DO YOU NEED A BLOCKCHAIN?

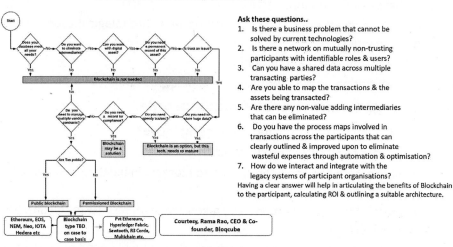

Ask these questions..
1. Is there a business problem that cannot be solved by current technologies?
2. Is there a network on mutually non-trusting participants with identifiable roles & users?
3. Can you have a shared data across multiple transacting parties?
4. Are you able to map the transactions & the assets being transacted?
5. Are there any non-value adding intermediaries that can be eliminated?
6. Do you have the process maps involved in transactions across the participants that can clearly outlined & improved upon to eliminate wasteful expenses through automation & optimisation?
7. How do we interact and integrate with the legacy systems of participant organisations?
Having a clear answer will help in articulating the benefits of Blockchain to the participant, calculating ROI & outlining a suitable architecture.

The main elements of the Blockchain based solution are:

A. Participants

- Define who can use the platform & conduct transactions. For example, the platform is for business to business or business to consumer or a consumer to consumer applications etc.

- Define who can query the information and for what reason

- Define who can authorize the transaction and what is the consensus approach that needs to be used is.

- Is there any prerequisite for authorizing and validating the transactions before accessing the Blockchain?

- Whether the participants can be potentially posing threat to the interests of the organization or fellow participants?

B. Administration & Management

- What is the role of the leadership/ promoter group?
- Whether the management will be an active part of the operation or will give supportive role with selective intervention?
- Is the management central to the organization or external support?
- What level of decision making and operation can be automated?

C. Transactions

- What are the transactions that are carried out by the participants?
- Whether the transactions involve transfer of value or title of an asset or exchange of information etc.?
- Will the transactions need to be stored in a chronological order or in any other manner?
- Who can approve the transactions?
- The arbitration process for resolving conflict scenarios

D. Storage & Infrastructure requirements

- Is the exchange of information storage intensive?
- Is the data to be stored on the Blockchain nodes?
- Will the amount of data stored, lead to Blockchain bloating and reduction in speed of operations?
- Any regulatory consideration to be taken care with respect to the data stored in the Blockchain?
- Any privacy issues that could be triggered, that would need to be managed?

E. Access control

- Whether all the data that is stored in Blockchain can be publicly exposed?
- Is there any data that needs to selectively masked, to be accessed by only selected parties?
- Identity management challenges in terms of creation of access keys, private and public and mapping of parties with respect to single/ multi user access

F. Security protocols

- Cryptographic encoding requirements for data, identities, transactions as they pass through the system
- Data isolation needs and potential threats to corruption of data on the Blockchain.
- Potential security threats that could cause failure of the smart contracts, cause damage to the decentralised applications along with the mitigation options.

G.   Incentivisation

- To ensure perpetuity of the operations, how are the various roles that are facilitating verification of genuine transactions, authenticity of the participants and the integrity of the Blockchain incentivized?

- How are the providers of resources like Storage, processing power, referral etc., incentivized?

- Are the transaction generators trust worthy or are they malicious & misleading? Are the validating/ mining nodes trustworthy and credible? The intensity of the work required to be done by the platform depends on the above questions. The more the trust between the nodes and transactors, the less the cost of mining process and corresponding is the need to incentivize the network maintainers.

Blockchain is a lot about automating the processes to reduce human intervention that could induce mistrust, latency and error. For that, it is very important to streamline the processes for an optimal Blockchain implementation.

Hence a SIPOC map of the organization where Blockchain is evaluated for implementation is a must. The same need further has to be streamlined for maximum efficiency. Otherwise, automation of redundant and wrong processes will lead to counterproductive results. A sample SIPOC matrix showing the flow of goods and services is given below:

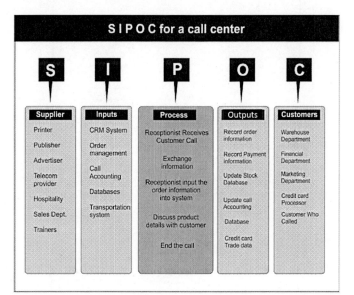

A clear project road map should be signed off by the top management before embarking on the project as this will provide the necessary commitment and resources required for a high involvement, path breaking project to implement Blockchain Technology. The purpose of the project charter is to document:

- Reasons for undertaking the project
- Objectives and constraints of the project
- Directions concerning the solution
- Identities of the main stakeholders
- In-scope and out-of-scope items
- Risks identified early on (A risk management plan should be part of the overall project management plan)
- Target project benefits
- High level budget and spending authority

Once signed, the project manager and the other stakeholders in the management, project charter will serve to get the necessary inputs, resources and organizational support to adopt a systematic approach for Blockchain project implementation.

Model The Solution

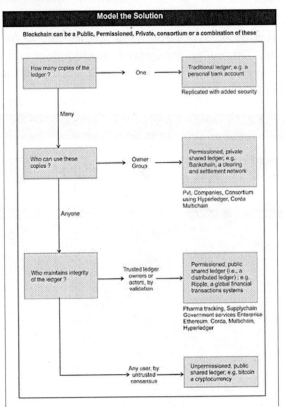

Blockchain can be a Public, Permissioned, and Private, Consortium or a combination of these.

The Consensus mechanism is the heart and soul of the Blockchain System.

The type of consensus mechanism that you find suitable for the industry also determines the type of Blockchain and the platform one can use for the solution.

There are different types of consensus mechanisms that will help arrive at the finality of the transactions in a conclusive manner with lowest probability of error occurrence. The consensus mechanisms are responsible for the governance and integrity of the platform.

Selection of the consensus mechanisms depends on the nature of interactions and the credibility of the interactions between the participants and those responsible for the governance of the network.

The lower the trust between the participants, the higher is the intensity and hence the amount of effort required to uphold the integrity of the network.

Bitcoin, the first implementation of the Blockchain protocol assumes, no trust between the parties transacting while any of the participants can take part in the decision making process.

The Proof of Work consensus mechanism implemented by Bitcoin Blockchain ensures that while the decision making that prevents the double spending is almost fool proof at the current level of technological paradigms. It results in an enormous expenditure in the form of electricity and computer processing power spent. The attackers wanting to upset the integrity of the system, consequently, have to spend economically unviable amount of resources to overturn the decision arrived through the consensus mechanism.

A similar consensus mechanism with a minor variation has been used by Ethereum, which apart from basic cryptocurrency dominated transactions, has implemented the concept of smart contracts.

The intensity of effort required by the POW mechanism has resulted in slow speed and drastically reduced scalability giving rise to a lot of improvisations in the subsequent implementation of the Blockchain protocol, albeit with at a trade-off across parameters, as per the need of the participants.

It is well understood that, as the trust level between the participants and also the leader consortium increases the consensus protocol can reduce the intensity of the work required and correspondingly allow for increased scaling without sacrificing the trust and integrity of the system.

A list of the various consensus protocols and their corresponding features and platforms is given below:

(1)   Proof of Work (POW)

(2)   Proof of Stake (POS)

(3)   Delegated Proof of Stake (DPOS)

(4)   Proof of Authority (POA)

(5)   PBFT & Derivatives

(6) Federated Consensus : Ripple & Stellar (Ripple fork)

(7) Tendermint

(8) Node to Node (N2N) : R3 Corda

(9) POET (Proof of Elapsed time)

(10) Round Robin

A comprehensive evaluation of the different types of Consensus mechanisms is given below:

BLOCKCHAIN CONSENSUS MODEL COMPARISON

Parameter	Proof of Work	Proof of Stake	Proof of Elapsed Time	DPOS	Practical Byzantine Fault Tolerance (PBFT & Variants)	Federated BFT	N2N	RoundRobin	TenderMint	Proof of Authority
Description	Unidentified participants can participate in Blockcreation through a gaming process to prove the amount of work done.	Participants with proven stake participate in a stake influenced chance in a lottery to select the leader to announce the block creation	Same as POW, without miners spending money but randomly announcing a wait time, one with the minimum being the winner.	Similar to POS but eleted participants nominated by stake holders participate in Block creation	Identified participants participate in Transaction approval	Multiple rounds of voting from trusted pool of validators	Transaction level agreement between nodes endorsed by a Trusted third party	Transactions are approved by nodes generating subsequent blocks in a round robin manner.	Pluggable Proof of Stake with weighed validators.	Reputed Validators approving transactions as per their stakes.
Blockchain Type	Public	Public	Public/Private	Public	Private/ Consortium	Private/Consortium	Private/Consortium	Private/Consortium	Public	Private
Node Identity Management	Open, Entirely decentralised	Open, Entirely decentralised	Depending on use case	Open, Entirely decentralised	Identified	Identified	Identified	Identified	Open, Entirely decentralised	Identified
Tolerance	< 25%	<50%	<25%	<33%	<33%	<33%	<33%	<25%	<50%	<33%
Platform Token	Yes	Yes	No	Yes	No	No	No	No	Yes	No
Node Scalability	High	High	Limited (under valida	High	Limited (Tested upto maximum of 100)	High	High	High	High	High
Client Scalability	Excellent	Excellent	high	Excellent	Very High	High	High	High	Excellent	High
Throughput	Low	High	Medium	High	High	High	High	High	High	High
Latency	Poor	Good	Good	Excellent	Excellent	Good	Good	Excellent	Good	Good
Transaction finality	NO	Almost 100%	No	Almost 100%	Yes	Yes	Yes	Yes	Almost 100%	Yes
Implementation cost	Low	Medium	Medium	Medium	Medium	NA	High	Low	Medium	High
Trust in validators	Untrusted	Bonded validators	Untrusted	Untrusted	Trusted	Trusted	Trusted	Trusted	Bonded valida Trusted	Trusted
Power consumption	Very poor	Negligible	Negligible	Negligible	Negligible	Negligible	Negligible	Negligible	Negligible	Negligible
Examples	Bitcoin, Ethereum (HS)	Ethereum (Casper)	Hyperledger Sawtooth	EOS/ Cardano	Hyperledger Fabric	Ripple	R3 Corda	Multichain	Cosmos	Ethereum Parity
Correctness Proof	No	No	No	No	Yes	Yes	Yes	No	No	Yes
Network Synchrony assumption	Yes	Yes	Yes	No	No	No	Yes	No	Yes	Yes
Developer Friendliness	High	High	Low	High	Low	Low	Low	Yes	High	Low
Cost of participation	Yes	Yes	No	Yes	No	No	No	No	Yes	No

The company has to decide whether they would like to:

1. Create a decentralised autonomous organization (DAO) that can be executed using smart contracts and use public Blockchain as a backend.

2. Be a part of a consortium of organizations transacting with each other to experience the benefits of automation for an efficient, paperless and secure operation for enhanced trust facilitated by smart contracts.

3. Have its own private Blockchain with all the parties dealing with it , suppliers, consumers, partners and its subsidiaries, branches, subdivisions and functions operating with shared distributed ledger and smart contract enabled automated operations.

4. Identify the level of information that can be shared and what needs to be held confidential with the organization and what are the role based permissions that need to be granted for different participants in case it is a permissioned operation.

5. What is the roadmap in terms of decentralization of operations into the future?

Disintermediation of existing operation by removing non-value adding and cost bloating middle layers:

One of the main use-cases of the Blockchain is removing the middlemen that add a lot of time and cost to the operations. Hence elimination of this waste, to make the operations Lean, mean and efficient is a key consideration while modelling the solution.

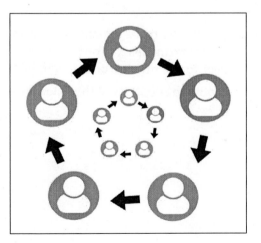

Decentralization and peer to peer transactions are then made possible for increased speed and efficiency.

Peer to Peer Transactions made possible by Blockchain:

- Decentralization brings in the need to relook at the existing Businessmodels and management structures.

Some of the models that need to be taken into account are considered as given below:

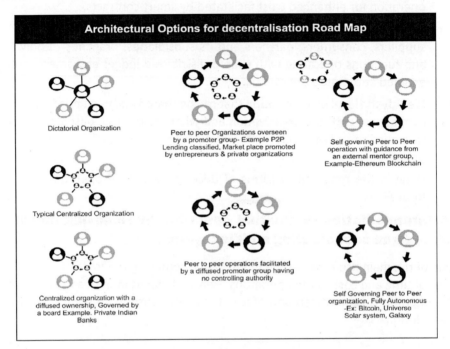

Architectural Options for decentralisation Road Map

Dictatorial Organization

Peer to peer Organizations overseen by a promoter group- Example P2P Lending classified. Market place promoted by entrepreneurs & private organizations

Self govening Peer to Peer operation with guidance from an external mentor group, Example-Ethereum Blockchain

Typical Centralized Organization

Peer to peer operations facilitated by a diffused promoter group having no controlling authority

Centralized organization with a diffused ownership, Governed by a board Example. Private Indian Banks

Self Governing Peer to Peer organization, Fully Autonomous -Ex: Bitcoin, Universe Solar system, Galaxy

Depending on the outlook of the management, the organization can consider a transition from the existing state mapping to one of the above modes of operation on the left side to the Peer to Peer models on the right side.

The organizations can choose to adopt any of the following end states in the short run:

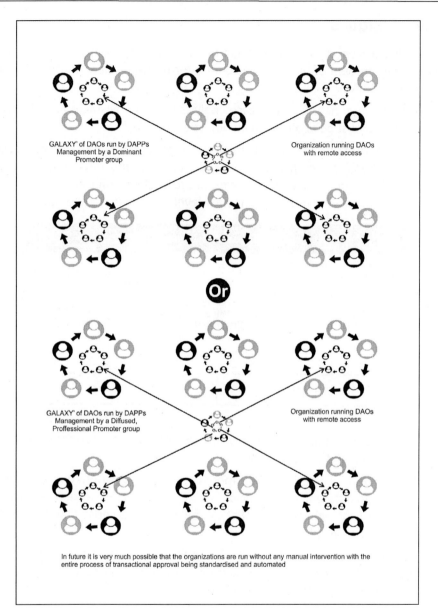

GALAXY' of DAOs run by DAPPs Management by a Dominant Promoter group

Organization running DAOs with remote access

Or

GALAXY' of DAOs run by DAPPs Management by a Diffused, Proffessional Promoter group

Organization running DAOs with remote access

In future it is very much possible that the organizations are run without any manual intervention with the entire process of transactional approval being standardised and automated

In future it is very much possible that the organizations are run without any manual intervention with the entire process of transactional approval being standardized and automated.

As we model our solution, it is important to understand the different types of Blockchains and their use cases.

In centralized organizations, the decision making is undertaken by a core group of leaders & promoters. Blockchain offers for a democratic approach to decision making with validators being anonymous. The approach is given below:

Analyze Options

Developing a Blockchain is a strategic move by an organization and involves a tremendous amount of planning and a long-term commitment by the promoters of the organization.

There should be a clear business case analysis in the early stages and all aspects of the project must be analyzed in an objective manner.

Business Model mapping: a useful tool that will help organizations to systematically and comprehensively map their needs, capabilities and environment and be prepared for the long haul with open eyes has to be signed off by the management before the organization moves to the next level after finalizing the options

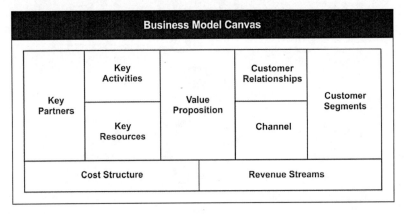

Once this is signed off, the company has to select the appropriate platform to develop and launch the application.

- Identify appropriate Blockchain model by evaluating various options available across the different spectrums of Private, Public or Consortium applications and select the right platform that can be used for its chosen model in light of the investments planned.

- For example, while, public Bitcoin and Ethereum platforms can be suitable for business to consumer applications, for enterprise applications, there is a wide choice of platforms ranging from:

- Ethereum

- BAAS (Blockchain as a service) from Microsoft,

- Hyperledger Fabric, Sawtooth, Iroha from Linux stable

- Quorum built on Ethereum platform by JP Morgan,

- R3 Corda

- Multichain,

- Chain etc.

Before selecting and finalizing a Blockchain technology platform for given user requirement, the CTO/CIO in conjunction with the Blockchain architect on board, must consider the following aspects:

(A) **Identity management:** How is the identity of the participants like, end users, consensus holders, promoters, transaction authenticator/verifiers, and miners etc., managed?

The complexity of the consensus mechanism is very much dependent on this as the management of 'Bad actor' influence and the corresponding risk needs to be mitigated through appropriate choice of the same. In case of Public Blockchains like Ethereum and Bitcoin, where the participants are unknown, complex mechanisms like POW (Proof of Work), PoET (Proof of Elapsed time), POS (Proof of stake and their variations are considered. These choices however, put a lot of limitations on the scalability of the platforms and the speed of transaction execution.

In case of private/ consortium Blockchains, where the identity of the participants is well known and documented through KYC (know your customer) and CoI (Certificates of identity for transaction participants) and all the transactions, the need for a complex Consensus mechanism that consumes a lot of resources like electricity and computer processing time for keeping a check on the participants with malafide intentions is considerably less. Here, one can consider, Consensus mechanisms like PBFT (Practical Byzantine Fault Tolerant) and its variations. In case a member is found to indulge in actions against the interests of the other participants, the member can be ostracized, or an appropriate action can be taken against the same. This helps the network to scale up substantially with increased speed & a better response. This is also helped by the fact that, a limited number of participants can participate in the decision making or transaction verification/ validation, unlike in public Blockchains, where all members must have the equal opportunity to participate.

(B) **Nature of participants:** The participants can be individuals, company officials, corporates, members within an organization or a group, members of an industry consortium & their designated staff etc. Depending on the nature of participants, the trust levels between the participants and the transaction endorses varies, which further influences the choice of the platform and the consensus mechanisms.

(C) **Governance models:** The platform can be managed autonomously in a democratic manner as in the case of public Blockchain like Bitcoin or by a consortium leader in the case of a private Blockchain. While it is important for the governing board and the team managing the Blockchain to assure and manage the decentralised aspect of the Blockchain in letter and spirit as much as possible, various aspects like management of the hardware

& technical infrastructure, smart contracts, databases etc., should be managed to ensure the confidentiality among the participants, continuity & permanency of the network in an appropriate manner. Otherwise, inability of the Blockchain platform initiators in assuring the participants can result in the project's failure.

(D) **Cryptocurrency/ asset digitization requirements:** The efforts of various participants who are involved in transacting on the network and assisting in maintaining its sanctity need to be rewarded in an equitable, quantifiable & profitable manner. Public Blockchains and the various peer to peer businesses that are sprouting with them as the backend use cryptoassets like tokens and platform specific currencies to remunerate the participants for their contribution and also to avail services on their networks. This has led to a whole new way of conducting business enabling value quantification and management through appropriate rewards for even microservices like blogging on the social media or providing valuable expert opinions.

However, in the case of enterprise applications, the need is for a platform that vastly improves productivity and efficiency while increasing automation and trust among the participants through programmatic execution. Hence a typical Enterprise application may not be in favor of using cryptoassets. However, asset digitation in the form of dividing the asset into a number of fungible uniform units and transacting by exchanging the same with units of fiat currencies or with equivalent value of other digitized assets could be considered more appropriate.

(E) **Security considerations:** As the usage and networks scale, there will be a need for accommodating different types of participants who come with their legacy systems and varying security implementations. Any chain is as strong as its weakest link. Hence it is imperative for the Blockchain platform initiators and manage to implement comprehensive security standards that protects all the aspects of the Blockchain like a) Hardware and IT infrastructure, b) Smart contracts & their connected applications, crypto/digitized asset related information and all transactional information c) Confidentiality of transaction etc., and d) highest data governance standards in line with the regulatory standards.

Appropriate choice of cryptographic techniques and risk management practices need to be put in place.. This is a major consideration in choosing the right platform and implementation partner.

(F) **Integration with existing systems of the organization and those of the other participants:** Implementation of Blockchain cannot be considered as an isolated activity by an organization. A lot of information that is required for the execution of transactions is derived on a runtime basis from various existing backend applications running within an organization and vice-versa.

Hence a comprehensive view of the Blockchain platform implementation in the case of enterprises and consortiums involves, a detailed look at the existing IT infrastructure and landscape across the participants. In a number of cases, it would be required to modify certain legacy applications to enable communication with the new Blockchain infrastructure. For example, integration of the Blockchain with the Big data analytics related applications should be considered in the future.

(G) **Infrastructure scalability and management:** In general, a number of organizations start their implementations in a small way for a limited set of applications and participants. As the comfort level and adaptation scale-up, there would be a need for a large amount of data to be stored across participants on a permanent basis. Hence the choice of platform and the implementation should consider aa scalable infrastructure based application. Cloud managed Blockchain as a service based implementations allow a quick installation and a rapid scale up in a secure and reliable manner, provided appropriate cloud vendor is chosen.

(H) **Investments and sharing of returns among participants:** One of the major factors that influences the investments in creating the Blockchain applications enterprises, is the ROI (Return on Investments) of such investments.

Hence it is important for the initiators of the Blockchain platform to objectively and comprehensively address the 'What is in it for me' question of all the envisaged participants. This alone can ensure the success and scalability of the projects.

(I) **Framework maturity and availability of community support:** Blockchain, being a nascent field, a number of developments are taking place rapidly and simultaneously across different aspects of the eco- system. While there are a number of new players entering the field with their own ideas and capabilities, it is imperative for the platform adaptors to ensure that they are backed by a sound and reliable ecosystem in their area of operation, that ensures, high service levels, continuous upgradation and scalability while making it convenient to understand, learn and follow the various developments. Depending on the leading available platforms with proven lineage offered by IBM/Linux, Microsoft, Oracle, Amazon coupled with comprehensive documentation available on pubic repositories like GitHub, Readthedocs etc. could help in mitigating the risk of being a pioneer implementer in a nascent field, thus ensuring higher returns on the enterprise's investments in a reliable manner.

(j) **Use-case availability and Environment scanning:** In the case of public Blockchain based services, there are a huge number of companies who have come out with their initial coin offerings and have published their white papers. A large amount of code is available on GitHub in public domain. These can be referred by new entrants. In the case of enterprise applications, leading companies like IBM have created a number of use cases with pioneering customers across industry domains. Studying the same and adapting suitable aspects for their own use case can help organizations have a quick start and a reliable implementation roadmap.

Design Your Application

Once the right platform is identified with appropriate characteristics, it is time to design the solution and decide on the following elements:

Select hardware, operating system, Cloud/ on premise or both, APIs, smart contract development by keeping into account the information on, how many nodes and who all can access, databases on chain or off-chain?

The following steps outline the designing process of the application. The architecture portion of the application development process is described through a real-life case study.

The steps are outlined as follows:

(a) Create a detailed process flow chart outlining the various parties involved and the transaction flow.

(b) List the data models relevant to the application. There are two types of information that are important:

o   The key ledger items

o   The different states of the ledger items as the transactions are carried out.

For example, if you are tracking the status of an order and payment for a television in a supply chain system, the data models are:

1.   Order- State of item, Order placed, Order billed, Order received, and Order in received, to vendor, to customer etc.

2.   Television- Status being ordered, in transit, received, billed to Customer, from Seller etc.

3.   The list of all the persons who need to use and those who need to interact with the application has to be listed.

4.   The Access control list that maps different players to the corresponding activities along with the read and write access has to be detailed to ensure that every party undertakes the appropriate activity without violating the sanctity of the application.

5.   Different components of the Blockchain application need to be thoroughly detailed. Some of them are listed below:

(a)   Ledger

(b)   Smart contract with the functionality

- Peer network details
- Membership criteria in case of permissioned network
- Wallet to store the identity keys
- Systems management
- Events triggered by contract and the impact on the state changes etc.
- List of all APIs and external applications and Integrations required.

6.   A typical Blockchain application will have the following interactions (example-Hyperledger Fabric)

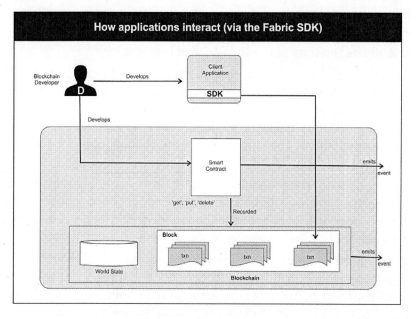

The Blockchain application will have a client facing application that interacts with the Blockchain through a program called smart contract or Chain code that is embedded into every node of the Blockchain. The smart contract when invoked by the client, will execute the transactions that are approved as per a Consensus mechanism to validate the same. Once validated, the approved transactions are then grouped into a block and appended to the existing blocks in the chain thus extending in a chronological fashion.

The presence of the transactions in all the nodes along with the necessary validations and approvals results in the immutability of all things, transactions and data stored on the Blockchain.

The transactions can then be queried using an explorer on a live basis.

1.   The complete list of transactions, party wise and timeline wise and the

business logic leading to the creation of blocks along with the information needed for creating appropriate user interfaces and the corresponding wireframes, tools and technologies to be used for the application is now ready.

2. The Blockchain platforms provide a number of open source tools, support system and development & testing frameworks that will help in creating the application, testing, compiling and migrating the same onto the Blockchain.

3. Smart contract development in appropriate language such as Java, Golang, and Solidity is done by the developers as per the needs of the application and deployed on the Blockchain nodes, initially on the test networks.

   The smart contracts in Ethereum are written in Solidity while in Hyperledger Fabric, the smart contract is known as a chaincode and is developed in GO.

   The chaincode in Hyperledger Fabric enables the users to create transactions and update the state as per the encoded business logic.

   Channels between different parties allow the respective parties to deal in a permissioned and confidential environment. The chaincode for each channel creates the assets pertaining to that channel, encodes the respective business logic thus managing the ledger state through transactions invoked by the applications. The chain code in one channel cannot be accessed by chaincode in another channel.

   Chaincode automates the entire process listed above allowing participants to collectively manage decentralised applications. The chaincode is installed in every peer node in Hyperledger, thus allowing the applications to interact with the Blockchain irrespective of the node they are connected to.

4. To download Hyperledger fabric and set up a network on can refer to http://hyperledger-fabric.readthedocs.io/en/release-1.1/build_ network.html.The build your first network (BYFN) scenario provisions a sample Hyperledger Fabric network consisting of two organizations, each maintaining two peer nodes, and a "solo" ordering service.

5. The front end of the application that allows users to access and interact with the chaincode is developed using tools like HTML, CSS and JavaScript.

   Once the testing is done successfully it is migrated onto the main network and scaled as per the needs of the user groups. Security is of utmost importance while launching a Blockchain application. The security has to be addressed at various levels:

   o **Ledger Level Security:** All the users and the members should be identified with proper registration on the network to be able to conduct transactions

6. **Network Level Security:** Communication between components of different nodes has to be secured through proper hardware isolation. Any unforeseen

and unplanned interconnections can compromise the sanctity of the system

7. **Transaction Level Security**: Transactions have to be encrypted end to end so that they are not compromised and reflect wrong outputs due to the same.

8. **Associated surrounding system security**: Since the applications interact with external databases and various applications, adequate firewalls and filters should be applied so that there will be no proliferation of external malware into and through the system

9. **Smart contract security:** Smart contracts offer the core functionality of the entire Blockchain project. Hence it is imperative that the Smart contracts are adequately shielded from all external links and APIs to prevent their infection.

Smart contracts interact with Oracles to connect to external data streams as required by the application. Any malware attacks on such external sources can spread through Oracles to the smart contracts and the ledger as well. Hence proper threat prevention and protection should be implemented to prevent Smart contract contamination.

Microsoft Azure offers Cryptlets for safe smart contract applications.

Cryptlets are off-chain code modules that are written in any language that can execute within a secure, isolated, trusted container and is communicated with over secure channels. Cryptlets can be used in Smart Contracts and UTXO systems when additional functionality or information is needed, upgrading the Blockchain "oracle" approach with a Cryptlet and Crypto-Delegate or adaptor.

Cryplet	Vs	Oracle
(+) Trust with verification-trust hoster (HTTPS), trust cryptlet key & trust enclave signature		(-) Requires trust but no formal verification
(+) Standard Infrastructure - Hardware based isolation and attestation via enclaves (SGX) available Globally in Azure		(-) Custom - write & host seperately and establishing trust difficult
(+) Integrated developer use with Aspects and tooling		(-) Custom-write your own
(+) Marketplace for publishing and discovery		(-) No common marketplace, no publishing or discover tools
(+) Bletchley Cryptlet SDK frameworks to get started quickly creating and consuming Cryptlets (Utility. Contract)		(-) Platform specific, documentation sparse
(+) Multiple language options as well as blockchain agnostic		(-) Custom

Microsoft Project Bletchley Blockchain as a service framework, promises to deliver a Blockchain Application Fabric that allows enterprises to re-invent business processes in a collaborative way. Cryptlets exist in this Cryptlet Fabric providing much needed functionality like integration, secure execution, privacy, interoperability, management and a rich set of data services.

You may browse for the Cryptlets from the existing libraries or you may want to develop your own Cryptlets in the language of your choice, that integrate data or logic from an external system like validating customer's data without disclosing it to the Blockchain itself and deploy to either Azure, Azure Stack or localhost* using the Bletchley SDK.

Validate Your Solution

Once the application is designed and completed, the same has to compiled and migrated on to the network.

https://codeburst.io/build-your-first-ethereum-smart-contract-with-solidity-tutorial-94171d6b1c4b

Depending on whether you are designing a DAPP for a pubic Blockchain or a private Blockchain, the corresponding steps have to be used. The steps in the case of Ethereum Blockchain which offers both private and public versions are given below:

In the simplest form, an Ethereum node is any device that is running the Ethereum protocol (Blockchain). While nodes are typically running on desktops & laptops, development for mobile is ongoing. When we connect to the Ethereum protocol we are on the Ethereum Blockchain network and are running a node. By running an Ethereum node we can connect to other nodes in the network, have direct access to the Blockchain, and even do things like mine blocks, send transactions, and deploy smart contracts.

1. Nodes are written in Go (Go Ethereum/Geth), C++, and Python. In this tutorial we're going to stick to the most popular of the three, Go. Important to also note that by downloading Geth we are downloading the ENTIRE Ethereum Blockchain. That said, make sure you have ~100GBs of storage on your hard drive before continuing.

    o   Visit the Go Ethereum website and install Geth.

    o   Visit here: https://geth.ethereum.org/downloads/

2. Download the latest release of Geth for Windows, or your operating system & make sure you download the 64-bit version. Geth Ethereum Downloadable Releases.

3. Once your download is complete, open the installer and click "I Agree".

4. Make sure the Geth box is checked and click "Next".

5. You'll be prompted to select a destination folder for your download. By default, Geth will install under C:\Program Files\Geth.

6. Close installation once complete.

7. Open up command prompt (I'll be using Git Bash — download here: https://git-scm.com/ , do make sure you add to PATH variables during installation) and navigate to the Geth directory by typing "cd C:\Program Files\Geth" **(Geth Path File)**.

8. Begin syncing to the Ethereum Blockchain by typing "Geth". Because this is your first sync you'll download the ENTIRE Blockchain from other peers. This will take some time so get comfy...

What you'll see when launching Geth for the first time (post download).

Establishing Our Own Private Ethereum Network

Now that we have access to the Ethereum protocol via our node, we're going to setup our own private server to develop & deploy our smart contract. Note that none of this will actually be deployed on the Ethereum Blockchain, instead we'll deploy on our own Blockchain. We'll start by initializing the very first block in our Blockchain, the genesis block (genesis.json).

1. Create a new folder on your desktop called "Private Chain".

2. Open command prompt in this folder and create a data directory folder for our chaindata by typing "Mkdirchaindata". You can open a command prompt in this folder by holding shift and right clicking, then select "open command window here".

3. Next, we need to create and save our genesis.json block in our Private Chain folder, as the genesis block will be used to initialize our private network and store data in the data directory folder "chaindata".

4. Open up notepad, copy & paste the code below into a new file called "genesis. json" and save this file in our Private Chain folder.

    Learn more about genesis.json parameters visit the link below: https:// ethereum. stackexchange.com/questions/2376/what-does-each-genesis-json-parameter- mean

5. Now we want to initialize our private network in the chaindata directory by using our genesis.json file. We're going to tell Geth we want the data directory in the "chaindata" directory and where the genesis.json file can be found (make sure genesis.json is NOT in chaindata folder) by entering the code below into our command line pointing to the Private Chain folder. geth --datadir=./chaindata/ init ./genesis.json

6. You should then see that the genesis state was successfully written.

7. Now we can start Geth and connect to our own private chain. As you will see the geth.ipc endpoint socket connection will be opened and so will port 30303.geth --datadir=./chaindata/

Launch application on 2 nodes and test. Increase the number of nodes in stages and test scalability.

Testing is an important part of Blockchain solution development. Since Blockchain provides for immutable recordkeeping and automated transaction processing any errors, if unnoticed can lead to potentially large and irreversible losses. Also, as the size of the databases and amount of transactions rise, the platform scalability can become a bottleneck. Hence a number of scenarios depicting all things that can go wrong need to be simulated and validated.

A case in point is the loss that occurred due to a flaw in the smart contract code of the first ever Decentralised organization called 'The DAO'. The DAO raised over 150 million US Dollars to be invested as an automated decision making process to invest in over 50 project (as of the day of launch of the ICO) and reward the investors and the 'The DAO; token holder. A flaw in the contract code allowed a token holder to withdraw over 3.6 million US Dollar worth of Ethereum through a recursive loop that repeated the withdrawal transactions before they are confirmed. This resulted in a huge furor and the Blockchain program had to be halted for a few days in an unprecedented manner. Subsequently the smart contract functionality has since been improved to prevent the specific faults that led to this situation. Main Ethereum network is currently following the upgraded version while the older version from which a number of miners and participants refused to shift due to ideological issues is known as Ethereum Classic.

Though the issue was settled by removal of the block causing the faulty transaction (due to mistake in the program) and the money later returned to all the investors (at least partly after accounting for the loss of value of base crypto currency, namely, Ether), the incident highlighted the tremendous importance of the smart contract Testing related issues.

Most of the platforms and IDE (Integrated Development Environments) that help in developing smart contract programs offer an excellent in built support to develop flawless applications.

Smart contract audit is a mandatory service that is required to be undertaken by anyone wanting to launch an ICO today.

For a detailed & structure audit, one can sign up on platform **https://audits. quillhash.com/smart-contract-audit**. There you can upload your smart contract code and get a report generated, if that doesn't work, there are a number of companies like M/s Quillhash who also perform a manual analysis which can detect all possible issues

Appropriate in advance warning mechanisms for things that can go wrong, automated fall over and correction mechanisms should be put in place and tested.

Provision for continuous improvement of the performance, in the form of a mechanism to generate evaluate implement the improvement proposals is required to keep in pace with the technological developments and keep the system, fine-tuned to performing at the best always.

CHAPTER 24

Scaling up the Blockchain Project

Implementing a Blockchain application for your organization is a very involved and resource consuming activity. Following a systematic approach enables organizations to plan with a strategy and end in mind.

It is imperative to keep an eye on the very business goal for which the company has embarked on a Blockchain project and should put in place a continuous review mechanism to see that the organization is moving in the right direction.

BLOCKCHAIN SCALE UP TRACKER consists of the following steps:

A. A cross functional team of 7 members for each and every project whether it is a DAO or a private Blockchain or a consortium project must be put in place for every project.

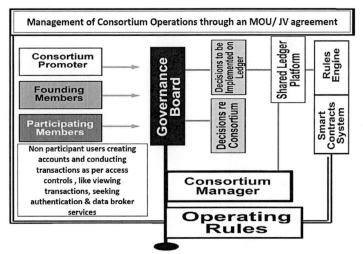

Figure: Consortium approach balancing the interests of members for a balanced ROI & benefit

B. Specific goals linked to the benefits the organization seeks to derive from the project have to be given to the concerned employees in the organization. For example

o Decrease in operational expenses due to automation by 25%

o Reduction in cycle time by 30% etc.

o The same have to be split into team and individual goals across the organization and driven through a reward system to reinforce a positive approach and behavior.

C.   Positivity and hope for the future for implementing new and path breaking initiatives has to be encouraged and persons in the organization who are having any indication of negative or un-cooperative behavior should be dealt with appropriately. Any cynical or negative approach in even a small corner of the company can have the potential to burst the bubble of enthusiasm and passion driven approach needed to make the new projects a success.

   o   Adequate resources across all the steps needed for implementing & monitoring the project and leading it to conclusion should be provided as this would have a long standing impact on the **security & risk management** of the organization in the long run.

   o   A persistent and systematic approach to not only ensure that the projects are going on at desired pact but also look to expand the success stories to new corners of the company have to be explored and capitalized.

This will ensure that the organization and its ecosystem derive the maximum benefit of the investments and successfully scale up the excellence on all fronts setting a stage for growth into new frontiers with a manageable risk and high rewards.

CHAPTER 25

Blockchain as a Service- Various Platforms Available

Setting and Scaling up a Private Blockchain

Microsoft, IBM, Oracle, Amazon and Huawei are offering cloud based services to set up and scale the Blockchain applications in a seamless manner

The following are the prerequisites for any Blockchain as a Service application:

1. Scalability

2. High Availability

3. Disaster recovery

4. Secure access and Key management services

5. Single sign-on to a variety of integrated applications

6. Ability to conduct private transactions over secure channels in a confidential manner.

Blockchain as a Service offering from global leaders like Microsoft, IBM, Amazon, Oracle and Huawei offers dependable, scalable and secure platforms with all these features.

HUAWEI: Blockchain as a Service (BCS)

https://static.huaweicloud.com/upload/files/pdf/20180416/20180416142450_6
1761.pdf

Leveraging its strengths in Mobile and Telecommunications, Hardware technologies, Cloud, Connected cars, IoT and cutting edge security technologies, Huawei is offering an end to end integrated Blockchain development, deployment and maintenance services encompassing activities like

• Planning

• Purchasing

• Configuring

• Development

• Product Launch

• Operation and Maintenance of Blockchain technology for organizations.

Based on Hyperledger Fabric platform, Huawei offers versatile features like

secured & encrypted peer to peer network with high level of security for all account and transactions, pluggable consensus algorithms, smart contract functionality and secured cloud services to clients for applications in IoT, Supply chain, Financial Services and auditing, connected cars, Identity verification, telecom carriers, cloud network, tokenization of assets and securities etc. This will enable clients across the world to leverage the power of Blockchain technology and also be in tune with the advancements across all the cutting-edge technologies, without being overawed by the same.

IBM LinuxONEBlockchain Services

(www.ibm.com/LinuxONE/Blockchain)

Based on Hyperledger platform, IBM offers production ready Blockchain platform to easily build, manage, scale and govern Blockchain applications.

- IBM LinuxONE Blockchain assures 99.999% uptime,
- End to end encryption for all data
- Transactions with security of highest level commercial security classification.
- Scale up to 30 billion queries in a day
- 170 dedicated cores with 8000 Virtual machines and 32 Tera bytes of memory.
- Reduced development time and speedy activation and management of ongoing management of the entire business network with a variety of collaborative tools.

IBM has over 400 in production Blockchain instances across Supply chain, Finance, Healthcare, Pharma, Education, IOT industries and for Government applications reflecting its immense experience, stability and dependability of its platforms.

Amazon BAAS

(https://aws.amazon.com/blogs/aws/get-started-with-Blockchain-using-the-new-aws-Blockchain-templates/)

In collaboration with Digital Services Group, Amazon offers Blockchain services on the cloud. Amazon offers Hyperledger and Ethereum platforms on a pay as you go basis. It offers open source platforms for easy and instant deployment of smart contract applications with permissions and access controls for peer to peer transactions with distributed consensus algorithms.

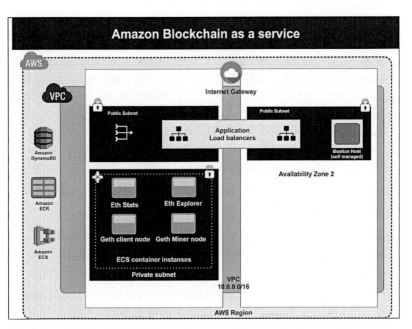

Microsoft Azure BAAS (https://azure.microsoft.com/en-in/solutions/Blockchain/)

Microsoft offers secure, scalable and versatile Blockchain as a service platform to rapidly develop and deploy secure Blockchain applications that are interoperable across all the enterprise applications like CRM, Big Data, Analytics, Project management, Social media and the like.

Microsoft in collaboration with Blockapps offers a comprehensive Platform to develop application on Ethereum enterprise platform using STRATO client.

STRATO is the best way to build apps on Ethereum. Our client, written in Haskell, provides a highly scalable Ethereum compliant Blockchain with an industry standard RESTful API. Blockapps provides the fastest development platform for building and deploying Ethereum Blockchain applications. Our quick deployments and RESTful API enables developers to build, test and deploy smart contracts faster than ever.

With Azure BAAS, clients can pay & scale as they go. Depending on a trusted Cloud provider, they can run their applications from anywhere in the world. In collaboration with Alpha Point, Microsoft offers Digital Asset exchanges to facilitate enterprises to store, track and trace digital assets.

In collaboration with IOTA Tangle, Microsoft offers a variety of solutions the IoT and Microfinance Industries.

IOTA Tangle is a DAG (Direct Acrylic Graph) based distributed ledger that offers an absolute light weight CORE that will enable applications to run on Micros sensors, very much needed by IoT devices. IOTA offers huge scalability with a unique consensus schema that will enable more transactions to be handled as the number of participants' increases, with zero mining fees.

IOTA's architecture allows setting up a settlement and transactional network for IOT clusters and a built in transfer layer allowing easy coupling of streams of compensation. With IOTA, Microsoft enables clients to set up one click payment channels for IOT devices, Oracle connectivity to collect and connect live external data as required, and also develop ultra-fast and versatile side chains. To set up a Blockapps STRATO virtual instance of a Blockchain platform in a few minutes, please visit **https://developers.blockapps.net/install/azure/.**

Azure Blockchain Development Kit (https://github.com/Azure-Samples/ Blockchain/tree/master/Blockchain-development-kit)

The **Azure Blockchain Development Kit** is built on Microsoft's server less technologies and seamlessly integrates Blockchain with the best of Microsoft and third-party SaaS.

This kit extends the capabilities of our Blockchain developer templates and **Azure Blockchain Workbench**, which incorporates Azure services for key management, off-chain identity and data, monitoring, and messaging APIs into a reference architecture that can be used to rapidly build Blockchain-based applications.

Azure Blockchain Workbench is far more than UI within client apps. Workbench provides a rich developer scaffold for you to develop and integrate blockchain solutions within your enterprise.

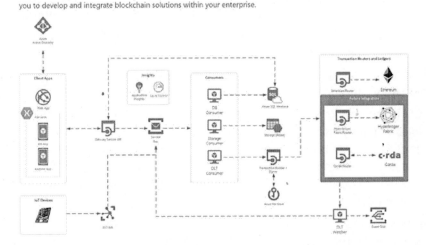

These tools have become the first step for many organizations on their journey to re-invent the way they do business. Apps have been built for everything from **democratizing supply chain financing in Nigeria** to **securing the food supply in the UK**, but as patterns emerged across use cases, our teams identified new ways for Microsoft to help developers go farther, faster.

This initial release prioritizes capabilities related to three key themes: connecting interfaces, integrating data and systems, and deploying smart contracts and

Blockchain networks.

Oracle BAAS https://cloud.oracle.com/en_US/Blockchain:

Oracle offers enterprise Blockchain applications on Hyperledger Fabric platform to enable clients to:

- Provision Blockchain networks
- Join other organizations
- Deploy and run smart contracts to update and query ledger
- Conduct trusted transactions with suppliers & banks
- While integrating seamlessly with existing new cloud based or on-premise applications.

Oracle BAAS enables organization to expand enterprise boundary through trusted dependable, enterprise grade managed platform as a service in a speedy manner with the following features.

Build Trusted Business Networks

Simple Provisioning

Provision a Blockchain cloud service (BCS) instance and get all required infrastructure services as embedded resources: compute, containers, local storage, identity management, object store, network, etc.

Complete Blockchain Platform

Start with a complete, production-ready Blockchain platform based on Hyperledger Fabric, including membership services, peer nodes, ordering service, with Oracle-added REST proxy and operations console tools.

Add Partner Organizations

Add partners locally or in different geographies easily. Provision a new service instance in any supported Oracle Cloud Infrastructure region and complete the guided process to join the new organization.

Hybrid Networks

Join partners running Hyperledger Fabric outside of Oracle Cloud by importing the organization's certificate into an Oracle Blockchain cloud service (BCS) instance.

Integrate Blockchain Transactions in Applications

REST API-driven development

Simplify integrations by invoking transactions running chaincode methods through REST proxies. Use REST APIs to run transactions and queries synchronously and receive a response when transaction commits.

SDK-based Development

Enroll members, add peers, create channels, deploy smart contracts, register for events, and run transactions or query ledger data using Java, GO, or Node.js.

Plug-n-play Integration

Extend Oracle and third-party SaaS and on-prem applications to use Oracle Blockchain Cloud through enterprise application & technology adapters and workflow tools in Oracle Integration Cloud.

Build New Apps

Build new applications or SaaS extensions to running transactions on the Blockchain using Oracle Java, Application Container, Mobile, Application Builder, Integration or SOA Cloud Services.

Leverage OOTB support for Blockchain API

Leverage Blockchain out-of-the-box through the REST APIs in Oracle Digital Innovation Platform for open banking and NetSuite SuiteCloud Platform.

Comprehensive Administration and Monitoring

Intuitive Admin Console

View network status from dashboard or navigate to Network, Nodes, Channels, and Chaincodes tabs to view Blockchain components and manage the network.

Dynamically Change the Configuration

Manage the Blockchain network, peers, orderers and membership service dynamically. Configure network channels and set policies. Deploy or upgrade smart contracts.

Easy Monitoring & Troubleshooting

Monitor peer, orderer, and other network components status and view network topology. View channel and peer metrics, node utilization, browse ledgers and logs for troubleshooting.

Source: https://cloud.oracle.com/en_US/Blockchain/features

Leveraging its strengths in enterprise applications, database technologies, ERP solution and experience in open source technologies, Oracle stands to make rapid strides in the Blockchainification of organizations as a major enabler.

CHAPTER 26

Blockchain Application in Action - Case Study

Humanpower Group

Human power group (HPG), one of the largest third party manpower providers in the world, with over 6 lakh employees across the globe in its payroll, who are placed in various top level companies, mostly Fortune 500, is facing a peculiar situation.

- HPG deals with over 1000 corporates and raises on an average of over 1 lakh invoices every month by tallying them with the timesheets and number of days/ hours worked on the project by each employee and also by verifying with the respective agreements.

- HPG also deals with over 100 consultants across the world through which it sources its manpower for placing with its clients. HPG has to pay to all its vendor partners as per thousands of invoices generated on it.

- HPG has also a direct selection process wherein it conducts walk in interviews and selects professionals on a continuous basis. Lakhs of such persons are employed in its roles and it has to process their salaries.

- HPG also recruits manpower through the various employment portals like Monster, Naukri, and Shine etc.

The following are the serious problems HPG is facing:

Lack of trust from the clients is leading to a rejection of a significant portion of its time-sheet based claims.

1. Inability to connect its claims in time is leading to a huge leakage in its revenues, as it ends up paying to its employees and vendors in time, but gets significantly lower number of hours remunerated from its vendors.

2. It is taking an enormous amount of effort to collate and scrutinize the resumes from the employment portals as most of the resumes are either

   o Duplicated without version control across portals or within portals,

   o A number of the potential recruits have already moved on after posting their resumes but failed to clear their records on the multiple portals.

   o A number of potential recruits, once identified by its recruiters through the employment portals either through direct approach or through classified, have not been found suitable due to a number of factors like mismatch of profiles, integrity of information etc. This has led to an enormous wastage of time and productivity and loss of trust in the Employment portals.

The solution:

Human power management applied the DMADV approach and arrived at the following solutions:

1. Pay bill cycle leakage

A. Hyperledger Fabric based Blockchain implementation with multiple channels between its vendor partners, Clients and itself.

B. Validating and recording transactions between mutual peers, part of the respective channels.

    a. The business logic implemented in the form of chain codes specific to each relation and common front end that triggered respective endorsements as per an automated sequence, ensured that the paper work among all participants is minimized and the chance for disputes are significantly reduced

    b. Ordering service also acts as a common service for all channels acting as a settler to oversee that the differences among the parties are netted and settled in an efficient manner.

2. Wastage due to the Employment portal dependency

Human power group promoted a Decentralised Autonomous Employment exchange using the Hyperledger Sawtooth framework, namely HP-Match for establishing a Peer to Peer connection between corporates and Individuals.

Initially all its branches and group companies across the world were given the nodes and through the smart contract, they were allowed to publish the jobs.

Any new corporate wanting to leverage the network will have a commercial agreement with Human power Group with a license fee for each node.

While all the corporates can directly look up for the candidates as per their requirements, based on the metadata, Individuals with verified credentials have a chance to look up the job postings and directly connect with the companies, The recruiters at the respective companies operated as nodes to act as a bridge between the candidate agents and the other peers in the network.

On the smart contract of Human match launched on the Blockchain, any company can post their jobs along with a suitable revenue reward for the post. All the potential employees and referees of employees can look out for the suitable jobs or gigs. The potential employees represented on the Blockchain through their pseudonyms, can express their interest and interact with the companies directly. The selection process is them conducted off chain and once the process is completed, the respective company should announce closure of the job and the settlement conclusion to the agent.

Designing The Solution

The Blockchain based application that we will be creating for Human Power Group consists of two types of data like in any general Distributed Ledger: They are:

Blockchain: A Chain of Blocks containing the immutable record of transactions involving the company and processes through the application

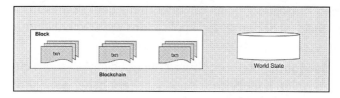

World state: Storing an access controlled and secure data base of the transaction output which may or may not be immutable.

1.   Paybill Cycle With Hyperledger Fabric

Hyperledger Fabric - A great choice for enterprise Blockchain applications:

Hyperledger platform is an opensource project hosted by Linux Foundation to promote cross company collaboration to further Blockchain adoption by leveraging collective strengths, use cases and experiences. IBM is one of the key participants along with Intel, in the development of Hyperledger platform, that offers a number of tools and frameworks required to develop cutting edge Enterprise grade Blockchain applications.

Some of the tools and frameworks offered under the Hyperledger framework are given below:

Tools

(i)   **Hyperledger Explorer:** Enables the administrators and authenticated users to query, view, invoke and deploy chain codes and all relevant network information.

(ii)   **Hyperledger Cello:** Helps in a smooth deployment of Blockchains and enables administrators to create, manage and terminate Blockchains effortlessly.

(iii)   **Hyperledger Composer:** Enables an easy development of smart contracts (chain code) and Blockchain applications as well the deployment of the same across the nodes to create distributed ledgers.

(iv)   **Hyperledger Quilt:** Offers interoperability of data across Distributed and normal ledgers

(v)   **Hyperledger Caliper:** Enables performance tracking of Blockchain impleme-ntations across use cases.

Frameworks

Hyperledger Fabric: A production ready versatile framework contributed mostly by IBM, Hyperledger Fabric offers a modular architecture with plug and play components for managing consensus, membership services to develop use case specific architecture based applications using Go language. The applications or Smart contracts, so developed are called Chain code and are hosted in secure containers offering versatility, scalability and tremendous reliability. For a detailed understanding of Hyperledger Fabric and its design, components, architecture and overall enterprise design, one can refer to the book, Handson Blockchain with Hyperledger- Building decentralized applications with Hyper Fabric and Composer by Nitin Gaur, et al.

Hyperledger Sawtooth: Intel contributed Hyperledger Sawtooth offers a versatile framework to develop both Permissioned and Permission less Blockchains. It uses PoET (Proof of Elapsed Time), as a consensus algorithm that is a variation of POW consensus algorithm offering a high level of economy & efficiency.

Hyperledger Iroha: Hyperledger Iroha is contributed by leading Japanese companies like NTT, Hitachi, Soramitsu etc., and is very much suited for Infrastructure oriented enterprises. It offers a Mobile application amenable design and uses a unique Consensus mechanism by name Sumeragi.

Hyperledger Burrow: Formerly known as ErisDB, Burrow offers a modular Blockchain client with a permissioned smart contract interpreter built in part to the specification of the most Popular Public Blockchain, namely Ethereum Virtual Machine. Thus it enables developers used to working on Ethereum based Blockchain applications using Solidity language, to leverage the strengths of the Hyperledger Project.

Hyperledger Indy: Originally contributed by Sovrin, Indy enables creation and management of decentralized, self-sovereign identities using distributed ledgers. Thus it helps in putting individuals in charge of decisions regarding the privacy and disclosure of any aspects regarding own profiles and identities

Being a part of the open source Hyperledger, ecosystem, Hyperledger Fabric, thus offers the following unique and versatile benefits:

(i) **Modular and Extensible approach:** Hyperledger Fabric offers a completely modular approach that enables architects and developers to use appropriate elements by using different layers for Identity Management (Certificate authority for users and transactions), Chain code, Application integration, Communication and Event Management, Database management, Consensus mechanism etc.

(ii) **Channels:** Hyperledger Fabric offers a unique concept of Channels, that helps in managing confidentiality of transactions and information across various groups of participants. Participants of Channel can share information and transact confidentially among themselves, while nonparties to the Channel will not be able to access the information, not relevant to them as per the application. This offers a huge scalability for enterprise applications, while addressing a key requirement in multi-party transactions.

(iii) **Security:** Hyperledger Project places a paramount importance on Security of the enterprise business networks derived from the lineage and offerings of its contributors like IBM & Intel.

(iv) **Crypto assets:** As required for most enterprise applications, Hyperledger Fabric offers, ability to tokenize assets thus offering a virtual form of various physical assets, but does not use Cryptoassets and Tokens, normally used in Public Blockchains.

(v) **Rich and easy to use APIs:** Hyperledger Fabric offers rich APIs offering the Blockchain systems to access enterprise middleware and other business networks. Hence it is easier to implement Hyperledger Fabric based Blockchain platform for cross enterprise application in a speedy and convenient manner without disturbing the existing operations.

(vi) **Opensource codebase and Vibrant contributing community:** The Opensource nature of the Hyperledger Fabric and a vibrant participating community ensures that the platform is continuously evolving, while it is easy to get resolutions for any runtime problems. This will also enable the participating companies and developers to be updated with the cutting edge technology required for developing and administering their Blockchain environments through continuous training of their teams.

All these and many more features make Hyperledger Fabric, a desirable option for developing Enterprise applications.

Hyperledger Fabric offers a channelized architecture across identified participants and a transaction flow that is simple and efficient for enterprise applications.

Transaction process flow contains the following steps:

(a) Certified users submit the transaction proposals to an application SDK to the Blockchain application.

(b) The proposal is executed by the chaincode and the result is endorsed by all the relevant parties and once the necessary endorsement are obtained, the ordering service accepts the same and delivers to all the parties in the corresponding channel by creating blocks of transactions as per the consensus algorithm.

(c) All the peers in the channel validate the transaction and commit the same to the ledger.

(d) Each peer may participate in multiple channels allowing concurrent execution of many transactions.

These steps can be understood clearly in the case study of Human Power Group, illustrated in this section.

Salient features of the Hyperledger Fabric Architecture

The main components of the Hyperledger Fabric are:

a.   Client- Generates orders and routes to the nearest peer node,

b.   Peers (Normal, endorsing and Committing) –

In the case of Human power group, we need the following:

Peer nodes in each organization, interfacing through a web application with the Blockchain through a Smart contract (also known as a Chain code) a program that captures the business logic, written in Go language.

The complete guide to developers for installing Hyperledger and the necessary dependencies to be able to set up the Hyperledger in your local environments is available at http://hyperledger-fabric.readthedocs.io/en/release-1.1/dev-setup/devenv.html.

A membership service provider that is responsible for all the participants to conduct safe and secure transactions in a confidential manner using their cryptographic identities.

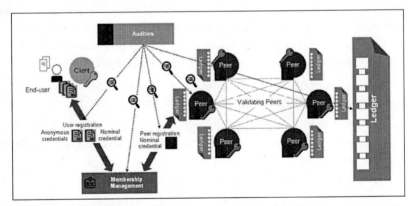

Each peer locally maintains the ledger in the form of the append-only Blockchain and as a snapshot of the most recent state in a key-value store

The clients in each organization generate a transaction and submit through the peer node in their organization.

Each peer node will verify the transaction and submit the output to the other endorsing nodes who verify and endorse the same or reject the same. Once all the endorsers verify the transaction and upon receiving the requisite number of approvals, the transaction generating peer submits the transaction along with the endorsements to the Ordered node application which will create a block of transactions and sends to the validator nodes which will once again verify the transactions. If the entire block is approved, the block is added to the chain and the next set of transactions are taken up by the application.

A high level transaction flow in case of interaction with a single organization is given below:

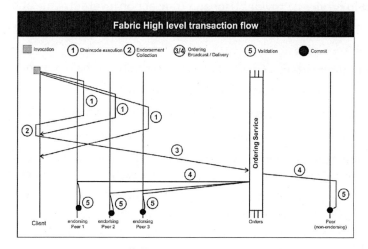

In the case of Human power group we will be creating two channels, one between the admin of the company and the client and another channel between the admin and the consultant. Both the channels will execute their respective smart contracts depicting the respective business logics and will have their own orders; the programs can interact with each other in case of any dependencies reflected by the business logic. For example, approve transaction 1 on receipt of confirmation of transaction in another channel.

Channel 1 depicts the interaction with Client and Channel 2 depicts the interaction of the Human power group with the Consultant.

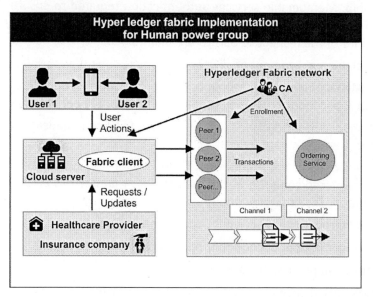

Actors in the Blockchain system

Membership services: Provides User and Transaction level authentication services

Architect: Studies all the processes and prepares an automation plan for migrating to Blockchain

Blockchain Administrator: Overall authority in the Blockchain network

Developer: Develops programs, APIs, Interfaces etc.

Tester: Checks if the program is functioning as per requirement and flags concerns

User: The Transaction generators who input data and communicate all aspects

Network Operator: The Technology Hardware and Software administrators in the respective organizations who take care of the Blockchain related operations.

Traditional Processing Platforms: The existing systems in the organization like CRM, ERP, Data Analytics, Accounting system which will be interacting with the Blockchain application Traditional Data Sources: Data generated from the traditional sources interacting with the application

Components of the Blockchain system

Ledger: State of transactions and current state data of respective channels.

Chain code/ Smart contract: Program to execute transactions as per the embedded business logic in respective channels to modify the assets (state or orders, proforma, disputes, resources etc.).

Peer network: List of interconnected nodes instrumental in executing the business logic and keeping a record of the Blockchain

Membership: Membership services authentication required to ensure that only approved users conduct the transactions and the confidentiality of transactions and identities of the respective parties are maintained.

Wallets: Secure management of all user credentials, their private and public keys.

Systems Management: Management of all IT aspects connected with the Blockchain application across the entire organization and peer network.

Events: Notification alerts of all significant actions to be communicated to relevant parties triggered the smart contract actions

Data Models Used in the Application: Order, Proforma, Invoices and Resources (employees) placed comprise of the data models that need to be considered in the application. They could be described as follows:

- Order Placed, Order Received, From Client, To Consultant
- Proforma raised to Client, Proforma received from Consultant
- Proforma approved, Proforma disputed
- Invoice raised, Invoice received, Invoice paid, Payment received

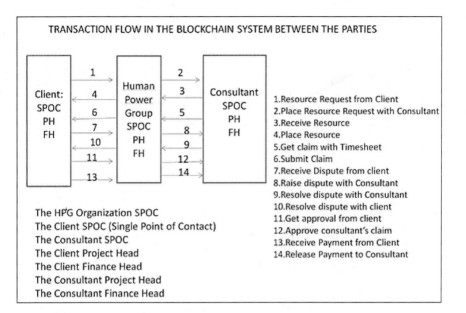

TRANSACTION FLOW IN THE BLOCKCHAIN SYSTEM BETWEEN THE PARTIES

1.Resource Request from Client
2.Place Resource Request with Consultant
3.Receive Resource
4.Place Resource
5.Get claim with Timesheet
6.Submit Claim
7.Receive Dispute from client
8.Raise dispute with Consultant
9.Resolve dispute with Consultant
10.Resolve dispute with client
11.Get approval from client
12.Approve consultant's claim
13.Receive Payment from Client
14.Release Payment to Consultant

The HPG Organization SPOC
The Client SPOC (Single Point of Contact)
The Consultant SPOC
The Client Project Head
The Client Finance Head
The Consultant Project Head
The Consultant Finance Head

The Blockchain representation of these activities once the chaincodes start executing will be added sequentially in the following format of the Blockchain, wherein each element will contact updated values of all data sets.

Block GENESIS	BL OC K-1	BL OC K2	BL OC K3	BL OC K4	BL OC K5	BL OC K6	BL OC K7	BL OC K8	BL OC K9	BLO CK 10	BLO CK 11	BLO CK 12	BLO CK 13	BLO CK 14
STATUS OF TRANSACTIONSREQU ESTS, PLACEMENTS PROFORMAS, DISPUTES, PAYMENTS RECEIPTS														

Once the mapping is done, the access controls for each peer have to be recorded for the development team to implement.

ORGANIZATION	PEER	Resource request	Place request	Resource received	Resource Placed	Claim received	Claim placed	Dispute Received	Dispute Raised status	Payment received	Payment made
HRG	The HPG SPOC	READ	WRITE	READ	WRITE	READ	READ	READ	READ	READ	READ
HRG	HPG Project Head			READ	READ	READ	WRITE	READ	WRITE	READ	READ
HRG	HPG Finance Head			READ	READ	READ	WRITE	READ	READ	READ	WRITE
CLIENT	The Client SPOC (Single Point of Contact)	WRITE			READ		READ	READ		READ	
CLIENT	The Client Project Head				WRITE	READ	READ	WRITE		READ	
CLIENT	The Client Project Head				READ		READ	READ		WRITE	
CONSULTANT	The Consultant SPOC		READ	WRITE		READ			READ		READ
CONSULTANT	The Consultant Project Head			READ		READ			WRITE		READ
CONSULTANT	The Consultant Finance Head			READ		WRITE			READ		WRTE

Write implies Read as well.

The typical Hardware and software requirement of a Hyperledger based Blockchain system is given below:

Hardware

Validating Peers- 8 Xeon core, 32GB RAM,

Application Server- 4 Xeon core, 16GB RAM

Certificate Authentication Server- 4 Xeon core, 16 GB RAM

Software

Operating System- Ubuntu 17.10

Validating peers- Hyperledger Fabric 1.1.0

Application server- Node.js, React, Redux with Fabric Node SDK, Go

The application is then developed by the developers and the contract is migrated to the Hyperledger Blockchain platform with the roles assigned to all the participants managing the platform across the client and the consultant organizations.

The Complete architecture is provided below:

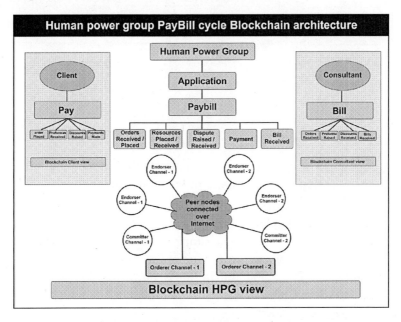

The application is then developed by the developers and the contract is migrated to the Hyperledger Blockchain platform with the roles assigned to all the participants managing the platform across the client and the consultant organizations.

The steps for Deployment, testing scaling and integrating the application are detailed in the Hyperledger developer guides available on the portal,

https://hyperledger.github.io/composer/latest/business-network/business-network-index.

Developers package the models, scripts and access control rules into a deployable Business Network Archive and use command line tools to deploy the archive to a runtime for testing.

Developers use popular JavaScript testing frameworks such as Mocha and Chai to run unit tests (against the Node.js embedded runtime) or run system tests against a Hyperledger Fabric.

Once the business network is tested and in place, front-end applications need to be created. Use the REST Server to automatically generate a REST API for a business network, and then a skeleton generate Angular application using the

Yeoman code generator.

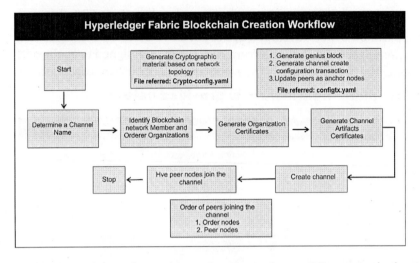

The REST Server can be configured to authenticate the participants in the business network, ensuring that credentials and permissions are enforced.

Hyperledger composer is a useful tool provided by the Hyperledger platform for developers to build and deploy functional are specific smart contracts embedding the respective business logics in a simple and speedy manner. Hyperledger Composer's Playground enables the developers to build user interface for the configuration, test and deploy the business network. The detailed guide for the developers are available at https://hyperledger.github.io/composer/latest/ playground/playground-index.

With this, Human Resource group is now ready to improve the transparency and profitability of its operations while also enabling its partners to become a part of a consortium that can vastly help their performance through automation and by leveraging the programmatic trust offered by the Blockchain technology.

Reducing Dependancy on Employment Portals as Middlemen

The following illustration outlines the steps in designing a Blockchain based application to reduce the dependencies on unreliable employment portals, who charge a lot of money while wasting organizational resources without desired results.

Blockchain Implementation to eliminate redundant job portals & save organisational resources

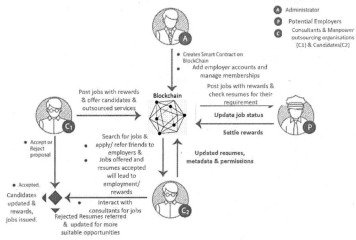

Step 1: Setting up the Sawtooth node

Our simple Sawtooth environment will include a single validator using the dev-mode consensus, a REST API connected to the validator, transaction processors, and a client container.

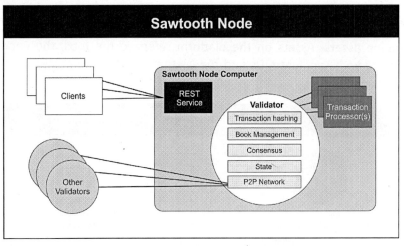

Download the following Docker Compose file as sawtooth:

default.yamlat https://raw.githubusercontent.com/hyperledger/education/master/LFS171x/sawtoot h-material/sawtooth-default.yaml.

In a Blockchain application, the Blockchain will store the state of the system, in addition to the immutable record of transactions that created that state.

A client application will be used to send transactions to the Blockchain. The smart contracts will encode some (if not all) of the business logic.

Here we focus on architecting a solution rather than on programming. Components of a Sawtooth Blockchain:

Transaction validators validate transactions.

Transaction families consist of "a group of operations or transaction types" (Dan Middleton) that are allowed on the shared ledger. Transaction families consist of both transaction processors (the server-side logic) and clients (for use from Web or mobile applications).

The transaction processor provides the server-side business logic that operates on assets within a network.

Transaction batches are clusters of transactions that are either all committed to state, or are all not committed to state.

The network layer is responsible for communicating between validators in a Hyperledger Sawtooth network, including performing initial connectivity, peer discovery, and message handling.

The global state contains the current state of the ledger and a chain of transaction invocations. The state for all transaction families is represented on each validator. The state is split into namespaces, which allow flexibility for transaction family authors to define, share, and reuse global state data between transaction processors.

Step 2: Creating the application

(A) **Define assets**- Assets on the platform refers to the Jobs, the Candidates posted with candidate IDs and the Meta data. Jobs are posted along with their specifications as well as agent remuneration.

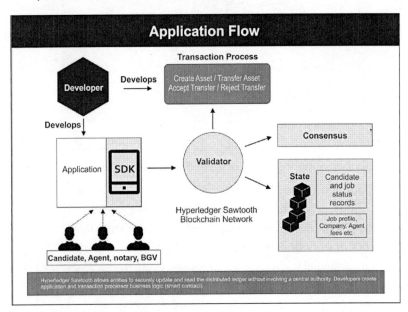

(B) **Transactions**- Transactions are Changes in status of the Candidates as well as the respective Jobs across the various stages of the selection process.

(C) Once the candidate selection is closed, the settlement of the corresponding agent or any other details about the job and candidate ids are recorded in the respective final transaction.

With this, Human Resource group is now ready to improve the transparency and profitability of its operations while also enabling its partners to become a part of a consortium that can vastly help their performance through automation and by leveraging the programmatic trust offered by the Blockchain technology.

CHAPTER 27

Blockchain Use Cases

BLOCKCHAINIFICATION OF THE WORLD - RISK MITIGATION IN THE REAL WORLD

IDENTITY MANAGMENT + DECENTRALISATION + AUTOMATION + CONSENSUS MECHANISM + SHARED LEDGER+ DISINERMEDIATION+ IMMUTABILITY

Offers a killer model for Risk proofing organization and unlimited scalability.

Originally introduced with the use case of a Cryptocurrency, the Blockchain transformed into a platform that facilitated a variety of transactions that mimicked many of the current global leading organizations across various domains while offering certain risk mitigating features.

https://www.cnet.com/news/Blockchain-explained-builds-trust-when-you-need-it-most/

Bitcoin and other cryptocurrencies have been the most overt application of Blockchain technology. However, this technology has many more potential use cases other than cryptocurrencies. In this section, we highlight the most popular Blockchain use cases

As we review the use cases, it is important to review the evolution of Blockchain eco-system:

BLOCKCHAIN 1.0 (PUBLIC BLOCKCHAINS)	2009 Onwards
Cryptocurrency Applications in Cash Crypto currency, transfer, remittance and digital payments Ex: Bitcoin, Litecoin, Monero, Z Cash, Bitcoin cash	
BLOCKCHAIN 2.0 (PUBLIC/CONSORTIUM)	2014 Onwards
Cryptocurrency & Smart Contracts Applications in economy, market, stocks, bonds, futures, loans, mortgages, titles, smart property smart contracts Example: Ethereum, Augur, Ripple, EOS, IOTA, Cardano	
BLOCKCHAIN 3.0 (PUBLIC/PRIVATE/HYBRID/CONSORTIUM)	2017 Onwards

Enterprise & Governance applications Health sciences, Insurance Government Applications

Supply chain, land records

Identity, Records

Hyperledger, BAAS, R3 Corda, Multichain, Quorum, Factom, BigchainDB, FlureeDB

BLOCKCHAIN 4.0 (WORLD OF BLOCKCHAINS)	2018 onwards
Interoperable Blockchain systems	
Communication & Updating across Chains	
COCO Platform (Microsoft)	
AION	
ARK	
COSMOS	

What are the features that make Blockchain so versatile?

Risk mitigation, Dramatic productivity improvement, Secured and encrypted identity management transactions are the critical value additions of the Blockchain Technology

IBM aptly describes Blockchain as 'The Peer to Peer Distributed Ledger Technology for a new generation of transactional applications that provide security, dependability, transparency and streamlined business processes.

By eliminating the single point of failure, anonymizing the identities, automating the process flows, Blockchain promises to disrupt every aspect of our personal lives in a positive manner.

Blockchain will help us manage the increased vulnerability of the world due to the rapidly growing population of Internet devices. By offering a secured access to the IoT gateways and also tilting the risk reward against the cyber criminals and malware perpetrators, Blockchain offers a new paradigm in approaching the future in a secure way.

Some of the biggest use cases of Blockchain are found in Finance, Supply chain, Health care and Pharma.

Banking and Finance:

1.   Capital markets.
2.   Settling of international payments.
3.   Trade financing
4.   Regulatory compliance and auditing
5.   Provision of protection against money laundering.

6.   Insurance.

Peer-to peer-based transactions:

In business, the technology can help facilitate and enhance the following activities:

1.   Streamline supply chain management

2.   Ensure the privacy of healthcare data.

3.   Expedite the selling and purchasing of real estate.

4.   Intellectual property rights.

5.   Improve the regulation, compliance, metering, billing, and clearing processes in the energy sector.

Governments are harnessing Blockchain's power to:

1.   Manage public records and identities

2.   Improve voting exercises

3.   Improve tax collection

The following industries are increasingly adopting Blockchain's underlying technology:

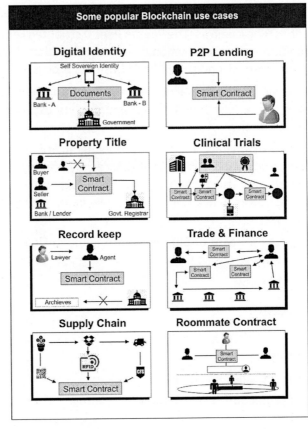

Blockchain offers a tremendous opportunity to manage risks and eliminate unproductive costs and improve the effectiveness of and return on our investments.

The benefits due to the Blockchain can be visualized in the following diagram:

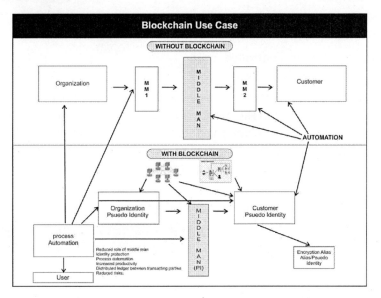

For more than 25 years, we have been used to the LAMP mode of application development and interacting with the web. While scripting languages like PHP are used to writing applications with MySQL databases storing the content served through Apache servers built on Linux.

Open Data Institute (ODI) raised the need for a "Blockchain ecosystem to emerge that mirrored the common LAMP web stack" and was "compatible with the Web we have already."

A typical Blockchain eco-system consists of the following layers:

- Application layer for development of smart contracts

- Data base layer where the data corresponding to the input files is stored

- Storage layer of the application data like IPFS

- DHT layer consisting of the key value pairs that underpin the state of the Blockchain.

- Blockchain data base that stores the blocks with transaction details, linked to each other in a chain

- A storage layer that consists of all the Distributed applications that run on the platform

- A network of nodes that transact with each other in a peer to peer manner that store all the blocks of the Blockchain.

The databases are generally characterized by the following:

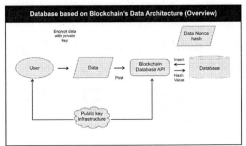

(a) All data is stored within itself or links to an external location

(b) Database is centralized or distributed or replicated

(c) Access to data is controlled or open to everyone.

The data in Public Blockchains is open to all while the access to conducting transactions are restricted to the participants with Public and Private Keys. While Blockchains generally provide option to store data in the form of words or in any other format, it is prohibitively expensive to store data in the Blockchains as it will increase the storage and processing requirement manifold due to the replication across all the nodes.

For example, a comparison of the cost of storage of 1 GB of data done in July 2017 is given as follows:

In contrast, data stored in Distributed data bases on the cloud like IPDB with replication factor of 6times is approximately 100 US dollars for the life time.

Protocol	Storage Cost per GB
Bitcoin	$ 22,766,250
Ethereum	$ 4,672,500

Hence Blockchains are best suited for only storing key value pairs and the most basis information needed while the rest of the data is stored externally using technologies like IPFS / Storm to convert the same to hash values and the hash values are reference in the applications.

Ethereum uses Swarm to store the De-centralised applications (DAPPS).

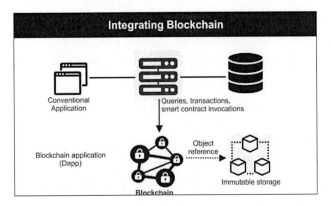

Thus, IPFS & SWARM have allowed the organizations to overcome the limitations of storing and processing the information contained in large files in a cost-effective manner.

Blockchain database consists of distributed hash tables, a mechanism used for indexing and distributing files in a Peer to Peer network, storing only the location(s) of a file along with a hash value (a unique reference that is the sum of the contents of the file). The hash value stored in the database can then be compared with that of the external file in order to qualify the integrity of the external file along with the Timestamp giving the chronological details of the file from creation to the time it was last accessed.

With a strong identity management system, smart contracts for automating business logic specific application, front end interfaces to interact with the smart contracts and an immense storage and versatile database handling capacity provided by IPFS, IPDB, SWARM, BigChain DB, Fluree an unlimited ability to scale the nodes across the world using cloud, the Blockchains are now enabled to handle versatile applications across industry in a scalable and cost effective manner.

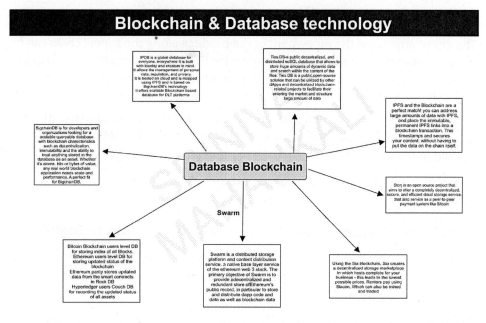

One of the biggest use cases is to track the ownership of goods across the supply chain as they move from one owner/ holder to another along with the recording of the various parameters registered using IOT devices and the timestamp every event triggered.

In Pharmaceutical it is now possible to track the movement of the medicine strip across the value chain from the manufacture to the last distribution point proving the source and differentiating it from a fake.

Similarly, in agriculture, the crop produce can be tracked from farm to fork, ensuring along the way using the IoT technology to monitor storage conditions like temperature etc. to ensure that it is not spoilt on the way.

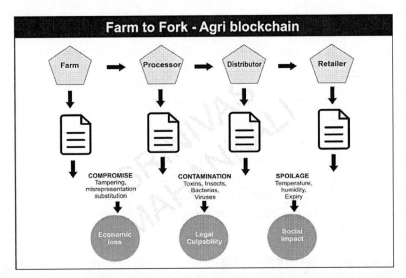

The entire process of the movement of the produce along the supply chain can be mapped, automated and tracked by leveraging IOT and Blockchain technologies to ensure that the spoilages & wastages are minimized, contamination is controlled and also tracked to the farm that produces the crop, in case required.

The perfections of the process using methodologies like Lean Six sigma, eliminates non value adding middle entities, ensuring maximum profitability to the farmers leading to their prosperity.

Source: https://www.ibm.com/blogs/internet-of-things/iot-Blockchain-use-cases/

World food Program's Aid disbursements to Syrian Refugees

World food program (WFP) has created a private Blockchain fork of Ethereum with the help of an engineering firm Parity and is transferring the aid to the Syrian refugees directly through Blockchain.

Before

World food program used to provide vouchers on account of aid provided to the refugees, which they used to encash in the retail outlets and supermarkets against their purchases. This amounted to huge leakages on account of wrong voucher submissions, bank charge and time delays.

Now

With the help of the Blockchain, the refugees are provided accounts on the Blockchain, identified by their scanned image of their Iris. Now, upon purchasing any items at the supermarkets, the refugees are identified by iris scanners by the supermarket staff and the due amounts debited to the World food program are credited to the supermarkets on account of the respective refugee's account.

This has saved the WFP over 98% in bank and other financial charges and now, they have a plan to spread it to refugees across all the regions over a variety of services.

Trade finance on Blockchain
Current situation

Companies request credit from Banks and finance companies for

- Working capital,
- Manufacturing costs,
- Temporary spurts in demand etc.

For this, they provide extensive documentation to the banks leading to high costs and also payments to intermediaries for facilitating documentation, relationships, contacts and other logistical issues.

With the help of Blockchain the companies can directly transact with the banks in a safe and secure manner with very limited paper work in a high trust environment.

Post Blockchain Implementation

The use of Blockchain technology enables with the following aspects:

a. Reduction in transaction costs due to elimination of middlemen.

b. Trust through system as all the transactions are recorded immutably on a distributed ledger, with established identities and time stamped for recording and monitoring.

c. Transparency and elimination of duplicity or mistakes in the invoices as all the records are managed through a streamlined process and verified formats that are encoded into the system.

d. All the parties can now operate in a safe and efficient environment, devoid of human dependencies.

Supply chain transactions between Manufactures and Distributors

Manufacturers of Consumer products undertake large scale distribution through a vast network of distributors and resellers.

Most often it becomes difficult to coordinate the billing and cash collection cycle due to skewed demands and supply patterns and limitation in manpower availability

Problems with the current system:

- Lack of trust between manufacturers and distributors resulting in delayed invoicing and payment cycles.
- High level of paper work leading to lot of unnecessary time delays and

expenses.

- Huge pressure on sales persons to reach targets resulting in excessive dumping at times and inordinate delays in payment.

- Distributors rotating their money among various manufacturers leading to work capital withdrawal from the business to fund other interests leading to working capital crunch.

Blockchain based supply chain management system offers the following:

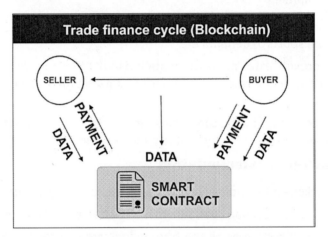

- Smart contract to automate the process of invoicing, dispatch , recording of end to end transaction

- Smart contract to interact with other applications like Production planning, ERP , CRM, analytics and other organizational systems to enable fine tuning of demand planning and product procurement/ manufacturing cycle to stream line operations.

- Reduced dependency on manual interventions to reduce relationship based requests and decisions causing delays in payment cycles

- Tamper evident and timestamped records to help monitor the trends of order-supply-dispatch-delivery-payment cycle and help in reducing the order to cash cycle through streamlined operations and reduction in working capital requirement

- Reduction in friction due to automation led management of issues causing friction like invoicing and money collection.

Cross Border Remittance

Cross border remittance is often a time-consuming process as it involves multiple countries, multiple banks and multiple regulatory and non-regulatory agencies. This result in

- Delays

- At times a lot of documentation
- High transaction charges across the various parties.

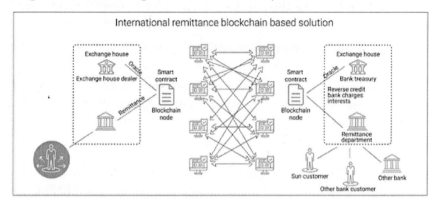

A Blockchain connecting all the interested parties as nodes in wither side of the border and also the regulatory agencies as the participants can speed up the process significantly taking care of all these issues. However, the concerned financial organization serving as the intermediary must be in tune with the regulatory environment to avoid any legal issues in the future.

A R3 Cords based distributed ledger system with a trusted third party based notary offers the best solution for a Blockchain application. The solution offers the following benefits:

A.   The details of the customer transferring the money and the one receiving money can be cryptographically encoded to ensure that their details will be confidential and known only to the relevant parties on a must/ already know basis.

B.   Instantaneous transfer of money through smart contract operation.

C.   Reduced transaction fees by cutting down on irrelevant intermediaries.

Bill Discounting

Invoice discounting is very often undertaken by medium and small scale industries dealing with large credit worthy organizations.

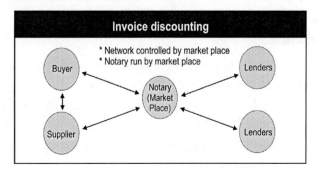

The process involves a lot of documentation and time consuming procedure. Since it involves a lack of trust between the borrowers and

lenders, Blockchain can offer the best solution by offering trust through the smart contract and cutting down a number of mediators between the parties.

R3 Corda offers an appropriate solution with a node to node secured and verifiable transaction.

The solution involves a trusted notary operated by a regulated and accredited entity who can ensure transaction sanctity without intruding into the confidentiality of the transactions.

Medical Records

Estonia, one of the smallest companies in the world, has digitized medical records of all its population and the same are uploaded onto the Blockchain on a live basis.

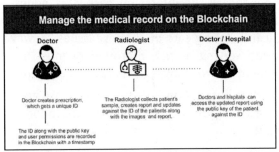

This enables doctors to have verifiable, tamper evident medical records of the patients with the entire history of the diagnostic tests etc., to offer right prescription.

Step 1: The radiologist and doctor update the record on the Blockchain to the patient's account.

Step 2: For more information and detailed working of Medical record Blockchain, please refer, https://medicalchain.com/en/whitepaper/

The patient uses his mobile device to access the information and also to provide the permission to the healthcare provider to access the health data for appropriate treatment.

Health Insurance

Singapore Government has implemented Blockchain based medical insurance for a certain segment of its population as a pilot.

An Ethereum based private Blockchain is implemented to connect the health insurance providers, hospitals and banks.

When a patient in a given risk category signs up for an insurance plan, the details of the concerned are recorded on the Blockchain.

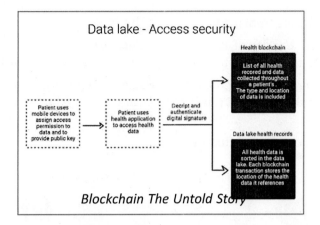

In case the patient needs to avail the insurance and undergoes the corresponding procedures, the smart contract gets triggered and the money is transferred from the insurance company to the hospital within 24 hours to clear the bills raised on the patient.

This has substantially eased the pain points of the patients who many times are not sure about the recoverability and settlement of their claims.

The following are some of the use cases emerging in the insurance domain.

- Automated comprehensive background and authenticity verification of all things insured

- Automated claim handling and settlement,

- Eliminate insurance fraud due to transparent recording and immutable data sets registered on the Blockchain that removes the propensity to defraud the insurance companies with inflated and multiple claims

- Automated settlement of Insurance for all IOT devices effective tracking on the Blockchain through smart contracts that get triggered on impacting events.

Supply Chain Management on Blockchain

Supply chain Management has emerged as the biggest potential user application for the Blockchain Technology. The following are some of the use cases being actively pursued by the Supply chain industry:

- Cross border transportation of goods

- Tracking the movement of automobile spare parts to ensure their originality at the service station

- Testing the purity of diamonds by tracking their movement across the supply chain from source to the ultimate consumer

- Ensuring the genuinity of medicines at the ultimate retail point at the time of purchase by consumer by recording in a verifiable manner, the movement of the medicine from manufacturer to the chemist shop

- Farm to fork tracking of agricultural produce to ensure optimal conditions for transportation and also traceability in case of any quality issues

- Tracking of refrigerated goods by recording the temperature across the value chain with the help of IOT devices to ensure they are not spoiled on the way etc.

An example use case is depicted below:

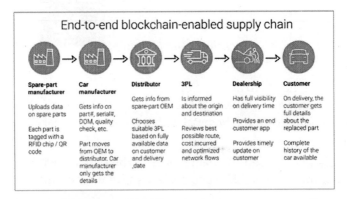

Classified and Ecommerce Exchanges

Blockchain offers an excellent platform for peer to peer exchange of a number of goods and services like automobiles, houses, rentals and educational services etc., which are handled by large Ecommerce organizations today. Blockchain enables the users to securely and pseudonymously trade any goods by minimizing the intervention of the centralised management prevalent today. In view of the impending regulations and the emerging Blockchain influenced decentralised environment, it is imperative that organizations in these businesses modify their business models to ensure they respect the privacy needs of the platform users and increase automation.

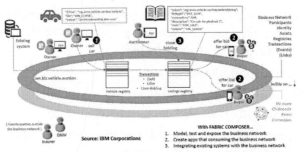

A Car exchange portal modelled on a Blockchain with Hyperledger Fabric

Energy trading is another opportunity that is increasingly viewed at for Blockchain adaption.

The producers of energy will be able to confidently trade their excess produce with the consumers in need of the same. Smart contracts can provide for listing, discovery, trading, settlement of all transactions pertaining to energy trading among the generators and users.

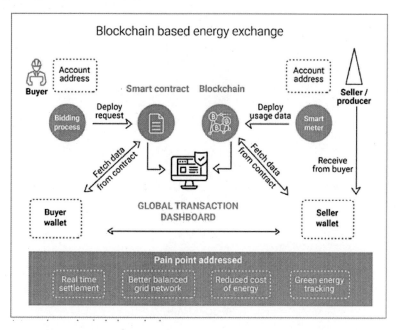

Education is another area that is emerging as a potential Blockchain use case.

Students can safely and securely store all their information in a public Blockchain.

Teachers and students can discover each other and offer peer to peer training and educational services as well.

Background verification and Identity management can be integrated into the Blockchain platform for educational resources and interactions.

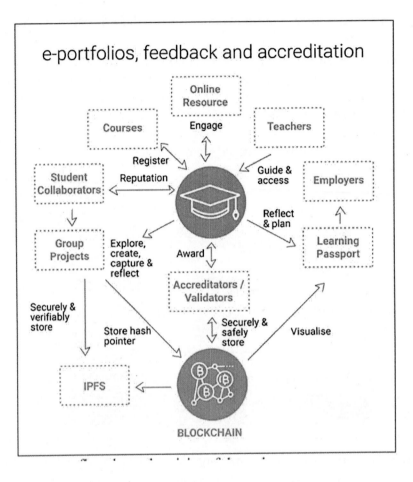

CHAPTER 28

Blockchainified Future - A Vision for Progressive Enterprises

Roadmap for Centralised Organizations for Blockchainification

The rapidly evolving dynamics of an increasingly tech enabled world is shaking the very foundations of the industry today. Where big was better and holding big data was a competitive advantage, the same are going to be perceived as an area of weakness.

While the penetration of Artificial Intelligence & Machine learning is leading to the increasing use of bots and reduced use of manual labour for repetitive tasks, the onus of safeguarding the information of vast number of people and also employing them in a productive fashion is making the organizations increasingly scout for reskilling opportunities and innovative entrepreneurial initiatives. Blockchain, by its very nature is an entrepreneurship fueling new age paradigm. The number of nimble and innovative organizations that have been created in the past 3 years in this domain is mind boggling.

The increasing threat of malware and cyberattacks is making centralised organizations shudder at the demolition of their 'Single point of failure. Risk is better managed through the example set by the Blockchain of increased decentralization, following open source technologies and leveraging SAAS based business models, rather than undertaking large asset investment programs.

Organizations can no more rely on the same business model of 'Big is Better' and should adopt the stance of micro organizations doing multiple things in a coordinated fashion.

The Blockchainified organization today is an organization which is participating in many activities in a safe, secure and nimble manner.

It can avail the services of a Public Blockchain, float a Private Blockchain, be a part of a consortium and also be a promoter of many Decentralised Autonomous organizations.

The increased penetration of IOT devices has resulted in an associated increase in vulnerability as reflected in the DDOS attack of October 2016 by Mirai botnet on a mere 1lakh devices.

The use of Blockchain for securing the IoT devices is another giant step forward for the mankind in effectively managing the risk in the future.

Given that in future automation is going to result in a 30-40% reduction in manpower and the number of robots, chat bot and connected devices is going to be 4 to 5 times the strength of the human beings in an organization, any vulnerability that is not addressed comprehensively would demolish an organization from the roots.

A number of world's leading companies including Cisco, Intel, IBM, Huawei, Hitachi, have been doing a great amount of work on strengthening the security of IOT devices.

In mid-October, the U.S. Patent and Trademark Office published U.S. Patent Application 20170302663, titled 'Blockchain Based IoT Device Identity Verification and Anomaly Detection' ,and assigned to San Jose, CA-based networking firm Cisco Systems (NASDAQ:CSCO). It discloses a method of receiving a network registration request from a particular node that includes information about that node, validating that node's information via comparison to a distributed Blockchain, causing an update to the Blockchain based on the node's information and using the updated Blockchain to control the behavior of the particular node and one or more other nodes. The resulting invention improves the authentication of devices operating on an Internet of Things (IoT) platform, which may have different authentication or registration while also detecting anomalies in device. Cisco announced that it was joining a consortium known as the Trusted IoT Alliance featuring a collection of 17 companies working towards a protocol for Blockchain-based IoT platforms.

How much ever insignificant this may seem, this is an important step in a world that is going to be deluged by IoT devices and securing them by leveraging the Blockchain technology is an imperative for us.

As we see the launch of more and more such platforms for different applications, we are increasingly faced with the world of many Blockchains.

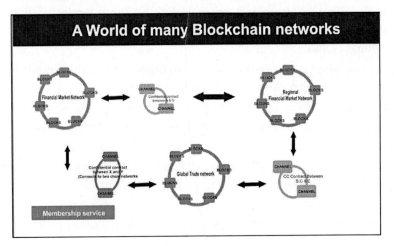

Many Blockchain platforms like Hyperledger Fabric, Cosmos, Ark, Ardor, Lisk, COCO platforms are offering the ability to create multiple channels, interconnected Blockchains or interconnect existing Blockchains.

Many Blockchain as a service platforms like IBM LinuxONE, Oracle BAAS, Huawei BCS, Amazon BAAS, Azure BAAS allow us not only to set up Blockchain applications quickly, but also enable us to integrate seamlessly with the existing legacy options.

Technologies like IPFS, Swarm and Big Data scale databases with Blockchain characteristics like BigChainDB, FlureeDB are enabling us to manage the rapidly evolving scale of replicated databases created during the Blockchain operations.

A typical centralised organization interacting with its peers and the ecosystem of vendors, customers, partners can be depicted in a simple way as per the following diagram:

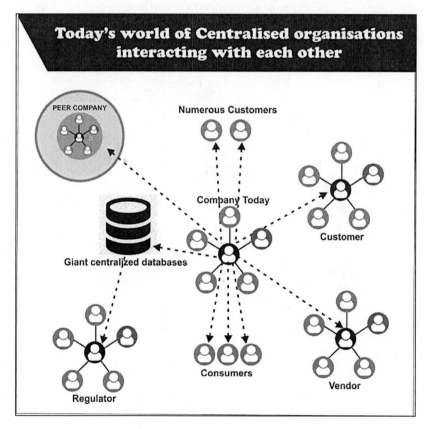

Blockchainified organizations of tomorrow could well look like:

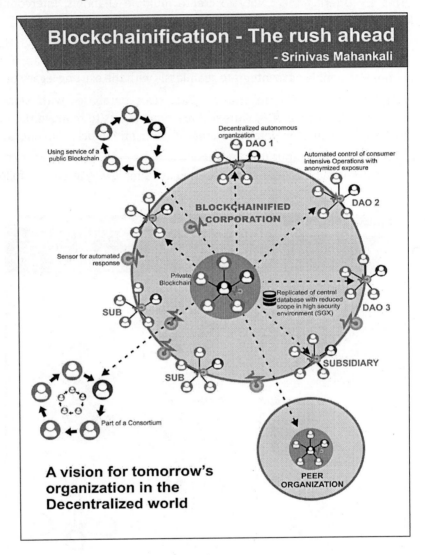

CHAPTER 29

Maneuvering in the World of GDPR

Secured Identity Management an imperative in the regime of GDPR

With the advent of advanced technologies like Artificial Intelligence like Big Data Analytics, Artificial Intelligence and Machine Learning, large companies like Google, Amazon, Facebook, Netflix and the like, have got substantial lead in the market place by leveraging these technologies and adopting predictive and prescriptive analysis to push the sales of their products and services. The recent malware attacks and data leakages as experienced in the Facebook issue, where data of over 87 million American citizens is unscrupulously compromised brought the issue of control of one's own identity to the fore.

European Union is set to implement the Global Data Protection regulation with respect to the personal data of the European Union citizens living across the world. These regulations have to be implemented by companies dealing with the EU citizens, irrespective of the country of their origin and noncompliance can lead to substantial fines and penalties.

However, these rules have been framed by taking into consideration, the centralised operations of the companies in the traditional way and need to be interpreted appropriately for records on the Decentralised and Distributed ledger Technologies like Blockchain. There are still a lot of grey areas with respect to implementation of GDPR for DLT based systems. European Union is conscious of the fact that the Blockchain Technology results in a huge movement towards application of innovation, process improvement and risk. EU wants to tread a cautious path to ensure that the Data privacy laws and the need to foster innovation are balanced at the same time.

The responsibility of adhering to the GDPR guidelines with respect to the data collected by the entities have to be taken care by identified Data Controllers. The responsibilities involve providing the appropriate information to the customers regarding

- Processing & Usage of the data
- Porting the data to other companies if requested
- Right to be forgotten or erasure of data if required by the subject

The controller has to ensure that the data is used as per strict guidelines and mutual agreement

The European GDPR regulations expected to be implemented from May 2018, propose to allow the individual's control of one's own data and also allow free transfer of data from one controller to the other, offer the following action insights/ action points:

- Every company that handles an individual's personal data has to take a number of actions with respect to the usage, storage and processing of the same.

- The subject whose data is being collected should have a complete visibility of the usage of the data by the company.

- In case of public permission less distributed ledger technologies, it is not clear as to who will be made accountable for the data on the Blockchain as it is freely available to everyone.

- The use of pseudonyms in Blockchain does not take the private data out of the purview of the GDPR as the data can still be linked to the corresponding subject.

- Since immutability of the data is a key feature of Blockchain and the data is supposed to be erasable, it is important for the creators of Permissioned Blockchain or any Public applications with identifiable Data Controllers to adequately ensure the encryption of the data so that no personal data is stored on the Blockchain.

- Hashing and storing the Public key and hashing the Meta data of the subjects and storing the personal data in data bases off chain with adequate replication and security, while storing the pointers in the Blockchain appears to be the best solution to the Blockchain Platform developers.

- This has huge implications for businesses holding huge personal data of consumers and non-consumers collected through a number of means over a wide period like:
  (i)   Finance companies
  (ii) Employment portals
  (iii) Social media portal
  (iv) HR consultants
  (v)   Exchanges of various types (ex: classified portals)
  (vi) IoT data processors
  (vii) Mobile platforms offering conveyance, boarding, lodging etc. And the list goes on...

These portals have been collecting the consumer data and monetizing them in a number of ways.

Blockchain facilitates the concept of Self Sovereign Identity of an individual that offers him control over his/her personal data.

In future, portals offering the above services will not only be required to take the permission from the individuals using their platforms with appropriate disclaimers, but also have to look at sharing the revenue earned by monetizing the same. There are a number of Blockchain enabled Peer to peer applications to empower and reward the users for using their platforms aimed at offering similar services.

Self Soverign Identity

Accenture and Microsoft's ID 2020 offers to enable the creation of a Self-sovereign identity for the global citizens.

The Accenture prototype is designed to interoperate with existing identity systems so that personally identifiable information always resides "off chain." It aligns to principles of the Decentralized Identity Foundation, of which Microsoft is a founding member, and uses the Enterprise Ethereum Alliance's private, or "permissioned," Blockchain protocol.

To solve problems faced by people who lack official identities face, Accenture will leverage its Unique Identity Service Platform to deploy a breakthrough biometrics system that can manage fingerprints, iris and other data. For example, the technology can provide undocumented refugees with a steadfast personal identity record, ensuring that they can receive assistance where and when they need it. The Accenture Platform is the heart of the Biometric Identity Management System currently used by the United Nations High Commissioner for Refugees, which has enrolled more than 1.3 million refugees in 29 countries across Asia, Africa and the Caribbean. The system is expected to support more than 7 million refugees from 75 countries by 2020, (Source Accenture News release https://newsroom. accenture.com/news/accenture-microsoft-create-Blockchain-solution-to-support-id2020. htm).

Today the consumers are dealing with a variety of parties:

The user creates a user name and password with all these entities and these centralised organizations then have complete control of access and information.

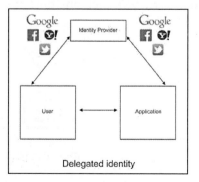

Delegated identity

The centralised providers not only can cut off access details but also share the same with any other third parties and applications and monetize the same, while the user does not get any returns.

The user is interacting with different types of parties who need different versions of his identity to verify 'Who they are dealing with'.

For example, financial institutions, educational institutions, social media & employers require different types of information for different needs

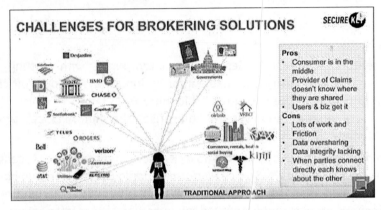

Secure Key is an exciting Canadian Identity Solutions company working closely with IBM.

Further, in the traditional approach, the user holds the key to all types of accounts in a potentially insecure manner and in a way ends up being a single point of failure. Using Blockchain, the consumer can create a self-sovereign identity, that is controlled by him and he can authenticate himself through the Blockchain in a safe and secure manner.

In the current system, KYC is conducted by the respective organizations needing the identity of the user by contacting the information providers in multiple ways and multiple times. It is time consuming and repetitive process for the individuals and all the organizations.

To circumvent this, the identity of the user is digitalized using all the documents and physically verified one time and stored on a Blockchain.

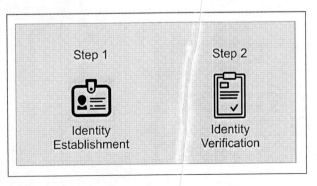

Once the identity verification is done, a user interface is created for the individual with a wallet and any institution needing access to the information of the user can obtain through the Blockchain.

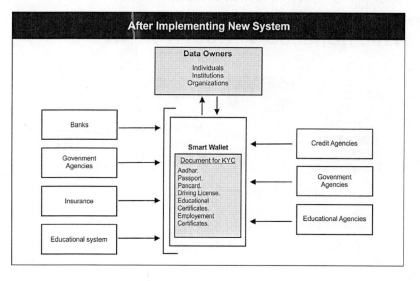

Thus a digital identity of the Blockchain is created and the access as required can be issued to the requisite party to verify the individual. IBM is building an identity verification platform on Hyperledger and is in the process of enrolling all the banks, financial institutions, government agencies to be a part of the system so as to seamlessly offer Blockchain enabled safe and secure Identity management services to all the citizens across the world, thus enabling them to control the access to their own identity.

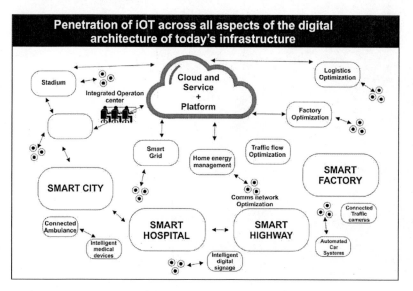

Once the identity is enabled on the Blockchain, the user will be able to sign in through his mobile with his private key and will be able to provide the access to the bank for the requisite information as illustrated below:

CHAPTER 30

A Safer and Secure World With Blockchain Based Solutions

Changing face of the new workforce - Makes Blockchainification -- a Must!

"I had 1000 employees last year. Next year I am targeting 800 humans, 25 robots, 10 chat bots and a 1000 connected things", Could well be the outlook of a 'Human Resource Head' in a thriving company of the future!

It is not just the organizations; the 'Bot' revolution is going to permeate every segment of our infrastructure. If the vision of global leaders like #Cisco has to be noted, connected devices are a part and parcel of every piece of our future landscape cutting across organizations, cities, functional areas and services, which is why, Cisco calls it, IOE, or Internet of Everything.

Cisco's Patent application 20170302663, "Blockchain Based IoT Things] Device Identity Verification and Anomaly Detection."

That enables a #Blockchain based system record changes to the conditions affecting and captured by sensors (i.e., smart objects) in a network and instrument network relationships and the data that the network generates in order to exercise control over those node, is one of the many patents filed to integrate IOT devices into the Blockchain eco-system. The need of the hour as we employ edge enabled devices, Fog computing to empower the once dumb IoT devices to do what they are supposed to do and not something dangerous!

It was in 1990 that John Romkey and Simon Hackett created the world's first connected device (other than a computer) in the form of a toaster connected to the internet, giving rise to the birth of Internet of Things. The world has come a long way since and as per the latest Spending Guide, IDC predicts that by 2021, global IoT spending is expected to total nearly $1.4Trillion in hardware, software, services, and connectivity that enable the IoT.

More importantly, by 2020, 25% of Enterprise attacks are projected to involve IoT, with 10% of overall security budgets allocated to IoT & over 50% of IoT implementations using Cloud security.

The October 2016 Mirai bot attack that infected unsecured internet of things (IoT) devices, like DVRs and IP cameras exposed the increased vulnerability of the centralised corporations depending more on the burgeoning number of Internet of Things. If the changing landscape of the workforce composition in today's companies, it is imperative to think Blockchain as one of the important paradigm to embed to secure your future! IBM & Samsung's ADEPT platform (Autonomous Decentralized Platform for Telemetry) is one of the landmark initiatives for securing the growing population of the IOT devices which is supposed to cross 10 times of the connected human beings in the next 2-3 years!

While the capability of the IoT devices is being vastly upgraded with the onset technologies like Edge, Fog and Mist computing, a strong identity management coupled with the decentralised approach of Blockchain Technology will help us secure the burgeoning IOT penetration and insure the safety of these networks.

Blockchain and Cybersecurity

Cybercrime is indeed growing exponentially. It is indeed a matter of common knowledge that the industry leaders across domains, Yahoo, Google, Sony, Equifax, Sears, Dropbox, Microsoft to name a few, have been subjected to malware attacks in the recent past.

Blockchain offers a tremendous scope for improvement in security of transactions and data management over the traditional approach of conducting digital transactions using unique identity management protocols in both Private and Public versions.

While understanding the security aspects of Blockchain transactions it is imperative for us to examine not only the security offered through Blockchain based approach, but also the security precautions to be taken to ensure security of Blockchain system itself.

Most of the malware attacks are implemented by masked identities, hoodwinking systems to gain access through camouflaged identities.

Blockchain led systems use cryptographic techniques to offer several layers of additional security to participants and transactions.

The important aspects of identity management for secure transactions already discussed elsewhere in the book are as follows:

(a) **Public Key infrastructure (PKI):** In the digital world, real people are identified by digital identities represented by a pair of cryptographic keys namely,

 Public key, which is known to everyone and a **Private Key**, which is kept a secret. A combination of Public and Private key of transacting and/or authenticating parties enables the participants of a transaction to conduct their dealings in a secure manner.

(b) **Cryptographic Hash Function:** A hash function can be used in cryptographic applications if it is collision resistant. It is said to be collision resistant if it is hard to find two inputs that **hash** to the same output; that is, two inputs a and b such that H(a) = H(b), and a ≠ b. SHA 256 used in most Blockchain applications is an example of Collision resistant Hash function.

(c) **ECDSA generated Digital Signatures:** Elliptical curve Digital Signature algorithm (ECDSA) is a Digital signature scheme i.e., an asymmetric cryptographic scheme for producing and verifying digital signatures.

Most of the public and private Blockchain platforms use ECDSA scheme for producing and verifying the digital signatures for their transactions.

(d) **Certification Authorities (CA):** A Certificate authority or Certification authority (CA) is a trusted entity that issues digital certificates certifying the ownership of a public key by the named subject of the Certificate. This is an essential part of a PKI infrastructure. X.509, is a widespread standard to manage certification.

For example, in Hyperledger Fabric 1.1, the Certificate authority managing member identities issues X.509 certificates to its members.

In the traditional digital world, mutually untrusted partners communicate through a centralised system with the help of these digital certificates issued by centralised authorities to different websites and portals.

However, there have been increasing cases of Certification authorities being attacked.

There have been several cases of fake digital certificates for famous publishers like Google issued by reputed Certification authorities like Gogo (Inflight internet service) and Symantec etc., while fake certificates used to target users of reputed banks to direct them to fake versions of their banks' sites.

In the case of Private Blockchains, the Certification authorities and the administrators need to take utmost precaution in identifying genuine participants through issues, identifying and revoking the certificates as the case may be appropriately. In the case of Public Blockchains, in 2016, Sead Muftic proposed a Blockchain based protocol that allows distribution and management of digital certificates (linking a subject with its Public key) without the need of Certificate authorities by offering BIX(Blockchain

Information Exchange) certificates maintained in BCL (Bix certificate Ledger). These can replace the system of X.509 certificates offered by Centralised authorities.

Properly managed identities and deployment of Byzantine fault tolerant consensus mechanisms ensures that the decentralised systems characterizing the Blockchain landscape are fault tolerant, attack resistant and collision resistant as they do not have the sensitive single central points of failure and also, it is almost impossible for malicious participants to come together and act against the interests of the other genuine participants, unlike in centralised corporations with single points of failure and power concertation in a central authority.

However, there are certain limitations that are inherent to the Blockchain platforms that needs to be looked at:

(a) The implementation of the consensus mechanism for arriving at the decision is contingent upon the opinion of the majority. Hence it is possible for majority to collude and manipulate decisions making a 51% attack feasible.

(b) Where there are a smaller number of participants in the Blockchain, that generally happens in enterprise Blockchains, closed groups or newly launched public platforms, the security is limited or missing at times.

(c) The Private key management is vulnerable to thefts and hence exploitable.

The trust in the Blockchain relies on the safekeeping of the private keys for a truly distributed identity management. Hence the cryptocurrency & token investors in the case of public Blockchains and cryptoasset based platforms and the node administrators in the case of private Blockchain should ensure adequate measures to record and store their private keys in a secure manner. Care should be taken that only authenticated users are able to transact on the respective platforms.

(d) Weakness in software implementation may compromise entire system. There have been a number of cases where smart contracts and chain codes have been exploited to the detriment of the participants in the Decentralised Applications. In the case of The DAO, the first Decentralised application launched on the Ethereum platform, about 50 million US Dollar (3.6million Ether) worth of tokens were syphoned off the organization through a bug that caused a recursive loop to remit the currency units to an attacker's account. (reference: https://en.wikipedia.org/wiki/The_ DAO_(organization))

(e) Blockchain's cryptographic techniques may assure the immutability of the ledger, but not that of the overall system. For example, there have been numerous attacks on the paraphernalia surrounding the Blockchain platform like exchanges, wallets etc.

(f) Blockchain aims at digitizing real world assets to enable a safe and secure exchange through implementation of smart contracts. The physical world data can be manipulated before being digitized.

Let us have a look at the typical malware attacks and see how the Blockchains manage the same:

(1) **Spoofing:** This involves use of a token or other credential information to pretend to be an authorized user of the platform. Many forms of attack like Sybil, Malware, Credential stuffing, Man in the middle (MITM) attacks involve the users being misled to fake sites or non-users gaining access to user's credential to transact on the system.

Hence key management and identity tracking through the operation are an important part of the security offered by the Blockchain system. Protocols like BIX protocol enable the correct identification of users and in enterprise applications, each user is provided a X.509 digital certificate that identifies and tracks his transactions. If any spurious transactions are detected that go against the interests of the participants, the identified participants are immediately rusticated from the system.

(2) **DDOS (Distributed Denial of Service attacks):** DDOS attacks are executed by botnets that compromise the identity of connected systems and use the same to flood targeted websites with unmanageable traffic, forcing their shut down. Strong identity management and access controls provided at each node, ensured that unauthorized participants cannot compromise and gain access to the connectivity of the compromised system, thus preventing the attack. Companies like Guardtime from Estonia are working on offering a Blockchain enabled system offering an additional bandwidth from connected peers, at times of increased load owing to such attacks, thus enabling them to see of the burden without a shut down.

(3) **Ransomware attacks:** Ransomware attacks involve the blocking of access to an institution to one's own data by the attackers. The distributed nature of the ledger in a Blockchain, such an attack improbable and ineffective as the attacker has to attack all the ledgers distributed across the system at the same time. Elimination of the Singe point of Contact and the replication of data effectively disincentivises the developers and perpetrators of Ransomware.

(4) **Tampering and Repudiation:** The improbability of the ledger manipulation ensures that the contents of the ledger are neither tamper able nor denied by a participant without leaving a trace of the credentials of those attempting the same. Hence Blockchain can be considered tamper evident, immutable platform and only way in which these can be done is by passing reversal/ modification transactions through subsequent approved transactions.

(5) **Information Disclosure:** In public Blockchains, the transactions are open for anyone to query, the identity of the participants is protected using pseudonyms or other appropriate programs in case of Blockchains offering anonymous transactions. In case of Private Blockchains, the transactions are protected cryptographically so that only authorized participants can view data relevant to them, by using their private keys. Further any entity or participant can only access the data that is programmatically approved by the access control mechanism approved by the administrators of the network. Any modification in access privileges must be authorized and approved by the authorities mentioned in the program.

Thus, it can be seen that, to ensure integrity and safety of Blockchain based systems, the implementers should ensure adequate control and employ best practices in:

(i)   Key management,

(ii) Software development and testing,

(iii) Connectivity with external data sources and integration with front end and backend systems,

(iv) Using appropriate digital signature & validation mechanism for authorizing transactions and

(v) Dynamic access control systems to ensure only the actual authorized participants and approved to transact by revoking the approval to those who cease to be members or are transferred to other positions in the organization.

It is a common practice for all Blockchain implementers to provision for a team that continuously scans the environment for evolving threats and also budget for and conduct hackathons to attack and compromise their own systems to identify and cover their weaknesses and overcome their vulnerabilities.

A summary of the various types of attacks along with the various counter measures that can be taken are well documented in the paper Blockchain Technologies for the Internet of Things: Research Issues and Challenges, Mohamed Amine Ferrag, Makhlouf Derdour, Mithun Mukherjee, Member, IEEE, Abdelouahid Derhab, Leandros Maglaras, Senior Member, IEEE, Helge Janicke (https://arxiv.org/pdf/1806.09099.pdf)

MAJOR ATTACKS ON BLOCKCHAIN

Threat model	Countermeasures	Resistant protocols
Key attack	- Elliptic curve encryption is used to calculate the hash functions	LNSC protocol [10]
DDoS/DoS attack	- Distributed SDN architecture	DistBlockNet protocol [36]
	- Decentralized mixing service	CoinParty protocol [37]
	- Ring signature using ECDSA	Liu et al.'s protocol [38]
	-Block size limitation, attribute-based signatures, and multi-receivers encryption	BSeIn protocol [39]
Replay attack	- Elliptic curve encryption is used to calculate the hash functions	LNSC protocol [10]
	- The freshness of public/private key pairs	BSeIn protocol [39]
Hiding Blocks	- An immutable chain of temporally ordered interactions is created for each agent	TrustChain protocol [40]
False data injection attack	- Blockchain consensus mechanisms	Liang et al.'s protocol [21]
Tampering attack	- Public-key cryptosystem	Wang et al.'s protocol [41]
Impersonation attack	- Elliptic curve encryption is used to calculate the hash functions	LNSC protocol [10]
	- Distributed incentive mechanism based blockchain and the node cooperation based privacy protection mechanism	Wang et al.'s protocol [16]
	- Attribute-based signatures	BSeIn protocol [39]
Refusal to Sign	- Not interacting with the malicious agent, or splitting the transactions in smaller amounts	TrustChain protocol [40]
Overlay attack	- Every transaction is embedded with a Time-Stamp to mark the uniqueness	Wang et al.'s protocol [41]
Double-spending attack	- Multi signatures and anonymous encrypted message propagation streams	Aitzhan and Svetinovic's protocol [22]
	- Time-Stamp and the Proof-of-Work mechanism	Wang et al.'s protocol [41]
Modification attack	- Elliptic curve encryption is used to calculate the hash functions	LNSC protocol [10]
	- The attribute signature and the MAC	BSeIn protocol [39]
Collusion attack	- Blockchain-based incentive mechanism	He et al.'s protocol [42]
Whitewashing attack	- Lower priorities are given to the agents of new identities	TrustChain protocol [40]
Quantum attack	- Lattice-based signature scheme	Yin et al.'s protocol [43]
Man-in-the-middle attack	- Elliptic curve encryption is used to calculate the hash functions	LNSC protocol [10]
	- Secure mutual authentication	BSeIn protocol [39]
Sybil attack	- An immutable chain of temporally ordered interactions is created for each agent	TrustChain protocol [40]

Challenges to Growth of Blockchain eco-system

Though there are a lot of drivers for the growth of Blockchain led eco-system, there are indeed a lot of challenges that need to be addressed.

(I)   The understanding of the Blockchain paradigm across the user industries and the technology implementers has a long way to go to trigger the widespread adaption. A lot of awareness, education of the technology and its potential breath-taking impact has to be undertaken by the early adaptors.

(II)   Blockchain has traditionally been associated with the 'Cryptocurrency' which is viewed as an anti-regulation and anti-establishment phenomenon. Hence while it is important for Regulators to weigh the real benefits of Blockchain based approach, they also need to accept and adapt the same to benefit from its disruptive potential.

(III) Many of the crypto currency protocols are currently employing the high resource intensive 'Proof of Work' consensus mechanism for mining transactions. This puts a huge limitation on scale while invoking opposition from the environmentalists and regulators.

(IV)   Security of the transactions is of immense concern as there is no legal recourse in most of the countries for transaction losses or thefts. Further, identity theft in the form of compromising Private keys in the case of Public Blockchains and improper key management by the Certificate authorities and Membership providers gives rise to a variety of system compromises and loss of property, information and value.

Microsoft is exploring decentralized digital identity solutions that leverage public Blockchains in order to create a secure encrypted digital hub where individuals can store their identity data and easily control access to it. Microsoft likewise has been promoting integrity and security in digital ID solutions using its cloud computing services.

SecureKey Technologies and IBM are collaborating to build a digital identity solution on top of the open source Hyperledger Fabric enabling large groups of individuals and enterprises to quickly board highly secured networks with minimal operational effort and minimal risk.

(V)   In many cases, there is no proper ground up approach and process mapping undertaken before the Blockchain platform selection, smart contract development and application launch. This has led a lot of failures among the Public Blockchain based entities and in the case of Private Blockchains, drain of resources due to avoidable mistakes. A systematic and methodical approach by taking into account , existing systems in the organization and considering all aspects for a proper integration with the same, will go a long way in making most of the investments in Blockchain based implementations by organizations.

(VI)   Blockchain implementation can dramatically alter the governance at organizations as it will eliminate non-value adding middlemen while freeing up a lot of wasted resources. While corruption and red tape is a biggest causality, this may cause a backlash for those used to thriving on such non-desirable practices. This has to be factored in while readying an organization for the new approach through investments in Blockchain systems.

(VII) While in the Public Blockchain domain, the investments could be raised through ICOs (Initial coin offerings) wherever allowed by regulatory authorities, in the case of Enterprise Blockchain, the investments have to be funded by the expected savings & cost benefits through automation, collaboration and process excellence. With a number of projects still under POC (Proof of Concept) stage, the trade-offs are not clear. Hence lack of clarity on the Returns on Investments, leads to a tremendous bottleneck for the adoption of Blockchain.

(VIII) The cross-border, cross-organizational, cross-platform nature of the Blockchain based businesses offers a great challenge for the regulatory and accounting authorities and practitioners. Hence a lot of co-operation among the participants and hand holding is required to get them on board for managing the transition.

It is imperative for the participants, industry leaders and regulators to come together and quickly evolve a set of global standards and references to ensure coordinated development of the eco-system in line with the standards of traditional IT products and services.

(IX) The traditional approach to Information technology practice in organizations is well managed with the availability of a number of guiding frameworks to better manage the safety and security of their operations.

In 2014, the National Institute of Standards and Technology ("NIST") published a Framework for Improving Critical Infrastructure Cybersecurity (the "Cybersecurity Framework" or the "Framework"), a voluntary framework designed to help organizations better understand, manage, and reduce their cybersecurity risk. It provides a high-level, strategic view of the lifecycle of an organization's cybersecurity risk management and can be tailored to specific business sectors and companies. Although it is voluntary, many companies across industries, particularly financial institutions, are developing cybersecurity programs aligned with the Framework.20

The Framework describes five broad functions – identify, protect, detect, respond, and recover – that define the high-level goals of a cybersecurity risk management program. It also identifies specific categories of cybersecurity outcomes that elaborate on the functions and are tied to activities. (Reference: Advancing Blockchain Cybersecurity- Technical and Policy Considerations for the Financial Services Industry by Chamber of Digital commerce, Microsoft).

The same needs to be adopted for the Blockchain infrastructure to which the organizations are exposed to ensure that the organization is not exposed to unforeseen & unknown threats and thus manage their risk better.

(X) Vulnerability of Smart contracts and Chain codes as well as their integration with external systems poses a big threat to the integrity of managing Blockchain applications.

This has to be properly addressed by the developers & the applications should be properly tested and integrated with trusted external applications and sources.

One Microsoft solution that addresses the risks inherent in oracles is the use of "cryptlets." Cryptlets operate outside of the permissioned Blockchain network and are designed to provide a secure, trustworthy way to serve as an oracle to a smart contract and reduce data quality risks.

Blockchain's removal of the single point of failure, shared and distributed ledger, secure authentication of Identity with appropriate permissions and authorizations in place to interact and end-to-end encryption of transactions, apart from many other advantages, fortifies the IoT devices and all other IT systems comprising our digital life against any Malware attack, disincentivising them and de-risking the entire economic eco-system.

Blockchain activities across various countries

Let us take a look at the global scenario of Blockchain activities of governments and public sector organizations in embracing Blockchain across the world.

United Kingdom

UK was among the early ones to recognize the importance of Blockchain technology. UK government's chief scientific advisor Sir Mark Walport, in a report, highlighted how Blockchain could help in areas such as reducing benefit fraud, protecting critical infrastructure, and registering assets.

Some of the key use cases identified by UK government are:

- Cyber security and infrastructure protection through use of Blockchain.
- Improvement of efficiency across all the operation of the government and its enterprises by leveraging Blockchain based automation
- Elimination of corruption and wasteful expenditure by ensuring traceability of government expenditure
- Support and encouragement to SMEs in a transparent and productive fashion, promoting the innovation & economic growth.
- Improve the KYC process by implementing digital identity like in Estonia.

Singapore

Singapore boasts of a conducive environment for Blockchain technology companies with a supportive policy. Under Project Ubin, using the concept of Digitized Singapore Dollar, the Monetary Authority of Singapore has successfully conducted a pilot for interbank payments. It is now testing Blockchain technology for cross-border payments, bonds trading, and insurance settlements.

Singapore has over 15 Blockchain startups that have together raised over $500 million in the last two years to invest in Blockchain platforms and projects.

Japan

In April 2017, Japan passed a law recognizing bitcoin as legal tender, and permitted 11 companies to operate cryptocurrency exchanges. The Financial Services Agency of Japan, along with three leading financial institutions - Bank of Tokyo-Mitsubishi UFJ, Sumitomo Mitsui and Mizuho - are creating a Blockchain-based digital ID for all Japanese citizens. These digital IDs will be used to create a national property registry including the sale prices, and to award government contracts.

A consortium of Japanese banks has joined hands to launch a new national digital currency, J coin, to wean away citizens from excessive cash usage.

China

In late 2016, capital markets and financial services company Juzhen Financials closed on a $23 million Series A, in which Fenbushi Capital, a China based Blockchain-focused VC firm participated. In early 2018, the Chinese government banned the use and trade of cryptocurrency in the country. China has, however, announced its strong appreciation and support for Blockchain technology. It has filed more than 225 Blockchain-related patents last year and the country is home to over 4,000 companies with Blockchain in their name, at least five times more than its nearest competitor, the US. China's state-backed Bank of China and financial services corporation, China Union Pay have announced plans to jointly explore Blockchain applications to develop a payment system. There are also talks that China plans to release its own digital currency as a play against bitcoin with a motto of 'dis intermediation' instead of 'decentralization'. China is also home to one of the most popular public Blockchain platforms, NEO.

Chinese President Xi Jinping, has become the world's most senior global figure to mention Blockchain technology as a disruptive technology, in a speech at the opening of the joint annual conference of the Chinese Academy of Sciences and Chinese Academy of Engineering. China is using Blockchain technology to reform its tax administration laws and eliminate corruption by bringing transparency in its government processes and activities

Dubai

As part of its plan to adopt latest technologies and innovative practices at the global level, 'Dubai Future Foundation' announced the establishment of 'Global Blockchain Council' consisting of 46 members who are potential key players in the Blockchain industry. The objective of the council is to explore and discuss current and future applications, and organize transactions through the Blockchain platform.

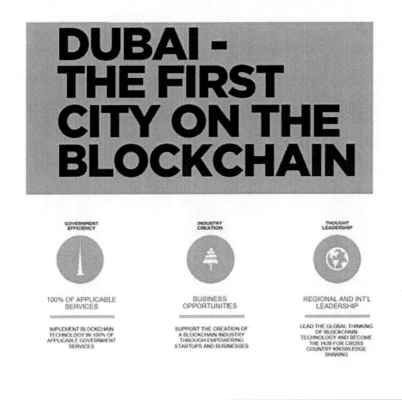

| | | | |

The Crown Prince of Dubai has announced plans to secure all government documentation on Blockchain by 2020 as part of the Smart Dubai initiative. The Dubai government has partnered with IBM to implement paperless smart contract-based supply chain solutions, and has launched proof-of-concepts for Blockchain projects across departments covering health records, diamond trade, title transfer, business registrations, digital wills, tourism engagement, shipping, and the court system.

Estonia

Considered to be a leader in the adoption of Blockchain technology, Estonia's citizens and e-residents are issued a cryptographically secure digital ID card powered by Blockchain infrastructure on the backend. This allows access to various public services like health, judiciary, security, legislative and commercial code systems. On a Blockchain platform, citizens can verify the integrity of records held in government databases, and control who has access to them.

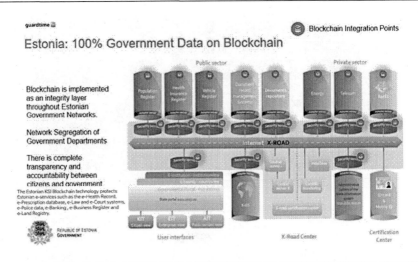

Estonia is also adopting Blockchain technology to secure the country's 1 million health records. Every update and access to healthcare records is registered on the Blockchain, preventing medical fraud and making it impossible for hackers to hide their trail. It also provides real-time alerts to attacks, enabling the government to respond to incidents immediately before any large-scale damage. Estonia is also planning to launch its own cryptocurrency, ESTcoin. It has an e-Residency program that allows persons across the world to become digital citizens, and register their companies in the country.

Guardtime offers servicers to enterprises aimed at establishing transparency & auditability of financial records by enabling them to store the hashes of their records on KSI Blockchain.

Sweden

The land registry authority Lantmäteriet, is working with startup ChromaWay and consultancy Kairos Future, and SBAB and Landshypotek banks to test whether private Blockchains can serve as a means to carry out property transactions. Also, financial services group SEB, along with Nasdaq, are planning a joint venture to revamp the $431 billion mutual fund industry by implementing Blockchain technology to improve efficiency in fund order management, payments and settlement. This is expected to accelerate the transaction cycle, increase transparency, ensure asset safety and security as well as reduce costs. This calls for cooperation and coordination from multiple parties like fund companies, service providers, banks, distributors and auditors.

South Korea

South Korea has identified Blockchain as one of the prominent growth areas along with AI and Big Data for the future, and has earmarked investments of

$918 million for the year 2019, up over 80 percent from 2018. The South Korean government is actively promoting Blockchain education among its youth and is considering a proposal from one its provinces, Jeju island, to become a special zone for Blockchain and cryptocurrencies from where startups can issue their ICOs despite a ban on them in the country.

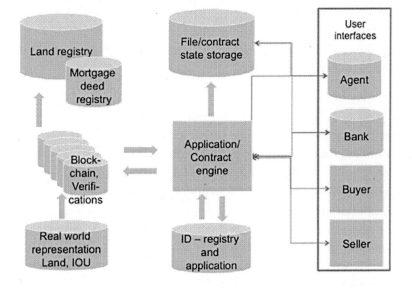

Overview of ChromaWay Postchain architecture for registration of Swedish property

Source:

[61] Mats Snäll, 'Blockchain and Land Register – a new "trust machine"?' (World Bank Land and Proverty Conference, 22 March, 2017)
https://www.conftool.com/landandpoverty2017/index.php?page=browseSessions&form_session=547&presentations=show

Malaysia

Malaysia has taken a proactive role to implement Blockchain. Malaysian government actively supports the public Blockchain platform NEM and has recently announced the adoption of Blockchain for issuing academic certificates issued by the leading educational colleges and universities in the country. Besides this, the Malaysian government is actively exploring opportunities to implement Blockchain in a variety of uses cases in supply chain of agricultural products grown in the country.

Switzerland

Switzerland is ranked among the most Blockchain and cryptoasset friendly countries in the world. Four of the 10 largest ICOs in 2017 were launched from Switzerland. Many companies and traders in Switzerland accept payments in bitcoins. The town Zug, where Ethereum was originally incorporated is rated as the epicenter of crypto activity in Switzerland, with the first bitcoin ATM in the country set up there.

Switzerland's Financial Market Supervisory Authority (FINMA) introduced a new fintech license with "relaxed" requirements that is applicable to Blockchain and cryptocurrency-based firm. On December 14th 2019, FAMA issued a report on Friday, providing a legal framework for distributed ledger technology (DLT), or Blockchain. The framework extends all the regulations & acts like Anti Money Laundering, ownership of assets & securities applicable to the normal financial market entities to all the companies in the Blockchain & cryptoasset ecosystem.

USA

In March 2018, a report submitted by the Joint Economic Committee of the US Congress made several recommendations for policymakers, regulators, and entrepreneurs regarding applications of Blockchain technology. The committee recognized the potential of Blockchain technology to conduct secured transactions and protect technology infrastructure against malware attacks.

While a number of states are still adopting a wait and watch approach towards cryptocurrencies and Blockchain technologies, states like Delaware, Illinois, Arizona Colorado (government record keeping), West Virginia (mobile voting) have taken an active approach to promote Blockchain based applications. Delaware announced the Delaware Blockchain Initiative in 2016, to spur adoption and development of Blockchain and smart contract technologies in both private and public sectors. Illinois announced the Illinois Blockchain Initiative, aimed at utilizing Blockchain and distributed ledger technologies to transform the delivery of public and private services, redefine the relationship between government and the citizen in terms of data sharing, transparency and trust leading to digital transformation."

The US Food and Drug Administration issued a "sources sought" notice late in 2017 for an application of Blockchain for portable interactive devices "to enable exchange of patient-level data within the United States Critical Illness and Injury Trails Group network."

The US Department of Defense Transportation Command has also showed interest in Blockchain.

US Army Medical Research and Materiel Command (USAMRMC), in coordination with the Medical Technology Enterprise Consortium (MTEC), is evaluating the application of Blockchain to streamline its supply chain operations.

Malta

Malta government has announced a strong intention to promote Blockchain technology with a vision to transform Malta into the **"Blockchain Island"** & an economic superpower in the emerging crypto-economy with Blockchain based businesses contributing to 10% of Malta GDP by 2027.

The following are the key activities proposed by the Malta government in line with its vision for creating a Blockchain centric ecosystem:

- Migrate all Public Registries & Records onto Blockchain to enable transparency
- Create a center of excellence in Malta by promoting Blockchain education and develop a body of knowledge in legal engineering
- Regulate and legalize Blockchain based decentralised organizations, cryptoassets, cryptocurrency exchanges and ICOs.
- Implement a Blockchain based identity systems for all citizens and also enable secure identity management system for Internet of Things and Decentralised autonomous organizations.
- Leverage Blockchain for creating a transparent and efficient tax administration and eliminate red tape while improving transparency.

India

Indian government has welcomed the use of Blockchain with its Honorable Prime Minister, Narendra Modi, repeatedly stressing the importance of Blockchain and the need to leverage Blockchain technology for all aspects of government and corporate functioning to be successful and relevant in the coming age of technology enabled disruption. He also stressed the need by all Indians to equip themselves with the knowledge of Blockchain technology to be successful in the future.

Government of Rajasthan, a state in India, has actively leveraged Blockchain technology for creating a transparent & the most efficient benefit distribution system, implemented by India's leading organization, M/s Auxesis group. The system is given in the following diagram:

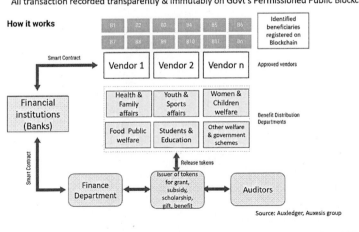

Benefit Distribution Program

All transaction recorded transparently & immutably on Govt's Permissioned Public Blockchain

Source: Auxledger, Auxesis group

Source: Auxesis foundation

The implementation of the benefit distribution on Blockchain has resulted in a dramatic reduction in wastages and fraudulent transactions with the benefits reaching the intended & deserving recipients in a fool proof manner.

West Bengal Government took a big leap in the implementation of Blockchain when it announced that the birth certificates of its citizens are stored on Blockchain henceforth.

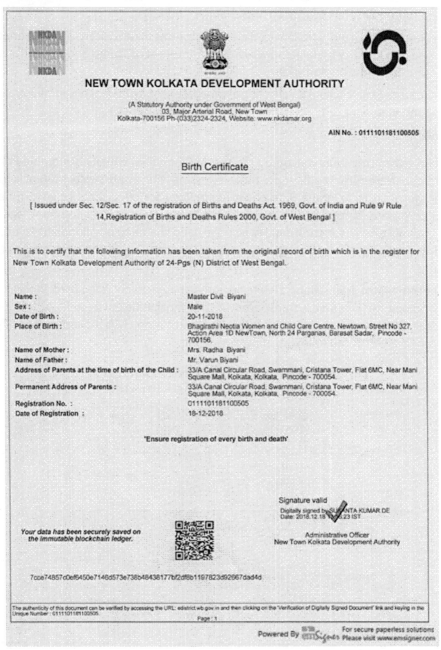

NEW TOWN KOLKATA DEVELOPMENT AUTHORITY

(A Statutory Authority under Government of West Bengal)
03, Major Arterial Road, New Town
Kolkata-700156 Ph-(033)2324-2324, Website: www.nkdamar.org

AIN No. : 0111101181100505

Birth Certificate

[Issued under Sec. 12/Sec. 17 of the registration of Births and Deaths Act. 1969, Govt. of India and Rule 9/ Rule 14,Registration of Births and Deaths Rules 2000, Govt. of West Bengal]

This is to certify that the following information has been taken from the original record of birth which is in the register for New Town Kolkata Development Authority of 24-Pgs (N) District of West Bengal.

Name :	Master Divit Biyani
Sex :	Male
Date of Birth :	20-11-2018
Place of Birth :	Bhagirathi Neotia Women and Child Care Centre, Newtown, Street No 327, Action Area 1D NewTown, North 24 Parganas, Barasat Sadar, Pincode - 700156.
Name of Mother :	Mrs. Radha Biyani
Name of Father :	Mr. Varun Biyani
Address of Parents at the time of birth of the Child :	33/A Canal Circular Road, Swammani, Cristana Tower, Flat 6MC, Near Mani Square Mall, Kolkata, Kolkata, Pincode - 700054.
Permanent Address of Parents :	33/A Canal Circular Road, Swammani, Cristana Tower, Flat 6MC, Near Mani Square Mall, Kolkata, Kolkata, Pincode - 700054.
Registration No. :	0111101181100505
Date of Registration :	18-12-2018

'Ensure registration of every birth and death'

Signature valid
Digitally signed by SUSANTA KUMAR DE
Date: 2018.12.18 16.23 IST

Your data has been securely saved on the immutable blockchain ledger.

Administrative Officer
New Town Kolkata Development Authority

7cce74857c0ef6450e7146d573e738b48438177bf2df8b1197823d92667dad4d

The authenticity of this document can be verified by accessing the URL: edistrict.wb.gov.in and then clicking on the 'Verification of Digitally Signed Document' link and keying in the Unique Number : 0111101181100505.

Page : 1

For secure paperless solutions
Powered By emSigner Please visit www.emsigner.com

Andhra Pradesh (a state in India) Government was one of the first to see the potential of Blockchain technology and has kick-started incubation focused on this area. Companies supported by it are now able to not only develop competency to execute government orders, but also expand their offerings across segments and go global.

Across the world, we have many accelerators working on supporting the Blockchain ecosystem through a variety of programs. Some of them are depicted in the following table:

Sl No	Name	Web site	Country	Focus areas	Modus operndi	Salient feature
				Global Blockchain focused Venture startup accelerators		
1	Adel	https://www.adelphoi.io/	Isle of Man	Platform agnostic blockchain projects	DAO approach for venture investment	Own ecosystem with Adel token (ADL)
2	Bank of England Fintech Accelerator	http://bithub.africa/incubator/	Nairobi, Kenya	Bitcoin & Blockchain adoption in Africa	Training, consultancy and subsidised working space	Africa focus
3	Blockchain Trust Accelerator	https://trustaccelerator.org/	Amsterdam, Netherlands	Blockchain technology for social impact	Connecting startups with funders and governments for support	Promoted by Bitfury group
4	Blockchain Business Camp, Tokyo	https://www.seisakukikaku.metro.tokyo.jp/bdc_tokyo/english/bizcamptky/blockchain/	Tokyo, Japan	Accelerating Blockchain businesses in Japan	2 months intense training camp for foreign Blockchain companies to set up business in Japan	Promoted by Tokyo Metropolitan group
5	Blockchain Business solution Accelerator	https://www.h-farm.com/en/acceleration/accelerators/blockchain-accelerator	Italy	Blockchain based business solutions	4 month intesive program to support selected innovative startups, 20000 Euros investment from H-Farm fund for 3-6% equity	Promoted by Deutsce Bank
6	Boost VC	https://www.boost.vc/	SanMaeto, California, USA	Blockchain based startups on Bitcoin & Ethereum platforms	Upto 50000 US Dollars for 7% equity and co-working space for 3 months.	Open for citizens from all countries.
7	Chicago Blockchain center	https://chicagoblockchain.org/	Chicago, Illinois, USA	Blockchain and Distributed Ledger Technologies	Coworking space, networking meetups and training workshops	Promoted by Government of Illinois
8	Consilium	https://www.coinsilium.com/	London, UK	Early stage Blockchain & Cryptoasset companies	Financing, mentoring and consultancy to promising startups	Incubated leading companies like Factum, RSK Labs, Indorse etc.
9	DC Blockchain center	http://dcblockchaincenter.com	Washington DC	Blockchain applications for Government and Public sector	Forum for public and private sector to collaborate and develop innovative Blockchain applications	By Chamber of Digital commerce US and 1776
10	Digital Currency Group	https://dcg.co/	New York, USA	Bitcoin & Blockchain Technology startups globally	Investing in promising comapanies and leveraging its network to promote them.	Over 70 investments in 20 countries
11	IBM Blockchain Accelerator	https://www.ibm.com/blockchain/in-en/accelerator/	Bangalore, India	Hyperledger Fabric	Guidance, support and technical expertise to founders for bringing new blockchain networks into production	Fee based program ($100K +)
12	Outlier Ventures	https://outlierventures.io/	London, Toronto, Chicago	Integrated approach to Blockchain, IOT, Data tech	Decentralised businesses focusing on Industry 4.0, Smart Cities, Mobility & Health	Believes in Convergence through opesource, decentralised, tokenized economies
13	Satoshi Studios	https://www.linkedin.com/company/satoshi-studios/	Delhi, India	Intensive training on Blockchain technologies	Three month residency training program and access to funding support. $50K for 10% equity	Supported by Roger Ver, Michael Terpin, early bitcoin investors and angels
14	SparkChain Capital	http://www.sparkchaincapital.com/	California, USA	Blockchain and Cryptocurrency innovations	Early stage Venture capital investment	Strong presence anf networking in US, Japan, China and South Korea
15	Syncheron's Finlabs	https://www.synechron.com/finlabs/blockchain	New York, USA	All leading enterprise Blockchain platforms	Assistance to enterprises in developing Blockchain COEs	Over 100 well trained Professionals
16	Shanghai Blockchain Enterprise Development Promobon Alliance	https://www.zhongan.io/en/about-us	Shanghai China	Enterprise Blockchain applications	Promote education, research and practical applications of Blockchain Technology	Founded by 20 member alliance including Alibaba group company

Growing applications of Blockchain- A close look at the real-world use cases

On 22 May 2010, Laszlo Hanyecz made the first real-world transaction by buying two pizzas in Jacksonville, Florida for 10,000 BTC. In five days, the price grew 900%, rising from **$0.008** to **$0.08** for 1 bitcoin.

Over a period, Blockchain has grown beyond the bitcoin's representation as a store of value or a medium of exchange of a value unit.

M/s Deloitte one of the leading consultancies in the world, has facilitated many Blockchain based PoCs and is taking a significant role in furthering the usage of Blockchain and the realization of its disruptive potential. Some of the PoCs facilitated by Deloitte are summarized below:

- Customer onboarding
- Smart identity
- Cross-border payments
- KYC utility
- Claims distribution
- Re-insurance
- Transaction reporting
- Personal event history
- Funds management
- Healthcare data management
- Art tracking
- Loyalty & Rewards
- Digital asset trading
- Room booking
- Voting
- Regulatory reporting

These different types of applications can be broadly classified into two main categories,

(i) as a static secure store of information or

(ii) a dynamic store of transaction information

They can further be divided into 6 sub categories (3each) as depicted in the following table:

Needs addressed by Blockchain		Description	Real world example applications
Record keeping: Stores of static information	Static registry	- Manage registry of asset ownership - Provide automation of specific assets	- Land title - Gift card ownership - Chain of custody
	Identity	- Secured store, confirm and distribute identity related info - Revised personal/ other data	- Store bank/credit card identity on blockchain to enable user to easily access proof of identity
	Smart Contracts	- Create and execute semi-autonomous contracts on distributed ledger platform	- Insurance claim payouts - Cash equity trading - Release of new music
Transactions: Stores of tradeable information	Dynamic Registry	- Exchange of digital and physical assets on a digital platform	- Streamlined low transaction on settlements to address the liquidity mismatch in loans
	Payments infrastructure	- Efficient payment transfer with lower friction	- Peer-to-Peer lending through the bitcoin blockchain, dis-intermediating banks
	Verifiable data	- Store of information and easy access to secure, dynamic information	- Event tickets - Registry of independent artists' work protection of intellectual property work

We have discussed certain killer applications of Blockchain across various verticals like 'Tokenization, Finance, Supply chain, Ecommerce, IoT, Automobiles and Registries' in the following chapters.

Blockchain Killer Application- Tokenization

Asset tokenization that represents digital representation of physical assets and financial assets is a key to implementation of Blockchain application. There are different types of token that represent the different forms of asset on a Blockchain.

While tokens represent an asset in the hands of the holders, they represent a liability in the hands of the issuers. The problems arise when the tokens are issued without subsequent discharge or the intention to discharge of the respective duties of the issuers, especially in an unregulated scenario like that of ICOs.

The emergence of Ethereum as a platform that supports DAPPS or decentralised applications gave rise to the phenomenon of crowdfunding through ICOs (Initial Coin Offerings). Different types of tokens came into existence depending on the public Blockchain platform they were launched on.

ICOs led to a rampant increase in unregulated early stage funding and in 2018 alone over 7 Billion US Dollars were raised through this route. These also marked the spectacular destruction of public investor wealth and the loss of face and faith of all those who swore by means of issuing tokens through ICOs backed by esoteric whitepapers promising utopian business models & extraordinary returns.

ICO offered the Web 3.0 version of crowdfunding, that allows entrepreneurs to raise money quickly through launch of tokens and ICOs by using whitepapers. ICOs overtook the traditional means of fund raising by far in 2017 and a record 7 Billion USD has been raised in 2018 so far. Most of the times, the vision proposed looks very rosy and the stage of fund raise is too early.

There are some fundamental flaws in the business models governing the launch and use of cryptoassets that are going to see the destruction of most of these in the future evaporating billions of dollars from the cryptomarket cap in the future.

Vitalik Buterin ✓ @VitalikButerin · Feb 17
Reminder: cryptocurrencies are still a new and hyper-volatile asset class, and could drop to near-zero at any time. Don't put in more money than you can afford to lose. If you're trying to figure out where to store your life savings, traditional assets are still your safest bet.

Crypto tokens are supposedly raised in lieu of the shares of the company as they confer certain rights to token holders. But token holders also use them to undertake transactions on the DAO and also exchange for the products & services offered with other participants.

The cryptoassets are given away as bonuses in promotions, airdrops and also to those offering services to improve the platform. Most of the times, these activities are undertaken by the promoters in unaccountable manner (read irresponsible and quixotic manner) without pricing services rationally.

This leads to unreasonable dilution of the stake of the promoters further bolstering the argument that DAOs are supposed to have negligible promoter's stake in line with the spirit of decentralization. In other words, the initial promoter group will gradually phase out as they reduce the stake in a number of ways (some of them fraudulently selling away & vanishing from the management scene).

Vitalik Buterin ☑
@VitalikButerin

Follow

Protip: if an ICO does volume bonuses ("buy at least $50000 of coins, get 20% more") then they do not understand the first thing about the egalitarian spirit of crypto (or at least, the egalitarian spirit that I believe crypto *should* have). Skip them.

That is the reason why, you find the token prices shooting up initially as promoters' use their new-found riches to canvass and promote heavily and vanish after selling them at high prices.

In real life the organizations keep changing their business models in tune with the times and adapt to the external environment while pivoting their models suitably. The promoters are always vested as the shares are with some responsible stake holders always. In DAPPS, the models cannot be changed once put in place and later when the time rises to do so, there are no promoters vested with reasonable stake to update through Improvement programs (like EIPs).

Hence left with no adaptability and no promoter stake by design itself, the DAOs have no other go but to fail.

The only way out is if the promoters use the coins/ tokens in a most responsible manner and leave the option open to buy back and convert to shares in business thus giving legitimacy in financial markets. Then, there could be a hope as those holding the shares can steer the companies forward. In other wards the ICOs should be seen as a pre-angel fund round of raising money and should be gradually brought into the main stream either by converting them into fiat by burning tokens or by converting the stakes into listed shares with minimal leakage. The DAPPs could then be governed like the banks of today with low promoter stake but responsible boards and vested shareholders who derive benefits from dividends, value appropriation and hostile take overs.

No wonder, many countries and top investors are still very wary about investing & trading in cryptoassets like tokens, currencies and coins

However, there still exists a sufficient business case for regulated and well controlled types of cryptoassets that are responsible for the growth of Blockchain ecosystem. Some of them are described below:

(a) **Security / Asset tokens:** Security Tokens are comparable to real world physical/ financial assets like real estate, things, equities, bonds and derivatives etc. They represent on the Blockchain, digital representation of physical assets and financial entitlements. Security Token Offerings or STOs, which area fully regulated form of ICOs, if used in an accountable manner, offer the best form of investments powering Blockchain applications globally.

DX.Exchange, a digital exchange in partnership with MPS Market Place Securities Ltd which has offices in Estonia and Israel, plans to offer, digital security tokens on the Ethereum network, backed by corresponding holdings of shares of 10 Nasdaq-listed companies like Facebook, Apple & Tesla. Each digital security is expected to track closely the performance of the corresponding shares on the stock exchanges and also entitle the holders to the same cash dividends, even though the companies themselves aren't involved. This offering of the virtual stocks, marks a significant move in the cross-pollination of cryptocurrency & he main stream financial markets.

(b) **Utility tokens:** Utility tokens enable the holders to use the services of the applications that they live on and are derived from the digitization of the rights and entitlements of the holders for a price or otherwise.

Utility tokens that live on the respective Blockchain platform, without any life outside in the open ecosystem are very much a norm in a number of real world and Blockchain applications.

(c) **Cryptocurrencies/Payment tokens:** Like bitcoin, Ethereum etc., crypto-currencies are native currencies of their respective public Blockchain and are supposed to possess certain inherent value depending on the demand and supply scenario, that can be used for purchasing goods and services in the real-world platforms that accept their existence and usage.

The concept of the cryptocurrencies as instruments for payment is not yet accepted by the financial regulatory authorities and it is a matter of time, the world comes around the fact that, digital currencies are a necessary part of the ecosystem and hence are to be respected in some form or the other, albeit with due regulatory framework in place.

Blockchain Killer Applications in Finance

Banking and Financial world has always been intrigued by the questions as below

- Whether the old processes and paperwork can be replaced by cooperation, innovation and speed between multiple parties in the financial world?
- Whether the costs for transactions between multiple parties in the financial industry can be reduced?
- Whether the fraud and crime could be put to rest by collective trust?
- Whether the highly secure shared single source and view of the truth can be established between multiple parties in the financial ecosystem?

The attributes for application of Blockchain has the natural capabilities to give yes as the answer for the above questions.

The implementation of Blockchain in the financial world can be characterized into 5 major parts:

a. International trade finance

Trade finance has become one of the top focus issues for Blockchain technology use. The number of pilots and other trials that are looking into the opportunities of Blockchain technology for trade finance and supply chain have dramatically increased in 2017 and intensified this year. The sheer complexity of trade finance is reflected in the variety of potential solutions. Different parts of the 'trade finance & supply chain' have their own Blockchain initiative.

Trade finance is a complex process. Various parties from exporters, importers, banks, truckers, shippers, custom agents and regulators all require checks and verifications at various points along the chain. Each interlocking part of the chain depends on successful completion of the previous phase and on reliable information.

Banks play a large role in the trade finance chain, notably in the supply of letters of credit (LC) and other financing mechanisms. Letters of credit are the most widely used way of financing between importers and exporters, helping guarantee trade transactions. At the moment, buyers and suppliers use a letter of credit typically concluded by physically transferring paper documents to underpin transactions. This process however creates a long paper trail and it may take between five and ten days to exchange documentation.

Trade finance is a network business. It is an activity that often involves multiple counterparties in various and far-away parts of the world.

Creating a Blockchain trade finance ecosystem that combines all the different stages of trade from production to end-delivery is a must as it would enable trust and speed, brining in the monetary benefit to each party in the entire system. Various parties who are involved in the trade finance and supply chain business increasingly become aware that stand-alone solutions are not the answer to the various challenges in the trade finance industry. The success of using Blockchain in trade finance purposes stands or falls with network effect and if it is adopted widely. They are increasingly convinced that as well as developing a platform and Blockchain solution, a network must be in place that covers all the parties in the trade finance chain so that the full transaction can be completed on the Blockchain.

Blockchain enabled shared ledger between different transacting parties can be visualized as follows.

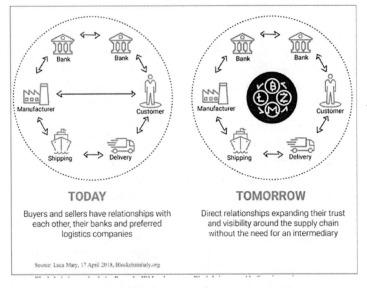

TODAY

Buyers and sellers have relationships with
each other, their banks and preferred
logistics companies

TOMORROW

Direct relationships expanding their trust
and visibility around the supply chain
without the need for an intermediary

Source: Luca Mary, 17 April 2018, Blockchainitaly.org

In the above system, where there are cross-border transactions and payments it would involve verification and authentication process by the regulatory authorities like customs department as well.

Thus, it is evident that for Blockchain trade finance platforms would require on-boarding of banks, regulators such as customs, entities, transporters and every other part of the trade cycle. This asks for the setting up of Blockchain-enabled trade finance platforms or networks with common standards enabling interoperability.

- Mahindra & Mahindra group and IBM have developed a Blockchain solution to reinvent supply chain finance across the country. This will help supplier's access instantaneous credit due to enhanced trust. Live information available to finance companies allows them to design and offer innovative products and solutions quickly

- In November 2019, India's largest private enterprise, Reliance Industries announced that it successfully executed a trade finance transaction on the Blockchain. *This Blockchain-enabled financial dealing has cut down time taken for such transaction from 7-10 days in a conventional route to now less than a day*. HSBC India and ING Bank Brussels have successfully executed a Blockchain enabled, live trade finance transaction jointly with Reliance Industries and Tricon Energy.

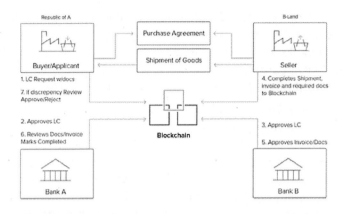

Letter of Credit (LC) through Blockchain- An illustration: Source: IBM

The steps are outlined below:

- Buyer and seller enter into a sales contract
- Buyer requests LC to his bank, Bank A
- Buyer's bank approves LC request and sends the same to Seller's bank, Bank B and records it on the Blockchain.
- Seller completes shipment and forwards the receipt confirmation to his bank through the Blockchain.
- Seller's bank reviews document and sends the same to buyer's bank through Blockchain.
- Buyer's bank reviews all the documents and if there is no discrepancy, records its approval and pays the seller's bank
- Seller's bank pays the seller after authorizations are recorded through Blockchain
- Buyer takes delivery of the goods.
- Buyer settles his bank liability within designated time.

Issuing a letter of credit through the Blockchain dramatically reduces the time required to exchange documents and simplifies the process while increase trust through an automated process.

Let's look to the recent Blockchain trade finance networks that have been announced recently. These may give some new insights in the various stages Blockchain works in the trade finance chain.

1. Batavia Platform

One of these new networks is Batavia, a Blockchain-based trade finance platform that is being collaboratively developed by a consortium of banks and IBM, in consultation with transportation industry experts as well as the banks' customers.

The Batavia platform derives from an initiative launched by UBS and IBM in 2016 to build a new global trade platform based on Blockchain technology. Since than four additional banks were joining its ongoing Batavia initiative, including Bank of Montreal (BMO), CaixaBank, Commerzbank and Erste Group, collaborating to bring the Blockchain-based trade finance platform to life.

Aim of the Platform: The idea behind the platform is to simplify the trade finance process by moving away from the trade finance sector's reliance on paper-based records. The Batavia platform is designed to support more efficient, transparent, secure and cost effective transactions. This by digitizing and automating the arranging, securing and financing of international trade transactions. The Batavia platform will as a result eliminate the necessity to handle and compare documents, allowing buyers, sellers and their banks to execute transactions with a high degree of efficiency and transparency.

How does the platform work: The Batavia trade finance platform is built on the IBM Blockchain Platform and powered by the Hyperledger Fabric Blockchain framework as an open ecosystem. The system aims to cover the end-to-end process of a trade, encompassing the closing of trade agreements and execution of smart payments, which can be automatically triggered by specified events in the supply chain and recorded in the Blockchain. Other features of Batavia include track and trace key events in the supply chains and risk management tools, while key events can prompt the execution of smart contracts that close trade agreements.

Information about pilot: Batavia, has successfully passed its first set of live pilot transactions on the network with corporate clients. The consortium involved two trade transactions, one that tracked the transport of Audi cars from Germany to Spain and the other, textile raw materials for furniture production from Austria to Spain. The pilot transactions used various modes of transport, geographies and trading parties of differing sizes, in order to highlight Batavia's ability to scale and manage diverse transaction types.

2. Marco Polo

Another interesting project is Marco Polo, named after the famous Venetian explore. Blockchain consortium R3, trade finance company TradeIX and several global banks are collaborating on this new Blockchain-based trade finance solution. It initially involved BNP, Commerzbank and ING to explore how to deploy Blockchain to enhance trade finance operations. Since launching the project in September 2017, the project has since also included Standard Chartered, DNB and OP Financial Group. Earlier this year, Marco Polo expanded again to add more third-party players, including credit insurers, logistics companies and more as they begin testing the solution.

How does the platform work: The Marco Polo initiative has developed a solution for post-shipment trade financing. A "fully interoperable" open-source trade finance network that is built with R3's distributed ledger technology product Corda providing the underlying Blockchain and delivered via TradeIX's open TIX platform, a Blockchain-based system of applications and tools for trade finance. Microsoft is also involved as it provides its Azure cloud solution to "speed this solution to market". The Marco Polo initiative uses distributed ledger technology to manage data and enable smart contracts, with the goal of making trade finance more secure, efficient and transparent.

Marco Polo enables end-to-end, real-time, seamless connectivity and real-time trade links between trade networks, systems and entities through an open-standard technology infrastructure for banks, credit insurers, shipping and logistic providers, B2B networks and other technology providers, "eliminating the data silos which prevent free flow of information causing inefficiencies and discrepancies". Initially the solution is focused on three distinct areas of trade finance: risk mitigation by provision of payment commitments based on the matching of trade data, payables finance and receivables finance.

Information about pilot: The various partners recently announced that they have moved their Marco Polo trade finance platform from a successful proof of concept that started last September in partnership with BNP, Commerzbank and ING to the pilot stage.

3. We.Trade

European banks have taken a crucial step to making Blockchain available to their corporate clients, creating a legal entity for the expansion of the Digital Trade Chain platform. The joint venture incorporated under the name We.Trade, includes the nine founding banks as equal shareholders: Deutsche Bank, HSBC, KBC, Natixis, Nordea, Rabobank, Santander, Société Générale and Unicredit. The company will manage and distribute the platform, with the target of bringing it to commercial clients in the summer of 2018. In the first stage, it will cover 11 European countries: Belgium, Denmark, Finland, France, Germany, Italy, the Netherlands, Norway, Spain, Sweden and the UK.

How does the platform work: Powered by the Hyperledger Fabric Blockchain framework, We.Trade is a platform for managing, tracking and protecting trade transactions between SMEs. It will connect all parties involved in a trade deal, including buyer, buyer's bank, seller, seller's bank and transporter in one place (online and via mobile devices), help SMEs initiate new trading relationships as well as provide easy access to trade finance.

The app registers the entire trade process from order to payment, displaying it in a flowchart and guaranteeing payment when all contractual agreements have been met. The platform is fully automated and available 24×7, so that the order-to-payment process is much quicker than the traditional exchange of documents. It also requires far less back-office administration.

The DTC platform will allow onto it the nine banks and their networks of small and medium-sized enterprise (SME) clients that have already undergone know-your-customer and anti-money laundering checks with those lenders and so are known and permissioned entities. It will also bring in logistics companies using the latest track-and-trace technology to verify the arrival of goods in agreed condition at key points in the journey from supplier to buyer that will then trigger payments automatically.

4. HSBC's International trade finance platform

HSBC and ING had performed the world's first commercially viable trade finance transaction using a single Blockchain platform, in a "push to boost efficiency in the multi-trillion-dollar funding of international trade". HSBC and ING completed the deal for US food and agriculture firm Cargill when a bulk shipment of soybeans was transported from Argentina to Malaysia. The bank thereby issued a letter of credit to ING that backed the shipment.

How does the platform work: The Cargill transaction was an end-to-end trade between a buyer and a seller and their respective banks that was completed on one shared digital application rather than multiple systems. HSBC and ING announced that the exchange of this letter of credit was performed in 24 hours, compared to the five-to-10 days it normally takes to complete such exchanges through a paper-based system.

The reason why letters of credit have persisted is because of two real challenges — the absence of digital infrastructure and the challenge of coordinating multiple parties. Blockchain platform can help overcome both these limitations.

The transaction was executed on the R3 Blockchain consortium platform Corda. The Blockchain application used in the Cargill transaction is supported by 12 banks, which could help bring the technology to the market more broadly. Efforts are on to onboard regulators, other financial institutions (FIs) and customs players and on-boarding them to the tool to ensure entire trade finance processes can be completed through Blockchain.

5. Hong Kong Trade Finance Platform

An area where we see a growing number of trade finance networks based on Blockchain arising is Asia, including the Hong Kong Trade Finance Platform (HKTFP), the India Trade Connect and the ICI Trade Finance Blockchain platform. This is not surprising given the big problems of getting trade finance for trade transactions with countries in the Asia area.

How does the platform work: The Hong Kong Monetary Authority (HKMA) led Blockchain trade finance initiative was started in December 2016. Recently it completed a proof-of-concept distributed ledger platform for trade finance, called the Hong Kong Trade Finance Platform (HKTFP). A collaboration between the Hong Kong Monetary Authority (HKMA) and the Monetary Authority of Singapore (MAS), and supported by Deloitte and five of the city's top banks including HSBC.

A number of other banks have now joined their recently announced Blockchain-based trade network.

Information about pilot: The DLT pilot - which is described as a "global trade connectivity network" (GTCN) – is aimed to digitize trade finance using distributed ledger technology (DLT). It is expected to set "new global standards" for the industry and aims to trace global trade flows between Singapore and Hong Kong. The project is designed to demonstrate the feasibility of using Blockchain to reduce the risk of fraudulent activity while increasing business transparency, operational efficiency and productivity in trade finance.

Expected to be launched by early 2019, the new network will now involve participation from over 20 global banks and financial institutions including Bank of China (Hong Kong), The Bank of East Asia, Hang Seng Bank and Standard Chartered Bank (Hong Kong). It is expected that European financial institutions will get involved in the project as it progresses.

6. Infosys India Trade Connect

India's IT Company Infosys has announced the development of a Blockchain-based trade finance network in partnership with seven private-sector banks. Aim of this network called India Trade Connect (ITC)is to increase security and raise efficiency in trade finance, while also broadening its product offerings.

How does the platform work: The Blockchain-based network will be designed to digitize trade finance business processes and covers areas such as ownership validation, certification of documents and payments. According to Infosys, ITC has been built to be Blockchain "agnostic" in order to "future-proof" the network against future changes in technology.

Information about pilot: ITC is currently being used by the banks for a pilot project, using the Blockchain-based solution to increase automation and transparency, and help manage risks in trade and supply chain financing. Banks currently testing the Blockchain-based network includes are ICICI Bank, Axis Bank, Kotak Mahindra Bank, Yes Bank, IndusInd Bank, RBL Bank and South Indian Bank. Infosys is also in talks to sign up more Indian and overseas banks to the network.

7. ICICI Trade Finance Blockchain Platform

Indian ICICI bank recently announced it has successfully on-boarded over 250 corporates, who have signed up on the bank's Blockchain application to "experience a more time and cost efficient and secure way of undertaking domestic & international trade transactions on its custom developed Blockchain platform".

How does the platform work: The Blockchain application created by ICICI Bank digitizes the paper-intensive international trade finance process as an electronic, distributed and unalterable ledger giving the participating entities, including banks, the ability to access a single source of information.

The platform allows all parties in the trade to have a real-time view of data at domestic and overseas branches of ICICI. It also allows them to track documentation and authenticate ownership of assets digitally and execute a trade finance transaction through a series of encrypted and secure digital contracts. Further, it allows each participant to check online, the status of the application and transmission of original trade documents through the secure network.

Information about pilot: Already in 2016, ICICI became the first in India to test a cross-border transfer pilot project on a customized Blockchain, specializing in facilitating trade finance and remittances. The successful pilot transaction transferred funds in real time from a branch of ICICI Bank in Mumbai, India, to an Emirates NBD branch in Dubai. The initiative aimed to simplify the paper intensive trade finance process by bringing counterparties on the same platform, enabling decision making in almost real time.

b. Clearing and settlement

The current collateral processing has been challenged by several market changes like extended trading hours and the need to centrally clear derivatives traded over the counter under the European Market Infrastructure Regulation (EMIR).

Due to an increasing amount of buy-side market players, such as money managers at hedge funds and institutional firms who want to clear their derivatives trades, the need to provide an efficient securities collateral solution has become essential. In particular, these firms need to cover margin calls despite operating in different time zones.

A Blockchain based system is an ideal solution for the above system as explained in the following examples.

1. Nasdaq

Stock exchange operator Nasdaq's clearing arm, along with securities services provider ABN AMRO Clearing and financial services firms EuroCCP and Euroclear, developed a joint proof-of-concept (PoC) Blockchain platform. The aim, is to cover margin calls – a need to deposit funds or securities to cover potential losses – through a distributed network among collateral givers, takers and intermediaries,

Nasdaq developed the PoC for the distributed network, while ABN AMRO Clearing and EuroCCP created a front-end interface and managed integration into the services.

Further, Euroclear, one of the world's largest settlement houses, processed the underlying collateral transfers, ensuring the settlement was final and monitoring regulatory compliance.

2. Depository Trust & Clearing Corporation (DTCC)

In October 2018, global financial giant Depository Trust & Clearing Corporation (DTCC), the premier post-trade market infrastructure for the global financial services industry demonstrated that distributed ledger technology (DLT) is capable of supporting average daily trading volumes in the US equity market of more than 100 million trades per day or 6,300 trades per second for five continuous hours.

c. Remittances, payments & credit systems

A remittance is a transfer of money by a foreign worker to an individual in his or her home country. These cross-border transfers are economically significant for many countries that receive them. Remittances often compete with foreign aid as the largest capital inflow for developing nations. It is safe to say that many economies rely on remittances to survive.

For the remittances to be possible, the traditional banking systems involve high percentage of transaction fees up to as high as 15%.

There are also "Money transfer operators" which undertake the activity of money transfer (e.g.: Western Union) in the lieu of Banking systems in any economy. Below is the architecture of the payment system:

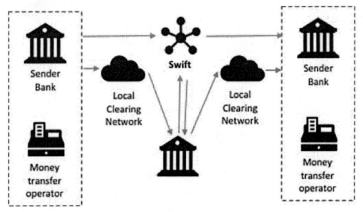

The above SWIFT system being a centralised system, carry a risk of reconciliation and thereby possibilities of fraud by way of fake instructions at one part of the system. The example of the same is the recent scam in the swift management system at the Punjab National Bank is a very good example of a high risk of centralised system operating for the remittance and the payment in bank.

Two employees at the branch of the bank by passed the core banking system, wherein the fake letter of undertakings (LOUs) were issued involved to overseas branches of other Indian banks, including using the international financial communication system, **SWIFT**. The LOUs were issued for the purpose of making available a credit of approximately INR 14,000 crore to Nirav Modi owned business.

While Blockchain and connected smart contracts can take care of the audit trail and procedural compliance, the connected ecosystem can ensure all the parties share the collective intelligence. If the core banking system is integrated with Blockchain, willful defaulters and clients breaching individual or group borrowing limits can be immediately identified.

In the case mentioned above issuance of fake LOUs would not have been possible on Blockchain, as the smart contract would have identified inconsistencies based on automatic reconciliation with core banking system. Following the established limits, it would have restricted the payment initiation over SWIFT network.

The Blockchain based architecture of the same is as follows:

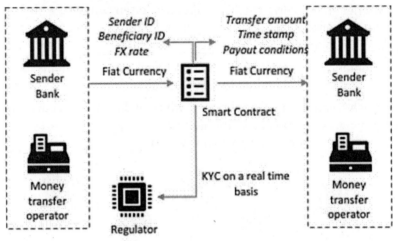

Some of the examples that can be quoted here are:

1. South Indian Bank completed a PoC for foreign currency remittance from the UAE in partnership with a Gulf-based currency exchange house

2. Singapore Government successfully tested Blockchain applications for Interbank money transfer vide a combination of a Private Ethereum network to digitize 225 Million SGD for facilitating the transfer of balances seamlessly over a R3 Corda based DLT Platform.

Apart from above, in September 2017, the Institute for Development and Research in Banking Technology (IDRBT), the research arm of Reserve Bank of India, released a white paper on the 'Applications of Blockchain Technology to Banking and Financial Sector in India.' It also announced plans to launch a Blockchain platform for different applications relevant to banking. The IDRBT also announced that India could use Blockchain to digitize the rupee.

Blockchain Killer Applications in Supply chain

Supply chain today has billions of dollars' worth of wasted investments locked in unproductive assets over a long period of time due to the inefficiencies and redundancies of the supply chain processes across contracting organizations spread all over the world.

There is a huge requirement of eliminating wasteful processes and tracking the movement of goods across the supply chain in a reliable and immutable manner also facilities a huge trust in the origin and the conditions being met during transit for a variety of goods.

Manufacturing by its very nature used a variety of processes including transport of raw material and finished goods which is directly linked to the the supply chain activity. Let us take a look at some of the areas in which Blockchain can be used in manufacturing activity. Source: Applications of Blockchain technology in manufacturing industry: Vincent Dieterich, Marko Ivanovc, Thomas Maier, Sebastian Zapfel, Munchen Manuel Utz, Philipp Sandner published by Philips Sanders, Frankfurt School, Blockchain centre, November 2017.

Overview of blockchain use cases in the manufacturing industry

Use case	Examples	Description
Supply Chain Management and Digital Product Memory	– IBM and Maersk	– Tracking of containers during the shipping process
	– Provenance	– Recording of all important product information throughout the entire supply chain
	– Everledger	– Registers certifications and transaction history of diamonds on blockchain
Internet of Things and Industry 4.0 applications	– Factom Iris	– IoT device identification over blockchain
	– Super Computing Systems	– Sensors that timestamp data on the blockchain to save them from manipulation
	– Tile Data Processing – tilepay	– Marketplace to allow customers to sell their data from IoT devices
	– IOTA	– Cryptocurrency and blockchain protocol especially developed to meet the demands for IoT applications
	– IBM Watson IoT	– Platform to save selected IoT data on a private blockchain and share it with all involved business partners
3D printing	– Genesis of Things	– Platform to enable 3D printing via smart contracts
	– Moog Aircraft Group	– Ensuring safe 3D-printing of aircraft parts via blockchain

Tracking of pharmaceutical products, high value goods like diamonds, food items and perishables like fish and organic vegetables through Blockchain platform is a huge area of focus for organizations across the world.

IBM has formed multiple partnerships with leading global companies like Everledger, Maersk, and Walmart and has successfully executed POCs that are now expected to move into production.

It has already been highlighted in the book earlier that, across the supply chain ecosystem, a number of opportunities exist for implementation of Blockchain versions of DLT technologies.

The model architecture of Blockchain implementation in supply chain is as follows:

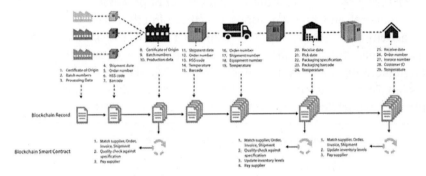

The Blockchain implementation has been explained in detail below across multiple sectors below:

a. **Pharmaceutical Supply chain**

Pharmaceutical supply chain is affected today primarily by counterfeit drugs. Following would demonstrate the intensity of the problem:

One in every 10 drugs sold are fake; 1,70,000 deaths annually happens due to fake malaria drugs in countries like Africa; and Approximately USD 75 billion values of drugs sold are fake drugs

The problem of the counterfeit drugs can be kept in check by way of traceability established across the entire pharmaceutical eco system, which would require existence of single source of truth about the product evolving with the every party in the chain of custody.

Inherent nature of Blockchain to establish a single source of truth across the entire application becomes ideal solution for the above problem. The below architecture would provide you an idea about how across the entire pharmaceutical supply chain Blockchain would operate.

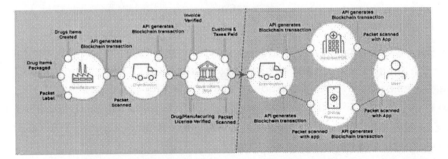

A classic implementation of Blockchain in patient safety and drug supply security is Mediledger, a Blockchain based project to address the issue of counterfeit

medicine and create trust machine for communication between multiple stakeholders in the Pharmaceutical supply chain. Mediledger is initiated by the Pharmaceutical giants Pfizer, Genentech, Mckesson and Abbvie.

Mediledger brought up some unique problem solving capacities of Blockchain in pharmaceutical supply chain, which are as follows:

- Keep an immutable record of transactions and data to demonstrate regulatory adherence and improve security

- Enforce cross-industry business rules without ever revealing your valuable, private data. This makes it easy to certify the authenticity of raw materials and drugs, stop counterfeit items from invading your supply chain and easily manage payment contract terms

- Protect your business intelligence, so your data stays behind your firewall and under your control. Use permission-based private messaging to share only the data you want to share with the partners you want to share it with

- Connect with trading partners and trusted service providers at the vanguard of emerging solutions for the pharmaceutical industry today

The below diagram would communicate better how multiple objectives for different parties in the pharmaceutical eco system are met by the Blockchain implementation

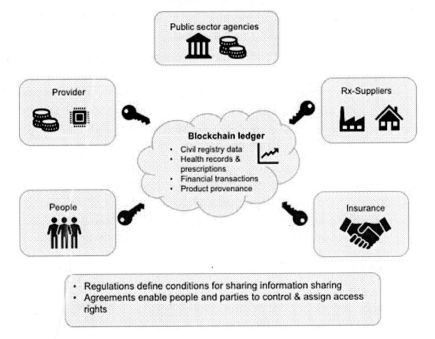

The architecture can be understood at the participant perspective as well from the below diagram:

One of the very important facet for the Blockchain implementation in pharmaceutical is its capacity to meet regulatory compliances.

Regulatory compliances for the supply chain traceability in pharmaceutical industry are becoming stringent, wherein serialization is required at lowest saleable level vide the 2013 Drug Supply Chain Security Act (DSCSA), wherein US FDA has prescribed a set of compliance requirements for pharmaceutical supply chain participants over a ten year period (2013-2023).

Within which all supply chain participants are required to store certain product, production, trading partner and ownership change data. Of importance to the industry is that, in 2023, "interoperable, electronic tracing of product at the package level requirements" shall go into effect.

It has been mentioned by the white paper released by Drug Supply Chain Security Act that, "Blockchain technology has demonstrated a strength in creating a single source of truth that is highly resistant to corruption – either accidental or intentional. It also holds promise for being able to restrict access to competitively valuable transaction data only to those parties with a defined "need to know," providing the confidentiality sought by trading partners"

This act warrants a serious examination of the utility of Blockchain to ensure compliance, thus leading to a huge interest in the implementation of relevant PoCs by all the pharmaceutical manufacturers across the world. This not only will result in a big boost to the usage of Blockchain technology, but also lead to manifold savings across the value chain & resultant dramatic improvement in profitability.

b. Food

The perishable nature of the product and impact on the human health and wellness, becomes important factor why the traceability and source of the food becomes necessary.

Fake Italian virgin oil, fraudulent labelling of fish in developed countries, fake wine etc., are common place across the world.

Blockchain attributes have capabilities to make available the consumer journey and information from farm to product level.

The flowchart of the food supply chain traced under the Blockchain system is presented below:

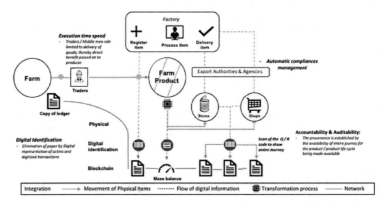

There is scope and requirement of IoT as well, to make possible real time recording of the conditions in which the good reloaded & transported. An IoT system coupled with verifiable data on the Blockchain, will ensure that suppliers and transporters maintain the ideal transportation conditions as, any variations that could affect the quality of the food products will be instantaneously and irrefutably highlighted leading to prompt corrective actions.

c. **Minerals**

The Blockchain implementation in minerals could be understood by categorizing it into implementation for precious metals and base metals.

In the precious metals Blockchain has seen a classic implementation example in the diamond industry:

Tracking of diamonds through its journey from the mines to the hands of discerning customers globally is a huge value to global trade as it assures the authenticity of the product and that the diamonds are not manufactured in conflict zones. It further facilitates a P2P commerce without any trusted intermediaries, which is currently the order of the day. Supply chain tracking through Blockchain that assures authenticity of transported shipments along with P2P ecommerce offer a undeniable and huge disruption to the way the ecommerce is done today through centralised global giants operating with single points of failure.

Everledger is a leading exponent of Blockchain technology for tracking supply chain of diamonds across the world to ensure the authenticity and source of the diamonds on a Hyperledger fabric based platform.

Base Metals

The regulations for Tin, tantalum and Tungsten, (the metals critical for the

Electrical batteries and Electrical vehicles) specifically require proof of ethical and sustainable sourcing of metal for the buyers

Metal supply chain has complex networks making the proof of transparency of supply chain hard to achieve. Today, the provenance of minerals simply cannot be assured after it has passed through the global supply chain

Further the child labour and unsafe mining practices are also one of the biggest problems in the base metals mining. Buyers require provenance of the fair practices adopted in mining. The intensity of the problem can be understood as follows:

	31%	**1.7 billion**	**$430 billion**
Smartphones	of world population owned smartphones by end 2017	projected annual sales by 2021	industry revenue in 2016

	13%	**14 million**	**50%**
Electric Vehicles	of all passenger vehicle sales in 2025 will be EVs	projected sales in 2025, up from 1 million in 2017	2025: European & North American share of market

The above statistics demonstrate that the requirement of proof of ethical and sustainable sourcing of metals – Tin, Tantalum and Tungsten critical for the production of smart phones, Electrical Vehicles & Electrical batteries will substantially increase

A solution is required, that would establish a single source of truth with multiple parties the requirement, to

- Establish authenticity of the source of metal; and
- Provenance of the fair practices in the mines

Blockchain becomes a perfect technology with the attributes of the above solution for the above problem. The users of mining chains will have a distributed ledger with immutable record of the trace of the metal across the life cycle, material composition, identity and chain custody. The same would act as trust engine between multiple parties in the supply chain

The traceability and provenance feature of Blockchain is expected to save a lot of lives

A high level architecture of the Blockchain in the mining for base metals is demonstrated below:

d. Construction Industry- where Blockchain performs the best with IoT, AI & Analytics

Construction industry offers significant opportunity for improvements in productivity and profitability with use of advanced digitization and automation technologies.

A case study of using Blockchain along with digitization, IoT implementation and AI & Analytics based digital support system is outlined here

Problems faced by construction company are mentioned:

- Lack of **coordination, collaboration and commitment** between vendors, architects, and contractors.
- **Design problems** from Architect (many changes and inconsistent information)
- **No timely detection** of poor quality of materials and component supplied
- Inefficient information transfer
- **Incorrect equipment maintenance** cycles
- Inefficient performance measurement and control scale for labour and other parties
- **Most importantly**, lack of visibility on supply chain of multiple projects leading to operational inefficiencies
- Limited **visibility on the project status** and the transparency of the project

The above problems are summarized in the below architecture:

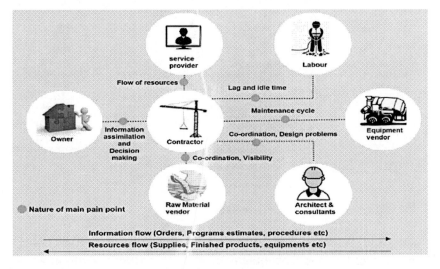

The above problems faced by the construction company could be categorized below:

Operational management of raw material, equipment and labour: It could be solved using IOT based architecture at appropriate levels, which would

- monitor the inventory levels of raw material;
- monitor the equipment usage as per the standards; and
- labour attendance and performance management

Data integrity: The data and information flowing across multiple parties through IoT based systems and manual interactions could be recorded and reconciled using a data platform built on the Blockchain system

A unified view on the construction supply chain and decision support system: Analytics operating across the historical data with comparisons to the multiple supply chain systems, could give results providing insights, decision support tables & graphs over a dashboard to the company. A Decision Support System could be further built to give a unified view over the multiple supply chains in construction industry and help decision making at the inventory, labour and cash management.

Further, a self-learning system using Artificial Intelligence could be built, which would learn the patterns of abnormal events in the past and the decision making during such events by management. The learning could be used to provide red flags to the management in where the current and future circumstances at the supply chain of construction company indicate risk of abnormal events. Further, the system could be trained to suggest solutions to the management.

The above implementation could be explained by way of following diagram.

Step wise adoption of the Data platform, IOT, Decision support system and AI

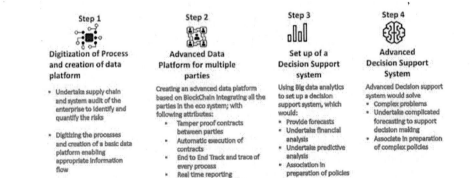

Step 1	Step 2	Step 3	Step 4
Digitization of Process and creation of data platform	**Advanced Data Platform for multiple parties**	**Set up of a Decision Support system**	**Advanced Decision Support System**
• Undertake supply chain and system audit of the enterprise to identify and quantify the risks • Digitizing the processes and creation of a basic data platform enabling appropriate information flow	Creating an advanced data platform based on BlockChain integrating all the parties in the eco system; with following attributes: ▪ Tamper proof contracts between parties ▪ Automatic execution of contracts ▪ End to End Track and trace of every process ▪ Real time reporting ▪ Single source of truth in multiple party system; Visibility of all projects together	Using Big data analytics to set up a decision support system, which would: • Provide forecasts • Undertake financial analysis • Undertake predictive analysis • Association in preparation of policies	Advanced Decision support system would solve • Complex problems • Undertake complicated forecasting to support decision making • Associate in preparation of complex policies

One of the doubts that the construction company carry is that, whether the above technology adoption could be integrated with the current systems and if so, how would be the integration mechanics:

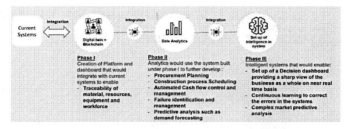

An architecture post implementation of all stages is as below:

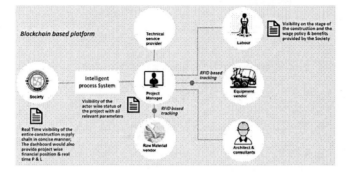

The combined implementation of 'Blockchain, IOT , AI & Analytics' is expected to have a reduction of over 10% in costs through proper monitoring, input provisioning and tracking.

Source: Sanat Bhat (Founder, Credence, and AVP, Strategy & Finance at Infinichains, Patent holder of BlocCal – Tool that calculates the Blockchain value at ROI level.

Auxeldger, India's leading enterprise Blockchain application company innovated the concept of 3 Dimensional non-duplicable and unique tags that can be used in place of the normal QR codes and bar codes.

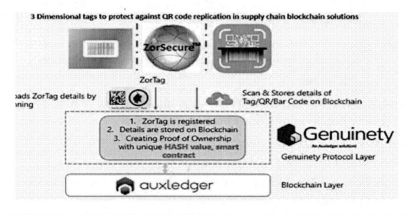

Courtesy: Auxledger, Auxesis foundation

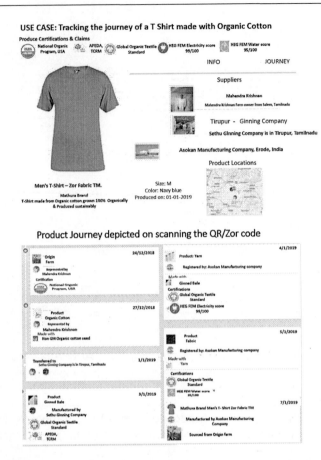

Product Journey depicted on scanning the QR/Zor code

Blockchain Killer Applications in Loyalty Management

The conventional loyalty management is a system where individual organizations have to undertake enormous efforts to manage their own programs. There is a lack of trust and transparency as well as, limited options to redeem for the members to whom loyalty points are issued.

Loyalty Management on the Blockchain is one of the biggest disruptions caused by Blockchain technology. Blockchain can be created to allow interactions among various stakeholders like

- Retail, ecommerce & other partner organizations marketing their services and issuing / redeeming loyalty points;

- Members who access the network and redeem their loyalty points from any of the partner members and

- Auditors and other service providers offering various services to the partner members to validate & authenticate transactions, audit point conversions and redemptions to create a smooth interface & dispute resolution between partner companies and members.

This allows an aggregation and versatility of the platform as against the isolated and suboptimal way in which most of the loyalty programs operate today.

A sample and basic reference architecture for managing the loyalty points seamlessly leveraging the Hyperledger Blockchain framework is given below.

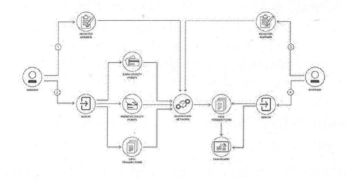

Courtesy: IBM

The technical adoption and operation of the above architecture of the above is explained below:

The network will have multiple members and partners

- Member is registered on the network by the admin of the Blockchain promoter

- Member can sign-in to make transactions to earn points, redeem points and view their transactions

- Partner merchant is registered on the network

- Partner merchant can sign-in to view their transactions and display dashboard

Identity and access management module, payment module and loyalty rewards management modules are created and managed through the respective modules and connected to the Blockchain through APIs. Various participants like admin users, businesses, auditors, developers, service providers, auditors and retail customers are connected to the Blockchain and access the system benefits through their respective interfaces.

The sample code pattern prided on the Github by IBM Hyperledger fabric team allows for the following steps:

- Create basic business network using Hyperledger Composer framework

- Deploy the network to an instance of Hyperledger Fabric locally or on IBM Blockchain Starter Plan

- Build a Node.js web application to interact with the Blockchain network using Composer API. The web application shows a basic dashboard for the partner displaying the total points that they have allocated and redeemed to members. As transactions get complex, the partner can perform analysis on their transactions to create informative dashboards.

The customers walking into various partner retail points can be tracked through IoT based systems like beacons placed in the partner institutions and integrated into the Blockchain vis edge servers and respective APIs.

Thus a versatile Blockchain based system that connects different types of online and offline customers of various platforms acting as partners, redemption services, payment gateways and various other relevant services can be integrated seamlessly to conduct the transactions in an utmost trust with each other, powered by distributed ledger technology & smart contracts.

Blockchain Killer Applications for managing IoT devices, drones and automobiles

Internet of Things (IOT) is deemed to be one of the fastest growing phenomena in the coming days with estimates pointing to tens of billions of connections being added to the internet through connected things that define the way we live in the future.

IOT is deemed to have wide spread usage in industries, manufacturing, retail, consumer, health care, smart city, transportation & logistics, energy management, agricultural, environmental, financial, automobile, government and military applications.

IOT also becomes an easier target to the malware attackers to penetrate and flood the internet with unwanted traffic creating nuisance to global population at large. The havoc caused by the Mirai virus that attacked a mere 6 lakh devices to shut down a large number of publisher sites in October 2016 is a pointer of the things to come.

The following figure gives a brief overview of the Mirai attack that shut down a number of websites and portals globally in September-October 2016:

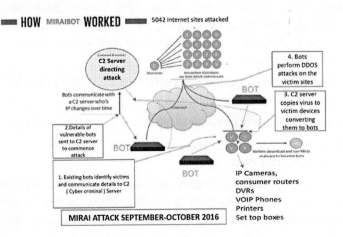

There have been a number of instances, where, cyber-attacks have been used as a weapon of state sponsored act to penetrate adversary computer systems and shut down their activities.

StuxNet was one such attack apparently conducted by US & Israel forces on Iranian Nuclear weapon program.

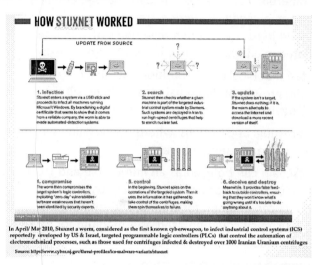

In April/ May 2010, Stuxnet a worm, considered as the first known cyberweapon, to infect industrial control systems (ICS) reportedly developed by US & Israel, targeted programmable logic controllers (PLCs) that control the automation of electromechanical processes, such as those used for centrifuges infected & destroyed over 1000 Iranian Uranium centrifuges

Source: https://www.cyber.nj.gov/threat-profiles/ics-malware-variants/stuxnet

The advent of the 'Smart City' concept is leading to a number of IoT devices being used across the landscape of modern infrastructure for leveraging automation of building, home, corporate and convenience facilities. The vulnerability of many of these IoT devices have been well exposed in a research study undertaken, namely the 'Chain Reaction' attack.

ZigBee Chain reaction Attack

Chain reaction is an academic simulation project that demonstrates he vulnerability of a set of IoT devices to penetration by unauthorized worms that can enter the system through a single device like a Philips Hue bulb

> **Source:** (https://eprint.iacr.org/2016/1047.pdf).

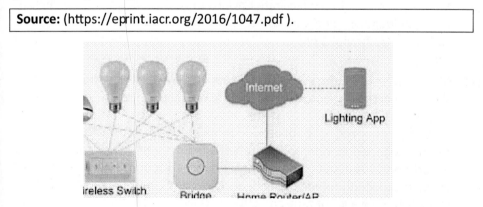

IoT Goes Nuclear: Creating a ZigBee Chain Reaction (research paper website), IACR

E-print submission. Eyal Ronen, Colin O'Flynn, Adi Shamir and Achi-Or Weingarten

By gaining an unauthorized access through a single infected bulb and placing it in a network controlled by ZigBee protocol, the hackers were able to take over an entire IoT network of devices showing the vulnerability of an entire Smarty populated with different IOT devices. Though the vulnerability associated with this device was later plugged, it demonstrates the real cyber threat faced by IoT dominated world in future where a new types of vulnerable communication networks are created in addition to the numerous already existing networks.

Hence it is expected that Blockchain adoption is a must to protect the IOT devices. Needless to say, the growth of Blockchain technology will therefore closely track the growth of IOT devices.

Some of the interesting applications where Blockchain is being leveraged to protect the IOT devices are outlined here.

(a) **Energy:** Blockchain can be used as an immutable and trusted repository of data for the source and performance of various renewable energy devices. Smart contracts can be used for trading and exchange of energy produced while, cryptocurrency could be used as a medium for facilitating the trade between the producers and suppliers.

(b) **Building automation:** Blockchain can be used to identify and offer trusted access to IoT devices that are used extensively in facility automation projects and facilitate authorized interactions with the devices for building access controls, parking lot automation, energy & utility management.

(c) **Industrial automation:** Blockchain can serve extensively in 3D manufacturing by serving as a trusted repository of patented & specialized designs, facilitating trusted interactions between machines and in tracking the provenance of genuine spare parts. Robots and drones can be managed in a secure manner to deliver desired outcomes without the threat of being hacked for unwanted outcomes.

(d) **Mobility:** Blockchain can facilitate tracking of vehicles on the move, Vehicles could be identified and various fees collected by authorities towards, toll, parking or traffic violations as well, without any room for dispute and lack of trust.

(e) **Disaster Management:** Drones can be used extensively for various purposed like photography, environmental hazard tracking, security and mapping in geographic information systems. Blockchain can be used extensively in ensuring authorized usage of drones. By mapping the information and visual records collected to various authorities like police, emergency services, fire department, local self-governmental agencies etc., through a Blockchain enabled distribution ledger, incident responses could be done in a rapid manner to save a lot of time and effort in times of distress.

(f)   **Insurance:** Blockchain can be extensively used to track and monitor the insurance record management and redressals of cases in all industries and for all automobiles.

(g)   Bosch one of the global leaders in developing & implementing cutting edge technologies in the automobile & medical electronics and TUV, have made significant contribution in developing Blockchain applications to manage automobiles through smart phone applications connected to the Blockchain. The connected cars can safely and securely track and record various performance and status related features of the automobile like odometer readings, fuel tank readings, mileage of car and tyre performance etc., a data which is very much useful for preventive maintenance. This also prevents the odometer frauds associated with drivers maintaining fuel usage records, travels and used car transactions.

IBM Watson IoT platform is an excellent initiative by IBM to seamlessly integrate the IOT devices to the Blockchain eco-system to enable them to enjoy the benefits and safety of distributed ledger applications. By using Watson IoT Platform on Blockchain, Internet of Things (IoT) devices can send data to and invoke smart contract transactions on IBM Blockchain Platform or on the open source Hyperledger Blockchain. For more information one may refer https://www.ibm.com/support/knowledgecenter/en/SSCG66/iot-Blockchain/overview/architecture.html Figure- Courtesy, IBM

Secured Access and Management of automobiles using Blockchain

Autonomous driving vehicles are expected to come onto roads in large numbers and are an amazing extension of IOT technology combined with artificial intelligence and machine learning applications. However, they are extremely vulnerable to hacking by cyber criminals. Blockchain offers the best possible security to the autonomous vehicles to ensure they are manipulated and their owners held to ransom.

In December 2017, an exciting disruptive technology company, XAIN and the global leader in automobiles, Porsche announced a partnership to take Blockchain technology to the management of cars.

XAIN and Porsche successfully tested a proof of concept in which an Ethereum client is fused to the car's systems and is connected to the Blockchain network comprising of IPFS and BAAS nodes in the azure market place. The car is tracked and managed through smart contracts and owner wallet present in the smartphone of its owner. The car's systems are tracked and all the parameters recorded in the vehicle wallet that keeps track of various aspects about the car's performance and activities etc.

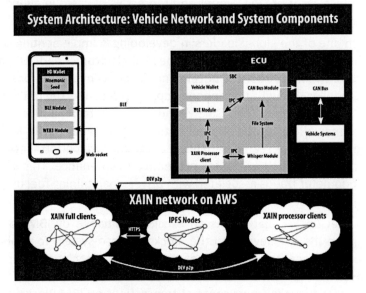

Porsche - XAIN Vehicle Network System Architecture

System architecture of Blockchain powered car management implemented by Porsche & XAIN

Figure courtesy: Porsche Digital Lab (https://medium.com/@porsche_tech)

Source: https://medium.com/next-level-german-engineering/the-porsche-xain-vehicle-Blockchain-network-a-technical-overview-e1f48c40e73d

The system will allow the authorised owners to access and communicate with their cars using the smartphone connected to the network and do the following from anywhere in the world through internet or through Blockchain powered direct offline connection in a secure manner:

- Lock, unlock doors and luggage compartments from distance securely
- Communicate with other cars in the network and exchange information
- Record and manage all critical information on a decentralised trust less system
- Prevent hacking by cyber criminals.

Blockchain Killer Application as Registry

Registries come in various forms like land records, motor vehicle records, medical records, personal records, academic records , scholastic records, municipal certificates, building approvals, corporate records, audited financials etc.

Blockchain could be an excellent system for the record maintenance, reconciliation, single truth and recall capacity. A high level architecture is below:

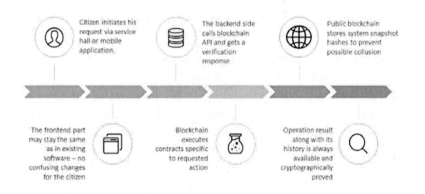

While in most cases the records are updated in the Blockchain after due authorization by the issuing authorities, in a number of cases they are represented on the Blockchain through hash of the actual record that is maintained in an IPFS/ normal database depending on the privacy issues in the respective countries and the given situation.

It has to mentioned that, in some countries, data privacy regulations like GDPR of European Union, warrant that the personal data of the clients and constituents to be mutable. In such a scenario, instead of storing large data files on the Blockchain or in IPFS, the private data has to be stored in normal databases and only their hashes have to be stored on the chain.

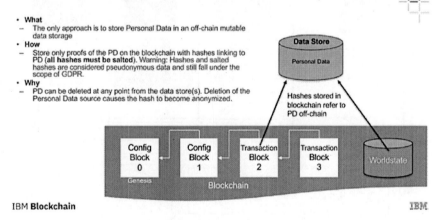

Some of the implementations and PoCs are listed below:

- The Andhra Pradesh Government in India is using Blockchain to record land titles and resolve disputes (Source http://economyria.com/ Blockchain-india/)

- In August 2018, a Hyderabad-based Blockchain startup announced it would launch Blockchain to digitize educational certificates, with IIIT Basar as its first customer

- The Union Government has mandated CDAC to develop a pilot for a Blockchain-based land registration system

- Eleven01 Foundation announced it plans to develop an India-specific Blockchain protocol defining the standards for its usage in India

- Niti Aayog is working on launching Indiachain, one of the largest Blockchain platforms in the world for governance. It plans to link Indiachain to IndiaStack and other governmental databases built around the India's unique identity project, Aadhaar that will enable the development of products and services on the country's digital infrastructure.

India's leading Blockchain development company, Auxledger has pioneered implementation of Blockchain in Universities for storing academic and non-academic records. The representation of the Blockchain based system by Auxledger is given in the following diagram.

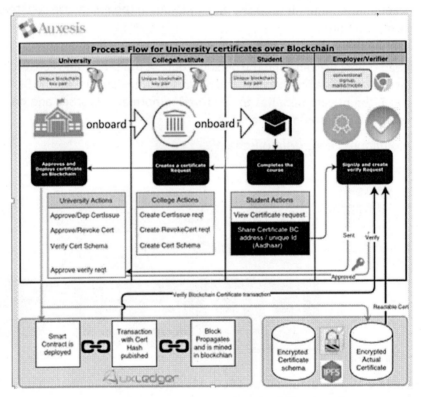

The representative flow of events is depicted in the following diagram.

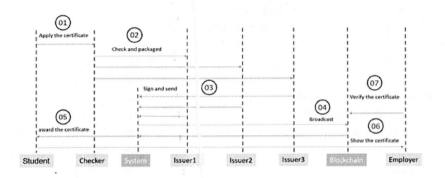

The solution architecture for the academic certificates Blockchain is depicted as follows:

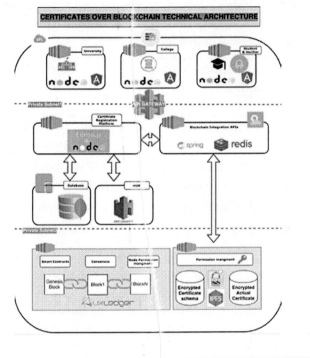

Source: Auxledger (Auxesis foundation)

Blockchain Killer Application - Disrupting Ecommerce

Ecommerce today is a US Dollar 5 Trillion industry globally. There are many ecommerce marketplaces that act as middlemen between buyers and sellers between the interested parties and offer various services. In return they pocket a lot of margin for providing and ensuring the trust between various parties. Ecommerce sites which are most trusted by third parties, with good practices become highly valued global players and attract millions of customers. They implement advanced AI & Analytics solutions to manage the information & mine maximum value out of it. They undertake targeted advertisements and promotions controlling and commercially exploiting the information of their customers more and more. While in many ways, these have positive outcomes enhancing the convenience of their customers, the movement towards decentralization and the tendency on the part of these various centralised organizations as suspected single point of failures either knowingly or unknowingly or by being subjected to malicious ransomware and cyber-attacks has led to the people realizing the potential of Blockchain based marketplaces as an attractive alternative to most of these businesses.

The ability of Blockchain to offer the provenance of the goods implies that the genuinity & authenticity of the products can now be assured by automated Blockchain based platforms. When combined with decentralised payment mechanisms of the Blockchain, it is possible to envisage an application that potentially can be a huge disruptive force.

Blockchain based Ecommerce	Marketplace's stack without Blockchain	Market Place's stack with Blockchain
Network	Trusted Third party	Trust on Automation & Cryptographic security
Technology Infrastructure	Payment gateways Data Exchange protocol	P2P Payments Blockchain protocol
	Hosted on centralised servers	Decentralised hosting
Data	Owned by the ecommerce provider	Individually owned and Private

At the simplest level, ecommerce DAPP on a platform is like an escrow service that collects money from the buyers and remits the seller, once the supply is made and conditions are met. There could be arbitrators or third parties who act as and when required to resolve the differences that may arise during the transactions.

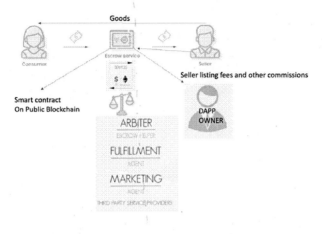

Figure: Goods and Funds flow in Ecommerce DAPP

The promoter of the ecommerce DAPP will be programmatically credited with the sales margins and the various service providers with their fees and incentives from the sales proceeding for successfully conducting their parts. All these transactions are transparently and immutably recorded on the Blockchain and the promoters will not get any access to the personal information w.r.t the customers on the platform.

Blockchain based market place applications are well suited for virtual goods. The Ethereum platform based DAPP, 'Cryptokitties' that facilitates investing in uniquely created 'cat shapes' in a programmatic manner, captured the imagination of many Blockchain followers. Each cat shape is a uniquely created token based on the ERC 723 standards as a collector's piece.

It is possible to create many such games where in different types of shapes that of aliens, animals, robots etc., can be generated and traded on the Blockchain. These items can be tracked from the origin, indefinitely as they pass from one owner to the other and can also be redeemed into cash electronically, without need of a third party, which is not possible in ordinary market places.

Thus, Blockchain based marketplaces offer a lot of unique advantages over the normal marketplaces.

Blockchain disrupting 'Hotel booking '

We have a number of platforms that act as a market place between customers of boarding & lodging services and property owners offering their properties for rent or lease for temporary purposes.

The LockTrip application is an open source application allowing different operators to create their own Blockchain DAPP for connecting property owner and the customers with a scope for earning margin and value for their services offered, to facilitate the transactions on their respective platforms.

The comparative architectural study of current solutions for Hotel Booking vs Decentralized systems under LockTrip is explained in the below diagram:

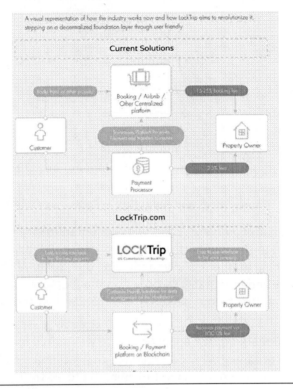

Source: Locktrip whitepaper

The application architecture consists of:

- Database of all listings and requirement posted along with descriptive details that include documents, user ratings, photographs, certifications, audit reports etc., in databases with the respective nodes of the platform operators. The meta tags of this information along with their identifiers are stored on the Blockchain

- All the transaction details are recoded on the blockchain like listings, bookings, settlements and expiries of listings are updated and maintained on the Blockchain

- The Blockchain applications are accessed by the users and partners using web interfaces with convenient user interface through web and mobile clients and transactions are pushed into the system through the same

Blockchain disrupting cab sharing business

Mobile application based transport service platforms have become synonymous with the public taxi system in almost all the countries of the world. From providing the rental cab to the personal cab, carpool, bike rides, and luxury cab services, such platforms offer every possible conveyance system to lure their customers. But the current ecosystem has many loopholes due to the centralized approach to manage the business operations. Like other industries, Blockchain is all set to bring disruption to app based cab service platforms.

With the increasing use of smartphone and internet connectivity, the on-demand transportation industry is expecting to grow eightfold by 2030. In the USA alone, more than 5 billion rides were completed in 2017. Users of taxi services are supposed to increase to 500 million users by 2021.

Some of the pain points that exist currently in cab service platforms:

- **High fees due to intermediaries:** As of now, when riders book the cab, the notification is first sent to the company and then the driver is allocated for a specific ride. The cab companies charge 10-20 percent of the total ride's pricing, increasing cost to the customers.

- **Lack of Transparency:** Also, due to the lack of transparency in the current ecosystem, it is impossible for the riders to understand how companies function, especially when subjected to surge pricing or sudden variations in prices.

- **Lack of Safety Standards:** One of the significant issues faced by cab companies currently is to take care of the safety of both rider and driver. Taxi organizations are spending millions of dollars on verifying the users, but despite their efforts, incidents of fraudulent identities and crime are still touching the skies.

Though appearing to be person to person dealing platforms, these are managed by centralised entities.

The platform's ecosystem works as follows:

- Riders submit the ride request on an app and the company receives that request
- Following the user's request, a vehicle and driver is assigned to the rider
- Riders complete the ride and they send payment to the company
- App company sends money to the driver by cutting a specific percentage of the amount as the commission fees

Therefore, we need a decentralized approach to overcome the above pain points in the current platforms.

Imagine you want to book a cab and you can directly find the drivers going in your direction without the involvement of cab companies. What if it becomes possible for the riders to see on what basis the ride pricing has been fixed? Blockchain can make this happen by bringing more transparency and efficiency to the system where verified users exchange / avail services without the involvement of third parties and centralised organisations.

High level architecture of Blockchain disruption in ride sharing business:

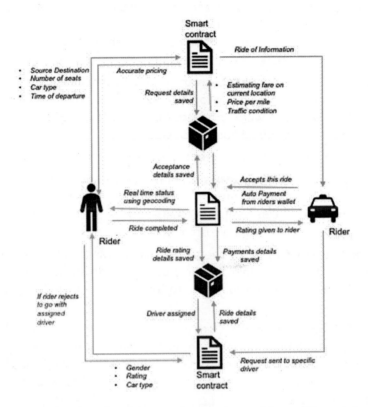

Smart contracts to undertake, driver assignment, provide real time status to users & process payments, ride sharing, fetch driver details, calculate & update fares.

Blockchain Killer Application- Disrupting Social media

The continuous data leakages plaguing the social media leaders and malware attacks exposing their centralised infrastructures as single points of failure are giving rise to the demands of decentralised social media vehicles where the users manage their own identities as self-sovereign identities and are rewarded for their contributions to the platforms or pay for their usage as well.

There are now decentralised versions of all leading social media platforms as mentioned in the annexures enclosed in the book.

The comparison of a typical social media platform e.g. Facebook and a Blockchain version of the same is given in the following:

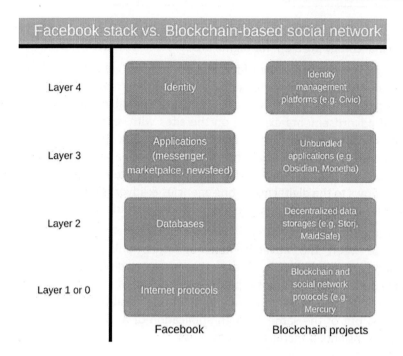

Blockchain Killer Application- Disrupting Advertising Network

The digital advertising market was worth $223.7 billion in 2017. The format is expected to see double-digit growth through at least 2020, eMarketer estimates. This includes promos, ads, content, and messages delivered through email, social media and search engines, as well as banner ads on mobile apps or Web sites and affiliate programs. But two very significant problems have turned this into an inefficient broken industry:

1. **Systemic Fraud:** for many years, all sorts of fraudulent tricks have been systematically used by a shady industry to make the human audience for most digital advertising appear significantly bigger than it actually is: software tricks and bots are used to create artificial viewers (more eyeballs) and artificial viewing intensity (longer attention spans, etc.) Brands are paying for human eyeballs that never looked at their product.

2. Middlemen take around 50% of the money spent on digital advertising, whereas content creators, publishers, and advertisers get less than 50%. (In some sectors, middlemen take as much 65 %.) Recent years have brought many new digital advertising formats to the market.

   New display formats, new social formats, new video formats, and even emerging formats like virtual reality are growing in the market. With the huge growth in digital advertising spending, there has also been a growth in inaccuracies and fraud. In the way that Blockchain solved the double spending problem for the digital currency, Blockchain can solve the ad fraud and inaccuracy problem for digital ads.

Advertising platforms form one of the biggest industry vehicles for placement of targeted advertisements on various sites as per the requirements of marketing and advertising organizations. There is always mistrust possible regarding the various aspects of advertisements exposed on the sites with respect to the veracity of claims on exposures, timing of insertions and the click through rates achieved. Blockchain offers an excellent alternative to act as a via media to eliminate this mistrust so that operations are carried with full transparency. This will also enable good cash flows to the digital marketing agencies & advertising networks, as many times, their invoices are disputed and hence are not settled on time.

AdOne is one such platform which leverages Blockchain to create an atmosphere of trust between the advertisement agencies, publishers and marketing organizations. The authenticity of data that is recorded regarding the insertions and their effectiveness across platforms, sites and associated description parameters offers an excellent quality data for analytical companies to mine and get the best out of the same through application of AI & ML techniques to get tremendous insights & increase effectiveness.

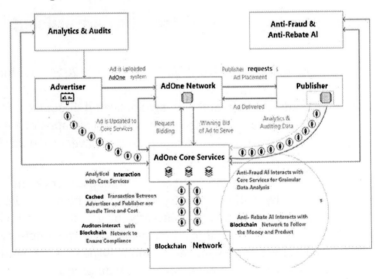

Source: AdOne Whitepaper

(**Credits:** Nausherwan Shah, Akash Gaurav, Cofounders, Auxledger, Auxesis group & Chaithanya Hiramath)

Network Flow

The basic network flow is easily understood and compatible to other ad networks in all the aspects familiar to traditional marketers. A publisher creates content with advertising spots then accesses the system to ensure those spaces are available through the AdOne network.

Advertisers access the system and put their ads into the system—ready to anticipate in the real-time bidding system. When the process is finished, the ad is delivered to the publisher's site and the system makes a payment from the advertiser to the publisher. When a certain threshold is reached, a bundle of transactions from an advertiser to a publisher is executed on the Blockchain network. The system logs data and metadata of these transactions and makes this available to the analytics and anti-fraud systems. The system uses artificial intelligence to offer unparalleled insight and fraud prevention.

Evolving Blockchain Business Models- The way forward

Blockchain at its heart is an infrastructure that allows the organizations to dramatically lower their costs and improves their productivity and profitability in the long run, Its akin to the telecom infrastructure for cellular companies or cloud service for a typical fast growing organization that needs a substantial upfront investment, but offers a long term return through cross company and cross department collaboration to streamline and automate processes, enhancing trust and accountability.

While implementing cloud services to enhance the network infrastructure of the company, one takes into account the following scenarios:

(a) **Private cloud:** Private cloud is a network and hardware infrastructure created by the company to take care of its expansion needs and caters exclusively for the needs of the organization and its subsidiaries. This is created & or managed by the company itself or by a third-party vendor and is managed on or off premises exclusively for its use.

(b) **Hybrid Cloud:** Hybrid cloud consists of a combination of public cloud and private cloud where private cloud is used for mission critical applications that are extremely confidential. This involves funding through a combination of capital expenditure and operational expenditure on the part of the company,

(c) Public cloud offers tremendous flexibility, a high level of security and is financially viable for the organization at times for a quick role out, pay as you use model that adapts to changing infrastructure needs. However, these are created & maintained by third parties with a massive investment that is remunerated through the payments made by the users on a SAAS/PAAS/IAAS mode. IBM, Amazon, Oracle, Azure offer cloud infrastructure as a service to most global organizations.

In a similar manner, it is expected that Blockchain infrastructure is expected to grow in the future with organizations creating their applications as private/public permissioned, hybrid and public permission less Blockchain applications in the future. Since the utility of the Blockchain is best felt in the collaborative and cooperative approach among the participants, consortiums and industry bodies are best suited to thrive in the coming years.

Currently permissioned Blockchain for enterprise applications is predominantly being implemented in the following 3 formats:

Consortium based network: A set of organizations come together and start a Blockchain network as equal participants. Later, they add a number of members who pay a subscription fees to avail the services of the consortium. This is like a cooperative society run by a governing body. The members could form a joint legal entity to collectively share the costs and benefits of the operations. IBM Food trust is an example of such a platform.

Founder directed network: In a founder directed network, a dominant player in an industry or the leading organization in a group takes a lead and initiates the implementation of Blockchain. The founder member acts as a leader and a sole administrator and provides the platform for more and more people to join the network and collectively benefit from such a platform. Blockchain applications for government applications generally fall in this category.

Community based networks: Initiated by industry bodies and associations, the community-based network forms the best form of new age Blockchain systems that have their foundation in a collaborative & collective fabric aimed to be promoted by Blockchain paradigm for a win-win approach. Sometimes regulatory authorities and most times, the evolving competitive scenario promote the move towards a massive adoption of community based Blockchain networks of the future. IBM Watson supply chain consortium is an example of such a network facilitated by IBM, the global leading company promoting the movement towards Blockchain adaption across entities.

While the formation of consortiums is going to greatly accelerate the adoption across the user group, it is very important to have a proper governance mechanism involving the stake holders and administrators to facilitate a systematic and productive evolution of the network. A strong 'Governing board' with a proper mandate, resources, competence and authority should be formed and handed over the governance of the consortium operating the Blockchain and to interface with all internal & external stake holders and technology vendors, collaborators and partners.

Hybrid networks that combine elements of public, permission less as well as permissioned Blockchains are seen to be the fastest growing segment of applications in the near future for enterprise applications. For example, land records & other registries maintained by governments need to be maintained in a permissioned ecosystem but, access needs to be provided to public at large to verify ownership & authenticity claims.

Blockchain implementation & integration challenges

The steps for implementing Blockchain have been comprehensively described in the earlier chapters. Broadly, they fall under the following set of activities:

(A) **Assessment:** Determine if implementation of Blockchain is deemed the appropriate solution to address the pain points,

(B) **Readiness:** Conduct workshops across the participant groups with in and across the organisation and user groups to prepare the groundwork for its acceptance and smooth implementation.

(C) PoC for the most appropriate use case: Initiate, develop and execute a proof of concept with a limited budget to solve the pressing problem on hand and assess its utility, while convincing all concerned about the potential of Blockchain led solution.

(D) **Implementation:** Full scale solution with all the relevant hardware, infrastructure, middleware and smart contracts are now ready to be developed and instituted across the organisation as per the use case. Once they are ready, they should be tested for their functionality and error free execution.

(E) **Blockchain integration with current systems:** It is a very important question for the industry as a whole as to what the challenges for Blockchain system are, to integrate with existing systems of the company and how they would be addressed.

   o   In case where the Blockchain is system of records, there do not exist any integration hurdles

   o   Smart contracts interact with the existing systems of the organizations by querying/ exchanging the information with them as needed,

   o   Most organizations have an integration module that exposes the internal systems as API services.

   o   Gateways are used to bridge the formats and connect peers in the Blockchain network and the existing systems

Interaction between the Blockchain and the existing system is also captured in the below diagram:

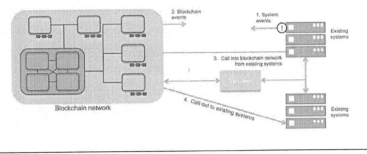

Source: IBM

In April 2018, IntellectEU, a global leader in Fintech integration announced the launch of Catalyst, a platform to integrate traditional infrastructures with multiple Blockchain networks including networks built with Hyperledger Fabric. Catalyst served as the hub for connecting the insurance database, the car dongle (IoT device), end-user mobile application and Hyperledger Fabric itself. In a proof of concept for a car insurance company, Hyperledger Fabric and Catalyst were used to create a flexible, pay-per-mile insurance product based on the actual car mileage and condition of the vehicle. The prototype insurance product was connected to the insurance database, internet of things (IoT) devices and end-user mobile applications.

(https://www.nasdaq.com/article/intellecteu-launches-catalyst-platform-to-integrate-distributed-ledgers-with-financial-services-cm957024)

(F) **Testing before commercial launch:** Once a Blockchain platform is selected, smart contracts are created and are ready for launch, different aspects of the applications & platforms have to be tested before the final commercial go ahead is given. Some of the smart contract test types that need to be undertaken are, **Expert Code Analysis, Control Flow Analysis, Dynamic Code Analysis, Manual Code Analysis, Vulnerability-Based Scanning, Symbolic Execution, Taint Analysis etc.**

The following are the key factors to be minutely looked at for a successful and flawless execution of Blockchain projects that tend to be very complicated due to the interaction of various components and integrations there of internally & externally as well.

Testing practices and Governance mechanism:

1. Best practices have to be adopted to ensure that there is a systematic approach to every aspect of testing which should be agnostic of people performing it, but has to be driven by processes.

2. Test practices should be continuously reviewed incorporating the best practices and also updating with the learning for continuous improvement. This is very important to keep pace with the dynamic

nature of the various components internally and externally and also that of the evolving threat environment.

Blockchain platform specific parameter functioning of all components should be thoroughly tested and adherence ensued with respect to the following:

1.   Transaction lifecycle performance

2.   Validation of event notifications & transaction state change events across the life cycle

3.   Transaction security through the message propagation lifecycle

4.   Assets creation and there accuracy there of

5.   Functioning of the wallet and storage components

6.   Consensus mechanism performance with respect to the decision making and time stamping process

7.   Performance of the chain code/ smart contracts and the validation of adherence to business rules laid out

8.   Auditability & traceability of the assets

9.   Secured access features as per the access permissions granted etc.

Test Types:

Like in the case of testing routine IT applications, there are different types of tests that need to be performed and adherence established to the quality of the contracts and applications developed before they are put into production. They are:

1.   **Security Testing:** Testing all features with respect to the cryptographic protocols

2.   **Functional Testing:** Performance with respect to all the expected performance features of all aspects of the Blockchain like the different types of nodes, shared database & contract validation.

3.   Non-functional testing to check the performance of Blockchain with respect to the speed and scalability for various loads expected

4.   External component compatibility, integration and interactions should be thoroughly tested with respect to the various APIs, Cloud components and Oracles etc.

It is very important to create a meticulous schedule of testing process in the test server and 100% performance established before the go live event, to ensure scalability, security and smooth performance of the Blockchain applications.

Source: ABC frame work components from the Global Testing Retreat, GTR 2017.

References

http://phasm.co.uk/data-databases-distributed-network

https://assets.kpmg.com/content/dam/kpmg /pdf/2016 /06 /kpmg-Blockchainconsensusmechanism.pdf

https://query.prod.cms.rt.microsoft.com/cms/api/am/binary/RE1TH5G (Advancing Blockchain Security- Whitepaper by Microsoft)

https://www.persistent.com/whitepaper-understanding-Blockchain-consensus-models/

https://www.youtube.com/watch?v=hsq4s_l9ZDM (Enterprise Data Lake: Architecture Using Big Data Technologies - Bhushan Satpute, Solution Architect)

Blockchain Enabled Applications: Understand the Blockchain Ecosystem and How to make it Work for You by Vikram Dhillon (Author), David Metcalf (Author), Max Hooper (Author)

Blockchain: From Concepts to Execution by Debajani Mohanty (Author)

Hands-On Blockchain with Hyperledger: Building decentralized applications with Hyperledger Fabric and Composer by Salman Baset (Author), Luc Desrosiers (Author), Nitin Gaur (Author), Petr Novotny (Author), Anthony O'Dowd (Author), Venkatraman Ramakrishna (Author)

Ethereum for Architects and Developers with Case Studies and Code Samples in Solidity Author: **Mohanty, Debajani (Apress publication)**

Solidity Programming Essentials: A beginner's guide to build smart contracts for Ethereum and Blockchain by Ritesh Modi (Author)

Big Data in Practice: How 45 Successful Companies Used Big Data Analytics to Deliver Extraordinary Results by Bernard Marr

AI and Analytics, Accelerating Business Decisions Hardcover by Sameer Dhanrajani (Author)

NPTEL video course https://nptel.ac.in/courses/nptel_download.php?subjectid= 106105184)

Annexure 1 : Blockchain Glossary

GLOSSARY OF BLOCKCHAIN TERMS	
51% Attack	Majority miners colluding to allow double spending
ABI	Application Binary Interface -Interface generally between a library & user's binary modules
Alt-coin	Cryptocurrencies other than Bitcoin
API	Application Programming interface
bitcoin	First and leading cryptocurreny unit
Bitcoin Blockchain	First Blockchain platform on which bitcoin was launched
Blockchain	Structure of storing data in chronologically and cryptographically linked blocks
Business logic layer	Code embedding business rules
Casper	Proof of Stake based consensus algorithm proposed by Ethereum
CDN	Content Delivery network
Chaincode	Hyperledger version of Smart Contract
Coin	Representation of a digital asset enabling value transfer
Composer CLI	Hyperledger's command line interface for carrying out admin tasks
Consensus Protocal	Software coded mechanism for nodes to come to agreement
CRUD	Create, retrieve, update , delete
Cryptocurrency	Native digital asset created by a Blockchain platform facilitating value transfer
DAO	Decentralised Autonomous Organization like Bitcoin's blockchain with no human control
DARPA	Defence Advanced Research Projects Agency of USA's Defence
DAPPS	Decentralized applications
DDOS Attack	Distributed denial of service
Decentralised	Shared network making decisions without a central authority
Digital Signature	A mathematically generated proof for proving authenticity
DLT	Distributed Ledger Technology for shared, cryptologically secured database
ECDSA	Elliptical curve Digital Signature Algorithm using elliptical curve for generating DSA
Enum	Shortform for Enumeration
EOA	Externally owned Account
ERC	Ethereum Request for Comments
Fork	A change to the way a **blockchain**'s software rules define valid transactions, or **blocks**
Soft Fork	Bacward compatible change requiring majority node adoption
Hard Fork	Change requiring all nodes to comply generally resulting in a new Blockchain
Gas	Unit of value required to conduct a transaction on Ethereum platform
Genesis Block	The first block in any new Blockchain
Github	Web based distributed version control platform for developer collaboration
Gossip	Protocal for disseminating information across and between computer networks
Governance	The administration in a Blockchain platform setting directions
Hash Function	A cryptography tool to create an unforgeable digital fingerprint of any input
Mining	Process by which blockchains add new blocks and create new cryptoassets.
RPC	Remote Procedure Call for constructing distributed client server applications
Smart Contract	Computer program assuring automated guarantee of promise between transactors
Zero-Knowledge Proof (ZKP)	Method of proving that one has knowledge of a value X without revealing the secret information or anything else of ValueX

Annexure 2 - Big Dataanalytics - Applications Across Globalenterprises

Bigdata & Analytics Use Cases

S. No	Industry	Organization	Why	What	How	Results
1	Retail	Walmart	Maximize customer service, minimize stock outs& quick redressal of problems identified	Data Café for near real time analysis for taking immediate actions	Hadoop, Cassandra, Spark, R & SAS for storage, processing, analysis and presentation	Manages data from 200 billion rows of transactional data and from 200 external sources leading to a cycle time reduction from 3 weeks to 20 minutes.

S. No	Industry	Organization	Why	What	How	Results
2	Scientific Research	CERN	Monitor 100s of millionsofcollisions every second that result in subatomic debris existing for millionths of a second generating a huge data.	Millions of collisions emit images that are captured by 100megapixel cameras with high resolution and analyzed with the help of algorithms	LHC computing grid spanning 170 computing centers and 35 countries with 200000 core and 15 beta bytes of disc space analyzed by condensing 300GB per second of data to 300 MB of data , at partner institutions across theworld.	The parallel distributed system's processing power enabled the recording of the sought for Higgs boson particle in 2013.

S. No	Industry	Organization	Why	What	How	Results
3	Online Entertainment	Netflix	Unpredictability of demand with respect to the effort made to create content	Big data analytics on data collected about customer likes, dislikes, experiences, demographics, geography etc. to fuel recommendation engine and tagging of titles. Micro segmentation of customers targeting 80000 genres.	Extensive us of AWS, Big Data Technologies like Hadoop, Hive, Pig, BI tools like Teradata and Micro strategy, Spark for Machine Learning & Analytics, Proprietary tools like Lipstick and Genie	Predictive content programming that Netflix pioneered enables it to gain a big lead over its competitors with a CAGR of over 20%.

S. No	Industry	Organization	Why	What	How	Results
4	Automobile & Aviation	Rolls Royce	Failure of engines used by armed forces and over 500 airlines can cause death of valuable lives and irreparable losses.	100s of peta bytes of data generated during design phase of jet engines, data from IOT sensors fitted to every component of engines and propulsion systems generated during manufacturing, maintenance and after sales service and flight data of every airline is analyzed for proactive action & improvement.	Extensive use of IOT sensors, high powered cluster computers, BigData technologies for storage, processing and analytics across very operation from Design, Manufacturing, Maintenance, Aftersales service and on actual flight data in a live basis to proactively measure and prevent any potential cause of failure. Poka Yoke system for faultless performance of billions of its parts.	Tremendous reduction of design and production costs, innovative service models to charge customers by the hour for the use of their engines and an almost nil cost of failure much better than six sigma (3.6 defects in a billion opportunities).

S. No	Industry	Organization	Why	What	How	Results
5	Oil & Gas	Shell	Increasing costs of operation and dwindling resources for oil production leading to poor profitability and threat to existence	Data from sensors connected to drilling systems collected and analyzed. Monitoring seismic waves for new oil finds extensive use of performance analytics across retail, distribution and logistics Functions undertaken.	BigData infrastructure on Amazon Web Servers, 3D & 3D visualizations of oil fields and potential sources, BigData Analytics from SAS to power CRMfromglobal leaders	Significant improvements in efficiencies across all areas of operation including extraction, distribution and retail
6	Social Media	Facebook	1.5billion users and 2.5 million piece content poses a huge challenge to manage,mine,serve profitably	Data collected from users is matched with their buying patterns and used for mining for targeted ads & cross Promotions	Open source technologies likePHP,MySQL, Hadoop,Hbase, Hive etc.	Significant traction in visitor traffic that offers innumerable data points offering hugevalueunlocked through its digital marketing efforts.

S. No	Industry	Organization	Why	What	How	Results
7	Social Media	LinkedIn	410 million users offer a hue challengetoservein a profitable manner	Army of data scientists analyses every click of every customer to recommend news, connections, serve right ads and recommend subscription plans	Multiple Datacenters, Thousands of machines running ON Hadoop, & other platforms and tools like Oracle, MySQL, Pig,Hive,Kafka, Voldemort& Espresso for Data storage and pinot for analytics	Significant traction & consistent growth of over 10% n sales quarter on quarter with increase in profits.

S. No	Industry	Organization	Why	What	How	Results
8	Financial Services	RBS	Lack of personal touch with customers impacting sales and profitability	Through a philosophy called personology & Advanced Datamining and analytical Techniques Customized recommendation and personalized greeting were delivered with the help of technology	CRM Software by Pegasus, Big Data Hadoop platform by Cloudera, Cassandra for NoSQL and SAS for analytics	Significant improvement in customer satisfaction and better retention levels

S. No	Industry	Organization	Why	What	How	Results
9	Govern-ment	US Immigration	Increasing threat of global terrorism and potential entry of humans into the country to cause immense harm	AVATAR (Automated virtual agent for Truth Assessment) system deployed at selected entry points for immigration into the country to scan entrants and compare the results with suspicious profiles.	Extensive use of Robts, High precision Audio video surveillance systems, BigData collection, processing and Analytics. Extensive use of Artificial intelligence and Machine learning technologies.	Significant increase in levels of accuracy in profiling immigrants, almost nil threats executed since launch thus thesystem proving to be a deterrent and reduction in error prone usage of manpower that can be potentially disastrous at times.

S. No	Industry	Organization	Why	What	How	Results
10	Industrial Conglom-erate	GE	Smallest scale inefficiencies can cause humongous losses due to large scale of operations across different industries using GE Machinery and turbines	Data from Industrial IOT sensorsfittedonto lakhs of machines operating across thousands of customers is collected and analyzed on a real time basis.	Petabytes of data is collected from lakhs of IOT sensors from its industrial customers fed into its Hadoop based Data lake and data analyzed with proprietary tools like Productivity and Predix services and those developed with partners like Pivotal and Accenture.	Machinery supplied by GE operates with highest levels of efficiency and with lowest downtimes with respect to industry standards making GE synonymous with quality, reliability, precision & performance and thus making it a true market leader.

S. No	Industry	Organization	Why	What	How	Results
11	Media	BBC	Tremendous competition to attract and retain viewer's interest to deliver best possible media services that inform, entertain and educate.	Extensive use of algorithmic power predictive analytics to generate recommendation services for viewers. Social media analytics and predicative modellingtofollow predict and create right content for right audience at right time.	Intelligent journalists powered by the knowledge of programming tools, analytic skills & knowledge of tools like Excel, Google Fusion tables etc. Army of data analysts working with BigData technologies like Apache Solr& Data science related tools like MySQL, Python, R etc.	Extremely efficient operations that enable it stay afloat without too much dependence on advertisers, thus maintaining ethics and integrity of highest order, which is a fundamental value dear to the company from the start.

S. No	Industry	Organization	Why	What	How	Results
12	Hotels	Airbnb	Millions of listings across the world andcroresofguests offering/using the rent a stay service	Close tracking of customers' voice, host friendly tools to list and aid appropriate pricing, extensive useofdatascience and BigData analytics	HDFS clusters hosted on Amazon EC2 clusters, query languages like Hive, open source Presto database, proprietary Machine Language platform Aero solve, data analytics platform, Air pal for robust recommendation service and fraud detection & prevention systems.	Tremendous growth, analytics powered employees with more than 30% employees using data driven analytical platforms for decision making leading to all round participation that helpsseamlessscale up.

S. No	Industry	Organization	Why	What	How	Results
13	Financial Services	Experian	Banks, Finance and Insurance companies across the globe depend on Experian for credit references. Need to accurately determine the optimum lendability to potential borrowers and increasing trend of Identity theft and cyber fraud	Demographic, Psychographic, Geographic data of current and potential customers along for micro level segmentation and profiling across various dimensions and also harvesting data from public records, national fraud prevention services of respective countries etc., is collected and leveraged to predict the potential predisposition of borrowers to pay along with their payment capabilities.	Open source Hadoop Architecture along with Spark, Hive for storage, process and analyticsofhuge amount of high velocity data along with Data Visualization tool like Table.	Experian plays an active role in the global financial services industry and servesasa backbone to the same and is continuously evolving to keep up with theincreasing threats from cyber-attacks and keeping the activities of cyber criminals in check acting as a deterrent.

S. No	Industry	Organization	Why	What	How	Results
14	Technology Products and Services	IBM Watson	Computers are constrained by the limitations of their programmers while they are capable of learning by themselves to improveaccuracyof results	Natural language Processing, Machine learning approach with access to comprehensive global information repositories enabling the Watson engine to constantly improve its analytical capability and performance with amazing accuracy to enable partner companies to reap significant performance benefits	IBM Deep Analytics engine running on open source Apache Hadoop BigData framework over 90 IBM 750 servers with 16Terabytes of RAM processing 500 GB of data per second	IBM's partners across industries are able to leverage Cognitive Computing to dramatically improve their productivity, accuracy and profitability

S. No	Industry	Organization	Why	What	How	Results
15	Technology Products and Ser- vices	GOOGLE	Mountainous task to serve Consumers surfing relentlessly across the globe over Billions of pages to get the information they are seeking for bordering on the verge of impossibility.	WebCrawler'sand spiders powered by Google's Proprietary PageRank Algorithm search through 100 Million Gigabytes of information covering over 35 trillion web pages and 20 petabytes of information everyday,toserve the best possible information to the online surfers.	Propriety Database and analysis platforms, BigTable and Big Query, own cloud platform powered by proprietary tools like PageRank Algorithm and advanced Artificial & Machine earning technologies for accurate prediction of customer actions	Undisputed leadership in core areas of operation, growing revenue base and entry into new bleeding edge areas like Automated cars, Home automation etc,, successfully.

S. No	Industry	Organization	Why	What	How	Results
16	Transporta-tion	Uber	Mindboggling amount of data flow across the world from drivers, passengers, location maps and local conditions needing to be synchronized for operational, tactical and strategic purposes	Data from across the world is collected on a live basis including GPS data, driver information, driver ratings, traffic conditions, dynamic spot demand forecasts etc., streamed through BigData platforms and analyzed using powerful analytical engines and actions broadcasted continuously.	Hadoop data lake with Apache Spark to process the data	Rapid growth across the world and ability to forecast the demand accurately at every spot for every time interval thus enabling dynamic pricing and a price- value match for optimum profitability, partner satisfaction & retention.

S. No	Industry	Organization	Why	What	How	Results
17	Social Media	Twitter	Huge amount of information flowing through the portal could contain valuable insights an could be wasted if not analyzed in time	Partnership with IBM Watson to analyses the data concerning selected customers availing Analytics as a service to improve their performance	Big Insights Hadoop service from IBM powered by Watson Analytics	The POC with selected customers has resulted in significant improvement in customer attrition rates by combining their Twitter feeds with IBM Watson Analytics
18	Ecom-merce	Amazon	Customers confused due to too much of choice across categories and listed retailers.	360 degree view of browsers, customers and users of streaming services collected on a live basis to offer recommendation using Collaborative filtering, to find out patterns that assist customers to make right choice for their needs	Propriety platforms, Amazon Cloud services, powered by HewlettPackards hardware running Oracle on Linux	Significant jump in revenues and customers satisfaction levels enabling the company to raise towards the 100 Billion US Dollar annual revenue mark with profits.

S. No	Industry	Organization	Why	What	How	Results
19	Airlines	Etihad Airways	Severe competition, loss of revenue to the perishable nature of unutilized capacities and increasing costs leading to performance challenges	Intensive monitoring of airlines traffic, capacity utilizations, dynamic pricing and improved service for customer delight	.DataLake using Hadoopplatform powered by Cloudera support for advanced analytics powered by Artificial intelligence and Machine Learning. Extensive use of technology across all operations	Significant improvement in capacity utilization and additional turnover resulting in a high ROI from BigData investments.

For extensive use case of BigData analytics across companies and governments globally, one can refer BigData in Practice by Bernard Marr

Annexure 3 – Prominent Blockchain Based Applications and Daos

AREA OF OPERATION	TYPE OF SERVICE	Url	Brief summary
P2P MESSAGING	DECENTRALISED APP	https://bitmessage.org/wiki/Main_Page	Bitmessage is a decentralized, encrypted, decrypted, peer-to-peer, trustless communications protocol that can be used by one person to another person, or to multiple subscribers.
P2P HOME SHARING	DECENTRALISED APP	https://www.beetoken.com/	Beenest is a P2P home sharig network that connects homw owners and guests without any middlemen or commissions.
GIG ECONOMY	DECENTRALISED APP	https://www.bluewhale.foundation/	BWX Decentralized ecosystem for the self employed. A decentralized ecosystem to allow freelancers and the self-employed to reap rewards and benefits from their contributions
FINANCE & SHARE TRADING	DECENTRALISED APP	http://www.trakinvest.com/	Trakinvest is the world's first social trading platform for equities and cryptocurrencies AI engine by a proprietary
PROOF OF EXISTENCE	DECENTRALISED APP	https://www.po.et/	Po.et, generates immutable and timestamped titles for your creative works and register your assets to the Po.et network, secured by blockchain. The metadata attribution remains safe, verifiable and immutable.
Sample Whiteper			https://databrokerdao.com/whitepaper/WHITEPAPER_DataBrokerDAO_en.pdf

TOP BLOCKCHAIN BUSINESS MODELS, PLATFORMS AND DAOs

AREA OF OPERATION	TYPE OF SERVICE	Url	Brief summary
SOCIAL MEDIA REWARDS	BLOCKCHAIN BASED SERVICE	https://isola.ai/	Decentralised social media network using AI/ML techniques to generate revenue from ads for users and alse be immune to blocking and censorship
SOCIAL MEDIA REWARDS	BLOCKCHAIN BASED SERVICE	https://mewe.com/	Twitter like service that promises no ads, no censorship, no tracking
SOCIAL MEDIA REWARDS	BLOCKCHAIN BASED SERVICE	https://obsidianplatform.com/	Obsidian a proof-of-stake, Stratis-based blockchain Messenger service like that of Facebook, that can bypass "cookie" censors aud surveillance. The data used for analytics and advertising
SOCIAL MEDIA REWARDS	BLOCKCHAIN BASED SERVICE	https://nexusearth.com/	Quantum resistant cryptocurrency enables user to buy and sell in the marketplace, puchasing ad space, and donating to crowdfunding campaigns througccryptographically encoded transactious
SOCIAL MEDIA REWARDS	BLOCKCHAIN BASED SERVICE	https://Indorse.io/	Indorse is an Ethereum based alternative to LinkedIn that promotes a "skills economy" with its own currency
SOCIAL MEDIA REWARDS	BLOCKCHAIN BASED SERVICE	https://www.synereo.com/	Monetises original online published content for creators and curators with AMP without any involvement of publishers, media and middlemen.
SOCIAL MEDIA REWARDS	BLOCKCHAIN BASED SERVICE	https://akasha.world/	Twitter like platform for professionals to creative entrepreneurs, Akash combines Ethereum wih the power of IPFS technology to create an uncensoremedia platform.
SOCIAL MEDIA REWARDS	BLOCKCHAIN BASED SERVICE	https://leeroy.io/	Twitter lie service built on Blockchain that tips users for their content creation efforts and participation.
DECENTRALISED DNS	BLOCKCHAIN BASED SERVICE	https://blockstack.org/	Blockstack is a new internet for decentralized apps where users own their data. Blockstack's platform helps entrepreneurs and engineer these apps and deliver better end-user experiences
Tracebility	BLOCKCHAIN BASED SERVICE	http://www.blockverify.io/	Verification of counterfiet, stolen, diverted goods and fraudulent transactions across the domains of Pharmaceuticals, retail, Luxury, diamonds and
IDENTITY AUTHENTICATION	BLOCKCHAIN BASED SERVICE	https://www.cambridge-blockchain.com/	User controlled Digital identity service for authenticating customers by resolves the competing challenges of transparency and privacy, leading to stiregulatory compliance, lower costs and a seamless customer experience
IDENTITY AUTHENTICATION	BLOCKCHAIN BASED SERVICE	https://www.civic.com/	Mobility enabled, Secure user controlled KYC with ID theft protection to allow users monetise their identity .
IDENTITY AUTHENTICATION	BLOCKCHAIN BASED SERVICE	http://www.existenceid.com/index.html	Zero knowledge safe keeping and sharing of valuable identity documents. An amazingly secure and private identity capsule for all of your identity duthat lets you share the information as per your choice.
GAMING	DECENTRALISED APP	https://www.cryptokitties.co/	CryptoKitties is a blockchain based virtual game developed by Axiom Zen that allows players to purchase, collect, breed and sell variou virtual cats
LOYALTY	DECENTRALISED APP	https://bitrewards.network/	Cash backs and Lloyalty points in Cryptocurrency. Merchants get a premium AI-powered rewards platform for free. Shoppers are rewarded for purchcryptocurrency.
IOT DATA MONETISATION	DECENTRALISED APP	https://databrokerdao.com/	DataBroker DAO is the first marketplace to sell & buy sensor data. As a decentralized marketplace for IoT sensor data using Blockchain technology, Databroker DAO enables sensor owners to turn generated data into revenue streams.
DATA MONETISATION	DECENTRALISED APP	https://repux.io/	RepuX Monetizes Data from Millions of Small Enterprises helping Small and medium enterprises get the power of Artifical Intelligence And Machine through access to large pools of trusted data.
P2P ECOMMERCE	DECENTRALISED APP	https://www.openbazaar.org/features/	Openbazaar is a P2P Ecommerce platform without any centralised control online Amazon, Ebay etc, with no middleman to take a cut from each sale completely free e-commerce
P2P ECOMMERCE	DECENTRALISED APP	https://storiqa.com/	Sell and buy goods with cryptocurrencies. No financial borders, extra fees and fake reviews anymore.
INFRASTRUCTURE	DECENTRALISED APP	https://gladius.io/	Managing DDOS Attacks by allowing a marketplace of spare bandwidth. One can rent their computer's spare network bandwidth and earn Gladius
P2P TRANSPORTATION	DECENTRALISED APP	http://lazooz.org/	Peer to Peer Ride sharing application for collaborative transformation

TOP BLOCKCHAIN BUSINESS MODELS, PLATFORMS AND DAOs

AREA OF OPERATION	TYPE OF SERVICE	Url	Brief summary
AGRICULTURE	BLOCKCHAIN	http://agriledger.com/	Blockchain for the Greater Good. Using Distributed Cryptoledger And Mobile Apps To Create A Circle Of Trust For Small Farmer Co-Operatives.
SECURITY	PLATFORM	https://airbitz.co/	Airbitz is a single-signon security platform for blockchain apps.
STRATEGY	CONSULTANCY	https://alphapoint.com/	AlphaPoint helps institutions and companies to discover and implement blockchain strategies. It powers various exchanges around the world, including those for financial institutions. Alpha Point's core solutions are a general-purpose permissioned blockchain solution, digital asset exchange, order routing, and an automatic market making exchange.
SUPPLY CHAIN	BLOCKCHAIN	https://www.descartes.com/appterra	Blockchain: The Next Big Thing in the Supply Chain.
SERVICES	BLOCKCHAIN AS A SERVICE	https://www.ardorplatform.org/	Ardor is the next generation blockchain-as-a-service platform. It has been built on the successful Nxt technology and is designed with unlimited scalability, safe smart contracts, and customizable child chains. These features are designed to increase business profits, efficiency, and security.
ARTISTS & CREATORS	BLOCKCHAIN	https://www.ascribe.io/	Lockin contribution, securely store and share you works & protect copyrights
PREDICTION	SERVICE APP	https://www.augur.net/	An Open-Source. Decentralized, Peer-to-Peer Prediction Market Platform.
SERVICES	DATABASE	https://www.bigchaindb.com/	BigchainDB enables industry leaders to build performant & scalable enterprise applications, platforms, and networks.
CONSULTANCY	SERVICES	http://bitfury.com/products	The BitFury Group offers a full spectrum of products, both hardware and software, to allow businesses and governments to integrate Blockchain technology into their operations.
REAL ESTATE	BLOCKCHAIN	http://landing.bitland.world/	Bitland.World exists to provide the backbone in the effort to unlock land capital through the democratization of real property ownership utilizing leading edge technology.
BIG DATA	APPLICATION & SERVICES	https://bitmark.com/	Convert your Digital Asset s & Data into money
RECRUITMENT	APPLICATION & SERVICES	Bitwadge.com - Not opening	Remote Job Placement and Wage Management Solutions for Overseas Workers.
ARTISTS & CREATORS	BLOCKCHAIN BASED SERVICE	https://binded.com/	Introducing Binded, the world's first copyright platform
SERVICES	Blockchain Platform	https://blockapps.net/features/	deployment and management of enterprise blockchain applications.
HEALTHCARE	Blockchain	https://blockchainhealth.co/	Health app developers can populate data inside cards, which can be used by users to share with research institutions
INFRASTRUCTURE	WEB SERVICES	https://www.blockcypher.com/	BlockCypher is the infrastructure fabric for blockchain applications. Powering blockchains in the cloud. Easily build reliable blockchain applications with our Blockchain Web Services: http://dev.blockcypher.com
CONSULTANCY	SERVICES	http://www.blockness.io/	Consultancy and Advisory
PHARMA	BLOCKCHAIN	https://www.blockpharma.com/	Pharma Blockchain for drug traceability
FINANCIAL	SERVICE	https://thisisbud.com/	An online platform and app which allows users to manage their financial products, with personalised insights, on a single dashboard. Bud's marketplace introduces relevant services which users can interact with through API integrations.
HR	BLOCKCHAIN	https://www.cambridge-blockchain.com/	Identity Compliance Simplified. Cambridge Blockchain puts control of personal identity data back in the hands of the end user. Our platform allows financial institutions to meet the strictest new data privacy rules, eliminate redundant identity compliance checks and improve the customer experience.
CROWDSOURCING	DAO	https://colony.io/	DAO - decentralized autonomous organization, that replicates a company, except instead of being managed by fallible individuals, Colony harnesses the wisdom of the crowd using AI to make sure that the right things get done by the right people, at the right time. Now people can convene and collaborate on large scale projects, even startups, and have a way to manage and measure productivity, as well as provide the means for people to get paid. Colony allows creators to stock value in their own cryptocurrency called "nectar".

TOP BLOCKCHAIN BUSINESS MODELS, PLATFORMS AND DAOs

AREA OF OPERATION	TYPE OF SERVICE	Url	Brief summary
SERVICES	VALUE ADD ON BITCOIN	https://counterparty.io/	Counterparty extends Bitcoin's functionality by "writing in the margins" of regular Bitcoin transactions, opening the door for innovation and advanced features not possible with ordinary Bitcoin software.
SERVICES	DAPPS	https://wingsfoundation.ch/?whitepaper	Decentralized applications for Blockchain-based evaluation, funding and early adopter engagement. Crowd AI with Ethereum and IPFS.
REAL ESTATE	BLOCKCHAIN	http://epigraph.io/	Austin based real estate blockchain technology company building transparent, tamper-proof, next generation title registration solutions for domestic and international organizations."
	PLATFORM	https://ethereum.org/	Open source-platform to write and distribute decentralized applications. Ethereum uses smart contracts which are essentially applications that are run exactly how they are programmed without any possibilities of fraud, 3rd party interference, or downtime.
HEALTH RECORDS	BLOCKCHAIN	https://gem.co/health/	Blockchain based Health records management
COUNTERFEIT PROTECTION	SERVICES	http://www.hikitag.com/About-us.html	Hikitag is an exclusive registration and peer-to-peer authentication service designed to protect brands and fans against the threat of counterfeit. Your product carries a tag with a unique product ID number which, once activated and registered on Hikitag.com or via the app, is matched with ...
SERVICES	PLATFORM	https://hyperledger.org/	...by The Linux Foundation, including leaders in finance, banking, Internet of Things, supply chains, manufacturing and Technology.
RAPID DEPLOYMENT	PLATFORM	https://www.multichain.com/	Multichain helps organizations to rapidly build applications on blockchains and shared ledgers for a number of applications and processes across a wide range of industries.
BLOCKCHAIN 2.0	PLATFORM	https://nxtplatform.org/what-is-nxt/	The Nxt platform includes many core-level features, such as a Decentralized Asset Exchange, Marketplace, and Voting system, all in additional to the NXT digital currency itself
PEER TO PEER ECOMMERCE	APPLICATION & SERVICES	https://www.openbazaar.org/	"OpenBazaar is a different way to do online commerce. Instead of visiting a website, you download and install a program on your computer that directly connects you to other people looking to buy and sell goods and services with you. This peer to peer network isn't controlled by any company or organization - it's a community of people who want to engage in trade directly with each other"
HEALTH CARE	BLOCKCHAIN	https://www.patientory.com/	HealthRecord repository
FINANCE	BLOCKCHAIN	http://www.pufin.org/	Peer to Peer lending
ARTS & MUSIC	SERVICE	http://revelator.com/	Analytics for Music industry
FINANCE	SOLUTION	https://ripple.com/	The world's only enterprise blockchain solution for global payments
IDENTITY AUTHENTICATION	BLOCKCHAIN BASED SERVICE	https://shocard.com/	Digital identity card & the one identity verification system that works the way consumers and businesses need it to for security, privacy, and always-on fraud protection.
SOCIAL MEDIA REWARDS	BLOCKCHAIN BASED PLATFORM	https://steem.io/	Steem is a blockchain-based social media platform where anyone can earn rewards.
REAL ESTATE	BLOCKCHAIN	https://www.ubitquity.io/site/index.html	UBITQUITY - The Blockchain-Secured Platform for Real Estate Transactions & Record keeping
MUSIC	BLOCKCHAIN BASED PLATFORM	https://ujomusic.com/	"We're building a home for artists that allows them to own and control their creative content and be paid directly for sharing their musical talents with the world."
MANAGEMENT CONSULTING	BLOCKCHAIN BASED SERVICE	https://www.vanbex.com/	Vanbex Group is a blockchain professional services firm established in 2013, delivering innovative application development, product strategy, management consulting, and investment marketing.
SUPPLY CHAIN	BLOCKCHAIN	http://wavebl.com/	WAVE connects all members of the supply chain to a decentralized network and allows them a direct exchange of documents. WAVE's application manages ownership of documents on the blockchain eliminating disputes, forgeries and unnecessary risks.
SOCIAL MEDIA REWARDS	BLOCKCHAIN BASED SERVICE	https://ong.social/	ONG MEDIA is a social media dashboard for influencers and uers that runs on Ethereum and Waves at the backend
COMPUTER INFRA	BLOCKCHAIN BASED SERVICE	https://golem.network/	Decentralized supercomputer that allows its members to access their collective computer power and monetise the computing power in their machines
COMPUTER INFRA	BLOCKCHAIN BASED SERVICE	https://storj.io/	End to end encrypted decentralise storage with peer to peer trading of excess hardware storage space in the members' computers

Annexure 4 - Consensus Model Comparison

Parameter	Proof of Work	Proof of Stake	Proof of Elapsed Time	DPOS	Practical Byzantine Fault Tolerance (PBFT & Variants)	Federated BFT	N2N	Round Robin	Tender Mint	Proof of Authority
Description	Unidentified participants can participate in block creation through a gaming process to prove the amount of work done.	Participants with proven stake participate in a stake influenced chance in a lottery to select the leader to announce the block creation	Same as POW, without miners spending money but randomly announcing a wait time, one with the minimum being the winner.	Similar to POS but elated participants nominated by stake hollers participate in block creation	Identified participants participate in Transaction approval	Multiple round of voting from trusted pool of validators	Transaction level agreement between nodes endorsed by a Trusted third party	Transactions are approved by nodes generating subsequent blocks in a round robin manner.	Pluggable Proof of Stake with weighed validators.	Reputed Validators approving transactions as per their stakes.
Blockchain Type	Public	Public	Public/Private	Public	Private/Consortium	Private/Consortium	Private/Consortium	Private/Consortium	Public	Private
Node identity Management	Open, Entirely decentralised	Open, Entirely decentralised	Depending on use case	Open, Entirely decentralised	Identified	Identified	Identified	Identified	Open, Entirely decentralised	Identified
Tolerance	< 25%	<50%	<25%	<33%	<33%	<33%	<33%	<25%	<50%	<33%

Parameter	Proof of Work	ProofofStake	Proof of Elapsed Time	DPOS	Practical Byzantine Fault Tolerance (PBFT & Variants)	Federated BFT	N2N	Round Robin	Tender Mint	Proof of Authority
Platform Token	Yes	Yes	No	Yes	No	No	No	No	Yes	No
Node Scalability	High	High	Limited (under validation)	High	Limited (Tested upto maximum of 100)	High	High	High	High	High
Client Scalability	Excellent	Excellent	High	Excellent	Very High	High	High	High	Excellent	High
Throughput	Low	High	Medium	High	High	High	High	High	High	High
Latency	Poor	Good	Good	Excellent	Excellent	Good	Good	Excellent	Good	Good
Transaction finality	NO	Almost 100%	No	Almost 100%	Yes	Yes	Yes	Yes	Almost 100%	Yes
Implementation cost	Low	Medium	Medium	Medium	Medium	NA	High	Low	Medium	High
Trust in validators	Untrusted	Bonded validators	Untrusted	Untrusted	Trusted	Trusted	Trusted	Trusted	Bonded validators	Trusted
Power consumption	Very poor	Negligible	Negligible	Negligible	Negligible	Negligible	Negligible	Negligible	Negligible	Negligible
Examples	Bitcoin, Ethereum (HS)	Ethereum (Casper)	Hyperledger-Sawtooth	EOS/ Cardano	Hyperledger Fabric	Ripple	R3 Corda	Multi-chain	Cosmos	Ethereum Parity
Correctness Proof	No	No	No	No	Yes	Yes	Yes	No	No	Yes

Parameter	Proof of Work	ProofofStake	Proof of Elapsed Time	DPOS	Practical Byzantine Fault Tolerance (PBFT & Variants)	Federated BFT	N2N	Round Robin	Tender Mint	Proof of Authority
Network Synchrony assumptions	Yes	Yes	Yes	No	No	No	Yes	No	Yes	Yes
Developer Friendliness	High	High	Low	High	Low	Low	Low	Yes	High	Low
Cost of participation	Yes	Yes	No	Yes	No	No	No	No	Yes	No

Annexure 5 - Enterprise Blockchain Applications – Top Use Cases

S.	Application No	Crypto assets	Domain	Key issues	Execution Methodology	Key Point	Platform options
1	Agreements, Invoices, Bills, Timesheets, Multi party approvals	Platform Internal token	Enterprise- Consortium	Paperwork, Trust, De- lays, Mar- gin leaks	Consortium Blockchain with one to one smart contracts	Automation of Process flow & Consensus mechanisms	Hyperledger Fab- ric, R3-Corda,
2	Vehicle manage- ment, Delivery against customer agreements, em- ployee services	Platform Internal token	Enterprise- Consortium	Paperwork, Trust, De- lays, Mar- gin leaks	Consortium Blockchain with one to one smart contracts	Automation of Process flow & Consensus mechanisms	Hyperledger Fab- ric, R3-Corda,
3	HCM, CRM, Manu- facturing, Partner, Retail & Distribu- tion, Internal ap- provals, Mainte- nance, Asset and IOT Devices, IT infra- structure	Platform Internal token	Enterprise- Gover- nance	Trust, De- lays, Paper work	Private Permissioned Blockchain for all branches, depart- ments, employees with designations &pseudo names.	Automation of Process flow & Consensus mechanisms, Mutable external database with replication	Hyperledger Fab- ric, R3-Corda,

S. No	Application	Crypto assets	Domain	Key issues	Execution Methodology	Key Point	Platform options
4	Stock, Private Eq-uity, Crowd funding, Bonds, Mutual funds, Derivate etc.	Financial Assets	Platform Internal token	Enterprise-Gover-nance	Trust, De-lays, Paper work	Permissioned Block-chain, Private mutable access, Notaries, Regu-lators and Auditors to Qualify	Automation of Process flow & Consensus mechanisms, Mutable external database with replication	HyperledgerSaw-tooth, R3-Corda,
5	Cross Border Trade, Transpiration, Shipping	Import – Export	NA	Enterprise-Supply chain	Trust, De-lays, Paper work	Permissioned Block-chain, Private mutable access, Notaries, Regu-lators and Auditors to Qualify	Automation of Process flow & Consensus mechanisms, Mutable external database with replication	Hyperledger Fabric
6	Insurance- Citizen, Vehicle, Machine, Property	Risk Manage-ment	NA	Enterprise-Finance	Trust, De-lays, Paper work	Permissioned Block-chain, Private mutable access, Notaries, Regu-lators and Auditors toqualify	Automation of Process flow & Consensus mechanisms, Mutable external database with replication	HyperledgerSaw-tooth, R3-Corda, Enterprise Ethereum
7	Cross Border Remit-tance	Financial Assets	NA	Enterprise-Finance	Trust, De-lays, Paper work	Permissioned Block-chain, Private mutable access, Notaries, Regu-lators and Auditors toQualify	Automation of Process flow & Consensus mechanisms, Mutable external database with replication	HyperledgerSaw-tooth, R3-Corda, Enterprise Ethereum

S. No	Application	Innovation	Crypto assets	Domain	Key issues	Execution Methodology	Key Point	Platform options
8	Entrepreneurship, Startups, Incubators	Innovation	Platform Internal token	Enterprise-Finance	Trust, Delays, Paper work	Permissioned Blockchain, Private mutable access, Notaries, Regulators and Auditors to Qualify	Automation of Process flow & Consensus mechanisms, Mutable external secured database with replication, Pseudo platform identity	HyperledgerSawtooth, R3-Corda,
9	Marriage, Birth, Death certificates	Public Records	NA	Governance	Trust, Delays, Paper work	Permissioned Blockchain-Public access	Automation of Process flow & Consensus mechanisms, Mutable external secured database with replication, Pseudo platform identity	HyperledgerSawtooth, Enterprise Ethereum
10	Land, Property, Vehicle, Company Registrations	Public Records	NA	Governance	Trust, Delays, Paper work	Permissioned Blockchain-Public access	Automation of Process flow & Consensus mechanisms, Mutable external secured database with replication, Pseudo platform identity	HyperledgerSawtooth, Enterprise Ethereum

S. No	Application		Crypto assets	Domain	Key issues	Execution Methodology	Key Point	Platform options
11	Vehicle	Public Records	NA	Governance	Trust, Delays, Paper work	Permissioned Blockchain-Public access	Automation of Process flow & Consensus mechanisms, Mutable external secured database with replication, Pseudo platform Identity	HyperledgerSawtooth, Enterprise Ethereum
12	Pension ration subsidy, Benefits administration	Public Records	NA	Governance	Trust, Delays, Paper work	Permissioned Blockchain-Public access	Automation of Process flow & Consensus mechanisms, Mutable external secured database with replication, Pseudo platform Identity	HyperledgerSawtooth, Enterprise Ethereum
13	Passport, Identity, Voter, Driver cards	Identification Records	NA	Governance	Trust, Delays, Paper work	Permissioned Blockchain-Public access	Automation of Process flow & Consensus mechanisms, Mutable external secured database with replication, Pseudo platform Identity	HyperledgerSawtooth, Enterprise Ethereum

S. No	Application	Crypto assets	Domain	Key issues	Execution Methodology	Key Point	Platform options
14	IOUs, Agreements, Contracts, Wills, Trusts, Escrows, Bonds	Private Records	NA	IAS (Identity, Authentication, Security)	Trust, Delays, Paper work	Permissioned Blockchain-Public access	Automation of Process flow & Consensus mechanisms, Mutable external secured database with replication, Pseudo platform Identity	Hyperledger Fabric, Factun
15	IOT- Home Automation, Automobile, Machinery, Supply chain, Corporate Asset tracking,	IOT	Crypto currency	IAS (Identity, Authentication, Security)	Trust, Delays, Paper work	Permissioned Blockchain, Public access, Automated consensus, Advanced analytical, identity management and security integrations	Device level identity Management with External Protected, replicated database with Swarm, IPFS,StorJ, Maid safe support	Enterprise Ethereum, ADEPT, IOTA
16	Social Media	Consumer Services	Platform token	P2P- Information	Trust, Delays, Paper work	DAO (Decentralised Autonomous Organization)	Automation of Process flow & Consensus mechanisms, Mutable external secured database with replication, Pseudo platform Identity	Ethereum, EOS, NEM

S. No	Application		Crypto assets	Domain	Key issues	Execution Methodology	Key Point	Platform options
17	Employment portal	Consumer Services	Platform token	P2P Classified	Trust, Delays, Paper work	DAO (Decentralised Autonomous Organization)	Automation of Process flow & Consensus mechanisms, Mutable external secured database with replication, Pseudo platform Identity	Ethereum, EOS, NEM
18	Automobile Exchange	Consumer Services	Platform token	P2P Classified	Trust, Delays, Paper work	DAO (Decentralised Autonomous Organization)	Automation of Process flow & Consensus mechanisms, Mutable external secured database with replication, Pseudo platform Identity	Ethereum, EOS, NEM
19	Marriage portal	Consumer Services	Platform token	P2P Classified	Trust, Delays, Paper work	DAO (Decentralised Autonomous Organization)	Automation of Process flow & Consensus mechanisms, Mutable external secured database with replication, Pseudo platform Identity	Ethereum, EOS, NEM

S. No	Application		Crypto assets	Domain	Key issues	Execution Methodology	Key Point	Platform options
21	Real estate-Rentals, Buy, Sell	Consumer Services	Platform token	P2P Classified	Trust, Delays, Paper work	DAO (Decentralised Autonomous Organization)	Automation of Process flow & Consensus mechanisms, Mutable external secured database with replication, Pseudo platform Identity	Ethereum, EOS, NEM
22	Loyalty	Consumer Services	Platform token	P2P Market place	Trust, Delays, Paper work	DAO (Decentralised Autonomous Organization)	Automation of Process flow & Consensus mechanisms, Mutable external secured database with replication, Pseudo platform Identity	Ethereum, EOS, NEM
23	Etailing	Consumer Services	Platform token	P2P Market place	Trust, Delays, Paper work	DAO (Decentralised Autonomous Organization)	Automation of Process flow & Consensus mechanisms, Mutable external secured database with replication, Pseudo platform Identity	Ethereum, EOS, NEM

S. No	Application		Crypto assets	Domain	Key issues	Execution Methodology	Key Point	Platform options
24	Personal loans	Consumer Services	Platform token	P2P Market place	Trust, De-lays, Paper work	DAO (Decentralised Autonomous Organiza-tion)	Automation of Process flow & Consensus mechanisms, Mutable external secured da-tabase with replica-tion, Pseudo platform Identity	Ethereum, EOS, NEM
25	Training	Mentors	Platform token	P2P Market place	Trust, De-lays, Paper work	DAO (Decentralised Autonomous Organiza-tion)	Automation of Process flow & Consensus mechanisms, Mutable external secured da-tabase with replica-tion, Pseudo platform Identity	Ethereum, EOS, NEM
26	Expertise-Consulting	Mentors	Platform token	P2P Market place	Trust, De-lays, Paper work	DAO (Decentralised Autonomous Organiza-tion)	Automation of Process flow & Consensus mechanisms, Mutable external secured da-tabase with replica-tion, Pseudo platform Identity	Ethereum, EOS, NEM

S. No	Application		Crypto assets	Domain	Key issues	Execution Methodology	Key Point	Platform options
27	Logistics- Market-place	B2B Services	Platform token	P2P Market place	Trust, Delays, Paper work	DAO (Decentralised Autonomous Organization)	Automation of Process flow & Consensus mechanisms, Mutable external secured database with replication, Pseudo platform Identity	Ethereum, EOS, NEM
28	Rentals, Ride sharing	Physical asset-Keys	Platform token	P2P Market place	Trust, Delays, Paper work	DAO (Decentralised Autonomous Organization)	Automation of Process flow & Consensus mechanisms, Mutable external secured database with replication, Pseudo platform Identity	Ethereum, EOS, NEM
29	Hotels and Home sharing	Physical asset-Keys	Platform token	P2P Market place	Trust, Delays, Paper work	DAO (Decentralised Autonomous Organization)	Automation of Process flow & Consensus mechanisms, Mutable external secured database with replication, Pseudo platform Identity	Ethereum, EOS, NEM

S. No	Application	Crypto assets	Domain	Key issues	Execution Methodology	Key Point	Platform options
30	Discounts and Coupons, Loyalty	Platform token	P2P Market place	Trust, Delays, Paper work	DAO (Decentralised Autonomous Organization)	Automation of Process flow & Consensus mechanisms, Mutable external secured database with replication, Pseudo platform Identity	Ethereum, EOS, NEM
31	Prediction Markets, Expertise Trading	Platform token	P2P Market place	Trust, Delays, Paper work	DAO (Decentralised Autonomous Organization)	Automation of Process flow & Consensus mechanisms, Mutable external secured database with replication, Pseudo platform Identity	Ethereum, EOS, NEM
32	Pharma, Authenticity	NA	Provenance-Supply chain	Trust, Delays, Paper work	Permissioned Blockchain, Public access	Automation of Promcess flow & Consensus mechanisms, Mutable external secured database with replication, Pseudo platform identity	Ethereum, EOS, NEM

S. No	Application	Authenticity	Crypto assets	Domain	Key issues	Execution Methodology	Key Point	Platform options
33	Agri-Tracking	Authenticity	NA	Provenance-Supply chain	Trust, Delays, Paper work	Permissioned Blockchain, Public access	Automation of Process flow & Consensus mechanisms, Mutable external secured database with replication, Pseudo platform identity	Ethereum, EOS, NEM
34	Media	Authenticity	Platform token	Provenance-Information	Trust, Delays, Paper work	DAO (Decentralised Autonomous Organization)	Automation of Process flow & Consensus mechanisms, Mutable external secured database with replication, Pseudo platform identity	Ethereum, EOS, NEM
35	Artists, Creators, Brand owners marketplace	Authenticity	Platform token	Provenance-Intellectual Property	Trust, Delays, Paper work	DAO (Decentralised Autonomous Organization)	Automation of Process flow & Consensus mechanisms, Mutable external secured database with replication, Pseudo platform identity	Ethereum, EOS, NEM

S. No	Application	Crypto assets	Domain	Key issues	Execution Methodology	Key Point	Platform options
36	Patents, Copyright, Trademark, Reservation, Awards, Certifications	Intangible assets	Platform token	Provenance-Intellectual Property	Trust, Delays, Paper work	DAO (Decentralised Autonomous Organization)	Automation of Process flow & Consensus mechanisms, Mutable external secured database with replication, Pseudo platform Identity	Ethereum, EOS, NEM

**Ones' personal details freely exposed and monetised by Social media, classified sites, ecommerce portals, finance companies, mobile app platforms etc. GDPR risk to be considered

Annexure 6: Corda Key Concepts

R3 Corda is an advanced Distributed Ledger Platform that implements many properties of blockchain technology and is finding increasing acceptance in regulated industries. Here are some of the important aspects, features and Key concepts of Corda platform including the Trade-offs that were considered by Corda for developing this unique platform that helps us understand the differing aspects of Blockchain systems. (Source R3 corda documentation docs.corda.net).

Trade-offs

Permissioned networks are better suited for financial use-cases, Point-to-point communication allows information to be shared need-to-know & a UTXO model allows for more transactions-per-second are employed by Corda Distributed ledger platform.

Permissioned vs. permissionless

Corda networks are permissioned. Each party on the network has a known identity that they use when communicating with counterparties, and network access is controlled by a doorman. This has several benefits for regulated financial institutions, allowing off-ledger conflict management and averting Sybil attacks etc.

Point-to-point vs. global broadcasts

In Corda, each message is instead addressed to a specific counterparty, and is not seen by any uninvolved third parties enhancing privacy as data is shared on a need-to-know basis only. To prevent double-spends in this system, Notaries are used as an alternative to proof-of-work.

Transaction tear-offs: Transactions are structured in a way that allows them to be digitally signed without disclosing the transaction's contents using a data structure called a Merkle tree.

Key randomisation: The parties to a transaction are identified only by their public keys, and fresh keypairs are generated for each transaction. As a result, an onlooker cannot identify which parties were involved in a given transaction.

UTXO vs. account model

Corda uses a UTXO (unspent transaction output) model. Each transaction consumes a set of existing states to produce a set of new states, vastly increasing the network's potential transactions-per-second. In the account model, the number of transactions-per-second is

limited by the fact that updates to a given object must be applied sequentially.

Code-is-law vs. existing legal systems

All code contracts are backed by a legal document describing the contract's intended behavior which can be relied upon to resolve conflicts

Build vs. re-use

Wherever possible, Corda re-uses existing technologies:

Standard JVM programming languages for the development of CorDapps, existing SQL databases and existing message queue implementations

Identities

- Identities in Corda can represent legal identities of organisations or service identities
- Participants in Corda network are determined by their participation requirement and not on the basis of acceptance by the majority of the members.
- Identities are attested to by X.509 certificate signed by the Doorman or a well known identity . Any node verifies the identity of owner of a public key using its X.509 certificate.
- Well known identities are published in the network map
- Anonymous-to-wellknown party mappings are resolved as a part of IdentitySyncFlow
- Confidential identities are only shared on a need to know basis to only those nodes in the network who are involved in transactions with the identity & hence their X.509 certificate is limited
- A field in a state can contain an anonymous identity and is defined as having the type AbstractParty

Network

- A Corda network is made up of nodes running Corda and CorDapps
- The network is permissioned, with access controlled by a doorman
- Communication between nodes is point-to-point, instead of relying on global broadcasts.
- The Network Map is used by the nodes to look up information on the other nods in the network.

Nodes

- A node is JVM run-time with a unique network identity running the Corda software Each node, shares its states in its Vault
- The node has two interfaces with the outside world: A network layer, for

interacting with other nodes, RPC, for interacting with the node's owner

- Nodes store all relevant objects of transaction in their vaults.
- Nodes communicate with each other using AMQP.
- When a node goes offline, all its messaged will be retired until the remote has acknowledged the messages and the connectivity restored.
- Each participant in a Corda netwrok must back up their own data.
- The node's functionality is extended by installing CorDapps in the plugin registry
- As Corda uses UTO methodology for tracking & verifying transactions, Each node receives a full copy of the Transaction history during verification.
- Regulator nodes can optionally be used in Corda as and when required for audit & authorisations.
- Regulatory node is a useful feature in Supply chain, Trade finance and Cross-border remittances.

Notary

- Notaries prevent "double-spends" & may optionally also validate transactions
- Notary is an important and necessary part of a Transaction builder.
- Notary is not required to notarize the transaction when the transaction has no input states and no timewindow
- A network can have several notaries, each running a different consensus algorithm
- The node can change a a states's notary using the NotaryChangeFlow
- Original Notary(s) have to sign when reassigning States with the NotaryChangeFlow?
- Each Notary maintains a list of state refs that have already been consumed. This way, Corda ensures that each Output state is only consumed once.
- A non-validating notary sees the input state references, the TimeWindow, and the transaction's notary when signing a transaction

Cordapps

- CorDapps (Corda Distributed Applications) are distributed applications that run on the Corda platform.
- Node's Cordapp folder contains the Cordapps installed on the node
- CorDapps can be written in either Java, Kotlin, or a combination of the two. Each CorDapp component takes the form of a JVM class that subclasses or implements a Corda library.
- CorDapp' goal is to allow nodes to reach agreement on updates to the ledger

by defining flows that Corda node owners can invoke through RPC calls:

- The CorDapp provider is where new CorDapps are installed to extend the behavior of the node.
- The node also has several CorDapps installed by default to handle common tasks such as:
- Retrieving transactions and attachments from counterparties, Upgrading contracts & Broadcasting agreed ledger updates for recording by counterparties.
- **Draining mode:** Node puts in a Flows Draining Mode, during shut down during which, commands requiring to start new flows through RPC will be rejected & scheduled flows due will be ignored
- **Event scheduling:** State classes may request flows to be started at given times
- Cordapps use Attachments to store contract related information in JAR files. Attachments are intended to be reused across transactions
- CordaSerializable marks a class as being eligible to be sent and received between nodes as part of a flow .
- Classes can be serialized by whitelisting them in Corda by implementing the Serialization Whitelist interface.
- Serialization allows Third party classes have to be explicitly added to the serialization whitelist in order to be sent over the network.
- For testing purposes, CorDapps may also include APIs and static web content.

States

- States represent on-ledger facts known by one or more peers.
- State can be exclusive to a peer and need not be shared by any others.
- Corda offers option to expose part or all of contract state to an Object Relatiional Mapping to be persisted in a ORM tool
- For running Human readable , SQL-like queries in the nodes local database against these states ContractState has to execute Queryable states interface.
- States are evolved by marking the current state as historic and creating an updated state
- Each node has a vault where it stores any relevant states to itself.
- ContractState interface defines the Participants in the Network '
- OwnableState represents Fungible asset owned by a single party which can be split and merged with other states of the same type
- Corda offers intermittent start for flows at different points in time in the future through SchedulableState command.

Ledger

- The ledger is subjective from each peer's perspective
- Ledger update requires network participants to specify exactly what information needs to be sent, to which counterparties, and in what orde
- Two peers are always guaranteed to see the exact same version of any on-ledger facts they share
- There is no single central store of data. Each node maintains a separate database of known facts.
- Each peer only sees a subset of facts on the ledger and no peer is aware of the ledger in its entirety.
- Facts shared by multiple nodes on the network, evolve in lockstep in the database of every node that is aware of it:

Transactions

Transactions are proposals to update the ledger , A transaction proposal will only be committed if: It doesn't contain double-spends, It is contractually valid, It is signed by the required parties.

- Any member/ party of the Corda network can propose a Transaction.
- Including a command in a transaction allows us to indicate the transaction's intent, affecting how we check the validity of the transaction.
- Each command is also associated with a list of one or more signers. By taking the union of all the public keys listed in the commands, we get the list of the transaction's required signers.
- A transaction is a proposal for an unlimited number of involved participants to update their ledgers and has one corresponding notary. Inputs cannot be assigned to multiple notaries.
- Corda uses a UTXO (unspent transaction output) model where every state on the ledger is immutable.
- Transactions represent a single link in the state sequences seen in States.
- Transactions are atomic: either all the transaction's proposed changes are accepted, or none are.
- There are two basic types of transactions: Notary-change transactions (used to change a state's notary & general transactions (used for everything else)
- Transactions are filtered to ensure that the participants see only the components relevant to them.
- Transactions use commands mandatorily and they provide a hint on the intent of a Transaction and list of public keys required to sign the transaction
- Transactions identify the contracts used to verify the same from the hash

of the JAR file containing the contract and the fully qualified contract class name .

- A transaction fails if any of the state objects created or consumed during its execution are not valid

- The signed transaction is identified by the root hash of the transaction's Merkle tree.

- Transactions combine at least one or more input/output states accept zero or more input states produce zero or more output states.

- Transactions are distributed to all the concerned parties involved in its approval and execution.

- TransctionBuilder holds the input states in StateRef interface and the output states in TransactionState that links the states and contracts together and a notary Is a must to instantiate a TransactionBuilder

- Before being verified by the code ContractVerifiy, the transactions have to be resolved to a LedgerTransaction For this, inputs must be converted from state references into state objects and the attachments must be converted from hashes into actual attachments.

- Once the Transaction Builder is signed by the concerned signatories (not included in the transaction), the transaction becomes immutable. The attachment hashes are included in the classs , Signed transactions.

- The hash of the transaction that created the input state and the state's index in the output of the transaction is included in a StateRef to identify the consumed state.

Contracts

- Contracts represent the sets of constraints that govern the evolution of state object

- Each state points to a contract

- The contract code can be written in any JVM language, and has access to the full capabilities of the language.

- A contract takes a transaction as input, and states whether the transaction is considered valid based on the contract's rules

- A transaction has to be contractually valid to update the ledger

- A transaction is only valid if the contract of every input state and every output state considers it to be valid

- Contract has single method, Verify which takes a LedgerTransaction as input and returns nothing.(Void). The proposal are valid if none of the Verify calls throw exception

- A valid transaction must be accepted by the contract of each of its input and output states an all contracts referenced by a transaction will be used for its verification.

- Transaction verification must be deterministic - a contract should either always accept or always reject a given transaction

- Contracts are written in a JVM programming language (e.g. Java or Kotlin)

- Contract execution is deterministic and its acceptance of a transaction is based on the transaction's contents alone and hence non deterministic libraries cannot be included in them to fulfil the business logic.

- Contract has no access to information from the outside world, it can only check the transaction for internal validity.

Time Windows

Times in transactions are specified as time windows, not absolute times. In a distributed system there can never be "true time", only an approximation of it.

Time-windows specify the time window during which the transaction can be committed

If a transaction (Times based option contracts) includes a time-window, it can only be committed during that window

The notary is the timestamping authority, refusing to commit transactions outside of that window.

It is assumed that the time feed for a notary is GPS/NaviStar time as defined by the atomic clocks at the US Naval Observatory

Time-windows can have a start and end time, or be open at either end , or they can be fully bounded.

If a time window needs to be converted to an absolute time (e.g. for display purposes), there is a utility method to calculate the mid point.

Flows

- Flows automate the process of agreeing ledger updates

- Flow is a sequence of steps that tells a node how to achieve a specific ledger update, such as issuing an asset or settling a trade.

- Constructing Transactions using TransactionBuilder is an important aspect of a flow.

- Corda provides a library of flows to handle, a)Notarising and recording a transaction, b) Gathering signatures from counterparty nodes & c)Verifying a chain of transactions

- Communication between nodes only occurs in the context of these flows, and is point-to-point

- Flows can be composed by starting a flow as a subprocess in the context of another flow. Parent flow waits till subflow returns. Multiple sessions between same parties cannot be opened in the same flow and they are sequentially executed.

- In case an exception needs to be propagated back to a Node waiting for it in suspended state, the same instance can be wrapped in Flow exception instance.

- During a Node reboot, flows are automatically serialized and persisted to the disk to be eventually finished.

- Built-in flows are provided to automate common tasks. Flows verify that all the signatures on the transactions are valid

- You can specify which responder flow to use via the node configuration. Initiated by is used to specifiy which initiator flow, a flow responds to.

- Flows can remain in a suspended state for indefinite amount of time and guarantee eventual finality.

- The node's owner can instruct the node to kick off this business process at any time using an RPC call using the notation Startable by RPC

- Nodes acknowledge only those messages for which they register a response flow.

  FinalityFlow instance is used to notarise the transaction and record it in every participant's vault

Consensus

To be committed, transactions must achieve both validity and uniqueness consensus

Validity consensus requires contractual validity of the transaction and all its dependencies

Uniqueness consensus prevents double-spen Two types of consensus

Determining whether a proposed transaction is a valid ledger update involves reaching two types of consensus:

Validity consensus - this is checked by each required signer before they sign the transaction

Uniqueness consensus - this is only checked by a notary service

Oracles

- Oracles are network services that, upon request, provide commands that encapsulate a specific fact (e.g. the exchange rate at time x) and list the oracle as a required signer.

- Oracles provides data external to the ledger into a Transaction and signs the Transaction.

- A node can request an Oracle to ascertain a fact included in a transaction as part of a command, An oracle is a service that will only sign the transaction if the included fact is true.

Oracle services can be used both when building and when verifying transactions for a fee.

Corda enterprise documentation - Release Corda enterprise 3.2 , available at https://docs.corda.r3.com/_static/corda-developer-site.pdf offers a commendable &!considerable information on all aspects of Corda platform. Salient features of the documentation are provided below:

Corda Enterprise Documentation, Release Corda Enterprise 3.2

Welcome to the documentation website for Corda Enterprise 3.2, based on the Corda 3.x open source release. Corda Enterprise adds:

- High performance, thanks to multi-threaded flow execution and extensive tuning.
- Support for more database backends:
  - SQL Server 2017
  - Azure SQL
  - Oracle 11g RC2
  - Oracle 12c
  - PostgreSQL 9.6
- The Corda Firewall, for termination of TLS connections within your network's DMZ.
- High availability features to support node-to-node failover.
- Support for advanced database migrations.

You can learn more in the *Release notes*.

Corda Enterprise is binary compatible with apps developed for the open source node. This docsite is intended for administrators and advanced users who wish to learn how to install and configure an enterprise deployment. For application development please continue to refer to the main project documentation website.

Note: Corda Enterprise provides platform API version 3, which matches the API available in open source Corda 3.x releases. Although the shipped JARs may contain new classes and methods that do not appear in API level 3, these should be considered preliminary and not for use by application developers at this time.

Annexure 7: Example of Technical Introduction Paper

Auxledger
Enterprise Blockchain Infrastructure
For Decentralized Internet

Akash Gaurav

akash@auxledger.org

www.auxledger.org

Auxesis Engineering Team

auxledger@auxesisgroup.com

www.auxesisgroup.com

Release version 1.0 | June 26th, 2018

Abstract

Since the birth of Bitcoin, Blockchain technology has opened up innumerable ways for enterprises to enhance their existing business process with an in-built layer of trust. However, the implementation of technology in core enterprises process and mass stream adoption is still limited due to the challenges of scalability, privacy, interoperability and flexibility, while designing systems. This paper outlines a proposal to build a new generation Blockchain infrastructure, aiming to solve the above outlined challenges. Microservices oriented protocols power Auxledger; as a flexible infrastructure allowing enterprises to deploy distributed networks easily and securely, while ensuring their business requirements are aligned with their network's core protocol. Auxledger provides methodologies to deploy multi-tier Blockchain networks and ensures cross-chain transactions and communication is possible in a trustless manner with complete data integrity. Auxnet, the genesis implementation of Auxledger is a highly scalable, first of its kind enterprise Blockchain network introducing high functioning virtual machine and self-regulating economic incentivization.

Contents

1.   Introduction

Technology infrastructure plays a significant role while building a scalable platform. The infrastructure must provide a sufficient level of flexibility for developers to choose and adopt core protocols for the platform while designing it. Also, the infrastructure must empower an application to allow high performance during its runtime execution. While discussing specifically about building Blockchain platforms, such an infrastructure is required to allow multi-tiered networks and inter-Blockchain communication, all while ensuring the entire ecosystem is trust-free and the data integrity is maintained at its best.

Over the past 3 years, while building and deploying Blockchain networks for governments and large enterprises, the Auxesis team has revealed significant findings, followed by research-based analysis.

By managing to solve all the business challenges encountered at first hand, the Auxesis team has gained the ability to propose an infrastructure which is reliable, secure and that meets the requirements of the complex business needs of today's world.

The paper intends to propose a one of a kind Blockchain infrastructure, which caters the high scalability requirements of businesses and thus introduces readers to the following:

- Background of Auxledger infrastructure with proposed implementation of a powerful virtual machine aligned with horizontally scalable micro-services-based architecture.

- The core offerings and protocols, the ability of building hybrid multi-tier network and allowing a full consensus based interchain operability.

- Introduction of Auxnet, a public Blockchain network and genesis implementation of Auxledger, ensuring the data integrity across chain.

- Mathematical modelling for a self-regulating economic ecosystem with the ability to dynamically control token supply depending upon network's demand.

2.   Background

Auxesis started the internal project in 2017, with the idea of implementing Blockchain network for one of the world's largest democratic country and to act as a value chain for the country's economy, enabling trust, transparency and efficiency in various business processes. During its operation, with the support of the Indian state governments, Auxesis team has on boarded a population of 53 Million users on its government operated Blockchain network. The Blockchain network was designed with the highest technical standards and with an inbuilt ability of executing robust smart contracts and deploying mass scale networks.

During the implementations of Blockchain on larger scale and the trials with the enterprises and governments, the Auxesis team realized that the basic elements and capabilities were missing from the Blockchain and thus hindered the adoption for the mainstream business processes. Solving the puzzle of these missing pieces of technology (not offered by any Blockchain project in the world) "gave birth" to the Auxledger.

After the "birth" of the Auxledger, the Auxesis team has further analyzed complex business use-cases and after summing up with on-going research, it has built a design of the next generation Blockchain infrastructure which is robust, secure and is able to support real-life complex business scenarios.

3.   Blockchain Evolution

Blockchain technology has been evolving rapidly and can be classified in the following major generations:

3.1   First Generation Blockchain

In the first generation of Blockchain stage we have observed that Bitcoin has successfully acted as a purely peer-to-peer version of electronic cash, which allows online payments to be sent directly from one party to another without going through a financial institution. [1] The network is secured cryptographically, verified by a decentralized global network and recorded into an immutable public ledger.

3.2   Second Generation Blockchain

Ethereum was introduced to the world in 2015 as a second generation Blockchain with a built-in Turing complete programming language; allowing anyone to write smart contracts and decentralized applications where they can create their own arbitrary rules for ownership, transaction formats and state transition functions. [2]

By offering ways to write distributed application easily on top of inherently secured Ethereum, the Blockchain network opened up unlimited possibilities for innovators across the world to build powerful trust-free applications. Applications with novel use cases further demonstrate, and validate, the technology's ability to evolve beyond just a means of transferring value.

While businesses have been adopting concepts of private networks to ensure scalability, privacy and low operation costs, they have started losing some of the inherited core values provided by a public Blockchain network. These private Blockchain networks also started acting similar to "small islands located in the middle of a sea", with no economic and information transfer being possible in a trust-less environment. This inability led to a serious hindrance in Blockchain realizing its true potential and is in a number of ways analogous to the early part of disconnected intranet, which disrupted with the introduction of the Internet.

3.3   Auxledger: The Third Generation Blockchain Infrastructure

A Blockchain generation empowered with hybrid networks where businesses would be able to enjoy the scalability, security and privacy of a private Blockchain while maintaining the ability to prove data integrity and maintain overall consensus through cross-chains. Networks can be deployed on a multitier basis, while the thousands and millions of Blockchain networks are able to communicate swiftly. A network supported by improved virtual machine able to process transaction and information in a more reliable environment. Auxledger is being created as an infrastructure supporting these third-generation features that require Blockchain technology to move in mainstream adoption.

At the heart of Auxledger we have designed a powerful enterprise grade public Blockchain network that will be the genesis implementation of Auxledger infrastructure; supporting the creation of multi-tier networks and handling consensus while allowing inter-chain operability.

The network is being secured and incentivized by two native token implementations:

- **AuxChips:** Providing administrative access into the Auxnet and the ability to create tiered networks

- **AuxGas:** Fuel in the Auxnet to empower computation, ensuring consensus among tiered networks and the ability to enable inter-chain operability.

4.   Infrastructure Design Architecture

From core architectural standpoint, Auxledger is revamped, ensuring to deliver a powerful virtual machine, flexible architecture and making horizontally scalable Blockchain network possible

4.1   Microservices Oriented Protocol

Microservices are the lowest level of autonomously defined function which are bundled together to build a fully functioning application. We have studied the wide differences in protocol requirements for different businesses, and thus we are building our infrastructure in a fully configurable manner to ensure network owners meet the level of flexibility required.

4.1.1 Deploying Flexible Blockchain Network

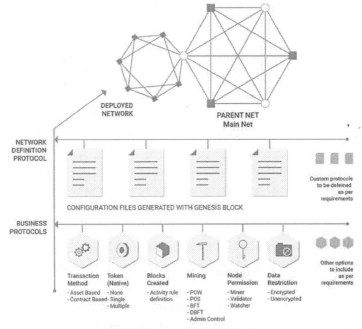

Figure 1: Microservices protocol for tiered networks

With the evolution of Blockchain we have noticed that many different infrastructures and platforms are made available for network owners to choose from; however, each infrastructure has enforced owners to use their pre-defined Blockchain protocols and thus network owners end up choosing different infrastructure for different business requirements. With Auxledger, we want to provide the network owners with the possibility to choose from a wide range of different Blockchain protocols available into the network, in a microservices format.

Implementing the concept of a simple Smart contract-based network configuration file defines the required protocols of the network. Some of the configurable items while deploying a network can be:

- Network native token
- Block creation activity
- Node permissioning
- Consensus / mining methods
- Transaction methods
- Privacy and data restriction

4.1.2   Horizontal Scalability of Microservices

Regarding the designing system - it has been considered that most of the Blockchain protocols suiting different business needs are yet to be defined and thus it is very crucial that our design must support horizontal scalability in terms of new protocols being added. By implementing the idea of microservices, we are ensuring that as new protocols are being defined by the community, they can be easily made available in their respective buckets for an even more flexible network deployment.

4.2   Auxviom – Auxledger Virtual Machine

Auxviom is a variant of LLVM[3] specialized to execute smart contracts on the Blockchain. Its design, definition and implementation has been done at the highest mathematical standards, following a semantics-first approach with verification of smart contracts as a major objective. Specifically, we have defined the formal syntax and semantics of Auxviom using the K framework, which in return gives us an executable reference model in addition to a series of program analysis tools, including a program verifier. Unlike Ethereum Virtual Machine, which is a stack-based machine, Auxviom is proposed to be designed as a register-based machine, like LLVM. It has an unbounded number of registers and also supports unbounded integers.

4.2.1   Design Implementations

During Auxviom design implementation, design rationale has been followed:

*   Serving as a uniform, lower-level platform for translating and executing smart contracts from higher-level languages. The contracts can interact with each other by means of an ABI (Application Binary Interface). The ABI is a core element of Auxviom, and not just a convention on top of it. The unbounded integers and unbounded number of registers should make compilation from higher-level languages more straightforward and elegant and looking at the success of LLVM, more efficient in the long term. Indeed, many of the LLVM optimizations are expected to carry over; for that reason, Auxviom followed the design choices and representation of LLVM as much as possible.

*   Providing a uniform gas model, across all languages. The general design philosophy of gas calculation in Auxviom is "no limitations, but pay for what you consume". For example, the more registers an Auxviom program uses, the more gas it consumes. Or the larger the numbers computed at runtime, the more gas it consumes. The more memory it uses, in terms of both locations and size of data stored at locations, the more gas it consumes; and so on.

*   Making it easier to write secure smart contracts. This includes writing requirements specifications that smart contracts must obey, as well as making it easier to develop automated techniques that mathematically

verify / prove smart contracts correct with respect to such specifications. For example, pushing a possibly computed number on the stack and then jumping to it regarded as an address makes verification hard, and thus security weaker, with current smart contract paradigms. Auxviom has named labels, like LLVM, and jump statements can only jump to those labels. Also, it avoids the use of a bounded stack and not having to worry about stack or arithmetic overflow makes specification and verification of smart contracts significantly easier.

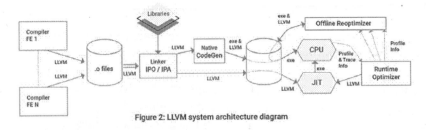

Figure 2: LLVM system architecture diagram

4.2.2 Machine Execution and Improvements

The LLVM based compiler framework exploits the code representation to provide a combination of five capabilities that is believed to be important in order to support lifelong analysis and transformation for arbitrary programs. In general, these capabilities are quite difficult to obtain simultaneously, but the Auxviom design does so inherently:

Persistent program information

Offline code generation

User-based profiling and optimization

Transparent runtime model

Uniform, whole-program compilation

The above figure shows the high-level architecture of the LLVM based Auxviom system. Briefly, static compiler front-ends emit code in the LLVM representation, which is combined together by the LLVM linker. The linker performs a variety of link-time optimizations, especially inter-procedural ones. The resulting LLVM code is then translated to native code for a given target at link-time or install-time, and the LLVM code is saved with the native code. It is also possible to translate LLVM code at runtime with a just-in-time translator. The native code generator inserts light-weight instrumentation to detect frequently executed code regions (currently loop nests and traces, but potentially also functions), and these can be optimized at runtime. The profile data collected at runtime represent the end-user's not the developer's runs, and can be used by an offline optimizer to perform aggressive profile driven optimizations in the field during idle-time, tailored to the specific target machine.

The LLVM representation is language independent, allowing all the codes for a program, including system libraries and portions written in different languages, to be compiled and optimized together. The LLVM compiler framework is designed to permit optimization at all stages of a software lifetime, including extensive static optimization, online optimization using information from the LLVM code, and idle-time optimization using profile information gathered from programmers in the field.

4.3 Smart Contracts and Scripting Language

Smart contracts are computer programs which execute through Blockchain transactions that are able to hold state, interact with decentralized cryptocurrencies and take user input. We have studied different cases analyzing attacks on Ethereum Smart Contracts[4] and we have also analyzed the root causes which lead to exploiting the code vulnerabilities. The analysis has been continued further to test EVM and Smart Contracts over K Framework[5] and thus formalize on the required improvements.

Auxledger language is being created and complied as a subset of Java programming language specifications. The libraries developed will implement the horizontal scalability of architecture and will provide an easier method to implement microservices oriented protocols into the system. As an infrastructure company, our focus is to provide an easy to use and simple infrastructure, but yet enforcing developers to use best defensive programming techniques to derive overall security in the ecosystem.

4.3.1 Language Characteristics

Under the light of recent smart contracts that have been found compromised, Auxledger scripting language enforces defensive programming scheme to provide a better security. Defensive programming is a loosely defined collection of techniques to reduce the risk of failure at run time. The technique is to make the software behave in a predictable manner despite unexpected inputs, parameters or in case of internal error. From our experience in several works of safety analysis[6], we have identified aspects that are required to be verified in such applications and further we have assembled the techniques which are proposed to be inbuilt in Auxledger scripting language. Scripting language will enforce the implementation output for different failure cases and thus providing overall security into the system.

Problems	Programming Techniques
Inconsistent or not-expected input values	Test of valid values
Inputs out of synchronism Lack of synchronization	Test of synchronism
Inputs obtained out of expected interval time Generation of outputs out of expected interval time	Test of execution times
Incapacity to treat a great number of interrupts signals Excess of input signals in a determined period of time	Verification of capacity
Non-generation of outputs Non-acquisition of inputs	Test of time-outs
Improper use of memory areas Stack overflow	Test of memory areas
Overflow/underflow	Test of valid values/ Exception handling
Endless loop Loop control	
Error in parameter passing	Checking function arguments
Error in values return	Returning error codes
Improper exit from a routine Improper entrance in a routine	Input/output tests
Excessive execution duration of routines	Test of execution times
Use of incorrect type of constants and variables	Check function arguments/ variables/ constants
Deadlocks	Test of resources use
Non-return of routines	Test of execution times/ Return from routines

Auxledger language is thus targeted to be built as a robust and secure platform with implementation of techniques discussed for defensive programming and the secure runtime environment with inbuilt defensive constraints inside Auxviom to limit the unintentional activities to be executed.

4.3.2 Execution Environment

As a smart contract executes, the most frequently execution paths that are executed are identified through a combination of offline and online instrumentation. The offline instrumentation (inserted by the native code generator) identifies frequently executed loop regions in the code. When a hot loop region is detected at runtime, a runtime instrumentation library instruments the executing native code to identify frequently-executed paths within that region. Once hot paths are identified, we duplicate the original LLVM code into a trace, perform LLVM optimizations on it, and then regenerate native code into a software-managed trace cache. We then insert branches between the original code and the new native code. The strategy described here is powerful because it combines the following three characteristics:

- Native code generation can be performed ahead-of-time using sophisticated algorithms to generate high-performance code

- The native code generator and the runtime optimizer can work together since they are both part of the LLVM framework, allowing the runtime optimizer to exploit support from the code generator (e.g., for instrumentation and simplifying transformations).

- The runtime optimizer can use high-level information from the LLVM representation to perform sophisticated runtime optimizations.

4.4 Data privacy & Encryption

Auxledger ecosystem aims to enable enterprise Blockchain solutions where data privacy is of utmost importance. Here we are proposing a tested framework enhanced upon the usability of Auxledger ecosystem. Auxledger privacy component rides upon a combination of two models – (i) Enigma based decentralize computation platform, and (ii) Hawk model for privacy preserving smart contracts.

Using Enigma's secure multi-party computation[7] (sMPC or MPC), data queries are computed in a distributed way, without a trusted third party. Data is split between different nodes and they compute functions together without leaking information to other nodes. Specifically, no single party ever has access to data in its entirety; instead, every party has a meaningless (i.e., seemingly random) piece of it.

To maximize the computational power of the network, we introduce a network reduction technique, where a random subset of the entire network is selected to perform a computation. The random process preferentially selects nodes based on load-balancing requirements and accumulated reputation, as is measured by their publicly validated actions. This ensures that the network is fully utilized at any given point.

Another component of Auxnet privacy remains in the portion of privacy preserving of smart contracts. The on-chain privacy and contractual security is based upon Hawk model[8]. On-chain privacy stipulates that transactional privacy can be provided against the public (i.e., against any party not involved in the contract) – unless the contractual parties themselves voluntarily disclose information. Although in Hawk protocols, users exchange data with the Blockchain, and rely on it to ensure fairness against aborts, the flow of money and amount transacted in the private Hawk program is cryptographically hidden from the public's view. Informally, this is achieved by sending "encrypted" information to the Blockchain and relying on zero knowledge proofs to enforce the correctness of contract execution and money conservation.

While on-chain privacy protects contractual parties' privacy against the public (i.e., parties not involved in the financial contract), contractual security protects parties in the same contractual agreement from each other. Hawk assumes that contractual parties act selfishly to maximize their own financial interest. In particular, they can arbitrarily deviate from the prescribed protocol or even abort prematurely. Therefore, contractual security is a multi-faceted notion that encompasses not only cryptographic notions of confidentiality and authenticity, but also financial fairness in the presence of cheating and aborting behavior.

5. Multi-tier Network Implementation

Auxledger introduces the concept of the most powerful multi-tier Blockchain architecture design, where multiple networks are able to be deployed upon a single network and further maintaining full network consensus and data integrity of all networks are maintained at any tier. In this section, we are also proposing an analysis methodology to make successful interchain transactions, communicate throughout different chains swiftly and the zeroth-tier implementation of the proposed protocol.

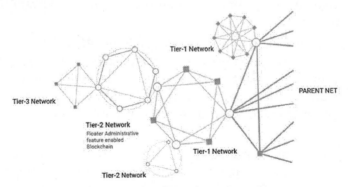

Figure 3: Representation of multi-tiered networks

5.1 Node Switching Protocols

Particular nodes in a network (provided they meet the requirements for the core protocol of deploying subnets as discussed later in the paper - section 6.4.1) can have the ability to deploy a tiered Blockchain network. The particular node will become a participating member of multiple networks and thus will be maintaining the switching states of multiple networks in a single virtual machine. Node switching also ensures that the idea of full consensus in the created subnet and the parent chain is maintained throughout the networks; with deploying nodes being the lifeline of the data integrity throughout the chains.

5.1.1 State Methodology

Auxledger introduces the concept of state switching in order to ensure a clear segregation in the virtual machine for executing contracts and transactions, while maintaining state elements clearly separated for the different participating networks. With proposed protocols of state switching and state functions, nodes can flow data and elements from one network to another.

The participating node will also be acting as a network governor for the created subnets and thus will be responsible for broadcasting data into the private network, which is required for the successful implementation of interchain transaction and interchain communication. The participating node will be responsible for the subnet governance and the consensus management, as for the deployed subnet across parent chain.

5.1.2 Consensus Management

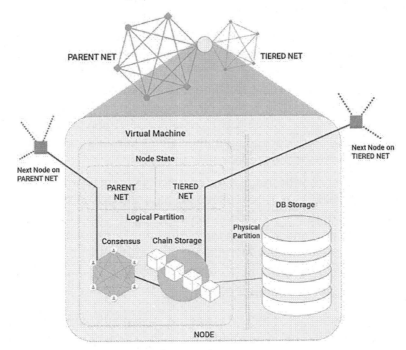

Figure 4: Internal layout of a connecting node

Participating nodes in the connecting network follows the core protocols for subnets governance. The participating nodes sync up the subnet activities to its parent chain on a checkpoint basis. The Merkle root data of the creating block in the subnet, along with other critical information's in encrypted manner is transferred and stored to the parent chain. While a transaction is being initiated, the cross chain participating node would verify the data consensus inside the subnet and then broadcast it to the parent chain. The parent chain is further responsible for testing the data integrity of the broadcasted transaction or broadcasted information, using the previous checkpoints and Merkle root's data. Post the data verification and participating nodes rating, the parent chain will broadcast payload information to the recipient chain, where transactions are to be executed and state change is required.

5.2   Interchain Transaction

Interchain transaction in Auxledger ecosystem is defined as a trust-less method to exchange native assets of different subnets. This transaction can also be followed and resulted into execution of a smart contract in their specific networks, resulting the change of other states data. This function allows any connected Blockchain networks to exchange assets, contracts and permissions. This provides the ability to take the current internet a step forward by allowing participants to not only share information, but also valuables in a trust free manner

5.2.1 Validation and Initiation

An interchain transaction can be initiated by any node of a particular network, payload data along with the transaction is attached to return the event in some form of desirable action. The transaction is created and broadcasted inside the network first, where other nodes test the authenticity and credibility of the created transactions. The transaction is then further tested by the participating nodes, which are connecting the subnet with its parent chain. Upon the validation of the transaction by the participating nodes, they are responsible for broadcasting the transaction to the connecting parent network.

The initiating node also ensures that the transaction is sent forward with sufficient transaction fee, wherever it is required to pass through different connecting networks. Since different connecting networks (which may be deployed as a public or private implementation on top of the infrastructure) have the flexibility to build different native tokens, the initiator must ensure that the transaction fee is sufficiently covered for passing through all the connecting networks

5.2.2 Connecting Blockchain Consensus

The transaction is broadcasted in the form of encrypted packets to ensure that the data can travel through a number of connecting networks, while maintaining data privacy, security and integrity. Each connecting network tests the transaction data with the help of existing checkpoints available in the connecting networks, or it can be made available by the parent network. The packet travels through different connecting networks, ensuring consensus is maintained throughout each network.

In Auxledger ecosystem, the transaction is pushed with sufficient fee as per different native tokens that are required for connecting networks to be incentivized and thus brining consensus in participation. The transaction fee incentivizes the connecting networks to participate in the consensus process, by testing the transaction and the relevant states in a decentralized manner

5.3 Interchain Communication

With its implementation of high fidelity, Auxledger, ensures the data integrity to be maintained throughout its lifecycle. We propose to build a relay system layer for implementing cross network query and data transfer mechanism.

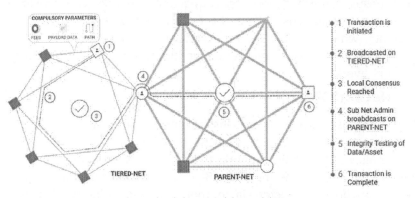

Figure 5: Interchain transaction/communication

5.3.1 Requesting data cross chain

A communication protocol for exchanging information off chain route, for non-critical data elements. Information and messages sent across the protocol will be facilitated through a secure P2P direct messaging protocol. The protocol will allow nodes across different networks to be able to communicate without going through the connecting networks route and thus by-passing all complex steps and procedures.

This protocol can also be used to request information from a Blockchain node to another network. After receiving the information, the network handler node will verify the authenticity and will allow permission of request and thus forward that information for processing. The requesting may be followed by sending back information off-chain route in case of non-critical data or sending information on-chain, so the receiving party ensures the data integrity is maintained

5.3.2 Sending data cross chain

An interchain data is sent across chain in the form of an encrypted packet along with the Merkle proof, allowing connecting networks to check the data integrity of the transmitted packets. Packets can be originated by any node, however the first consensus of sent data must appear from the sent network, which will be tested by the participating node and then further transmits the data to the connecting network.

The encrypted data packets, along with the data integrity testing proof, travel through the connecting networks and are finally delivered to the recipient network. The process is in many ways similar to an interchain transaction, where all core protocols along with the requirement of fee must be taken care of, in order to bring different networks to consensus. However, the core difference from interchain transaction is that no exchange of assets happens, but only information is transmitted.

The consensus is reached upon by connecting networks in a similar method of interchain transactions, where the transmitted packet is tested upon the checkpoints, while the data is broadcasted by each network to their parent connecting network. Post the successful verification, the data is delivered to the recipient network.

5.4 Network Tiering

Auxledger proposes to provide consensus in any cross chain transmission, because of its ability to remain connected via some joints in the Blockchain network. Auxledger allows Blockchain networks to be created and deployed by the idea of tiering only. This form of tiering of the Blockchain in vertical direction will ensure that each network is connected via another, in a direct or indirect shape.

5.4.1 Genesis Ledger Implementation

Auxledger proposes to build a genesis Blockchain network for Auxledger as a zeroth-tier network publicly available for anyone to connect and participate in this network. The implementation of the genesis ledger is being done to ensure that the highly distributed structure of real-life complex businesses can remain interconnected with each other due to this zeroth tier implementation. Zeroth tier implementation of Auxledger aims to act as a publicly available decentralize form of

Internet, ensuring that all the data available is trusted, verified and sealed together with the power of cryptography consensus.

5.4.2 Tiering Subnets

The zeroth-tier implementation of Blockchain network opens unlimited possibilities to create subnets in or around this network. A participating node in a network will have the capability to start their own network, which is tiered upon the nodes existing network. However, there are core protocols required to be followed in order to ensure all subnets remain in sync with the genesis ledger implementation.

Participating nodes are the ones who are representative of a subnet in their parent chain and thus fulfilling the requirements of parent chain in order to ensure the smooth functioning of the subnet. The participating nodes who are maintaining networks to remain tiered also ensure that the checkpoint data, as well as the Merkle root data of the deployed network is timely transferred to the parent chain, and so the parent chain can have the ability to prove consensus in the subnet.

6.   Auxnet

Auxnet is the genesis implementation of Auxledger infrastructure and thus acts as zeroth tier Blockchain implementation. It is an open Blockchain network, built with enterprise grade security, privacy and scalability. Auxnet is built to perform the role of the "heart" in the Auxledger ecosystem, capable to fulfil the requirements that have been listed in the multi-tier Blockchain network architecture. As a public Blockchain network, Auxnet, is built with following design goals:

- Act as an infrastructure to build powerful DApps interacting with multiple networks and services.

- Powering organizations to deploy a hybrid Blockchain network on top of Auxnet.

- Providing a sustainable network through robust and sustainable economic incentivization.

- Acting as a source of consensus for all networks deployed in the ecosystem and regulating them.

Auxnet targets to bring on board large enterprises, to start building consortium networks, as well as early entrepreneurs for providing reliable infrastructure and supporting them alike to leverage the ability of distributed applications in daily operations. Our vision will successfully implement the full potential of the Blockchain, where a decentralize application can sit over connecting networks and logically driven by communicating through a multitude of Blockchain networks.

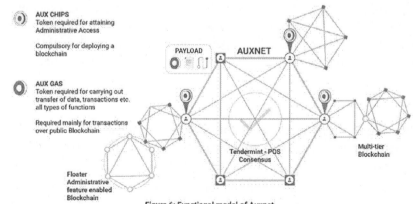

Figure 6: Functional model of Auxnet

6.1   Node Roles

In Auxnet ecosystem, multiple roles in the public network have been defined on the basis of their engaged activities. They can majorly be classified in 3 roles:

6.1.1 Stakers

These are the nodes which hold AuxChips (the administrative token of Auxnet) and stake it towards the network, returning the stakers with the ability to mine new blocks and thus collect AuxGas as mining rewards. The stakers are promoted to be the nodes involved in maintaining overall consensus of the public network.

Stakers will get a chance to mine block with the probability equivalent to the proportion of AuxChips staked by a miner, in comparison with the total of AuxChips staked in the network. Once a staker is selected, it will propose the block which will be validated by other nodes and thus the block formation process will be completed.

6.1.2 Validators

All participants in the Auxnet public network are considered as validators; this set also includes all those nodes which don't hold any AuxChips, but participate in the network as a developer or approver node, and thus helping in bringing overall security to the network. These nodes are additionally incentivized by Auxnet public network in order to continue participating in the network, acting as validators in the form of AuxGas.

6.1.3 Candidate

A candidate is the node in the Auxnet network which is initiating a transaction. This candidate node can either be a stand-alone node broadcasting transaction, or it can be a participating node which is also active in a tiered network and thus broadcasting transaction on behalf of its network.

6.2   Ecosystem Governance

Auxnet focuses on building a high growth and sustainable economy model, which incentivizes the early entrants into the platform that acquire administrative tokens; as well as the community of developers and Blockchain enthusiasts who will help us secure the network, by offering in return the Blockchain fuel that powers the entire network.

6.2.1 AuxChips

AuxChips are the administrative tokens available in Auxnet ecosystem. They are limited in number and are created as a one-time process, which means no new AuxChips will be mined in the Auxnet ecosystem.

AuxChips hold a critical value with the following major functionalities on-chain:

- Ability to participate in block formation process as Stakers node and earn the right to mine new blocks. Mining new blocks will result into generation of new AuxGas, a fuel used inside Auxnet public network.

- Ability to deploy a tiered network on top of Auxnet, depending upon the number of AuxChips being hold by the network owner, more number of nodes will be able to join with the created subnetwork.

- AuxChips holders will enjoy participation in voting rights, while making important network governing related decisions.

As our core protocols require subnets to broadcast checkpoint information into the public Auxnet network to ensure consensus among connecting network and that the subnet remains in sync, we have kept in mind that our mining process will generate sufficient volume of new gas for the AuxChips holder to be able to sustain its deployed network in a self-sustainable manner.

The total supply of AuxChips has been fixed at 100 Million, out of which 60 Million will be made available to be acquired by the public in the crowd-sale that Auxledger company will organize in the second half of the year 2018. The remaining 40 Million AuxChips will be retained by the company for community development and for the growth of the company.

6.2.2 AuxGas

AuxGas is the fuel in Auxnet ecosystem, which incentivizes the network to participate in any consensus process, to make computation and to allow storage, and thus securing the integrity of the network. 300 million pre-mined AuxGas will be made available and distributed proportionally to AuxChips holders while launching Auxledger's Auxnet network. New AuxGas can further be mined by AuxChips holders while participating in a hybrid proof of stake consensus model.

AuxGas can be utilized for following purposes:

- Enabling native assets transactions i.e. AuxChips and AuxGas transfer in Auxnet ecosystem

- Cost for computation and contract execution in Auxnet.

- Computation cost for interchain communication.

- Transaction cost for interchain transaction and contract implementation.

- Fee for node/address/assets based permission or ownership transfer

We are proposing a unique, first of its kind self-regulating economic model for AuxGas. While other models proposed by different networks are based on time/block wise pre-decided token supply, we are proposing a more sustainable and dynamic way to control the supply of AuxGas as per demands being created on the network. The model will ensure that the network can self-regulate the supply of AuxGas in a controlled and more systematic manner.

Mining reward consists of two portions:

- Block generation reward
- Transaction fees

We are proposing to split the block generation reward in two parts with proportion of a and b;

Block generation reward, M at zth block is given as summation of Fixed reward and Regulated reward.

$$M(z) = a * F(z) + b * R(z)$$

Quantity of Fixed reward & Regulated reward will be calculated by the below proposed mathematical model:

Assume:

Initial fixed reward = A

Fixed reward adjustment (no. of blocks) = m

$$F(z) = \frac{A}{k^{|z/m|}}$$

Fixed reward reciprocal factor = k

$$\lim(z \to \infty) \equiv Fz \to 0$$

Regulated reward considerate (no. of blocks) = n

Rz is being calculated by finding out the change in gas consumptions through last n blocks and last 2n blocks. With the below equation we can check the trend and predict the consumption of gas in the coming blocks:

$$G(z) = \sum_{n=0}^{N} \frac{G^n(z)}{n!} x^n + \frac{1}{N!} \int_0^x f^{(N+1)}(t)(x-t)^N dt$$

Simplifying the above equation and predicting the change of gas consumption we derive:

$$\frac{dG}{di} = \frac{\sum_{i=z-n}^{z} Gi - \sum_{i=z-2n}^{z-n} Gi}{n}$$

The above equations will govern and predict the requirements of gas in the coming times and thus the parameter for R(z) can be adjusted accordingly to ensure that a dynamically controlled gas can be generated and released.

$$R(z) = b * \frac{dG}{di}$$

Further, for contingency management and risk assessment, the system must ensure that there are no sudden changes in the data. To realize this we highlight the risk areas by calculating a derivative of the change in gas per block. A threshold parameter, k, is defined where at any given point below must hold true:

$$\frac{d2G}{di2} < k$$

The areas where derivative will exceed the threshold parameter are highlighted as risk areas and thus will be normalized to ensure a smooth curve of generating number of gases is received.

There is an overall cap thresholding number of gases that will be released in a block and throughout time network is expected to meet the supply-demand curve and align itself in a self-sustainable model leading to new generation of gases to become zero. An additional hard cap of 2 Billion is kept as a total number of AuxGas in the ecosystem.

The AuxGas that is being collected with every block formation is distributed equally among all the validator nodes participating in the consensus process. This process ensures incentivization for new entrants into the ecosystem and further securing the overall network.

6.3 Consensus

The complexity of the Auxledger ecosystem (the ability of connecting networks, participating nodes and interchain transactions) raises the need of building up a novel consensus model, which is properly regulated and maintains sufficient decentralization, but is still quick enough in coming up with a decision.

Auxnet uses BFT powered proof of stake mechanism to create blocks and bring consensus:

6.3.1 Incentivization

The Blockchain network is incentivized in the form of AuxGas to maintain a fair and secure ecosystem. AuxChips holders participate in the block formation process and work towards creating a block in order to earn newly generated AuxGas. The nodes which don't hold AuxChips (but act as a validator node to vote for the proposed block) are also incentivized by the network with equal distribution of AuxGas collected as a transaction fee in the operating Blockchain network.

6.3.2 Hybrid Tendermint Staking Model

In Auxledger's Auxnet ecosystem, we have categorized nodes into 2 types, which play a major role in the consensus process. On one hand, there are Stakers node, holding AuxChips in their active wallet participating to mine blocks. On the other hand, we have validator nodes, who are a part of the ecosystem to explore the Auxledger infrastructure / running applications on top of Auxnet. Acknowledging the ecosystem members of both groups is of the utmost importance, especially when it comes to securing an ecosystem.

With dedicated analysis for recording a high performance consensus method we implemented Tendermint[9] protocol. Tendermint is a protocol for ordering events in a distributed network under adversarial conditions.

The consensus part of the Byzantine Fault Tolerance[10] protocol occurs through a "gamified" form of block verification among Staker nodes. Staker nodes are identified by the amount of AuxChips they are holding. The network chooses a Staker node to propose a new block, the decision is made randomly with probability in equal proportion of AuxChips being held by the Staker. The chosen Staker node broadcasts its version of the Blockchain to the network. If 66% of the other nodes agree with the information, then consensus is achieved. If this threshold is not to be met, then a different professional node is appointed to broadcast its Blockchain version until consensus can be established.

In Auxnet, the hybrid consensus mechanism will take about 10 to 15 seconds to generate a block, the transaction throughput is measured in orders of thousands of TPS, which is excellent performance among the public chains. Through appropriate optimization, there is potential to reach 1 Million TPS, allowing it to support large-scale commercial applications

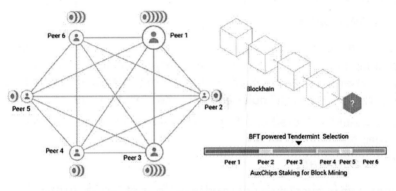

Figure 7: Hybrid Tendermint-POS Consensus Model

6.3.3 Node Ratings

All nodes in Auxnet ecosystem is rated on the basis of decision making process. A Staker node can earn positive rating by proposing a block which gets widely accepted and a negative rating whenever the proposed block doesn't pass through. Similarly, a validator node is appreciated with positive rating when their voted block is confirmed, or their rejected block has also been rejected by the network's majority. A validator node will earn a negative rating in case of false positive or true negative during the block formation process

6.4   Subnets Governance

All subnets in Auxledger ecosystem are directly or indirectly being regulated by the Auxnet core protocols for subnets governance. This is done to ensure that at any given point, data trust and integrity can be secured. For a node to deploy subnet it needs to follow the below pointers and requirements:

- A participating node must hold a sufficient number of AuxChips for a successful operation of subnet. The total number of AuxChips required is dependent upon the number of nodes in operation in the deployed subnet or any network that has been tiered upon the Auxnet connecting subnet. The lack in number of AuxChips will result in connection loss by the participating nodes on the tiered network.

- The Auxnet participating nodes (or subnet admin nodes) must broadcast checkpoint information, including network health and status in encrypted format to the public Blockchain network. The participating node is also responsible for collecting the checkpoint data of all the networks that maybe tiered upon the subnet and broadcast their bundled data to the Auxnet public network.

- Depending upon the size of the subnet (including the size of tiered networks on top of the subnet) the network must nominate more numbers of participating nodes to ensure a sufficient level of decentralization is always maintained in the network.

7.   Conclusion

Auxledger, as proposed in this paper, is designed after several years of experiments and practice. The team has been involved in working with some of the world's largest enterprise Blockchain projects and thus have experienced at first hand many issues in the current infrastructure. This paper has been designed by keeping in mind the most complex of the real world's business use cases and requirements. Auxledger intends to solve the problem of flexibility, scalability and interoperability within the current Blockchain infrastructure and thus enable the mainstream adoption of Blockchain. The Auxledger research team have made incredible findings, required for the next generation Blockchain infrastructure to be able to operate and function smoothly. In the coming months we are intending to work aggressively towards completing the necessary research & development of Auxledger, as well as building our community, so early adopters can join in our project.

References

[1]   S. Nakamoto, *"Bitcoin: A peer-to-peer electronic cash system"* 2008.
      Link: https://bitcoin.org/bitcoin.pdf

[2]   V. Buterin, *"Ethereum whitepaper"* 2014.
      Link: https://github.com/ethereum/wiki/wiki/White-Paper

[3]   C. Lattner and V. Adve, "LLVM: A Compilation Framework for Lifelong Program Analysis & Transformation" 2004.
      Link: http://llvm.org/pubs/2004-01-30-CGO-LLVM.pdf

[4]   N. Atzei, M. Batoletti, and C. Tiziana, *"A survey of attacks on ethereum smart contracts"* 2016.
      Link: https://eprint.iacr.org/2016/1007.pdf

[5]   E. Hildenbrandt, M. Saxena, X. Zhu, N. Rodrigues, P. Daian, D. Guth and G.

Rosu, *"KEVM: A Complete Semantics of the Ethereum Virtual Machine" 2017.*
Link: https://www.ideals.illinois.edu/bitstream/handle/2142/97207/hilden brandt-saxena-zhu-rodrigues-guth-daian-rosu2017-tr_0818.pdf

[6] *J. Almeida, S. Melnikoff, J. Camargo and B. Desouza, "Defensive Programming for Safety-Critical Systems".*
Link: http://www.wseas.us/e-library/conferences/brazil2002/papers/ 449-214.doc

[7] *A. Kosba, A. Miller, E. Shi, Z. Wen and C. Papamanthou, "Hawk: The Blockchain Model of Cryptography and Privacy-Preserving Smart Contracts" 2016.*
Link: https://ieeexplore.ieee.org/stamp/stamp.jsp?tp=&arnumber=7546538

[8] *G. Zyskind, O. Nathan and A. Pentland, "Enigma: Decentralized Computation Platform with Guaranteed Privacy" 2015.*
Link: https://arxiv.org/pdf/1506.03471.pdf

[9] *E. Buchman, "Tendermint: Byzantine Fault Tolerance in the Age of Blockchains" 2016.*
Link: http://atrium.lib.uoguelph.ca/xmlui/bitstream/handle/10214/9769/ Buchman_Ethan_201606_MAsc.pdf

[10] *M. Kastro and B. Liskov, "BYZANTINE FAULT TOLERANCE" 2003.*
Link: https://patentimages.storage.googleapis.com/d6/5d/2c/6a38734909 3621/US6671821.pdf

Annexure 8- More on 3 Cs of Blockchain- Consensus, CIA & CAP

Consensus is the core element of Blockchain to come to the correct decision on the transaction parameters.

CIA triad, aka confidentiality, integrity and availability often confused with Central Intelligence Agency is a model designed to guide information security related policies of an organisation.

One of the ultimate aims of Blockchain implementation is to neutralise designs of cyber-attackers.

Hence while integrity of data is given maximum preference by most platforms, availability of all data to everyone in the system including the miners or decision makers is balanced with confidentiality of the transactions. Here, confidentiality & availability relate to the terms & sharing of transactions between transacting/ non-transacting parties and availability to all and sundry across the world regarding transactional information, respectively. These operate within the constraints imposed by the CAP theorem of distributed IT systems, namely consistency, availability and partition tolerance, which states that any IT system can only & must at-least satisfy a minimum two of the three features. The availability in CAP theorem represents the time window of data availability in non-byzantine and up & operating nodes.

It will be interesting to see the trade-offs chosen by the permissioned and permissionless blockchain implementations within these constraints or features.

Public Blockchains with unknown and mutually non-trusting members working with each other & competing for a monetary incentive through a competition based on game theories call for the highest level of complexity of the Consensus Algorithm. This is where resource intensive applications like PoW score big as they make it increasingly difficult for attackers to out-compute the collective PoW related wall of resource expensed to propagate the transactions and safeguard integrity. Here the focus is more on integrity, availability (CIA) availability & partition tolerance (CAP) while confidentiality and consistency and sacrificed in favour of utmost transparency and eventual consistency by resolution of forks in favour of the longest chains over short but varying time periods.

Thus though Bitcoin Blockchain implements, highest level of security, but lower levels of confidentiality (though identities of transactors are protected by tough to track pseudonyms) and consistency , its choice limits the scalability of transactions throughput.

While public Blockchain platforms like Ethereum are planning a shift to a POS

(Proof of Stake) consensus mechanism that in a way converts the competition to approve to a block from competition to cooperation with the mining probability based on the staked coins, there are still potential downsides in the system that can cause centralisation due to higher probability of block creation by dominant stakers.

Some of the Blockchains like EOS, Hashgraph offer innovative variations of Proof of Stake that guarantee speed, scalability and offer byzantine tolerance.

EOS utilises DPOS. DPoS, the delegated proof of Stake, is a new consensus algorithm born on the basis of PoW and PoS. It can not only solve the problem of a large amount of energy consumption caused by PoW in the mining process, but also avoid the problem of the "trust balance" bias that may arise under the distribution of PoS rights, thus it stands out for becoming the representative consensus mechanism for the consensus mechanism 3.0. Typical examples include Bitshares, Steem, and EOS. (https://eosbootcamp.com/lesson/what-is-delegated-proof-of-stake/).

Hedera Hashgraph used a unique consensus model, that offers speed, scalability and highest level of trust that balances the needs of permissionless and permissioned applications in favour of a higher degree of permissioned behaviour. In other words, it uses a trusted group of 39 organisations to govern the blockchain, albeit with no control to any single party to control the system. (https://s3.amazonaws.com/hedera-hashgraph/hh-whitepaper-v1.1-180518.pdf) Termed ABFT (Asynchronous Byzantine Fault Tolerant system) Hedera governance is comprised of two parts: Council Governance, used for the management of the business of the council, and POS based Consensus for determining the consensus order of the transactions. The Council Governance model concerns the election of the Board of Managers of Hedera (Governing Board) that establishes policy for council membership, regulate the network tokens, and approve changes to the platform codebase and the Consensus Model concerns the process by which the nodes reach a consensus on the order of transactions in the platform. This is designed to prevent consolidation of power over a few parties.

On the other hand, permissioned blockchain platforms deal with known identities that vastly reduces the need to safeguard against collusion and subversive attempts to compromise the systems. Hyperledger Fabric supports pluggable consensus service for all 3 phases of endorsement, ordering, and validation depending on their requirements. In particular, the ordering service API allows plugging in BFT-based agreement algorithms. Though pluggable consensus depending on the type of management and platform applications is the desirable methods, Apache Kafka in Hyperledger Fabric, RBFT in Hyperledger Indy, and Sumeragi in Hyperledger Iroha use a voting-based approach to consensus that provides fault tolerance and finality within seconds. PoET in Hyperledger Sawtooth uses a lottery based approach to consensus that provides scale at the cost of finality being delayed due to forks that must be resolved.

Here the clear focus is more on Confidentiality, instant finality & high speed while availability (CIA) is restricted to transacting parties, thus preferring a 'Shared ledger' to a widely 'Distributed ledger'.

Some of them are worth looking at here. Let us look at what is Byzantine Fault Tolerance. A **Byzantine fault** is a condition of a computer system, particularly distributed computing systems, where components may fail and there is imperfect information on whether a component has failed. In a Byzantine fault, a component such as a server can inconsistently appear both failed and functioning to failure-detection systems, presenting different symptoms to different observers. It is difficult for the other components to declare it failed and shut it out of the network, because they need to first reach a consensus regarding which component has failed in the first place. A Byzantine fault is any fault presenting different symptoms to different observers.[3] A Byzantine failure is the loss of a system service due to a Byzantine fault in systems that require consensus. Byzantine fault tolerance (BFT) is the dependability of a fault-tolerant computer system to such conditions. Byzantine fault tolerance mechanisms use components that repeat an incoming message (or just its signature) to other recipients of that incoming message. All these mechanisms make the assumption that the act of repeating a message blocks the propagation of Byzantine symptoms. For systems that have a high degree of safety or security criticality, these assumptions must be proven to be true to an acceptable level of fault coverage. (Source- Wikipedia). While bitcoin was the first digital asset generation and maintenance system, that demonstrated Byzantine fault tolerance in a fool proof manner with PoW consensus mechanism, there have been several improvements and improvisations depending on the needs of the respective blockchain or distributed ledger applications.

Tendermint: BFT based POS: Implemented by Cosmos platform that chose a BFT based POS as against a chain based POS (Casper by Ethereum), Tendermint claims to be a faster and safer approach to consensus by by selecting a validator with unpredictable IP address, that is difficult to attack.

The simplified explanation of how the algorithm works looks like this:

1. Validator weight is established
2. Validator is elected, their turn to propose a block
3. Weight is recalculated, decreases some amount after round is complete
4. As each round progresses, weight increases incrementally in proportion to voting power
5. Validator is selected again

Notary node based consensus

R3 Corda has "pluggable" consensus, allowing notary clusters to choose a consensus algorithm like RAFT, BFT-SMaRt, based on their requirements in terms of privacy, scalability, legal-system compatibility and algorithmic agility.

Each Corda network can have multiple notary clusters, each potentially running a different consensus algorithm. This provides several benefits:

- **Privacy:** we can have both validating and non-validating notary clusters on the same network, each running a different algorithm. This allows nodes to choose the preferred notary cluster on a per-transaction basis
- **Load balancing:** spreading the transaction load over multiple notary clusters allows higher transaction throughput for the platform overall
- **Low latency:** latency can be minimised by choosing a notary cluster physically closer to the transacting parties

This provided immense flexibility to R3 Corda distributed platform in different, complex and regulated use cases as well while allowing for high through put.

PBFT- Practical Byzantine Fault Tolerance

Proposed by Miguel Castro and Barbara Liskov of MIT in 1999, the model offers a practical approach to byzantine fault tolerance in asynchronous environments like Internet through a number of improvisations to the then existing algorithms through a new state machine replication algorithm.

The algorithm works roughly as follows: 1. A client sends a request to invoke a service operation to the primary 2. The primary multicasts the request to the backups. 3. Replicas execute the request and send a reply to the client. 4. The client waits for 1 replies from different replicas with the same result; this is the result of the operation.

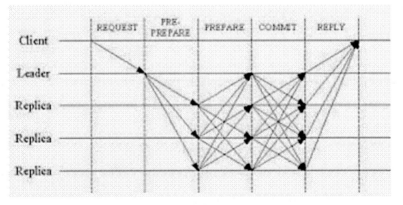

Figure- PBFT Steps (http://pmg.csail.mit.edu/papers/osdi99.pdf)

The good performance of this algorithm is due to a number of important optimizations, including replacing public-key signatures by vectors of message authentication codes, reducing the size and number of messages, and the incremental checkpoint-management techniques. (Source: http://pmg.csail.mit.edu/papers/osdi99.pdf)

RBFT- Redundant Byzantine Fault Tolerance

In RBFT, the client is sending a request to nodes. It does not have to send to all nodes because sending to f+1 nodes is sufficient. After receiving the client request, the nodes do a dissemination process through PROPAGATE in which every other node is made aware of the request. Each primary creates a proposal from the received requests called a PRE-PREPARE and sends it to all other nodes. If the nodes accept the primary's proposal, they send an acknowledgement to the proposal by a message called PREPARE. Once a node gets a PRE-PREPARE proposal and 2f PREPARE messages, then it has sufficient information to accept the proposal and sends a COMMIT message. Once a node gets 2f+1 COMMIT messages, then the batch of requests can be ordered and added to the ledger since a sufficient number of nodes have agreed that a majority of nodes have accepted the proposal. The primary does not require one proposal to complete before it can send the next proposal.

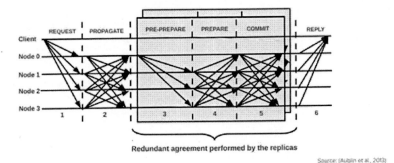

Redundant agreement performed by the replicas

Source: (Aublin et al, 2013)

Hyperledger Indy uses RBFT to handle ordering and validation, which results in a single ledger containing both ordered and validated transactions. This is unlike many blockchain networks that use a Byzantine Fault Tolerance (BFT) protocol only for ordering

The following table gives the glimpse of the comparison among various consensus models employed by Hyperledger platforms.

Consensus Algorithm	Consensus Approach	Pros	Cons
Kafka in Hyperledger Fabric Ordering Service	Permissioned voting based. Leader does ordering. Only in-sync replicas can be voted as leader. ("Kafka," 2017).	Provides crash fault tolerance. Finality happens in a matter of seconds.	While Kafka is crash fault tolerant, it is not Byzantine fault tolerant, which prevents the system from reaching agreement in the case of malicious or faulty nodes.
RBFT in Hyperledger Indy	Pluggable election strategy set to a permissioned, voting based strategy by default ("Plenum," 2016). All instances do ordering, but only the requests ordered by the master instance are actually executed. (Aublin, Mokhtar & Quéma, 2013)	Provides Byzantine fault tolerance. Finality happens in a matter of seconds.	The more nodes that exist on the network, the more time it takes to reach consensus. The nodes in the network are known and must be totally connected.
Sumeragi in Hyperledger Iroha	Permissioned server reputation system.	Provides Byzantine fault tolerance. Finality happens in a matter of seconds. Scale to petabytes of data, distributed across many clusters (Struckhoff, 2016).	The more nodes that exist on the network, the more time it takes to reach consensus. The nodes in the network are known and must be totally connected.
PoET in Hyperledger Sawtooth	Pluggable election strategy set to a permissioned, lottery based strategy by default.	Provides scalability and Byzantine fault tolerance.	Finality can be delayed due to forks that must be resolved.

Fig: Hyperledger consensus model comparison

Source: https://www.hyperledger.org/wp-content/uploads/2017/08/Hyperledger_Arch_WG_Paper_1_Consensus.pdf

Proof of Authority, POA

PoA uses identity as the sole verification of the authority to validate, meaning that there is no need to use mining. PoA only allows non-consecutive block approval from any one validator, meaning that the risk of serious damage is centralized to the authority node.

PoA is suited for both private networks and public networks, like POA Network, where trust is distributed. Since PoA security is centralized in the form of the authority node, a lot of PoA critics wonder the point of using a blockchain for this kind of usages - stating that PoA blockchains are not really decentralized and a simple DB would be more efficient, faster, and cost effective.

While there is a lot more research is being done and more consensus algorithms may emerge, the important point is to remember that the philosophy of the platform immensely impacts the choice and also the acceptance of the corresponding target user segments, while securing the transactions.

While discussing the consensus mechanisms in the Blockchain, it is important to address another concept, namely the 'Scalability Trilemma' coined by Vitalik Buterin, the legend behind Ethereum platform. Scalability trilemma refers to the tradeoff that a Blockchain platform, has to make between 'Decentralisation, Security & Scalability'.

Decentralisation refers to the delegation of decision making regarding validation of transaction to the constituents of the network as against centralisation or concentration of decision making authority in the hands of the founders or a central authority.

The degree of decentralisation depends on a number of factors like the proportion of the members that can take part in the process , degree of anonymity between the participating nodes and method of choosing the mining nodes etc. While this is considered to be at the highest in platforms using POW consensus like Bitcoin and Ethereum, it is limited in the case of DPOS based platforms like EOS that use a set of 21 nodes to arrive at the consensus.

The high level of decentralisation and anonymity that exists in POW based platforms results in a very high security level with respect to the malicious attackers who need to use extremely high energy and processing power to break the system and this is deemed improbable and almost impossible & unviable. A downside here is that the transaction throughput and speed of processing transactions is considerably compromised as well.

To provide the same level of security in platforms using alternate consensus mechanisms, we need to have considerable information on the participating nodes & the validating nodes that are provided with known identities . This reduces the degree of decentralisation by a considerable level while dramatically increasing the transaction throughput and processing speed.

Thus it can be observed that, the architects of any Blockchain solution need to consider and evaluate the tradeoffs between these three aspects; by keeping in mind, the needs of their clients and platform users who have differing weightage for the three factors, Decentralisation, Security & Scalability'.

Annexure 9: Concepts Addressed in the Book

1. What led to the discovery of internet and how was the project started?
2. Who are the major personalities behind the launch of internet and how did their work influence the launch of internet?
3. When was the first internet data transfer made?
4. When was internet dedicated to the world?
5. What were the objectives of internet?
6. What are the various stages of evolution of the web?
7. When was the first IoT product made?
8. When did the first Blockchain come into existence & in what form?
9. What are the major desirable features of currency?
10. How does bitcoin compare to Gold and US dollar across the desirable features of currency?
11. Why is bitcoin better than money as per Bill gates?
12. Explain the origin of Bitcoin Blockchain and the major works that contributed to the launch of Bitcoin
13. What is solution to Byzantine General problem and how does it address double spending?
14. What is the relation between Microsoft, Apple and their founders and the evolution of Blockchain?
15. What are the key benefits of a Blockchain?
16. What are the salient features of a Blockchain?
17. What are the three major trends that are leading to the fast growth of cutting-edge technologies including Blockchain?
18. What are the characteristics of enterprise Blockchain?
19. What are differences between public and private Blockchains?
20. How is Bigdata analytics leveraged by leading companies?
21. Top 25 Public Blockchain based use cases
22. Top 25 enterprise use cases
23. History and evolution of Digital marketing,
24. History and evolution of AI/ML,

25. History and evolution of IOT
26. History and evolution of Blockchain technologies
27. What is a cryptographic hash?
28. What is a consensus mechanism?
29. What is a Digital signal algorithm?
30. What is PKI?
31. IoT data connectivity to creating value
32. What are the various sources for IoT data?
33. What is the technology road map for IoT?
34. What are the projections for IoT data by 2020?
35. IoT- Difference between consumer and industrial internet
36. IoT use cases
37. IoT & smart infrastructure
38. What are data lakes and where are they used?
39. Data Management architecture in large organisations
40. Types of cyberthreats
41. Risks of centralization and SPOF
42. GDPR and Blockchain- What is GDPR?
43. Types of data collected by organisations
44. 5S methodology for GDPR compliance
45. Poka-Yoke and its applications in Blockchain
46. Areas affected maximum by GDPR
47. What is the data stored in Bitcoin, Ethereum and Hyperledger Blockchains?
48. Who owns Bitcoin Blockchain?
49. How is Ethereum Blockchain managed?
50. How are private managed?
51. How are the public Blockchains planning to scale up and increase transaction throughput?
52. What is sharding?
53. What is segwit?
54. What are the advantages of side chains?
55. Facebook Cambridge Analytica incident
56. What are the various elements of a digital marketing strategy
57. What are the objectives of a CRM strategy?

89. Six Sigma based approach for architecting enterprise Blockchain applications-DMADV

90. Questions to ask for assessment of Blockchain requirement

91. Architectural road map for organizational decentralization

92. Comprehensive comparison of Consensus mechanisms

93. The DAO case study of smart contract vulnerability

94. Scaling up enterprise Blockchains

95. Blockchain as a Service- platform options and their description

96. Blockchain case study- Pay-Bill cycle, direct recruitment

97. Blockchain 1.0 2.0 3.0 4.0

98. Blockchain use cases in banking, finance, Government

99. Popular Blockchain use cases

100. Benefits of Blockchain use w.r.t Middlemen

101. Elements of a Blockchain eco-system

102. Blockchain integration challenges

103. Trade finance application use case

104. Farm to fork application use case

105. World food program- Aid distribution on Blockchain

106. Distribution led supply chain use case

107. International remittance use case

108. Bill discounting use case

109. Medical record use case

110. Supply chain management on Blockchain

111. Classified and Ecommerce exchanges on Blockchain

112. Blockchain based Energy exchange

113. Educational records

114. Identity Management on Blockchain

115. Blockchain enabled future for a decentralised world

116. Cyber security - components, PKI, CA and the limitations with examples

117. What are the major cyber threats faced by organisations?

118. How does Blockchain address security threats?

119. How do organisations address security of Blockchains?

120. What are the factors limiting the growth of Blockchain and how can they be addressed?

Testimonials

"This book gives a holistic idea about the Blockchain, touching all the aspects right from a basic idea of website to full-fledged Blockchain application. A true sense of Digitalization in a concise way".

Vineet Pandey

Head of Supply Chain at Future Consumer Ltd.

"The Story is excellent.."

G Suresh Kumar (GSK)

Head - Digital Enterprise API Programs

"The way concepts are explained smoothly across the book using simple words , is really amazing. Personally, I felt so interested while I was going through Blockchain use cases across various industries and its relationship with other future tech like IoT, AI, Big Data and ML..."

Jaswanth Reddy Vutukuri

MEAN Stack Trainer | Developer | Blockchain Enthusiast

"This book 'Blockchain - The Untold Story' indeed covers all that info a Blockchain enthusiast would like to know. Very well structured and easy to understand. Great discussion and exchange of futuristic ideas with Srinivas Mahankali on common interests of BCT, DLT, Bigdata, ML/AI."

Sesidhar Sahukaru

Blockchain & Analytics Consultant "This book is indeed a great effort to put Blockchain in a right perspective with respect to other cutting-edge technologies and its utility beyond the Bitcoin for Enterprises, NGOs, Government and Institutions. Enjoyed the journey from the birth of the Internet to Blockchain enabled future!"

Dr M Muneer, CEO & MD,

Customer Lab Solutions and Co-Founder &
Chief Evangelist Medical Institute.

Your book demystified Blockchain for me and was able to get across the message with simplicity. Enjoyed reading the story while learning a lot on this Complex subject!

JV Raman, EVP of Unilever, Russia, Ukraine and Belarus

It's a fantastic read for all techno and business leaders. From the various Blockchain platforms to the use cases.

Sunil Nambiar, IT Site Manager,
Infineon Technologies India, Pvt Ltd.

Srinivas is one the few individuals in the country who really understands Blockchain! His book truly demystifies this topic and has a lot of insights. It's a must read for anyone interested in understanding this new technology

Hari TN, HR Head Bigbasket &
Strategic Advisor to Fundamentum Partnership